Cognition and Personal Structure

COGNITION AND PERSONAL STRUCTURE

Computer Access AND Analysis

EDITED BY

James C. Mancuso

AND

Mildred L. G. Shaw

PRAEGER

New York
Westport, Connecticut
London

Library of Congress Cataloging-in-Publication Data

Cognition and personal structure.

Bibliography: p.
Includes indexes.
1. Cognition—Data processing. 2. Personal construct theory—Data processing. I. Mancuso, James C., 1928– . II. Shaw, Mildred L. G.
BF311.C5484 1988 153 87-13770
ISBN 0-275-92606-0 (alk. paper)

Library of Congress Catalog Card Number: 87-13770
ISBN: 0-275-92606-0

First published in 1988

Praeger Publishers, One Madison Avenue, New York, NY 10010
A division of Greenwood Press, Inc.

Printed in the United States of America

The paper used in this book complies with the Permanent Paper Standard issued by the National Information Standards Organization (Z39.48-1984).

10 9 8 7 6 5 4 3 2 1

Contents

Cognition and Personal Structure

1 A Constructivist Perspective on Assessing Personal Cognitive Structures

James C. Mancuso and Mildred L. G. Shaw

To build a theory of persons, a radical constructivist first accepts the premise that an organized cognitive system occupies any psychological context as definitively as does the energy-emitting event that interfaces with that system (Gergen 1985; von Glasersfeld 1984). A behavior scientist working from a constructivist/contextualist perspective builds explanations from the assumption that event-derived input will function as a psychological variable only when that input has been assimilated into a structured cognitive system. Further, that system ultimately can be represented quantitatively, so that one may relate its parameters to other aspects of psychological functioning. In other terms, meaning is assigned to a stimulus pattern only through its absorption into the acquired knowledge system the person has available, and the psychological process of assigning meaning can be studied through, among other things, assessing and quantitatively representing a person's cognitive system.

Empirically based constructivist explanation, as Shepard (1984) has illustrated, had been cogently advanced by Wertheimer's (1912) demonstration of the ways in which a person will impose the meaning "moving" onto the sensory input pattern that emanates from two stationary stimulus events. Shepard's recent (1984) work extends Wertheimer's studies well beyond their elementary significance. Shepard has amply shown that the trajectory of a light's movement across an intervening space represents an instance of a general principle of *kinematic geometry*. In a typical investigation of the ways in which people attribute motion to rigid objects, Shepard and his associates asked a subject to watch a surface in the picture plane spread before his or her line of sight. A multi-edged polygon was then projected onto that surface. The projection was terminated, and within an appropriate time interval the same polygon was projected, for example, onto a point to the right of the initial projection. Observers report having seen the polygon move across the space intervening between the two locations of the separate projections. Like the two single light points used in Wertheimer's phi-phenomenon demonstration, the two projections of the polygon, as input-producing events, are assimilated into a complex cognitive structure that imposes the meaning of "motion" onto the input. When the right-left alternation continues, observers see the two successive projections of the polygon as a single polygon moving rapidly back and forth across the intervening space.

Other transformations of the position and the orientation of the second presentations of the polygon more dramatically illustrate the proposition that apparent motion proceeds through the most direct, single unique axis between points on the surface of the consecutively presented polygons. For example, the second projection, presented to the right of the position of the first projection, might represent the polygon in enlarged size. With this arrangement, an observer "liberates" the polygon from the picture plane. The polygon would appear to pop out toward the observer while simultaneously moving from left to right. A similar liberation from the picture plane is effected when the investigator presents, as the second projection, a straight vertical line in the exact center of the field onto which the polygon had first been projected. In this case the observer reports that the polygon had rotated 90 degrees through the *near–far* axis (some observers see it move from the right to the left, whereas others see it move from the left to the right).

One can have little cognitive difficulty if he or she were to apply the constructivist assumption to these reported observations. Event-associated input becomes part of a psychological process only when that input is assimilated to an available cognitive structure. The sense of an event derives from the ways in which its input-producing energy patterns are translated into neural impulses at sensory endings and are then assimilated to a person's existing cognitive structures. In Shepard's demonstrations of apparent movement, a person's system functions to "fill in the space" between successive actual presentations, using an attributed representation of the rigid object. When it is necessary to do so in order to assimilate the input in a way that maintains the coherence of the system, the system will "fill in" within the third dimension. When, for example, the polygon is presented in the picture plane and is then replaced with a straight vertical line that can be experienced as an edge-on view of the rigid two-dimensional object, a person will make sense of the stimulus change by experiencing the figure moving through the third dimension.

In sum, then, these demonstrations of specific instances of constructive psychological functions provide validation of general constructivist assumptions, and they encourage investigators to search out and describe those aspects of a person's psychological system which, in conjunction with input from an event, form an integral part of any psychological action.

CONSTRUCTIVIST PRINCIPLES IN PERSONALITY THEORY, MEASUREMENT, AND APPLICATIONS

Concurrent with the cognitive scientist's affirmation of the utility of constructivist principles, other psychologists have explored the utility of constructivist approaches to explanations of person functioning (Averill 1982; Carver and Scheier 1981; Mancuso and Adams-Webber 1982a; Mandler 1984). With this redirecting of focus by general theorists, applied psychologists, as well, have increasingly investigated the advantages of using constructivist principles to guide their work (Adams-Webber and Mancuso 1983; Guidano and Liotti 1983; Goldfried and Robins 1983; Landfield and Leitner 1980; Neimeyer 1985; Neimeyer and Neimeyer, 1987).

A personality theorist using a total constructivist position would assume that a person would be defined in terms of the complete, integrated system of internal representations that he or she can retrieve to impose on and to anticipate the steady flow of input that he or she encounters in the continuous movement of psychological adaptation. From this position one would believe that every input must be processed in terms of the idiosyncratic, organized system the person has acquired in the pre- and postnatal period during which she or he has developed psychologically. The person, then, comprises that cognitive system — a system which is stored in long-term memory and which is carried from situation to situation.

With the rise of interest in and use of innovations by which to conceptualize cognitive processes, investigators have developed a variety of techniques for assessing the content and organization of a person's cognitive structures. Often investigators (Cantor and Mischel 1979; Murphy and Wright 1984) have borrowed directly from the technology that cognitive scientists (Posner 1978; Rosch and Lloyd 1978) have used in laboratory studies. In many cases the investigator's use of theory implicates a structure for the subject's cognitive systems through the assumptions that guide the study. The investigator then accepts the outcome of the study as a suitable demonstration that the implied, but not directly assessed, system had functioned to produce particular results.

The work of Bargh (1982) illustrates the use of standard laboratory technology to deduce the structural properties of the construction systems that people apply to processing self- and person-relevant input. Bargh set out to add to the demonstrative base for regarding a personality as the cognitive processing systems that a person takes into interactions with his or her world (Wyer and Srull 1984). Bargh (1982) explored the ways in which an existing cognitive organization becomes implicated in the directing of attentional processes. To demonstrate the validity of his assumptions, Bargh, among other procedures, classified the persons who participated in his study as either *schematics* or *aschematics*. He placed his subjects in one or the other category on the basis of their responses to self-report rating scales. Essentially, those participants who rated themselves on the high end of scales assumed to be "independence-relevant" were judged to be persons who would readily access independence-defining schemata as they processed the flow of inputs. Bargh then used the standard dichotic listening task (a separate message to each ear) to assess the extent to which *schematics* would apply automatic attentional processes to cognize adjectives judged to be synonymous with the term *independence*.

In his attempt to work from a base of constructivist assumptions, Bargh, as noted (1982), chose his schematics on the basis of participants' self-ratings with reference to scales purportedly describing self characteristics of independence. Bargh assumed that those persons who rated their selves (this pronomial construction is used deliberately to show that participants rated self as an object that can be ordered into categories) to be highly independent would have acquired a highly accessible independence construct; whereas persons who had rated themselves low on independence would not have done so. Although this assumption would have an immediate face validity, it cannot be accepted without further consideration, and its ultimate acceptance must depend on the availability of evidence based on technologies that allow quantitative representation of an individual's person-construing system. After those technologies have been developed, an investigator may better test the hypotheses that persons who rate their selves highly on a particular dimension also use that dimension as a superordinating self-construing dimension.

Note that Landfield and Schmittdiel (1983) report an exploration of the concept of *meaningfulness* within a person's construing system. Building on earlier investigations of the concept (Bonarius 1970a, 1970b), Landfield and Schmittdiel have shown the utility of a meaningfulness measure based on the assumption that the meaningfulness of a construct, in a particular person's system, is reflected by the person's use of *both* extreme ends of rating scales (which, in their studies, are embedded in a Role Repertory Grid Analysis; see Kelly 1955). Extending this proposition, then, one would need to conclude that Bargh's aschematic participants, who had been selected on the basis of their having rated their selves at the dependent end of the dependent–independent construct, would use that construct as "meaningfully" as would the schematics. One would hesitate, then, to endorse Bargh's expectation of a processing difference attributable to his schematics' ability to easily access an independence construct, whereas the aschematics would less readily access that construct.

In short, those investigators who would undertake studies based on constructivist assumptions will ultimately profit from having available a variety of sound methods for representing the cognitive systems that a participant brings into a study. Such methods will be useful not only for establishing the parameters of the cognitive system that participants can access while being exposed to the experimental procedures, but those methods can also serve to quantify the system's changes following the applications of experimental and clinical manipulations.

APPROACHES TO ASSESSMENT OF COGNITIVE STRUCTURE

Investigators who have worked to expand on personal construct psychology, which was originally formalized by George Kelly (1955), have given special attention to specific methods of quantifying and assessing the contents and structural properties of an individual's cognitive systems. In the original presentation of his theory, Kelly described a methodology by which to obtain quantitative summaries of patterns of organization within an individual's person-perceiving system. Kelly's first applications of *role repertory analysis* required that a respondent produce a grid or matrix whose rows would be labeled with bipolar, person-defining constructs and whose columns would be labeled as persons significant in the life of the participant. The completed role repertory grid, which contained ratings of each person relative to each construct, could then be subjected to a wide variety of multidimensional quantitative analyses. From Kelly's first explorations there grew a large body of investigations based on repertory analysis (Adams-Webber 1979; Stringer and Bannister 1979). To conduct these studies investigators (Fransella and Bannister 1977; Landfield and Schmittdiel 1983; Shaw 1980, 1981; Slater 1977) have adapted the original assessment techniques to the wide range of computing technologies that have appeared since the introduction of role repertory analysis.

Beyond this plethora of studies of people's constructions of people, investigators have adopted the technology of analyzing role repertory grids to the analysis of a wide variety of cognized elements. Construct grid technology has been used to study conceptualizations of seaside resorts (Riley and Palmer 1976), of architectural and environmental designs (Honikman 1976), of automobiles (Boxer 1981), and of postgraduate students' activities as they progress through research training (Phillips 1981). Shaw and McKnight (1981a) have devised and published methods of using grid technology for personal decision making. Role repertory technology holds particular promise as a method for the analysis of expert systems (Boose 1985a, 1985b; Shaw and Gaines 1984).

As personal construct theorists have pushed forward their techniques, investigators working outside of this specific framework also have provided methods to be used in the analysis of cognitive structures. Rosenberg and his associates (Rosenberg 1977; Gara and Rosenberg 1979), who have concentrated on person cognition, have developed extended analytic methods. Following their interest in communication processes, Woelfel and his associates (Woelfel and Fink 1980) have devised procedures by which to track the cognitive changes that follow from the deliver of a constant flow of information. Jaccard (Jaccard and Wood 1986; Jaccard and Wan 1986) has devised methods for extracting the idiosyncratic cognitive systems that underlie decision-making processes.

THE UTILITY OF MULTIDIMENSIONAL ANALYSES AND MICROCOMPUTERS

Much of this work has been enhanced by analytic procedures that have become feasible with the advent of high-speed computing. A variety of multidimensional analyses have been adapted to the assessment of construction systems (Massaro and Schmuller 1975; Rosenberg 1977; Shaw 1980; Tversky and Gati 1982; Woelfel and Fink 1980), and these applications have served particularly well to advance conceptualizations of cognitive processes. Such techniques allow quantitative representations of the structural properties of cognitive systems, and with such representations an investigator may frame hypotheses that are then amenable to additional quantified assessment.

In the last five years the rapid development of microcomputers, coupled with statisticians' greater attention to multidimensional analytic procedures, has created an ambience that presages a huge burst of activity in multidimensional approaches to analysis of cognitive structures. Portable, inexpensive computers now have the capacity to complete computations that recently were accessible to only the small number of investigators who could employ data tabulators and who could purchase expensive computer time. Additionally, the microcomputer allows for the easy collection and filing of data. In the recent past only well-financed investigators could collect data interactively by the use of computers. At this moment an investigator or an applied psychologist can collect and arrange large blocks of data by having respondents engage in tasks they find simple and stimulating. In short, one may now collect and analyze large data sets through relatively time-economical and inexpensive procedures.

Additionally, the use of the microcomputer facilitates the transmission of data, technologies, and information. Once collected, data may be transmitted in electronic form, either through direct linkage between computers or through the exchange of light-weight records of data (floppy discs, tapes). Investigators may similarly transmit programs designed to collect or process data.

ORGANIZATION OF THIS VOLUME

This volume has been planned to provide a wide range of potential readers with a readily accessible compendium of illustrative descriptions of techniques that have been developed to assess individual construct systems. A variety of these techniques have been developed by theorists and practitioners who have described their work in widely spread outlets. In many instances the techniques have been described incidentally as investigators have reported the results of investigations.

These descriptions should highlight the significance of this research in ways that have not been realized by the less systematic presentations that have thus far been assembled. In the first place, by the study of these juxtaposed descriptions an interested reader can become aware of the intertwined technological and theoretical problems the designers of these techniques have considered. It will be seen that the development of these methodologies depends on and facilitates the reciprocal refinement of theories about cognitive process and measurement.

Additionally, by consulting this single source a reader can become acquainted with the workings of a variety of techniques, any one of which might be adaptable to the kinds of problems that he or she might pose and might wish to explore. As a reader surveys the available techniques, he or she will become aware that the people who have developed these techniques have tried to develop their methods toward greater flexibility of application. Although many of these techniques had been developed originally for the assessment of a person's construction systems relative to one event domain (persons, for example), the inventors of the techniques have attempted to make allowances for adapting the techniques to any domain in which an investigator might be interested.

The presentations in this volume will also illustrate the constant interplay of applied and theoretical problems that have informed the work of those people who have developed the described technologies. As will be seen, some of the chapters focus primarily on measurement and theoretical considerations. Other chapters are written from an applied perspective. Nonetheless, the activity described herein attests to the investigator's belief that technologies can usefully guide thought about day-to-day psychological functioning.

Nine chapters in this volume describe programs the authors have developed for use on microcomputers. (The programs described in a tenth chapter have been used on a large computer, and are not yet translated for microcomputer use.) Each of the authors has worked toward the goal of devising a suite of programs that would allow a quantitative representation of the cognitive system a person would use as he or she processes the input from one or another set of events.

As a reader can see, the authors' work represents a range of concerns, as those concerns are reflected in the chosen elicitation techniques and in the analysis strategies. Shaw and Gaines report on an extended suite of programs (PLANET) that one can use to elicit and then to analyze, in a variety of ways, the cognitive system a person would use to think about any domain of events. They have designed elicitation and analysis programs of wide generality. Their chapter contains a description of the intricate detail that they have worked into their programs to ensure that clinicians and investigators will be able to take into account and adequately meet the many contingencies that can arise as one attempts to access and to assess cognitive systems relative to any domain of input a person might receive from his or her environment.

Landfield, one of the first investigators to develop computer programs to assess grids based on Kelly's Role Repertory Test, describes (with Cannell) the analysis programs Landfield and his associates have devised. These programs extract scores related to concepts that are important to the tenets of Personal Construct Psychology. With their programs Landfield's group has focused sharply on measure of hierarchy in the organization of those construction systems that people apply as they construe other persons. Landfield and Cannell describe the theoretical base of their measure of hierarchical organization, report on the computerized techniques by which the measures are extracted, and point to the research and clinical questions that one may answer with the extracted measures.

Mitterer and Adams-Webber take yet another task. They have programmed a method through which an investigator or clinician can construct a wide variety of instruments by which to elicit and analyze the system a person would use to construe events. They aimed at high flexibility in constructing and analyzing the data produced by any kind of instrument that would be of interest to the administrator of an assessment process. The content of their chapter illustrates the diversity of approaches that have become available to behavior analysts who wish to explore the complexity of personal systems of cognitive structures.

In Boose's chapter one sees the results of a more precise focus of cognitive assessment methodologies on the problems that interest a specific investigator. Boose set out to find an efficient method of extracting the knowledge system of experts. Building on the work of Shaw and Gaines (Shaw 1979; Gaines and Shaw 1981), Boose has developed a computer-assisted methodology for representing the knowledge base of an expert construer: the Expert Transfer System. Among other things, Boose's methods simulate the rules that would be embedded in the cognitive systems of experts, and constantly refine representations of the systems.

The work of Jaccard, Wan, and Wood parallels that of Boose, in that it reflects the development of techniques by which one can usefully quantify personal cognitive systems that are of interest to a special line of investigation. Jaccard and his co-workers have developed their methods to enhance work related to Jaccard's long-time interest in decision-making processes. The computerized operations, described in Chapter 7, facilitate the collection and analysis of information about the cognitive organizations that guide a person's decision-making processes relative to any product, event, or issue.

Knowledge of the cognitive systems underlying decision making would be of special interest to scholars and practitioners of communications technology. Woelfel, who studies communications processes, has built a highly refined system for analyzing the development and change of personal cognitive systems. In his chapter he describes programs with which he can analyze the ways in which people construe any topic, for example, that might be a matter of current public discussion. Woelfel's analysis programs are of particular interest to persons in communications, because they include procedures by which one can project the state of a person's system in the event that one or another part of the system changes.

Lehrer and Mancuso, who share a strong interest in developmental processes, write about programs that take an even narrower focus. Lehrer has been particularly interested in the structures that young people bring to their school learning. That specialization led him to consider the connections between learning to read, personal narrative grammar, and the ways in which a person constructs his or her self within the narrative grammar structure that he or she uses implicitly to process all input. Mancuso's programs have been put together to explore a specific area of personal role construction. His ParRep analysis programs systematize the cognitive organizations a person uses as he or she construes enactments of parent roles.

Ashbrook, Spaulding, and Cromwell have followed yet another direction. Their studies have focused on the cognitive processes of persons who have been diagnosed in clinical settings. They have followed a theoretical position from which they have explored the deficits in the processing functions these persons bring to their interactions with inputs. In their chapter they describe the instruments by which they, using microcomputers, have assessed the various cognitive functions psychopathologists have implicated in the processes underlying the development of deviant behaviors.

In the last chapter, Pruzek reminds readers that the selection and justification of methods of analysis demand constant attention to measurement theory. Pruzek has devoted years of his career to the study of the intricacies of factor analytic methods, and remains a strong advocate of model-based methods for psychometric and statistical inference. He presents a strong brief for common factor analysis as a means of drawing inferences. He illustrates the ways in which common factor analysis can be of special value to investigators who rely on the analysis of two-dimensional matrices, to develop representations of the structures one presumes to underlie cognitive processes.

A FINAL WORD

Ultimately, the contributors to this book intend to convince investigators of the immense possibilities of exploration that have been created by the development of useful theory and technologies. The field has progressed beyond the "blood and sweat era." Persons who have not mastered the first principles of computer programming may implement available programs, although one could safely guarantee that anyone who begins to use one of the systems described in this volume will not remain at that rudimentary level. In the long run, the further development of theory and technology will depend on the versatility of investigators who can envision the multiple possibilities of adapting programs for analysis and re-analysis of data.

The state of affairs presented by this volume can satisfy only the scholar of cognitive processes who has observed the recent immense acceleration of activity devoted to building a theory base from which to investigate cognitive processes, to inventing methods for accessing and representing cognitive structure, and to extending the territory under exploration. Consider that 15 years ago the ambience surrounding the behavioral sciences and the then current state of technological developments would have seriously constrained the assembling of a book like this. Currently, one can easily introduce undergraduate students to the contents of this book. What is more, some of those undergraduates will readily add elaborations to the conceptualizations and techniques discussed in these chapters.

As editors of this volume, we regard this collection of papers as an invitation. Some readers, we hope, will be invited to elaborate on this work by reasoned criticism. We want other readers to accept the book as an invitation to become acquainted with the diversity and ready availability of computer-assisted approaches to assessing cognitive systems. More than anything, of course, we invite readers to collaborate with the writers who have built these systems. Each of the authors anticipates the opportunity to share his or her excitement and enthusiasm.

2 Modeling Cognitive Processes

Mildred L. G. Shaw and James C. Mancuso

CONSTRUCTIVIST PARADIGM AND COGNITIVE SCIENCE

The constructivist paradigm that underlies personal construct psychology is an alternative to the positivistic, behavioristic approaches that have rested on mechanistic paradigms. Although mechanistic paradigms have been difficult to dislodge from the favored position they have held in the behavioral sciences, scholars have steadily moved toward constructivist approaches. It is not a surprise that a new metaphor, the computational model, has carried forward the constructivist metaphors. The development of computer-based modeling systems has allowed the operationalization of constructivist formulations. Work in artificial intelligence, the emulation of high-level human capabilities on the computer, has led to representations of systems that model human performance. Parallel to this, the acceleration of the development of cognitive science follows from the use of such computer-based emulations of human performance to provide a model of human functioning.

Whereas strict behaviorism legitimated only models of human functioning that could be inferred from human behavior, cognitive science legitimates mental models whose functioning parallels that of people, but whose processing structures cannot necessarily be inferred from observable output (Gentner and Stevens 1983). Such models are possible inferences from human behavior in that they are consistent with it, rather than necessary inferences in that they are strictly derivable from it. The influences of positivism and early computer technology are evident in the information-processing models of the first accounts of cognitive science (Lindsay and Norman 1977). However, in recent years the role of a wider variety of mental processes has been realized, and the models are being extended to account for such phenomena as emotions and consciousness (Norman 1980).

Parallel to this legitimation of mentalistic concepts through developments in artificial intelligence and computer modeling, one observes an increased acceptance of such concepts as those expressed in studies of the social construction of self and others (Gergen and Davis 1985) and in personal construct psychology. In particular, Kelly's (1955) construct of anticipatory construction (p. 46), which stands in his theory as the fundamental dynamic of human functioning, resonates with the cognitive science emphasis on the key role of planning and of hierarchical goal structures (Anderson 1983: 33). In effect then, personal construct theory and cognitive science share a heavy reliance on the concept of anticipation as a constructive process that underlies all human activity. With this reliance comes an ancillary dependence on the concept of a schema, which designates an inner representation of events that is constructed through the use of organized cognitive systems. This concept was first put forward by Head in 1920, and has had a long history in psychological science (Bartlett 1932; Kant 1934; Vernon 1955; Bruner, Goodnow, and Austin 1956; Neisser 1967), but it assumes new significance with the legitimation of mental models.

Bartlett (1932: 201) developed the idea of a schema in his widely cited work on remembering. He defined schema as follows:

> "Schema" refers to an active organization of past reactions, or of past experiences, which must always be supposed to be operating in any well-adapted organic response. That is, whenever there is any order or regularity of behavior, a particular response is possible only because it is related to other similar responses which have been serially organized, yet which operate, not simply as individual members coming after one another, but as a unitary mass.

Bartlett further suggested that there is a gradual buildup of such cognitive structures which are nonspecific, but organized, classifications of many events. These events are linked by a classification schema that he described as "effort after meaning," that is, the perception or construction of similarity in the events themselves. It seems that it is anticipation that determines the meaning of an event, and that one construes an event as being the same or different from the anticipated schema.

Piaget emphasizes the dynamic nature of schemata by stating that a person constructs events in his or her world by assimilating schemata, while accommodating these schemata to input-associated constraints (Flavell 1963). Neisser (1967, 1976) similarly suggests that a person forms cognitive structures that are the result of the constructive processes involved, and emphasizes their anticipatory role: "At each moment the perceiver is constructing anticipations of certain kinds of information, that enable him to accept it as it becomes available" (1976: 20).

Osgood, Suci, and Tannenbaum (1957) introduce the social aspect of schemata by noting that while each person has a unique system of dimensions that are used to perceive and judge the environment, some of these are common to large segments of people who share a common culture.

The underlying theme of all these approaches is that an individual uses a system of organization together with interrelationships between components in the system, which, by interacting with the structure, produce interdependencies. Kelly's (1955) personal construct psychology provides a systematic, comprehensive framework for this kind of cognitive psychology. In particular, Kelly suggests that if the person becomes aware of the structure and of the organization within the structure, he or she becomes more able to make adequate predictions and to act according to those anticipations. Kelly (1955) explains construing as a process of abstraction: "We look at the undifferentiated stream of circumstance flowing past us, and we try to find something about it that repeats itself. Once we have abstracted that property, we have a basis for slicing off chunks of time and reality and holding them up for inspection one at a time . . . this is done by construing" (p. 120).

He also describes the relation between construing and anticipation of events: "When one abstracts replicated properties in the events he has already experienced, it becomes possible for him to chart events to come in terms of these same properties. . . . What one predicts is not a fully fleshed-out event, but simply the common intersect of a set of properties. If an event comes along in which all the properties intersect in the prescribed way, one identifies it as the event he expected" (p. 121).

Kelly proposes that each person constructs his own version of reality using a hierarchical system of personal constructs. These processes, to him, constitute a personality — the ways in which each person constructs his or her view of reality and lives within it. In the context of a person learning from experience, the theory describes the ways in which one can negotiate a viable position in his or her own reality, review it, revise it, and refine it within his or her own world.

PERSONAL CONSTRUCT PSYCHOLOGY AS A THEORY OF THE PERSON

Kelly expresses personal construct psychology as a postulate and eleven corollaries. The Fundamental Postulate states that "a person's processes are psychologically channelized by the ways in which he anticipates events" (p. 46). It has been noted:

> Kelly was careful in wording the central statement of this theory to surmount or avoid three of the most persistently knotty problems in psychology — namely, why people do anything at all; why over a period of time, or at any choice point, they do certain things rather than others; and how people who are so obviously different in so many ways can yet be compared within some consistent conceptual framework. (Bannister and Mair 1968: 10)

The anticipatory emphasis of personal construct psychology is inherent in Kelly's approach:

> According to his Fundamental Postulate, all of our representation, including the represented action elements, are anticipatory. Human action, from the standpoint of Kelly's theory, flows from an intention to bring about a correspondence between a person's constructions of the future and his mental representations (personal constructions) of information-producing events. (Mancuso and Adams-Webber 1982b: 8)

ORGANIZATION AND DYNAMICS OF CONSTRUCTS

Kelly (1955) states the corollaries as necessary extensions of the foregoing proposition. They are attempts to expand the theory in a strict formulation, and hence they may appear to be of different types and levels. The Construction Corollary states that "a person anticipates events by construing their replications" (p. 46). In construing or placing an interpretation on events, the individual places into categories those which he/she determines to be similar to and different from others, building up a set of constructs which enable him/her to pick out recurring patterns that he/she can then use to anticipate and predict. It is this tendency which makes an adequate model an essential part of success in any field. One does not always build a new model when faced with new events, but anticipates on the basis of the models which he or she has already developed.

Kelly states his Individuality Corollary as follows: "Persons differ from each other in their constructions of events" (p. 55). This corollary expresses Kelly's stress on the personal nature of construing, but he emphasizes also that "persons can find common ground through construing the experiences of their neighbors along with their own" (p. 56), although "individuals can be found living out their existence next door to each other but in altogether different subjective worlds" (p. 56). He suggests that to obtain the best explanation of a person's organization of experience or behavior, one should find ways to inquire of the person who does the organizing.

The Organization Corollary states that "each person characteristically evolves, for his convenience of anticipating events, a construction system embracing ordinal relationships between constructs" (p. 56). Kelly recognized that "different constructs sometimes lead to incompatible predictions" (p. 56), and he saw a hierarchical relationship that ordered constructs relative to one another as a basis for explaining such contradictions. He conceptualized hierarchic functioning as a process in which the stability of the upper levels allowed for change in the lower ones, so that the arrangement of constructs in a particular hierarchy would be more a determinant of personality than are the constructs themselves.

On stating the Dichotomy Corollary, Kelly proposed that "a person's construction system is composed of a finite number of dichotomous constructs" (p. 59). Kelly saw concepts of similarity and contrast between elements forming the two "poles" of a construct. This does not necessarily involve a binary evaluation of elements; a person can locate an element somewhere between the poles of a construct.

On what basis would a human psychological system process an event in terms of one construction rather than another? To answer this quasi-motivational question, Kelly included a Choice Corollary in his theory: "A person chooses for himself that alternative in a dichotomized construct through which he anticipates the greater possibility for extension and definition of his system" (p. 64). To explicate the system's functions one must keep in mind that constructs are dichotomous, and that they are hierarchically organized. A person locates an event at one or another end of a hierarchically interconnected construct in ways that will maintain the greatest anticipatory power of which the system is capable. To contrast his contextualist motivational position with that of the mechanists Kelly explained that "there is a continuing movement toward the anticipation of events, rather than a series of barters for temporal satisfactions" (p. 68).

Correlatively, not every construct can allow convenient anticipation of every event. Convenience in psychological processes refers to the extent of revision and alteration of the hierarchical structure that would be occasioned by fitting one or another event into one or another pole of a particular construct. The necessary constraints on haphazard, immediate construing is expressed in the theory's Range Corollary: "A construct is convenient for the anticipation of a finite range of events only" (p. 68). This may be thought of as introducing a concept of relevance into the definition of construct systems.

Each of a person's attempted anticipatory constructions represents a hypothesis to be tested not only for its convenience in anticipation, but also for its extending and defining capabilities. Such continual experience leaves a residue of change in the person's system; to formalize his view that the resulting accommodations of the system constitute learning, Kelly stated an Experience Corollary: "A person's construction system varies as he successively construes the replications of events" (p. 77). In a way, the Modulation Corollary takes into account the metaphorizing character of a person's constructs. Novel inputs to the system will be anticipated and will change the system if the system can access permeable constructs, that is, constructs that are "so constituted that new experience and new events can be discriminatively added to those which it already embraces" (p. 81).

The theory's Fragmentation Corollary states that "a person may successively employ a variety of construction subsystems which are inferentially incompatible with each other" (p. 83). Through this corollary Kelly allows for the operations of different psychological systems and hence different methods of inference and forms of rationality within a single individual.

Kelly completed his system of formal propositions by giving two corollaries that relate construing processes to social interaction events. Another person's constructions of events, as well as the events themselves, provide input relative to those events, and, thereby, become a part of the experience of those events. A personal construct theorist must consider that "to the extent that one person embraces a construction of experience which is similar to that employed by another, his psychological processes are similar to those of the other person" (the Commonality Corollary, p. 90). This corollary complements the Individuality Corollary and allows for the "fact that certain groups of people behave in certain respects" (p. 93).

The Sociality Corollary states that "to the extent that one person construes the construction processes of another, he may play a role in a social process involving the other person" (p. 95). Kelly here acknowledges that the construal processes of one person can become elements for construal by another and hence can model the process by which we anticipate the actions of others.

CONSTRUCTIVISM AND CONSTRUCTIVE ALTERNATIVISM

In light of the difficulties in which personality theorists still become ensnared when they take up issues related to reality, or subjectivity, or objectivism, one could easily agree that Kelly's most radical departure from standard theorizing is reflected in his stance on the issue of constructive alternativism. Maddi (1984) very cogently disassembles Fiske's (1977) suggestion that small concrete data units are more real, and that objectivity is to be found in avoiding interpretation or abstraction. He neatly counters Fiske's effort to promote objectivity with the observation, "While there may be an immutable thingness out there, we have only our perceptual systems with which to apprehend it" (p. 18). But nowhere in his prescription for a personology for the 1980s does Maddi advocate, as did Kelly, that the behavioral scientist approach his target of study from that same ontological position. Maddi, as a representative mid-twentieth century scientist, seems unable to acknowledge that individual persons, like individual scientists, cannot render "objective" statements about the universe of events, and he seems unable to grasp the radical significance of Kelly's emphatic assumption that "all of our present interpretations of the universe are subject to revision or replacement" (p. 15).

Although Kelly specified his conclusion that "the universe is really existing and that man is gradually coming to understand it" (p. 6), he also was astute enough to avoid equating reality with "immutable thingness." He notes specifically that "within our universe something is always going on. In fact, that is the way the universe exists; it exists by happening" (p. 7). To come gradually to understand the universe, for both the scientist and the target of the scientist's work, is to come gradually to construct a system of understanding the processes of a "happening world." As personologists who adopt constructivism, and as construing persons (Mancuso and Adams-Webber 1982a), we take it as a given that we create the shared and the private meanings of events. A personal construct theorist cannot have the construct objectivity–subjectivity as a core construct because "it is fundamental to the constructivist's view that the environment can never be directly known but that conception determines perception. We know reality only by acting upon it. . . . The active interaction between the individual and the environment is mediated by the cognitive structures of the individual" (Nystedt and Magnusson 1982: 34). Or as Kelly (1955) said, "No one needs to paint himself into a corner; no one needs to be completely hemmed in by circumstances; no one needs to be a victim of his biography" (p. 15).

PROBING THE CONSTRUCT SYSTEM — REPERTORY GRIDS

Each person may be seen as a personal scientist (Shaw 1980), classifying, categorizing and theorizing about his/her world, anticipating on the basis of his/her theories, and acting on the basis of his/her anticipation. The personal scientist models his/her world, using his/her theory or model to make predictions or to act in the world, and experiencing events that may or may not be influenced by his/her actions. This experience of events is then fitted to the model, which may be reviewed or revised in light of experience to make more "successful" predictions.

> A theory is a device to enable man to deal comprehensively with what might otherwise be an overwhelming variety of events. . . . Strictly speaking, man invents his theory; he never discovers it. . . . The process by which a theory is derived is known as abstraction, and the complementary process by which it is extended to events is known as generalization. Both may properly be regarded as psychological processes, or even as aspects of the same psychological process. . . . Thus meaning is not extracted from nature, but projected by man upon it. (Kelly 1965: 289, 290)

THE REPERTORY GRID AS A REPRESENTATION OF PERSONAL MODELS

Kelly suggested the technique of the repertory grid to represent the repertoire of constructions that the individual has acquired from his or her personal observations of the world. A repertory grid or "construction matrix" is essentially a two-way classification of data in which events and abstractions, or constructs, are interlaced. In his own terms, "it expresses one's own finite system of cross-references between the personal observations he has made and the personal constructs he has erected" (Kelly 1965: 291).

The personal observations are known as elements. Elements were originally constituted from the role titles of significant people in the life of the particular individual. The personal constructs are bipolar dimensions that group the elements into varying clusters according to their similarities and differences within the individual's frames of reference. Kelly used the repertory grid as a tool to assist with psychotherapy, using significant others as elements. Since its introduction, it has been used in many settings to probe the construct systems of psychiatric patients, student teachers, effective managers, knitwear inspectors, and rivet selectors in the aircraft industry. The elements may be people, things, events, or experiences, which are related to the particular problem or purpose for using the grid.

PRECOMPUTER ELICITATION TECHNIQUES

Constructs may be elicited by many means, the most common being the minimal context form or triadic method (i.e., "Can you say in what way two of these elements are alike, and in the same way different from the third?"), and the full context form ("Considering the whole set of elements, think of an important way they divide into two [or more] groups"). Other methods derived from these are splitting the two most similar elements to put one on each pole of a new construct, and naming of a construct to describe the difference between the two most dissimilar elements.

Another useful form of construct elicitation is a technique developed by Hinkle (1965) called *laddering*. Initially, constructs are elicited by a standard method, then one construct is selected and the question asked, "Which pole is the one you would prefer to be rated on?" then "Why would you prefer that pole?" and "What is the opposite of that?" This then provides a new construct that is more superordinate or generalized than the original one. As this process is repeated, a hierarchy or heterarchy of superordinate constructs is elicited.

THE ROLE AND SIGNIFICANCE OF COMPUTERS

During the past 20 years, the digital computer has come to assume a role of increasing importance in psychology and in the application of psychological techniques. During this period also, the nature of available computer resources has itself changed dramatically. In the early 1960s we submitted massive computations of variance and factor analyses to some remote computing center that punched our data onto cards and sent back the results, often days later. By the early 1970s we had our own minicomputers in our laboratories giving a hands-on system for direct experimental control, but they were so expensive that they were available only as a shared resource to a group of researchers on a booking basis. The central computers also changed during that period, to allow some form of interactive time-sharing whereby we could enter our own data on a local terminal and receive the analysis back reasonably rapidly on the same terminal. In the last few years, a further development has taken place in that so-called personal computers have become available, offering us great power and a wide range of facilities at such a low cost that an individual can have one or more such machines dedicated to his or her work.

These advances in computer technology have offered opportunities for the automation of psychological testing, which have been widely taken advantage of (Elithorn and Telford 1969; Gedye and Miller 1969; Elwood 1972a, 1972b, 1972c; Klinge and Rodziewicz 1976; Thompson and Wilson 1982; Volans and Levy 1982). Direct interaction between patients and computers has now been shown to be successful and acceptable in an experimental environment (Card et al. 1974; Lucas 1977), and it has even proved possible for the computer to act as an effective therapist (Stodolsky 1970). Automated psychological testing has also been widely validated against experts administering the same test (Ridgway, MacCulloch, and Mills 1982; Calvert and Waterfall 1982; Watts, Baddeley, and Williams 1982; Acker 1982). These advances in technology have also offered the opportunity for new approaches to the testing process that are dependent on having powerful computational facilities in operation during the test. In particular, it has become possible to obtain test results speedily and in a manner that aids both expert interpretation and self-interpretation.

Many researchers have developed computer techniques for the elicitation and analysis of personal construct psychological data, some of which are reported in the following chapters. Many of these are interactive programs that allow a greater degree of autonomy and more control to be given to the user. It would be easy to assume that such interactive programs are merely more convenient ways of eliciting construct systems through extensions of Kelly's repertory grid and do not themselves add anything qualitatively new to the process. However, such an assumption would be missing certain crucial psychological factors in the person–computer situation and its differences from the person–person situation. For example, we have observed informally, in making the grid elicitation program PEGASUS (see Chapter 3) available to a wide range of people in a variety of situations, that those coming to it for the first time often seem to find it a very dramatic experience. They react to it intensely and become gripped by the interactive process of construct elicitation. They also feel that they are learning something new from the process and are prepared to use this in determining their behavior.

Probably such involvement is also significant in the elicitation of construct systems by a person rather than by computer interaction. However, we believe there are certain quite fundamental differences when the elicitation is done in such a way that interpersonal interaction is clearly absent. In particular, when a person is feeding back comments and guidance, it is a natural and ready assumption that the constructs are being injected rather than elicited. It is easy for the subject to believe that the elicited constructs do not come from him/herself, but that a tutorial or debating situation with another person is taking place. It is necessary to persuade him/her that this is not so, and the persuasion has to be stronger the more striking and significant the constructs elicited. However, when a computer is the tool by which his/her construct structure is being reflected or laid bare, then such an assumption of outside injection and interference is far less tenable.

When constructs are being elicited by a computer program, then it is more likely to be accepted that it is precisely and only oneself that is being portrayed. We trust a computer program to be doing just what it appears to be doing without deeper motivations and without attempting to persuade us to its point of view. No one is telling the user anything. One is seeing, in interacting with PEGASUS, possibly for the first time, the basis for one's own thought processes. Very often extreme surprise is the first reaction. If another person were eliciting the construct structure, then the surprise would be taken as an indication that he or she was incorrect, and one would ignore or argue with him/her. With computer elicitation, it is more likely that one will accept the reflected structures as self-generated, and the surprise will act as a motivation to know more.

That this knowledge can be totally private is another important feature of interaction with the computer. We do not like to be caught, as Kelly put it, with our constructs down. When another person is involved, we are more reluctant to expose and explore our constructs the more surprising they are, perhaps because the surprise is often the result of a conflict between our ostensive value judgments and the basis of our behavior. Or it may just be sloppy verbal behavior that we are naming two distinct constructs with the same label. For example, in using PEGASUS, a scientist found that he was using the word *time* to label several different elements and was generating confusion in his arguments because of this.

Another reason that we are reluctant to explore construct structures freely in interacting with another person, particularly a professional, is that we are acutely aware of the possible waste of their time. This phenomenon has been noted (Card et al. 1974) as a major reason for the preference expressed by patients to be interviewed through an interactive computer program rather than by their doctors. There are many pressures and artifacts of interpersonal relationships that can totally obscure and undermine such reflective processes that we require in the elicitation of personal constructs.

It is interesting to note that this argument has been put in reverse. Adams (1979) notes that children learn quickly to play games on a personal computer and conjectures that this is because of the lack of interpersonal complications. She suggests, however, that "one of the benefits of game-playing is that a child learns how to behave with and towards others, how to cope with success and failure, and what effect it has on others. In the human–computer relationship the child does not learn these valuable social skills" (p. 29). We are arguing conversely that the need to deploy such "social skills" is a burden that can seriously detract from the exploration of the self.

SIGNIFICANT APPLICATION AREAS

These cognitive modeling techniques have been used widely in many areas of work. The ones covered in this book are clinical psychology, education, management, and computer science. Commenting on clinical psychology, Shepherd and Watson (1982) state, "Personal meanings arise from events and relationships which a person interprets within his most basic frame of reference — his awareness of being an individual, conscious of personal agency and personal biography" (p. 1). Fransella (1982) explains, "To construe is to impose meaning or interpretations upon something or some things" (p. 47). Many clinical psychologists have used personal construct psychology to explore a patient's personal meaning system, and to make explicit the implicitly held models of the world that lead to behavior, that is, prediction or action.

In education and learning, many groups are using personal construct psychology techniques. Phillips (1981) has studied the development of research skills and the styles of supervision of doctoral students. She elicited information from the viewpoint of the students at stages during the progress of their research over three or four years, and from the viewpoint of their supervisors. Valuable insights were acquired by both parties about this process, and some interesting results were obtained. Pope and Shaw (1981) and Pope and Keen (1981) have related personal construct psychology to various philosophies or ideologies of education mainly as they applied to school learning, and they extended this to areas of educational research and to some of the current issues in education.

Personal construct psychology has been found to apply equally well in helping an expert articulate her skill, as it has been in more traditional uses, such as in helping a person referred for psychotherapy to articulate her problems, or a student her needs for learning. The initial success of expert system developments (Michie 1979; Gevarter 1983; Reitman 1984) and the development of a number of reasonably domain-independent software support systems for the encoding and application of knowledge (Hayes-Roth, Waterman, and Lenat 1983) has opened up the possibility of widespread usage of expert systems. In particular, the Japanese Fifth Generation Computing System development program (Moto-oka 1982; Gaines 1984) assumes this will happen and is concerned with knowledge processing rather than information processing. However, what Feigenbaum (1980) terms *knowledge engineering* (the reduction of a large body of knowledge to a precise set of facts and rules) has already become a major bottleneck impeding the application of expert systems in new domains. We need to understand more about the nature of expertise in itself (Hawkins 1983) and to be able to apply this knowledge to the elicitation of expertise in specific domains.

Shaw (1983) and Boose (1984) have used personal construct psychology techniques to elicit and structure expert knowledge, and to analyze and refine this knowledge into production rules. (An example of a production rule so obtained is: If a database is inverted, then it will not run on a Vax computer.) These rules can then be assembled into an expert system building tool or shell for immediate refinement and debugging. Boose (1985a) has developed over 200 expert systems, using personal construct psychology as a base.

PERSONAL CONSTRUCT PSYCHOLOGY IN THE ERA OF MENTAL MODELS AND THE PERSONAL COMPUTER

These are exciting times for psychologists. The constructivist paradigm, the development of cognitive science, the legitimation of mental models, and the availability of the personal computer together offer the vehicles to explore new territories. The remaining chapters in this book are by those who have constructed those vehicles and have begun to use them. All those who have participated in generating this book hope that the wider dissemination of these tools, techniques, and experience will encourage others to join in the exploration. Many different disciplines of psychology have much to gain from the constructivist paradigm and its operationalization through the personal computer. The following chapters should promote this symbiotic relationship.

3 PLANET: A Computer-Based System for Personal Learning, Analysis, Negotiation, and Elicitation Techniques

Mildred L. G. Shaw and Brian R. Gaines

Repertory grids have proved to be powerful tools in a wide range of disciplines and applications. However, elicitation by people requires skills in interviewing techniques, personal construct psychology, and the avoidance of interpersonal artifacts. Computer-based elicitation techniques have proved capable of supplying these skills, essentially acting as expert systems for grid elicitation. PLANET is an integrated suite of elicitation and analysis programs designed for widespread application by users with widely varying backgrounds. This paper presents our experience in the development, dissemination, and application of PLANET. The subprograms described are: PEGASUS, which elicits from a person the constructs he or she is using; SOCIOGRIDS, which analyzes the relationships between members of a group through their differing construct systems and determines consensual constructs; MINUS, which compares two grids; CORE, which extracts the invariant core constructs; FOCUS, which hierarchically clusters constructs and elements; PRINGRID, which gives a principal components analysis; and ENTAIL, which analyzes the logical dependencies between constructs and can be used to develop rules for an expert system shell that acts as a cognitive model of the person.

During the past 20 years, the digital computer has come to assume a role of increasing importance in psychology and in the application of psychological techniques. Also during this period, the nature of available computer resources has itself changed dramatically. In the early 1960s we submitted massive computations of analyses of variance and factor analyses to some remote computing center that punched our data onto cards and sent back the results, often days later. By the early 1970s we had our own minicomputers in our laboratories, which provided a hands-on system for direct experimental control, but were so expensive they were available only as a resource shared by a group of researchers on a booking basis. The central computers also changed during that period to allow some form of interactive time sharing whereby we could enter our own data on a local terminal and receive the analysis back reasonably rapidly on the same terminal. In the last decade, a further development has taken place in that so-called personal computers have become available, offering us great power and a wide range of facilities at such a low cost that an individual can have one or more such machines dedicated to his or her work.

This chapter is concerned with a set of repertory grid programs implemented as an integrated system on a low-cost microcomputer. This was done in such a way that all aspects of the operation and many aspects of the application of the system are self-evident to users who are issued with only a program disk and a simple manual. These users are widespread geographically, with a wide range of experience of computer systems, test procedures, analytic techniques, and information presenta-tion. It is also a requirement of some potential users that they be able to reprogram the interactive dialogue with their clients to reflect the particular purpose for which a grid is being elicited, for example personnel selection, career guidance, or industrial training. Some users also wish to translate the dialogue from English into their native language. The chapter also describes the techniques adopted to allow these modifications without requiring programming knowledge on the part of the users and without undermining the integrity of the program suite.

COMPUTER-BASED REPERTORY GRID ELICITATION AND ANALYSIS

The repertory grid and its applications are described in Chapters 1 and 2 of this book. In computer terms, the repertory grid is a simple data structure of entities (the elements) and attributes (the constructs) that is complete when each entity has been assigned a value for each attribute (the ratings). In these terms a grid can be seen as part of an entity–attribute database (Chen 1980). In addition, with each grid it is useful to maintain explanatory and classificatory data, such as a list of subjects from whom it was elicited, and the time and purpose of elicitation.

REPERTORY GRID ELICITATION

In the past the elicitation of repertory grids has been a task requiring a skilled psychologist who can draw out a person's constructs while not imposing his or her own ideas or personality. This has involved the development of a variety of techniques and methodologies for grid elicitation (Kelly 1955; Fransella and Bannister 1977). The advent of powerful, low-cost personal computers has made it possible to program some of the elicitation techniques in a form in which they can be applied automatically. It is also possible to codify some of the techniques in a form in which they can be administered through a conversational interactive computer program. PLANET contains two such programs: PEGASUS, which elicits a single grid from a person and feeds back comments and suggestions during the elicitation; and ARGUS, which elicits a set of grids from a person using a number of different perspectives.

PEGASUS is a set of programs, each of which elicits a repertory grid (details of the variants are given later). The most commonly used version incorporates continual commentary on patterns in the responses. Six elements are initially chosen by the user with special attention to the purpose for eliciting the grid. The first four constructs are elicited from fixed triads and thereafter random or chosen triads are offered. Real-time processing allows feedback about highly matched constructs and elements. Options offered are: to add an element to split highly matched constructs; to replace two highly matched constructs with one; to add a construct to split highly matched elements; to delete one or more elements; to delete one or more constructs; to add a construct without using a triad; to add an element; to change the level of feedback commentary; to redefine the purpose for eliciting the grid. A flow chart of control around these options is shown in Figure 3.1.

ARGUS elicits a set of grids simultaneously from one person holding several roles or points of view. First, the elements, which are also the roles or points of view, are elicited, followed by three constructs from fixed triads. These construct labels are then used for a new set of ratings

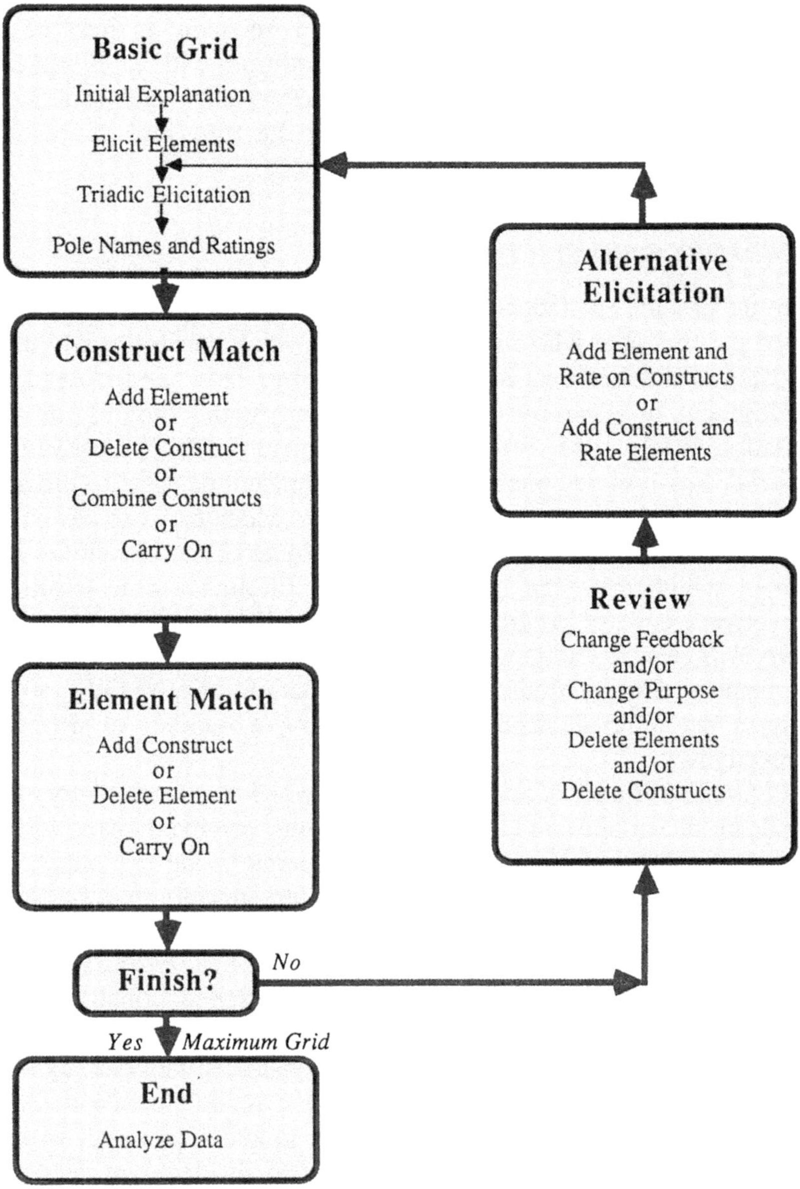

Fig. 3.1.
Flow of control in PEGASUS elicitation.

to be entered for each perspective in turn, and at each stage another construct that is felt to be important for that role is added. Eventually, each perspective has a grid using construct names from all the perspectives, but with unique rating values. The final set of grids, all with the same element and construct labels, can be processed with the structure analysis programs SOCIOGRIDS, CORE, or MINUS (described below).

REPERTORY GRID ANALYSIS

Repertory grids in themselves encode information about a person's way of looking at the world. This information can be used in its own right for some purposes, since it is an aid to remembering the basis for decisions and actions. It can also be analyzed in a variety of ways to bring out possible underlying structures, or construct systems, in a person's world view and its relationship to those of others. There are a number of forms of analysis that are widely used for different purposes, and PLANET offers all the commonly used techniques plus the developments of recent years. The form of analysis that should be used in a particular case is partly a matter of personal preference and partly a matter of purpose. Comparisons have been made in the literature of different analyses with the same data (Shaw 1981).

It is convenient to divide analysis techniques into three groups: those concerned with the analysis of a single grid; those concerned with a pair of grids; and those concerned with a group of grids.

ANALYSIS OF A SINGLE GRID

For any given construct we may regard the numbers in the grid as a vector of values, giving the assignment of each element in turn to one or the other of the poles of the construct. From this point of view each construct is represented as a point in a multidimensional space whose dimension is the number of elements involved. A natural relation to examine between constructs is then the distance between them in this space. Two constructs that are zero distance apart are such that all elements are construed in the same way in relation to them, and hence we might infer that they are being used in the same way; in some sense they are equivalent constructs. For constructs that are not equivalent, we may analyze the entire constellation in space to determine a set of axes such that the projection of each construct onto the first axis accounts for most of the distance between them, the projection on the second axis accounts for most of the remaining distance, and so on. This is a principal components analysis of the construct space (Slater 1976, 1977), and it is related to the factor analysis of semantic space used in the study of semantic differentials (Osgood, Suci, and Tannenbaum 1957). We may also group constructs that are close together in space, using some form of cluster analysis (Shaw 1980).

The FOCUS algorithm (Shaw 1980) is a distance-based hierarchical cluster analysis technique that sorts the constructs into a linear order, such that constructs closest together in space are also closest together in the order. It has the advantage in presentation that the sorting is used only to re-present the original grid reorganized according to the proximity of constructs and elements. It is left to the user to construe the result in terms of his or her own personal meaning and to confirm this directly in terms of the original data. Element and construct matching scores are computed by subtracting the rating values in each position of the two elements or constructs, summing them, then mapping the result into 0 percent to 100 percent similarity for the elements, and 100 percent to –100 percent similarity for the constructs. Two matrices are thus formed, one for elements and one for constructs. Clusters are computed by selecting the highest numbers form these matrices (that is, the most similar in terms of the ratings given) and continuing this process for the next cluster, until all elements and constructs are incorporated. The tree diagrams show these clusters and are imposed on the re-sorted original grid data.

The PRINGRID algorithm is another distance-based cluster analysis using standard principal component analysis techniques and giving the same results as Slater's INGRID (Slater 1976, 1977).

The alternative to distance-based methods of grid analysis is a logical analysis, looking at constructs as predicates applying to elements. The ENTAIL algorithm (Gaines and Shaw 1981) derives asymmetric implications between the construct poles so that one can infer how a new element might be placed on one construct, given how it is placed on others. This is discussed in more detail with an example given in a later section.

ANALYSIS OF A PAIR OF GRIDS

It is desirable to compare several repertory grids. Shaw (1980) discusses exchange grids for the measurement of understanding and agreement between either two people or one person on two occasions.

For example, two people may each elicit a grid in an area of common knowledge or experience. Each may choose his or her own elements independently of the other, and elicit and rate his or her constructs quite separately. Each then makes two copies of the grid, leaving out the rating values. Both these copies are filled in by the other person, one as he or she uses those constructs on those elements and the other as he or she thinks the original was completed. By comparing pairs of these grids it is possible to map the extent of overlap of the agreement and understanding between the two people.

There are three ways in which PLANET can be used to compare two grids. The first is to concatenate those grids that have the same elements, and then to use the algorithms of FOCUS, ENTAIL, or PRINGRID as if they were one large grid. One can then explore the interaction of ideas by examining mixed clusters of constructs from the two grids.

The MINUS algorithm requires the two grids to have the same element and construct names, and compares the two to indicate where changes in construing occur. This is done by superimposing one grid on the other and subtracting the equivalent rating values. The parts of the grids that are the same are then clearly visible, as is the extent of the variation elsewhere. The result shows where there was agreement indicated by areas of blanks, and grades of difference indicated by increasing numbers.

Again starting with two grids having the same element and construct names, the CORE algorithm examines the most changed element and construct alternately, identifies it, and allows it to be deleted from the grids. In this way the core elements and constructs that show agreement or understanding in the two grids are identified and recorded. This method has been used to chart change over time, and to evaluate courses by examining changes in the participant rather than using the traditional method of examining behavioral objectives.

ANALYSIS OF A GROUP OF GRIDS

The SOCIOGRIDS algorithms analyze a set of repertory grids elicited from a group that shares the same elements. SOCIOGRIDS compares every pair of grids using the FOCUS algorithm and produces a set of *socionets* which indicates the links of similar construing within the group. A *mode grid* is also produced that shows the constructs which are readily understood by the majority of the group, and this is filed for future processing on one of the structure analysis programs. Every construct that has been used is listed in order of how highly matched it is across all grids, with a description of where it originated.

This technique can be used for a wide variety of purposes concerned with group structures, cultures, and relationships. It has been used for investigating the relative positions of members of a small group, and the content of the shared terms and values. It has been used to investigate management hierarchies defined operationally through the interrelationships of construct systems, and in conjunction with the Delphi technique to promote common values and understanding in a group.

KEY FEATURES OF THE PLANET SYSTEM

PLANET runs as a system of programs under the DOS 3.3 operating system on the Apple II family of computers. It requires two disk drives (referred to by the normal convention as drive 1 and drive 2) with the controller installed in slot 6. It also requires a printer usually available through slot 1 on the Apple. This is a standard operating configuration for the Apple II and //e.

```
****************************************
* PLANET  PERSONAL LEARNING, ANALYSIS, *
* NEGOTIATION & ELICITATION TECHNIQUES *
*            COPYRIGHT 1982            *
*   CENTRE FOR MAN-COMPUTER STUDIES    *
****************************************

 <P> PEGASUS    - ELICITATION

 <A> ARGUS      - MULTIPLE ELICITATION

 <S> STRUCTURE  - ANALYSIS TECHNIQUES

 <D> DATA       - DATA FILES UTILITY

 <O> OUTPUT     - OUTPUT DEVICE UTILITY


WHICH DO YOU WANT?
```

Fig. 3.2.
PLANET main menu.

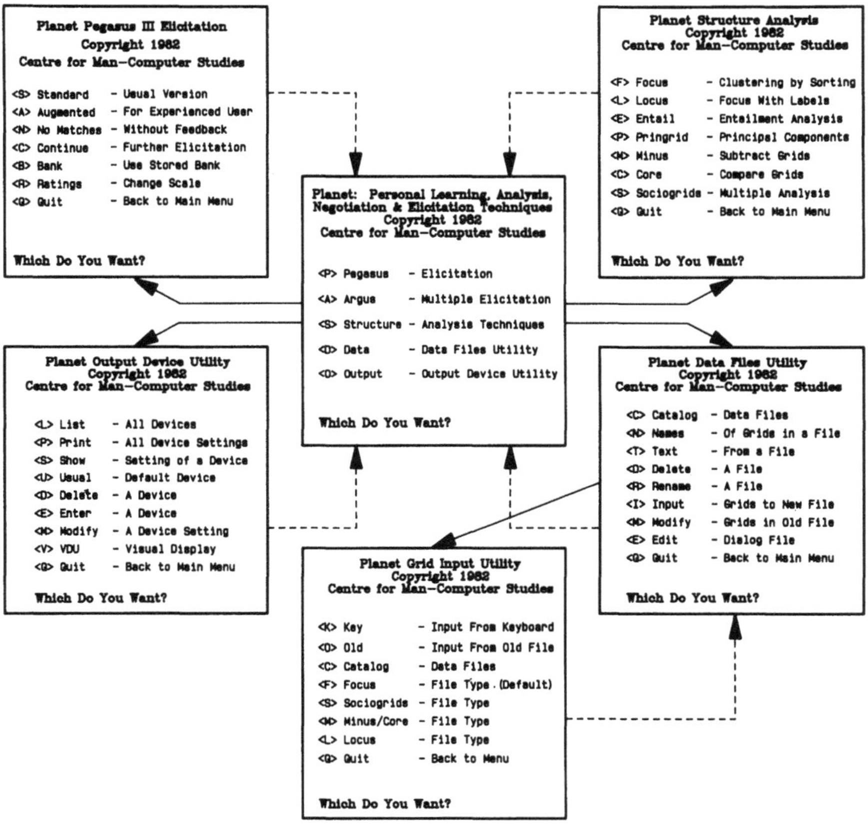

Fig. 3.3.
PLANET overall menu system.

To run PLANET, two disks are needed: the PLANET program disk and a data disk. The data disk can be any disk formatted for operation under DOS 3.3. PLANET is designed to check for possible errors in operation that may cause loss of valuable data, and checks that the data disk is valid before it commences any operations.

The main menu is both the starting and return point for all the PLANET programs. It has a PLANET logo as a heading followed by a list of the options, shown in Figure 3.2.

The reply to the question is simply the single character that appears in the angle brackets on the left-hand side of the chosen option. PLANET will fill in the rest and then call the program for the option requested.

When PLANET program options are complete they generally return to the main menu. If an error occurs in a program (such as a disk write being impossible because the disk is full), this is reported and a return is made to the main menu.

Figure 3.3 shows the overall PLANET system through printouts of the menus as they appear on the screen, together with the flow of control between them. Individual programs and utilities are described in the next two sections.

```
     PLANET PEGASUS III ELICITATION
             COPYRIGHT 1982
    CENTRE FOR MAN-COMPUTER STUDIES

<S> STANDARD    - USUAL VERSION

<A> AUGMENTED   - FOR EXPERIENCED USER

<N> NO MATCHES  - WITHOUT FEEDBACK

<C> CONTINUE    - FURTHER ELICITATION

<B> BANK        - USE STORED BANK

<R> RATINGS     - CHANGE SCALE

<Q> QUIT        - BACK TO MAIN MENU


WHICH DO YOU WANT?
```

Fig. 3.4.
PEGASUS menu.

GRID ELICITATION PROGRAMS

PEGASUS is an interactive program for eliciting a repertory grid that may have up to 15 elements and 15 constructs. Various versions that can be used are shown in the PEGASUS menu in Figure 3.4 and described in detail below. The menu in Figure 3.4 also shows the option to change the rating scale from the usual five points to anything from two points to nine points.

In the STANDARD version, six elements are chosen initially by the user, with special attention to the purpose for eliciting the grid. The first four constructs are elicited using fixed triads, and thereafter random or chosen triads are offered. Real-time processing gives continuous feedback about highly matched constructs and elements.

Options offered to the user in PEGASUS include:

- adding an element to split highly matched constructs
- replacing two highly matched constructs by one
- adding a construct to split highly matched elements
- deleting one or more element
- deleting one or more construct
- adding a construct without using a triad
- adding an element
- changing the level of feedback commentary
- redefining the purpose for eliciting the grid

The AUGMENTED version of PEGASUS is identical to the STANDARD version, except that extra elements may be added initially. It is intended for the fluent PEGASUS user.

The NO MATCHES version of PEGASUS gives a conventional triadic grid elicitation without any feedback, but with the opportunity to add and delete elements and constructs where the user wishes.

The CONTINUE version of PEGASUS allows the user to continue an elicitation started earlier. Otherwise, CONTINUE is identical to the STANDARD version.

The BANK version of PEGASUS provides an *expert* grid, which the user does not see at first but against which the elicited constructs are matched. Feedback is given not only on how the user's constructs match each other, but also on how they relate to the expert constructs. The final grid is put on file, and can be processed on FOCUS (or another of the

STRUCTURE programs) to show how the two sets of constructs are interrelated. The expert grid should be entered initially using one of the previous versions of PEGASUS.

The RATINGS option allows the rating scale being used in any version of PEGASUS to be changed. It is set by default to be 1 through 5, but the upper limit may be changed to be anywhere between 2 and 9. For those who frequently use a rating scale other than 1 to 5, a facility has been added to the PEGASUS menu where typing the value (i.e., 2 through 9) rather than R for RATINGS sets it up immediately. The rating scale range is now also shown in the menu.

ARGUS elicits a set of grids simultaneously from one person who is instructed to work from several roles or perspectives. First, the elements (significant others) are elicited, then three constructs are elicited from fixed triads in the usual way. These construct labels are then used for a new set of ratings, to be filled in from each perspective in turn. At each stage another construct that is felt to be important for that perspective is added. Finally the set of grids, all with the same element and construct labels but with different ratings, are filed for future processing on FOCUS, CORE, or SOCIOGRIDS.

STRUCTURE PROGRAMS

The STRUCTURE menu gives access to all the grid analysis programs available in PLANET. All of these programs analyze a grid (or grids) from a file on the data disk and produce output on the printer. The STRUCTURE menu in Figure 3.5 shows all the analysis programs available.

FOCUS gives the two-way hierarchical cluster analysis previously described. It will analyze grids with up to 54 elements and 54 constructs. Whether or not it has space to print them out depends on the printer being used. FOCUS checks the width specified for the printer and will print out the focused grid either in one piece complete with construct tree, or in two pieces with the construct tree separate, to be attached to the right-hand side of the focused grid.

LOCUS is a version of FOCUS that prints out the element and construct labels. It is especially useful with a PEGASUS grid or for displaying grids. It can be used for either the raw or the clustered version of the data, and will analyze up to 30 elements and 30 constructs.

ENTAIL gives the logical entailment analysis previously described. It will analyze up to 32 elements and 32 constructs. The implicational

```
           PLANET STRUCTURE ANALYSIS
                COPYRIGHT 1982
         CENTRE FOR MAN-COMPUTER STUDIES

     <F> FOCUS      - CLUSTERING BY SORTING
     <L> LOCUS      - FOCUS WITH LABELS
     <E> ENTAIL     - ENTAILMENT ANALYSIS
     <P> PRINGRID   - PRINCIPAL COMPONENTS
     <M> MINUS      - SUBTRACT GRIDS
     <C> CORE       - COMPARE GRIDS
     <S> SOCIOGRIDS - MULTIPLE ANALYSIS
     <Q> QUIT       - BACK TO MAIN MENU


     WHICH DO YOU WANT?
```

FIG. 3.5.
STRUCTURE menu.

relation of entailment is asymmetric, and hence ENTAIL gives a form of construct analysis that brings out order relationships and hierarchies if present.

PRINGRID is a principal components analysis program giving an analysis similar to Slater's INGRID (Slater 1976, 1977), presenting it both numerically and as graphic plots. It will analyze up to 30 elements and 30 constructs.

MINUS compares two grids as previously described. It highlights the differences between them by subtracting ratings in equivalent positions. A measure is given to indicate how similar the two grids are overall. It will analyze grids of up to 54 elements and 54 constructs.

CORE is an interactive program that compares two grids as previously described. The two grids of up to 54 elements and 54 constructs are processed by successively determining the element and construct that have changed the most between the two grids. The user is then offered the opportunity to delete the element or construct at each stage, finally leaving the core or unchanged part of the grids. The technique is essentially interactive, but the option is given to maintain a record of the matches, action taken, and final core grid on the printer.

SOCIOGRIDS analyzes a set of up to 20 repertory grids elicited from a group that shares the same elements as previously described. The number of elements can be up to 20, but must be constant across grids, as must the rating scale. The number of constructs can be up to 20 and can differ from one grid to another. More details on these programs, their operation, and applications are given in Shaw (1980, 1981).

THE DATA UTILITY

DATA is a utility enabling an experimenter to examine, update, and maintain the experimental data and records of a program of personal construct elicitation using PLANET. The menu is shown in Figure 3.6.

CATALOG allows the files on the PLANET DATA disk to be catalogued by the user, and the output to be directed to the screen or the printer.

The NAMES of the grids in a particular file can be output with the details of the sizes of the corresponding grids onto the screen or the printer.

The TEXT of any data file on the PLANET DATA disk can be printed onto the screen or the printer.

DELETE allows the user to delete a data file.

RENAME allows the user to rename a data file.

The INPUT program is used to enter data for processing on any of the STRUCTURE programs. It will accept grids from within existing files, or from the keyboard, and forms a new file of grids. Typical applications of INPUT are entering grid data elicited by means other than

```
              PLANET DATA FILES UTILITY
                   COPYRIGHT 1982
           CENTRE FOR MAN-COMPUTER STUDIES

    <C> CATALOG       - DATA FILES
    <N> NAMES         - OF GRIDS IN A FILE
    <T> TEXT          - FROM A FILE
    <D> DELETE        - A FILE
    <R> RENAME        - A FILE
    <I> INPUT         - GRIDS TO NEW FILE
    <M> MODIFY        - GRIDS IN OLD FILE
    <E> EDIT          - DIALOG FILE
    <Q> QUIT          - BACK TO MAIN MENU


WHICH DO YOU WANT?
```

Fig. 3.6.
DATA menu.

the PEGASUS and ARGUS programs, and bringing together a number of grids elicited by PEGASUS into a single file for analysis by SOCIOGRIDS, MINUS, or CORE.

INPUT first asks the user for a file name for the new grid file. If a file of that name already exists, the user is given the option to overwrite it or to choose a new name. The menu then appears as shown in Figure 3.7.

Note that the QUIT command is particularly significant for INPUT, since it is only when this command is given that the new file being created is closed. Hence, any number and mix of grids may be created from data entered from the keyboard or from old files.

The KEY option allows grid data to be entered from the keyboard. Checks are made that the actual data entered corresponds in numbers of elements, constructs, and scale range to that specified.

The OLD option allows grid data to be entered from an existing file of grids. Again, checks are made to ensure that the data in the file satisfies any constraints specified.

The file type can be indicated initially, or at any time, and INPUT will check that grids entered previously and thereafter are compatible with the requirements of that file type. FOCUS allows any mix of grids in a file to be analyzed. SOCIOGRIDS requires that all grids have the same number of elements and rating scale range. MINUS and CORE require, in addition, that the number of constructs be the same. LOCUS operates on

```
          PLANET GRID INPUT UTILITY
               COPYRIGHT 1982
        CENTRE FOR MAN-COMPUTER STUDIES

     <K> KEY        - INPUT FROM KEYBOARD
     <O> OLD        - INPUT FROM OLD FILE
     <C> CATALOG    - DATA FILES
     <F> FOCUS      - FILE TYPE (DEFAULT)
     <S> SOCIOGRIDS - FILE TYPE
     <M> MINUS/CORE - FILE TYPE
     <L> LOCUS      - FILE TYPE
     <Q> QUIT       - BACK TO MENU


WHICH DO YOU WANT?
```

Fig. 3.7.
INPUT menu.

a file containing only one grid, together with the construct labels and element names, and its file type is unique in incorporating this extra data; it is the file type generated by PEGASUS. Setting the file type enables INPUT to perform checks to validate the data being entered. The initial file type set by default is FOCUS.

The MODIFY program can be used to edit data already on file. It steps through the grids in the file one at a time, giving options to add or delete elements or constructs, change particular values in the grid, or change the grid name.

EDIT copies the PEGASUS dialog file onto the PLANET DATA disk, so that it can be edited or rewritten (see section on PLANET PEGASUS Dialogue below).

PRINTER CHARACTERISTICS

Whereas the machine configuration, operating system, and language on the Apple II are more highly standardized than that of most microcomputers, the printers used vary considerably. Since one of the key features of the analysis programs in PLANET is meaningful layout of the clustered data, exact printer control is very important. The OUTPUT utility controls a general interpreter that handles all printer set-up commands and does this uniformly throughout the system. The interpreter is driven by a printer device file set up with the characteristics of a wide range of printers. The user can modify these using OUTPUT, adding additional ones as required, and changing the default printer characteristics being used. The interpreter allows for all the many variations of control characters to be sent to printers, status words to be modified in memory, slot changes to be made, and so on, and allows messages to be put out on the screen as to which printer is being used and when. The OUTPUT utility menu is shown in Figure 3.8.

LIST lists the devices available by name on the screen or printer.
PRINT prints the contents of the device file on the screen or printer.
SHOW shows the setting of a specified device.
USUAL sets up the default device to be used as that specified.
DELETE deletes a device from the device file.
ENTER enters a new device into the device file.
MODIFY modifies the characteristics of a specified device.

```
      PLANET OUTPUT DEVICE UTILITY
              COPYRIGHT 1982
      CENTRE FOR MAN-COMPUTER STUDIES

   <L> LIST       - ALL DEVICES
   <P> PRINT      - ALL DEVICE SETTINGS
   <S> SHOW       - SETTING OF A DEVICE
   <U> USUAL      - DEFAULT DEVICE
   <D> DELETE     - A DEVICE
   <E> ENTER      - A DEVICE
   <M> MODIFY     - A DEVICE SETTING
   <V> VDU        - VISUAL DISPLAY
   <Q> QUIT       - BACK TO MAIN MENU

WHICH DO YOU WANT?
```

Fig. 3.8.
OUTPUT menu.

PLANET PEGASUS DIALOGUE

One of the new features of PEGASUS is that the actual dialogue with the user may be readily changed for different applications or national languages.

For example, the standard dialogue is intended to cover as many applications as possible and refers to general elements. It also has an explanation in terms of repertory grids. In a specific application such as market research for a particular class of products, psychiatric studies of particular problems, or personnel studies of relations with subordinates, it is desirable to have a dialogue reflecting the terminology usual in that application. Elements may become detergents, relatives, or staff; and the explanatory text may be revised to explain the particular activity being undertaken.

Clearly similar considerations apply to the use of PEGASUS for repertory grid elicitation in a language other than English. One important aspect of repertory grids is that they are language independent, with the entire vocabulary of the data coming from the person from whom the grid is elicited. However, in computer elicitation this also requires that the explanation and feedback be available in the language being used. PEGASUS now makes this possible.

The standard PEGASUS text file is issued on the program disk and is a DOS 3.3 text file (Type T). This file consists of blocks of free text on one or more lines separated by a line commencing with $$. Any text after the $$ is not used or stored by PEGASUS; it normally contains a number for the dialogue and possibly a comment on its use. An example is given in Figure 3.9.

The quotation marks show the whole of the text that is output, including extra new lines and spaces at the end of a line. A blank line causes a carriage return and a blank line to be output. There must be quotation marks if a , or " or : is included in the line, otherwise they are optional.

If a section of text needs to be omitted, the actual text lines must be deleted but not the $$ line following the text. For example, to delete the text in Section 8, it would become that shown in Figure 3.10.

If a line contains just # then a substitution occurs in the text either from a previous input by the user or calculated from the stage of the elicitation. An example is given in Figure 3.11, where the number of stored constructs is substituted in place of the #.

```
"$$15"
""
"Do you want to change the pole names"
"$$16 CHECK AFTER ELICITATION"
"Your element name is too long. Please choose a shorter one"
""
"$$17 CHECK AFTER ELEMENT ENTRY"
```

Fig. 3.9.
PEGASUS dialogue file showing the separators.

```
......
"These elements will then be used to elicit constructs."
""
"##"
"$$7"
"$$8"
"You have ......
```

Fig. 3.10.
PEGASUS dialogue file showing the effect of deletions.

If these parameters are required to be output in a different order or used more than once in the output sequence, they can be numbered to indicate this. An example of this is shown in Figure 3.12.

If the line that should contain a # is left empty, then the next line of text is omitted from the dialogue.

Where a line of text starts with a $ this has the effect of clearing the screen before outputting the following text (for example, see Figure 3.13).

If the $ occurs at the end of a line of text, it causes a carriage return (for example, in Figure 3.14).

```
"This grid already has "
"#"
"constructs$"
```

Fig. 3.11.
PEGASUS dialogue file showing the substitution of a number at runtime.

```
"Think of another element which is either"
"#4"
"and"
"#3"
"or"
"#1"
"and"
"#2"
```

Fig. 3.12.
PEGASUS dialogue file showing the output of parameters in a different order.

```
"$Name six elements."
""
......
```

Fig. 3.13.
PEGASUS dialogue file showing how to clear the screen before output of text.

```
"Your pole name is too long please use a shorter one.$"
"$$59"
```

Fig. 3.14.
PEGASUS dialogue file showing how to output a carriage return.

The text shown in Figure 3.15 is part of an interaction with the general PEGASUS dialogue as it appears on the screen. This is generated by the part of the dialogue file shown in Figure 3.16. The next piece of text in Figure 3.17 shows the interaction in a specific market research context. This was generated from a new dialogue file written specifically for this market research, part of which is shown in Figure 3.18.

```
The two elements Margaret and Jane are
matched at the 86 percent level.

This means that so far you have not
distinguished between Margaret and Jane
Do you want to split these?yes

Think of a construct which separates
these two elements, with Margaret on
the left pole and Jane on the right
pole.

Left pole rated 1?close to me

Right pole rated 5?remote
```

Fig. 3.15.
An interaction with the standard PEGASUS dialogue.

Note how the matching level parameter "86" is not used in this case. Note also how the word-processing facilities of the dialogue interpreter fit the text to the size of the screen regardless of the parameters passed, such as element names.

The dialogue file is in upper and lower case. On an Apple II+ it will still appear in upper case. On an Apple IIe or IIc the PEGASUS menu gives an option of UPPER to switch it to upper case, or LOWER to switch back. If the 80-column card is present it will be used, and the

```
$$49
"$The two elements"
#
"and"
#
"are matched at the"
#
"percent level."
""
"This means that so far you"
"have not distinguished between"
#
"and"
#
"Do you want to split these"
$$50
""
"Think of a construct which separates these"
"two elements, with"
#
"on the left pole and"
#
"on the right pole.$"
$$51
""
"Left pole rated"
#
$$52
""
"Right pole rated"
#
$$53
```

Fig. 3.16.
The PEGASUS dialogue file generating the dialogue in Figure 3.15.

```
The detergents DAZ and PERSIL
seem very similar to me.

None of the ways of thinking about them
that you have mentioned so far makes
DAZ or PERSIL very different for you.
Can you think of a difference?Y

Tell me the difference which puts DAZ on
the left end of a scale and PERSIL on
the right end

Left end rated 1?I LIKE THE COLOR

Right end rated 5?NOT SO MUCH
```

Fig. 3.17.
An interaction with a PEGASUS dialogue file specifically for market research.

option FORTY will appear in the PEGASUS menu to force 40-column display, or EIGHTY to switch back.

PEGASUS will also accept lower-case input for purpose, elements, and constructs. Other input in lower case is converted to upper case, so that both "Y" and "y" or "YES" and "yes" are acceptable forms of affirmative reply. Often in PEGASUS the user is asked for a yes/no response and then for a number. Users sometimes type the number directly, omitting the "Y" for yes. PEGASUS allows this as an option where it makes sense.

PLANET is available also for the IBM PC, with only minor differences from the Apple version.

APPLICATIONS OF PLANET

The PLANET system, or parts of it, have been used in many studies. Reported in Shaw (1980) are a study on inspection of knitwear that was conducted over a hierarchical cross section of the firm using FOCUS and SOCIOGRIDS; a study on staff appraisal with the management services department of a paints division of a large company using PEGASUS, SOCIOGRIDS, and CORE; a study of personal and family relationships of teenagers in a psychiatric adolescent unit using FOCUS and CORE; and a study of role perspectives in an individual, using ARGUS,

```
$$49
"$The detergents"
#
"and"
#
"seem very similar to me.
""
"None of the ways of thinking about them"
"that you have mentioned so far makes"
#
"or"
#
"very different for you."
"Can you think of a difference"
$$50
""
"Tell me the difference which puts"
#
"on the left end of a scale and"
#
"on the right end$"
$$51
""
"Left end rated"
#
$$52
""
"Right end rated"
#
$$53
```

Fig. 3.18.
The PEGASUS dialogue file generating the dialogue in Figure 3.17.

FOCUS, CORE, and SOCIOGRIDS. It has also been used in education to study the changing constructs of the postgraduate (Phillips 1981) and the training of teachers (Pope and Keen 1981), in clinical psychology to study patient interview data (Shepherd and Watson 1982), in management and training (Steward and Stewart 1981), and in the transfer of knowledge from an expert to an expert system (Shaw 1983; Boose 1984b, 1986).

BIAIT: AN APPLICATION OF PLANET TO EXPERT SYSTEMS

The initial success of expert system (ES) developments (Michie 1979; Gevarter 1983; Reitman 1984) and the development of a number of reasonably domain-independent software support systems for the encoding and application of knowledge (Hayes-Roth, Waterman, and Lenat 1983) has opened up the possibility of widespread use of ESs. In particular, the Japanese Fifth Generation Computing System (FGCS) development program (Moto-oka 1982; Gaines 1984) assumes this will happen and has targeted knowledge processing rather than information processing. However, as noted, *knowledge engineering* represents a major bottleneck impeding the application of ESs in new domains.

The problems of knowledge engineering have been stated clearly:

> Knowledge acquisition is a bottleneck in the construction of expert systems. The knowledge engineer's job is to act as a go-between to help an expert build a system. Since the knowledge engineer has far less knowledge of the domain than the expert, however, communication problems impede the process of transferring expertise into a program. The vocabulary initially used by the expert to talk about the domain with a novice is often inadequate for problem solving; thus the knowledge engineer and expert must work together to extend and refine it. One of the most difficult aspects of the knowledge engineer's task is helping the expert to structure the domain knowledge, to identify and formalize the domain concepts. (Hayes-Roth, Waterman, and Lenat 1983)

The problem of knowledge elicitation from a skilled person is well known in the literature of psychology. Bainbridge (1979) has reviewed the difficulties of verbal debriefing and notes that there is no necessary correlation between verbal reports and mental behavior, and that many psychologists feel strongly that verbal data are useless. However, the PLANET system has been used to bypass cognitive defenses, including those resulting from automatization of skilled behavior. An example of an application of some of the major PLANET programs is in the evaluation of expertise in business record keeping. Sowa (1984) describes the record-keeping needs of a business that can be prescribed through the BIAIT analysis technique (Carlson 1979), based on seven features:

1. Does the supplier bill the customer, or does the customer pay cash?
2. Does the supplier deliver the product at some time in the future, or does the customer take the order with him?
3. Does the supplier keep a profile of the customer, or is every transaction a surprise?
4. Is the price negotiated or fixed?
5. Is the product rented or purchased?
6. Does the supplier keep track of the product after it is sold or not?
7. Is the product made to order or provided from stock?

Sowa notes that these features "seem almost obvious once they are presented, but finding the right features and categories may take months or years of analysis. The proper set of categories provides a structural framework that helps us organize the detailed facts and general principles of a system. Without them, nothing seems to fit, and the resulting system is far too complex or unwieldy."

The BIAIT features are examples of constructs applied to orders placed between a customer and supplier. They provide a useful test case with which to evaluate the personal construct elicitation methodology provided in PLANET. An empirical study is being carried out to determine whether PEGASUS can be used to elicit the BIAIT distinctions from persons with some accounting or business knowledge. Hence, the initial experiments have been based on taking a spectrum of persons with assumed expertise in business record keeping, from businesspeople and accounts to accounting students at various stages of their education, and using PEGASUS to elicit their constructs relating to business transactions. Again, in the interests of an initial open-ended approach, the construing has not been tightly constrained to relate to the record-keeping aspects of the transactions. It has been interesting to determine what distinctions are made that do not relate to record keeping, or relate to it in ways different from BIAIT.

PEGASUS IN ACTION

PEGASUS commences its interaction by asking for the purpose of the elicitation and then for a set of elements relevant to this purpose, as shown in Figure 3.19. In the dialogue the computer output is shown in normal face and the human input in bold. One technique used by PEGASUS to elicit constructs is that of triadic comparison shown in Figure 3.20. Another technique is that of matching the ratings given to elements and asking for a construct that differentiates between two highly matched elements, as shown in Figure 3.21. A technique that allows PEGASUS to elicit additional elements is to match constructs across elements and ask for a new element that differentiates between two highly matched constructs, as shown in Figure 3.22.

Through a combination of triadic comparison, element matching, and construct matching, a PEGASUS interaction elicits from the user his or her system of constructs relating to the topic being studied. The PEGASUS flow chart shown in Figure 3.1 shows how the different parts link together. Figure 3.23 is a composite grid in which the top seven constructs are those from BIAIT applied to a standard set of elements related to business record keeping. The remaining nine constructs were elicited from a businessperson using PEGASUS.

ENTAIL IN ACTION

ENTAIL (Gaines and Shaw 1981, 1986; Shaw and Gaines 1982) gives a dependency analysis of a grid by listing logical entailments consistent with the data. The dependency analysis is also being extended to be interactive, so that it may lead to the elicitation of further elements if the system suggests dependencies with which the subject disagrees, or to the modification of ratings if the subject suggests dependencies that are not possible according to the data he or she has entered. The overall objective is to allow the subject to explore the dimensions of his/her conceptual structure, testing it against specific cases, and discussing its implications, until he/she is comfortable that the representation elicited reasonably represents his/her knowledge.

Figure 3.24 shows the ENTAIL analysis of the composite grid shown in Figure 3.23. The entailments are shown with two values, the first a truth value from 0 to 100 (e.g., L7 → L8, truth 75), and the second the uncertainty reduction generated by asserting this entailment, again in the range from 0 to 100 (e.g., L7 → L8 with truth 75 reduces the uncertainty in L8 by 57). The uncertainty reduction measures the information carried by the assertion and is used to ensure that trivial entailments consistent with the data are pruned (Gaines and Shaw 1985).

```
Type in your purpose for doing this grid?examining
business record keeping

You must choose a set of six elements keeping in mind
why you want to do this grid. They could be people,
events, pieces of music, pictures, books, or what you
want but whatever you choose they must be of the same
type and each must be well known to you. Try to
choose specific things. Now type each one after each
question mark.

Do not forget to press the RETURN key after each.

  Element 1?selling newspapers from a stand
  Element 2?selling antiques in a market
  Element 3?selling custom drapes
  Element 4?selling large appliances
  Element 5?hiring out a car to a customer
  Element 6?providing TV rental services

Here is a list of your elements.

  1  selling newspapers from a stand
  2  selling antiques in a market
  3  selling custom drapes
  4  selling large appliances
  5  hiring out a car to a customer
  6  providing TV rental services

Do you want to change an element?no

Can you think of another element that belongs with the
6 that you have got so far?y

  Element 7?selling car insurance
```

Fig. 3.19.
PEGASUS initial element selection.

```
Triad for elicitation of construct 1
  1 selling newspapers from a stand
  2 selling antiques in a market
  3 selling custom drapes

Can you choose two of this triad of elements which
are in some way alike and different from the other
one.
What is the number of the one which is different?1

Now I want you to think about what you have in mind
when you separate the pair from the other one. How
can you describe the two ends or poles of the scale
which discriminate selling antiques in a market and
selling custom drapes on the left pole from selling
newspapers from a stand on the right pole?
Just type one or two words for each pole to remind
you what you are thinking or feeling when you use
this construct.

  left pole rated 1 --?no. of different objects
  right pole rated 5 --?same object in quantity

Now assume that selling antiques in a market and
selling custom drapes are assigned the value 1 and
selling newspapers from a stand is assigned the value
5 according to how you feel about them please assign
to each of the other elements in turn a provisional
value from 1 to 5

   2 selling antiques in a market      1
   3 selling custom drapes             1
   1 selling newspapers from a stand  5
   4 selling large appliances         ?3
   5 hiring out a car to a customer   ?1
   6 providing TV rental services     ?2
   7 selling car insurance            ?4
   8 providing electricity for home   ?5
   9 providing dental services        ?2
  10 being agent for home purchase    ?3
```

Fig. 3.20.
PEGASUS triadic construct elicitation.

```
The two elements 1 selling newspapers from a stand
and 8 providing electricity for home are matched at
the 87 percent level. This means that so far you have
not distinguished between selling newspapers from a
stand and providing electricity for home.
Do you want to split these?Y

Think of a construct which separates these two
elements, with selling newspapers from a stand on the
left pole and providing electricity for home on the
right pole.

  left pole rated 1 --?supplied one at a time
  right pole rated 5 --?direct delivery

According to how you feel about them please assign to
each of the other elements in turn a provisional
value from 1 to 5

  1 selling newspapers from a stand  1
  8 providing electricity for home   5
  2 selling antiques in a market    ?1
  3 selling custom drapes           ?2
  4 selling large appliances        ?1
  5 hiring out a car to a customer  ?1
  6 providing TV rental services    ?4
  7 selling car insurance           ?3
  9 providing dental services       ?1
 10 being agent for home purchase   ?1
```

Fig. 3.21.
PEGASUS construct elicitation by breaking element match.

```
The two constructs you called
  5 direct delivery -- supplied one at a time
  9 'hands-on' delivery -- nonpersonal delivery
are matched at the 75 percent level

This means that most of the time you are saying
direct delivery you are also saying 'hands-on'
delivery and most of the time you are saying supplied
one at a time you are also saying nonpersonal
delivery. Think of another element which is either
direct delivery and nonpersonal delivery or 'hands-
on' delivery and supplied one at a time. If you
really cannot do this then just press RETURN after
the first question mark but please try.

Then you must give this element a rating value on
each construct in turn. After each question mark type
a value from 1 to 5

What is your element?
```

Fig. 3.22.
PEGASUS element elicitation by breaking construct match.

		1	2	3	4	5	6	7	8	9	10	
Billed	1	5	5	3	4	3	1	2	1	2	3	Pay cash
Deliver product	2	5	5	3	1	5	1	2	1	5	3	Customer takes
Keep cust. profile	3	5	5	3	5	3	2	1	1	1	3	Each trans. surprise
Price negotiated	4	5	1	4	5	5	5	5	5	5	1	Price fixed
Product rented	5	5	5	5	5	1	1	5	5	5	5	Product purchased
Supplier tracks product	6	5	5	3	2	1	1	2	3	3	4	Supplier forgets product
Made to order	7	5	5	1	5	5	5	3	4	2	4	Provided from stock
STANDARD PRODUCT	8	1	2	5	1	1	1	2	1	3	2	SPECIAL PRODUCT
SEND BILL	9	5	5	2	1	2	1	1	1	1	3	COLLECT CASH
CUSTOMER OWNS	10	1	1	1	1	5	5	1	1	1	1	WE OWN
SHORT TERM RELATIONSHIP	11	1	1	2	1	1	4	2	5	4	2	LONG TERM RELATIONSHIP
FIXED PRICE	12	1	5	2	2	2	1	1	1	1	4	HAGGLE
CHOICE	13	1	1	1	1	1	1	1	5	2	1	MONOPOLY
DELIVER	14	5	4	4	1	5	1	5	1	5	3	TAKE
CUSTOMER LOOKS AFTER	15	1	1	2	1	5	5	1	3	2	1	WE LOOK AFTER
EXPENSIVE	16	5	2	2	2	3	4	2	3	2	1	LOW-COST

BEING AGENT FOR HOME PURCHASE
PROVIDING DENTAL SERVICES
PROVIDING ELECTRICITY FOR HOME
SELLING CAR INSURANCE
PROVIDING TV RENTAL SERVICES
HIRING OUT A CAR TO A CUSTOMER
SELLING LARGE APPLIANCES
SELLING CUSTOM DRAPES
SELLING ANTIQUES IN A MARKET
SELLING NEWSPAPER FROM A STAND

Fig. 3.23.
Composite repertory grid. BIAIT constructs at top; constructs elicited from businessperson by PEGASUS at bottom.

```
Entail   Truth  Information (Cutoff 30)

L 7 -> R 8   75  57 Made to order -> SPECIAL PRODUCT
R 3 -> R 1   75  53 Each trans. surprise -> Pay cash
R 9 -> R 1  100  52 COLLECT CASH -> Pay cash
L 1 =  L 3   75  51 Billed  = Keep cust. profile
R11 -> L 1  100  51 LONG TERM RELATIONSHIP -> Billed
R11 -> L 3  100  51 LONG TERM RELATIONSHIP -> Keep cust. profile
R 1 =  R 3   75  51 Pay cash  = Each trans. surprise
R15 -> L 6  100  50 WE LOOK AFTER -> Supplier tracks product
R 3 -> L11  100  49 Each trans. surprise -> SHORT TERM RELATIONSHIP
R 9 -> R 3  100  45 COLLECT CASH -> Each trans. surprise
L 1 -> R11   50  43 Billed  -> LONG TERM RELATIONSHIP
R 1 -> L11  100  43 Pay cash  -> SHORT TERM RELATIONSHIP
L14 -> L 2   75  41 DELIVER -> Deliver product
L 5 -> L 6  100  40 Product rented -> Supplier tracks product
L 6 -> L 5   50  40 Supplier tracks product -> Product rented
L 4 -> R12   75  40 Price negotiated -> HAGGLE
L 5 -> R10  100  40 Product rented -> WE OWN
L 5 -> R15  100  40 Product rented -> WE LOOK AFTER
L 6 -> R10   50  40 Supplier tracks product -> WE OWN
R10 -> L 5  100  40 WE OWN -> Product rented
R10 -> L 6  100  40 WE OWN -> Supplier tracks product
R12 -> L 4   75  40 HAGGLE -> Price negotiated
R15 -> L 5   50  40 WE LOOK AFTER -> Product rented
R10 -> R15  100  40 WE OWN -> WE LOOK AFTER
R15 -> R10   50  40 WE LOOK AFTER -> WE OWN
L 3 -> L 9  100  39 Keep cust. profile -> SEND BILL
R 6 -> R 9   50  39 Supplier forgets product -> COLLECT CASH
L 8 =  R 7   75  38 STANDARD PRODUCT = Provided from stock
R 7 =  L 8   75  38 Provided from stock = STANDARD PRODUCT
R 9 -> R 2  100  38 COLLECT CASH -> Customer takes
L 1 -> L 9  100  37 Billed  -> SEND BILL
L 2 -> L 9  100  36 Deliver product  -> SEND BILL
R 6 -> L15  100  36 Supplier forgets product -> CUSTOMER LOOKS AFTER
R12 -> R 9   75  35 HAGGLE -> COLLECT CASH
R13 -> R11  100  35 MONOPOLY -> LONG TERM RELATIONSHIP
```

Fig. 3.24.
Entailment analysis of repertory grid in Figure 3.23.

In this example, the ENTAIL analysis is being used to see which BIAIT constructs may be recovered from the businessperson. Usually entailment analysis is used to derive relations between constructs for use in expert system shells. The entailments derived by ENTAIL can be converted directly to rules that may be loaded into a standard expert system shell, as Boose (1984) has shown. The truth value of the rule codes into the truth value representation used by the shell. The rules may be checked by the expert for their content but their prior evaluation for uncertainty reduction makes it unlikely that spurious rules will be generated.

FOCUS IN ACTION

Figure 3.25 shows the FOCUS analysis of the grid given in Figure 3.23. The construct matches are shown by the tree drawn on the right side of the FOCUS grid. It can be seen from the high construct matches that C5 and C10 are matched at 100 percent, — that is, we own products that are rented, whereas the customer owns products that are purchased; we haggle over products where the price is negotiated, whereas we have a fixed price if the price is fixed. Two highly matched BIAIT constructs show up in cluster 19. Each transaction is a surprise when the customer pays cash, whereas a customer profile is kept when the customer is billed. We look after rented products that we own, whereas the customer looks after purchased products that he or she owns, in cluster 20; and standard products are provided from stock, whereas special products are made to order, in cluster 21.

It is easy to see the highly clustered elements, and the ones that stand out on their own in the tree diagram above the grid in Figure 3.25. The element clusters indicate that the record keeping for providing dental services and for selling car insurance are the most similar (cluster 11); and selling newspapers from a stand is similar in record keeping to selling antiques in a market. The most different one is E4, selling large appliances, which is not highly clustered to any of the other elements. Providing TV rental services is quite similar in its record keeping to hiring out a car, but these two are unlike any other examples of record keeping in this grid.

Most of the entailments in Figure 3.24 appear in the clusters matched over 50 percent, that is, up to cluster 27. We get some confirmation in these results that ENTAIL and FOCUS produce very similar results, but in a slightly different form. The ENTAIL results can be translated directly

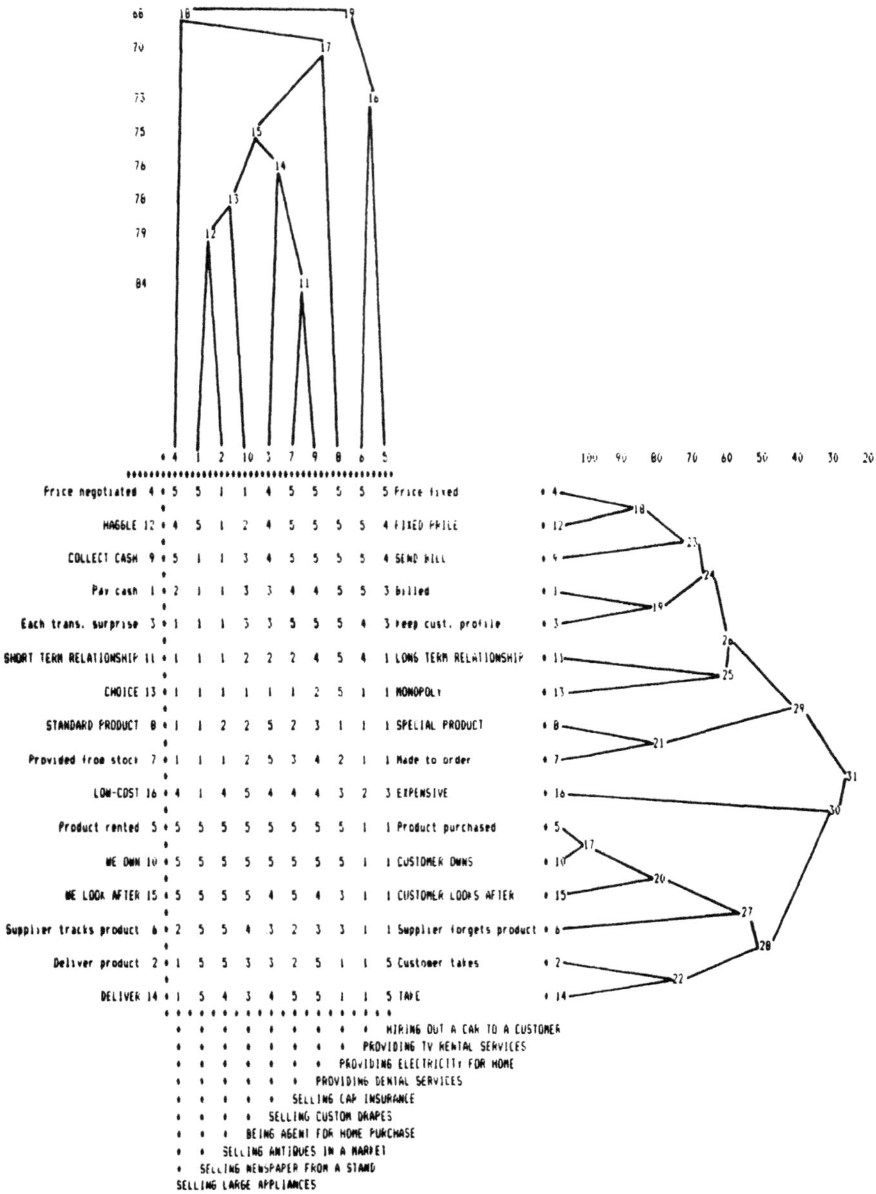

Fig. 3.25.
FOCUS analysis of repertory grid in Figure 3.23.

into production rules (Hayes-Roth, Waterman, and Lenat 1983). For example, the first one would become, "If a product is made to order, then it is a special product"; and the last one would become, "If there is a monopoly, then there is a long-term relationship with the customer." Most of these results seem intuitively obvious, even if one knows little of business record keeping.

SOCIOGRIDS IN ACTION

The construct elicitation described in the previous section is being carried out with a number of subjects, from those experienced in business record keeping to students with some knowledge of accounting. It is clearly possible to analyze for each subject whether the BIAIT constructs are among those elicited, how closely they are mimicked, and which ones are missing, and this analysis is being done. However, one can also see whether it is possible to reconstruct the ranking in expertise of the subjects through a SOCIOGRIDS analysis. For example, in an earlier study (Shaw 1980) of quality control for a garment company, the SOCIOGRIDS analysis reconstructed the management hierarchy of the firm from the construct systems of staff involved in construing garment faults.

The operation of SOCIOGRIDS is based on what Kelly (1955) terms the *commonality corollary*: To the extent that one person employs a construction of experience that subsumes that of another in a given domain, that person can understand the cognitive processes of the other person in that domain.

SOCIOGRIDS derives linkages between people (socionets) by comparing grids in pairs (A and B, say) to determine for each construct in grid A the best matching construct in grid B. The comparison is done by calculating the average over all constructs in grid A of the similarity of the best match for each construct in grid B. This measures to what extent the system of construction modeled in grid B subsumes that modeled in grid A. These subsumption averages are ordered and used to produce socionets showing the degree to which one person's construction system subsumes that of another. SOCIOGRIDS derives a consensual construction system (mode grid) by comparing each construct in turn with those in every grid and calculating the average over all grids of the best match for the construct in each grid. This measures to what extent a given construct is represented in the construction system of every person, and hence is consensual.

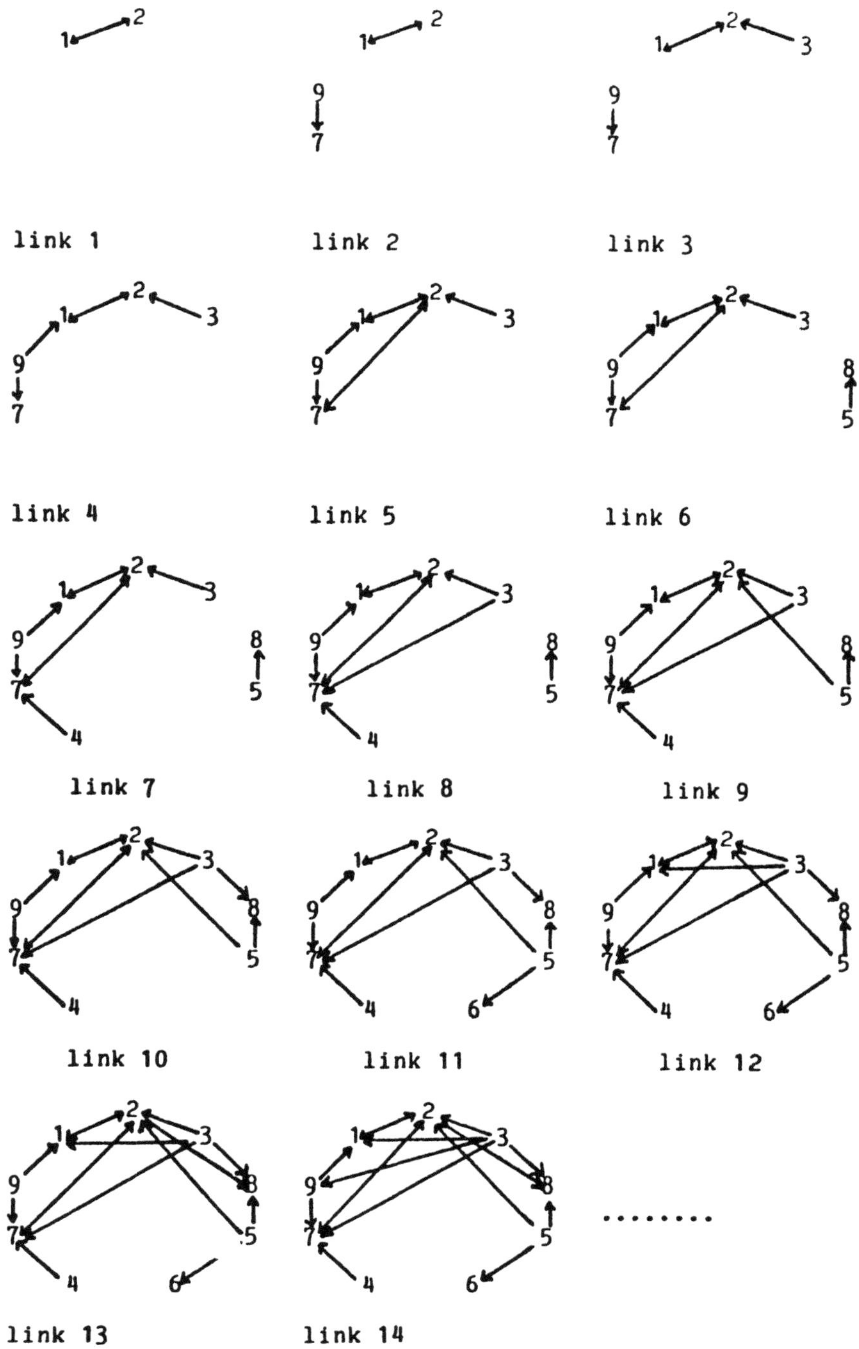

Fig. 3.26.
Series of socionets produced by SOCIOGRIDS from BIAIT validation experiment.

Link 1 in Figure 3.26 shows the most highly matched pair, which is BIAIT and a businessperson; link 2 shows another matched pair, which is an economics student and a visual arts student. As the links are formed these initial pairs are joined into one group at link 4. A new subgroup is formed at link 6, then gradually the other participants are brought in and joined into one group. The nodes forming the central part of the network are BIAIT, the two businesspeople, an economics student, and the visual arts student. This can be seen at link 14, which is shown more completely in Figure 3.27.

This is mainly what one would expect, with the businesspeople and the economics students closely related to BIAIT. The only disconcerting result is the position of the visual arts student, who is clearly a central part of the cluster. On inquiring into the background of this student, it was discovered that she had only recently become a student, having spent the previous 25 years as an administrative secretary in an insurance organization.

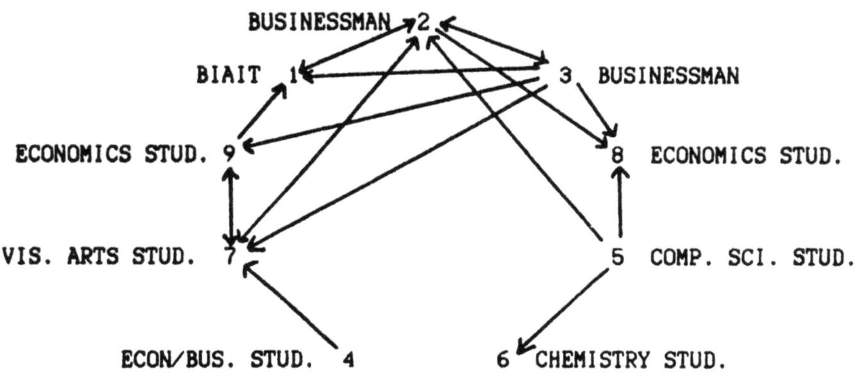

Fig. 3.27.
Socionet produced by SOCIOGRIDS from BIAIT validation experiment.

SUMMARY AND CONCLUSIONS

Repertory grids have proved to be powerful tools in a wide range of disciplines and applications. However, elicitation by people requires skills in interviewing techniques, personal construct psychology, and the avoidance of interpersonal artifacts. Computer-based elicitation techniques have proved capable of supplying these skills, essentially acting as expert systems for grid elicitation. PLANET is a complete suite of elicitation and analysis programs designed for widespread application by users with widely varying backgrounds. This chapter has presented our experience in the development, dissemination, and application of PLANET.

PLANET has most recently been applied to knowledge engineering for expert systems. The conceptual framework involved is of widespread interest because in educational, clinical and management applications we are involved in eliciting personal knowledge representing individual "expertise," its internal structure, and its relations to the "expertise" of others. PLANET contains a number of subprograms to do this. PEGASUS elicits from a person the fundamental distinctions, or constructs, he/she is using in applying his/her expertise; SOCIOGRIDS analyzes the relationships between members of a group through their differing construct systems and determines consensual constructs; ENTAIL analyzes the logical dependencies between constructs and can be used to develop rules for an expert system shell.

Note that in non-expert-system applications, the rules operating in a shell become a cognitive model of the person from whom the constructs have been elicited and hence a means for anticipating his or her cognitive, decision-making, and behavioral processes. Such shells can give feedback to individuals on the dynamics of their personal thinking and can further enhance the reflective processes of constructive alternativism that Kelly saw at the heart of personal construct psychology.

We see PLANET as an expert system incorporating the best features of elicitation from skilled people and making these available to those who do not have the time, experience, or personality to develop the necessary skills. Those writing elicitation programs should note that the advantages described do not come automatically with the use of a computer. The design of the human–computer interface requires great care and takes rather more effort than the writing of the elicitation and analysis procedures in their own right. To make person–computer interaction as attractive as the best person–person interaction requires that much of the expertise of good personal interaction be encoded for the computer. Certainly most of the faults of poor personal interaction can be programmed for the computer unless great care is taken!

APPENDIX

The PLANET programs and some of the more difficult to obtain books are available from the Centre for Person–Computer Studies. For a detailed price list please write to:

Dr. M. L. G. Shaw
Centre for Person–Computer Studies
4 Edgepark Mews NW
Calgary, Alberta
Canada T3A 3J7

For those people who do not have access to or do not wish to use a computer, many of the techniques used in PLANET and others are explained, with examples, for use with paper and pencil in Shaw and McKnight (1981b).

Since this chapter was written, a new set of programs has been developed for the Apple Macintosh. This incorporates many of the PLANET programs and new exchange procedures in an integrated package using the Macintosh graphic interface. It will be available shortly from the above address.

ACKNOWLEDGMENT

Financial assistance for this work has been made available by the National Sciences and Engineering Research Council of Canada.

4 Ways of Assessing Functionally Independent Construction, Meaningfulness, and Construction in Hierarchy

Alvin W. Landfield and John E. Cannell

This chapter is divided into four main sections. The first section, An Historical Overview, outlines the development of two kinds of grid methodology and computer programs. The second section, Two Grids, more specifically explains a particular 13-point scaling grid used with the well-known Rep Test and introduces a type of Implications for Change Grid. The Implications Grid helps one understand how construct dimensions relate in hierarchy. Further, this section presents concepts used with these grids, that is, functionally independent construction, meaningfulness, and construction in hierarchy. Section three, Computer Analyses, gives the reader some feeling for the kinds of information that will be shown on the computer printouts. The fourth section, Applications and Extended Possibilities, describes representative examples of research that have been conducted in the course of development of the techniques presented in the chapter. Several recent innovative studies are cited which may point the creative researcher toward a few of the extended possibilities for application of Rep Test methodologies. An appendix informs the reader about certain characteristics of the computer programs and how one may obtain them.

AN HISTORICAL OVERVIEW

Kelly (1955: 219–318) presented a Rep Test Grid in which a subject was asked to rate elements (e.g., acquaintances) on bipolar elicited construct dimensions. In this particular format, the subject checked the left-hand pole of a dimension whenever it applied to a certain acquaintance. When a pole was not checked (a void) for a particular acquaintance, the assumption was made that the opposite pole applied. This check-and-void method allowed the investigator to use conventional correlational statistics in determining the relationships between construct rating patterns. Unfortunately, this approach did not take into consideration the possibility that a subject might not apply either pole of a dimension to a particular acquaintance. This problem, suggested by Kelly's Range Corollary, was recognized by him (Kelly 1955: 271), but he hoped it would not create too great a difficulty.

Our own experience (Landfield 1971) with asking subjects separately to apply both poles to an acquaintance indicated a problem with normal persons and a more critical one with maladjusted persons. It was found that construct dimensions could not be usefully applied to all persons, a finding consistent with Kelly's Range Corollary (Kelly 1955: 68–72).

Landfield then developed a triadic rating system (i.e., left pole, right pole, not apply). The first computer program (FIC) for this approach was shown in his volume, *Personal Construct Systems in Psychotherapy* (1971). The first computer program, included in the 1971 volume (pp. 200–207), was written by a graduate student, John A. Gifford.

The first program then grew like Topsie as we added new modifications to the original triadic methodology. We became interested in rating scale polarization (Adams-Webber 1979; Bonarius 1970a, 1970b; Landfield 1977). In this context, we asked subjects to rate on 13-point scales (6–0–6). We treated the zero rating as a nonapplication rating to conform to our earlier triadic method. We also scored for total polarization on each element described, each construct, and the total for the system.

It is important to note that underlying our thrusts into methodology, was our primary interest in whether differently worded bipolar scales on a Rep Test Grid might have something in common as judged by the similar ways in which the scales were employed. If a person were to employ his or her differently worded scales all in the same way (e.g., intelligent persons are honest, happy, and prosperous, etc.), could it point to his or her greater simplicity of conceptual structure? A person might really have only one basic concept. In contrast, another person might employ many *independent* dimensions in which the presence of one characteristic need not imply others.

Later, we wanted to explore whether ratings toward the extremes or greater polarization on 13-point (6 – 0 – 6) scales might signify greater meaningfulness, that is, greater significance, importance, clarity, and certainty. Isaacson (1965) had demonstrated the linkage of scales derived from the person to the greater extremity of his/her ratings on these scales, his/her higher judgments of their importance, and, a greater certainty of his/her rating scale positions.

We then became interested in the complexity of a person's approach to certain personal scales, that is, using his/her own descriptive language scales in a simple either-or way, versus using them in a more differentiating way with varying degrees of application and meaning. In particular, we focused on the *within* construct variation of the polarization ratings, that is, the use of different degrees of extremity in ratings. As will be explained later, we wondered whether the use of many different degrees of extremity in ratings or greater variation in rating polarization might indirectly point to a greater capacity to form hierarchies of meaning.

This later theorizing was linked to our questions about whether independent construction, as conventionally measured from the Rep Test Grid, necessarily pointed to a lack of hierarchical relationships between constructs. As a brief illustration of hierarchy, a person might say that "a happy man can always be trusted, but a person who can be trusted may not always be happy." Thus, when we speak of hierarchy, we also imply a unidirectional relationship. In our example, happiness leads to trust, but trust may not always lead to happiness.

We began to question correlational methods as a way of understanding unidirectional or hierarchical relating. Landfield (1977) theorized that greater variation in rating polarization implied some capacity to form unidirectional or hierarchical relationships. It seemed reasonable to theorize that integrative activity would involve functioning within hierarchies of meaning.

Our concern with developing a Rep Test Grid scoring that would have implications for hierarchical functioning led to the development of the New Ord measure and finally to a familiar statistic, chi-square. The two latter measures correlate highly, and we feel that the chi-square measure may be the better one (Landfield and Schmittdiel 1983). At this point, the reader should not be surprised to learn that many graduate students helped in the writing and rewriting of this program, which we call the Scaling Grid. The current and more tidy program was written by a professional programmer, Kent Landfield.

Continuing the historical overview, our interest in hierarchical organization finally led us to Hinkle's implication grids (Fransella and Bannister 1977). In particular, we were interested in the idea of how a construed change on one dimension might lead to construing change on some other dimension. After several years of playing about with various kinds of hand scoring of an Implications for Change Grid, Landfield stumbled onto the idea of separating the search for implications into two separate processes called the upsearch and the downsearch. It was at this point that Kent Landfield made a breakthrough on the writing of the program. What finally emerged was a program that prints out levels of organization, taking into consideration strange phenomena like backlooping (where A leads to B and B to C and C to D and D back to A). This grid as well as the Scaling Grid is the product of years of revision and experimentation. The present form of both grids will now be described in detail.

TWO GRIDS: SCALING AND CHANGE

Rep Tests and Implication grids come in many forms and packages (Fransella and Bannister 1977). In this section, we describe our own version of a Rep Test Grid, referred to as the 13-Point Scaling Grid. We also introduce our form of an Implications for Change Grid. For the sake of brevity, we have shortened these titles to: Scaling Grid and Change Grid. Descriptions of these grids are followed by an introduction to the concepts of functionally independent construction, meaningfulness, and construction in hierarchy.

ELICITING THE CONSTRUCT

The Scaling Grid and Change Grid both begin with the elicitation of verbalized, bipolar, personal constructs. This elicitation procedure can take many forms, as shown by Fransella and Bannister (1977) and Kelly (1955), and in the forthcoming volume by Landfield and Epting, *Personal Constructs in Use*.

The most traditional *triadic* procedure (Kelly 1955) requires that the person consider three things (elements) to be described and to state how two of them are similar in some one important way that distinguishes them form the third. This elicitation procedure captures the processes of contrast and generalization.

A *dyadic* procedure (Landfield 1971) requires that the person consider only two things or elements at a time. If the person first perceives them as similar, a difference also is asked for. If the person perceives them as different in some one important way, the two polar contrasts are elicited. This procedure gets around the problem created by the subject, who perceives *three* elements as similar in the triadic method and thus does not provide a contrasting description.

A *monadic* procedure requires that the person, frequently a child or adolescent, describe one element at a time. Then contrasts or opposites are elicited for these single descriptions. Developmental and educational psychologist Phil Salmon (1976) has nicely described this monadic process with young children.

THE SCALING GRID

Following the elicitation of a specified number of bipolar descriptions of acquaintances, situations, and so on, either the investigator or the subject places these descriptions at the poles of 13-point scales (6–0–6), as shown in Figure 4.1. As you observe this figure, visualize a base sheet on which the descriptions are recorded. Then, imagine a set of 13-point-scale sheets placed between the bipolar description. Further imagine that each element described in the elicitation procedure has been written at the top of these sheets, one on each sheet.

If 15 constructs or bipolar descriptions are elicited from combinations of 15 acquaintances, 15 scale sheets would be employed, one for each acquaintance. At this point, one may speak of a rating grid of 15 person columns and 15 descriptive rows. Using a single rating for each scale, each of the 15 persons is rated across the 15 construct scales.

Typical instructions for filling out the rating sheets are as follows: Begin with the person on the first rating sheet. You will be rating him or her on each of your scales. This is done by circling *one* number on each 13-point scale, a number that best represents how you see this person. First, you choose whether the person is more to the left or more to the right of the zero point. You may need to use the zero if you *cannot* put the person more to the right or to the left. In general, the higher the number you use, the greater the quality or characteristic.

	Column 1	Element Written Here													**Column 2**
	Construct														Contrast
1	________	6	5	4	3	2	1	0	1	2	3	4	5	6	________
2	________	6	5	4	3	2	1	0	1	2	3	4	5	6	________
3	________	6	5	4	3	2	1	0	1	2	3	4	5	6	________
4	________	6	5	4	3	2	1	0	1	2	3	4	5	6	________
5	________	6	5	4	3	2	1	0	1	2	3	4	5	6	________
6	________	6	5	4	3	2	1	0	1	2	3	4	5	6	________
7	________	6	5	4	3	2	1	0	1	2	3	4	5	6	________
8	________	6	5	4	3	2	1	0	1	2	3	4	5	6	________
9	________	6	5	4	3	2	1	0	1	2	3	4	5	6	________
10	________	6	5	4	3	2	1	0	1	2	3	4	5	6	________
15	________	6	5	4	3	2	1	0	1	2	3	4	5	6	________

Fig. 4.1.
Thirteen-point scaling grid.

THE CHANGE GRID

The Implications for Change Grid is structured from as many as 12 dimensions, which are placed at the left side of the 12 x 12 matrix, as shown in Figure 4.2. These dimensions to the left are considered the *impliers*. These same dimensions become the *implied* when referred to along the top of the matrix. Cells in which a dimension intersects with itself are crossed out.

The implication process begins by asking the subject to indicate the preferred poles of his or her dimensions. Then the investigator starts with the *first* dimension, instructing the subject to imagine that a person (self *or* others in general) *changes from the preferred* to the less preferred role. "If a person (or self) changes on this scale, on what other scales would you expect to see change? Specifically, are there other scales on which you would definitely know or definitely wonder about change? Indicate whether your expectation would be that of *definitely knowing* or *definitely wondering*."

		Implied Constructs									
		1	2	3	4	5	6	7	8	9	10
	1	X		K				K			
	2		X			W					W
	3			X							
	4				X						
Impliers	5		W			X		W			W
	6						X				
	7							X			
	8		K		W				X		
	9									X	
	10				K						X

Fig. 4.2.
Implications for change grid.

If the subject definitely knows, for example, that a change on construct 1 would be accompanied by a change on construct 3, a (*K*) is inserted in the intersecting cell of row 1 and column 3. The response, "definitely wondering," would be recorded as a (*W*). After the implications from construct dimension 1 have been explored, the investigator proceeds to dimension 2, 3, and so on.

INTRODUCTION TO CONCEPTS

Before presenting the specific analyses of data generated by the Scaling and Change Grids, the concepts of functionally independent construction (FIC), meaningfulness, and construction in hierarchy will be defined. A fuller discussion of these concepts is found in Landfield (1971, 1977) and Landfield and Schmittdiel (1983).

FIC refers to the number of independent dimensions and dimensional clusters found on the Rep Test Scaling Grid. This analysis begins by defining each descriptive construct dimension, for example, friendly versus unfriendly, by the row rating pattern opposite the construct, for example, –1, +3, +5, –4, 0, –4, and so on. The minus sign designates left-side ratings of the scale (6 to 1). The plus or absence of the negative sign designates right-side ratings (1 to 6). Zero designates the midpoint of the 13-point scale (6 to 0 to 6).

Just as the pattern of row ratings defines the descriptive construct, column ratings may be used to define the people or situations being described. In short, the overlap between row ratings is used in finding independent dimensions and clusters of descriptive dimensions. The overlap or match between column ratings is used in locating the independence of people and people clusters or of situations.

To measure row pattern overlaps or column pattern overlaps, ratings across the 13-point scale are reduced to sidedness and midpoint ratings. Thus, all left-side ratings become 1; right-side ratings become 2; and center ratings are designated by 0. Using this triadic scoring, imagine the following grid ratings of 15 acquaintances in relation to two different descriptive constructs:

Construct 1:	1	1	2	2	0	1	1	2	1	2	1	0	2	2	2
Construct 2:	1	1	2	1	0	1	1	2	2	2	1	1	2	2	2

In this example, you will find 11 *directly* overlapping *application* ratings of 1–1 and 2–2. The *inverse* relationship of 1–2 and 2–1 is found in only two cases. The overlapping of the zero ratings is found in only one case. This overlap of 0–0 is a commonality in *nonapplication* ratings. Using this example, take the highest number of direct or inverse application relationships and add this score to the overlaps in nonapplication. Thus, the 11 direct paired cell application ratings are added to the one pairing of zero ratings, giving a total score of *plus* 12 — plus for the dominance of the direct over the inverse paired applications. A *minus* sign would be used if the inverse paired applications exceeded the direct paired applications.

Since we do not want the overlapping zeros (i.e., nonapplication overlap scores) to carry the weight of the relationship, one point is subtracted from the total score when the overlapping zero ratings reach 6. Two points are subtracted from the overlapping zeros when they reach 9. By using this correction, in conjunction with a 12/15 cell overlap total score (i.e., direct or inverse pairs added to the nonapplication pairs), the ratio of direct to inverse application relations found at the minimal 12/15 cell criterion level will be at least 2 to 1 or 1 to 2. The logic of this scoring has been clearly stated by Landfield (1971). In summary, it should be noted that the computer makes proportional corrections according to the size of the grid.

Following the determination of relationship scores between all rows and all columns, we are ready to obtain the FIC score for columns and for rows, and the total for columns plus rows. In this regard, imagine a 15 x 15 grid in which 15 acquaintances have been rated on 15 construct dimensions. An analysis of row relationships indicates that constructs 1, 2, 3, 4, and 5 are unrelated to each other, directly or inversely, and are not related to other constructs on the grid (see Figure 4.3). *Each* of these five constructs is assigned a score of 1 point.

Again referring to Figure 4.3, imagine that constructs 6, 7, and 8 are all interrelated. However, they are not related to other constructs outside the cluster. This cluster is assigned a score of 1 point. Further, imagine that construct 9 is related to construct 10. In this case, 9 is related only to 10. However, 10 is also related to constructs 11 through 15. Moreover, these latter constructs are not related to each other. Finally, constructs 9 through 15 are not related to constructs 1 through 8. In other words, we have a string of constructs with construct 10 integrating the whole. This cluster, in which constructs are not *all* interrelated, also is scored 1 point. Now we add 1 point for this latter cluster to the 1 point for the previous

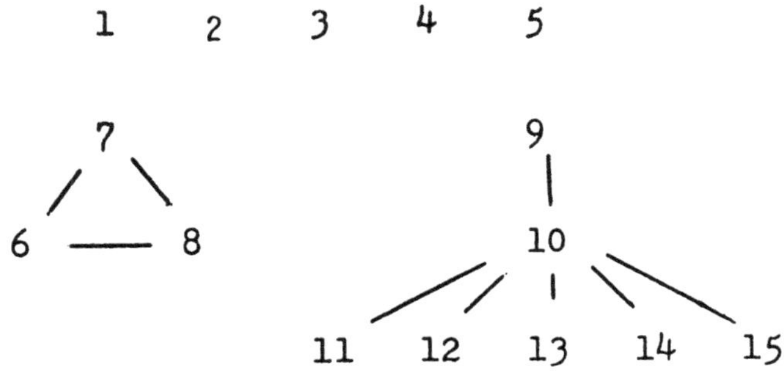

Fig. 4.3.
Example of FIC scoring.

one. Then we add the 5 points for separate dimensions. Thus the final FIC score for rows or concepts (FICc) is 7 points. Now *if* all rows had been strung together in some fashion, the score would have been only 1 point. If none of the rows had shown relatedness, the FIC would have been 15 points, that is, 15 independent constructions.

Using the same scoring process with columns (people described), an FICp is calculated. Then this column score is combined with the FIC row score to produce a total FICt with a possible range of 2 to 30 points. In combining the two FIC scores, it is important to note that the two scores are not redundancies, the average correlation between them being about .60. The combined scoring does extend the range from 1 to 15 points for each FIC to 2 to 30 points for the combination.

With regard to the extremes of a combined FIC, a score of 2 through 4 on a 15 x 15 grid seems related to persons best described as having a simpler understanding of life. The last person to receive a score of 30 points (signifying no relationships) was described as confused, fragmented, and schizoid. This person stated that only his dog understood him.

Meaningfulness, as we implied earlier, refers to the experience of greater importance, significance, clarity, and certainty. We chose to operationalize it in relation to how the person does his or her ratings on 13-point scales. In this context, meaningfulness refers to the degree or amount of rating scale polarization or extremity of ratings found on each column, row, or combined columns and rows. A high degree of polarization is exemplified by the person who uses only ratings of 6 on the scale 6–0–6. A low degree of polarization is shown by the person who typically center rates, mostly using scale points of 0 and 1. Persons who use varying degrees of polarization would be seen as more differentiating in their use of scales, pointing to variations in levels of assigned significance or meaningfulness. This meaningfulness interpretation of rating scale polarization has been elaborated by many authors, including Adams-Webber (1979), Bonarius (1970a, 1970b), and Landfield (1977).

As we elaborate further on our approach to rating polarization, the reader should remember that we have employed two different ways of understanding it. First, it is used as an absolute amount or quantity. Second, it is used in relation to the *variation* in the extremity of one's ratings.

Construction in hierarchy refers to the inferred capacity to employ vertical arrangements of constructs in which conceptions stand in superordinate and subordinate relationships to one another.

In his Organization Corollary, Kelly (1955: 56–59) stressed the importance of hierarchical organization. Landfield (1977), starting from this corollary, argued that organization in hierarchy implies an appreciation of "more and less," a vital factor in efficient decision making. Landfield further argued that an indirect measure of a capacity to "ordinate" or form hierarchies and to function in terms of "more and less" could be defined by *variation* in rating polarization on the Scaling Grid.

One of the first attempts to measure variation in rating polarization, or variation in levels of meaningfulness, was called New Ord (Landfield 1977). A second measure, negatively correlated .80 with New Ord, was called chi-square (Landfield and Schmittdiel 1983). Of considerable interest is the observation that neither New Ord nor chi-square correlates significantly with FIC. This lack of relationship between FIC, a "complexity" measure, and New Ord and chi-square would argue, *in theory,* against the assumption that many different constructs point directly to an ability to integrate one's constructs.

Our preoccupation with these indirect measures of hierarchical capacity led quite naturally to ways of assessing organization in hierarchy in more *direct* ways, in this case, to an Implications for Change Grid (Fransella and Bannister 1977) and our own version of it. It also has led to developing a system by which one may assess levels of construction and a corresponding computer program.

This development of a way of assessing implicative levels provides a vehicle for answering the following questions:

1. Do the more indirect measures, New Ord and chi-square, derived from the Scaling Grid, correlate with the more direct measure of hierarchical string levels on the Implications Grid?
2. How often do independent constructs on the Scaling Grid appear as part of the central system on the Implications Grid?
3. Do the extreme scores (very high and low) of FIC on the Scaling Grid point to a lack of hierarchy on the Implications Grid?
4. Do the more interrelating constructs on the Scaling Grid appear at higher levels of organization on the Implications Grid?
5. Do rating patterns on constructs from the Scaling Grid relate to hierarchical levels on the implications analysis?

The finding that independent construction on the Scaling Grid can be system related on the Implications Grid could lead to the development of more sophisticated ways of assessing independent structure on the Scaling Grid. Of course, the investigator should note that the questions being asked on the Scaling Grid (e.g., to rate individual elements) are more specific and less abstractly interpretative than the more general questions of the Implications Grid. The subject tells the investigator how things are generally related, for self or for others, on the implications task, whereas the investigator makes the interpretation of relatedness on the Scaling Grid. Thus, the question can be raised about whether one can satisfactorily relate two procedures that are pitched at different levels of subject awareness. Perhaps what is needed here is an implications task that requires less general awareness from the subject, allowing the investigator to make the overall assessment of implicative relationships. One laborious approach might focus on how the person perceives different changes within well-known acquaintances. This approach would allow the investigator to scan several grids on specific acquaintances, noting common implicative themes.

The remainder of this section will focus on three measures of hierarchy: New Ord and chi-square from the Scaling Grid and Implicative String Levels from the Change Grid. We begin with New Ord.

New Ord is a way of determining the variation in rating scale polarization as the person rates elements (acquaintances, situations, etc.) across 13-point scales anchored by his or her elicited personal construct polarities. As mentioned previously, these scales (6–0–6) allow the person to rate six degrees of polarity on either side of the midpoint of a scale. Thus, we are not concerned with sidedness. We are interested only in the degrees or levels of polarization as defined by the ratings of 1 through 6.

If we want to know the ordination level of a particular descriptive construct (e.g., humorous versus dull), we note how the subject has rated his or her elements on this construct. If the person has used four different levels of polarization or extremity (e.g., scale points 1, 2, 3, and 5), these four levels are multiplied by the difference between his or her highest and lowest ratings (i.e., 4) and thus the ordination score is 16. If we want to obtain the ordination level of a particular *acquaintance* described by the subject, we observe how he or she has rated that person across his or her descriptive construct dimensions. Again, the number of rating levels used is multiplied by the high–low rating difference.

In summary, the ordination score for a descriptive construct or for a rated acquaintance encompasses the number of levels and range of meaningfulness. The final ordination score (Ocp) is found by first averaging the different descriptive construct ordination scores (Oc), and the different acquaintance ordination scores (Op), and combining these two averages into Ocp. The highest possible average ordination score for descriptive constructs (c) or people (p) is 30. Therefore, the upper limit for the combined Ocp score is 60.

Hierarchical organization of constructs is of such critical importance if one wishes to capture the essence of Kelly's Organization and Fragmentation corollaries, that continuing efforts have been made to develop better measures of individual hierarchical potential. The New Ord measure has acquired a stable-mate, chi-square, in an effort to assess the capacity for higher-order perspective-taking with greater mathematical precision. Both measures resulted from a concern for restoring theoretical consistency to the study of cognitive complexity, which for a time appeared to have lost sight of its theoretical origins in personal construct theory (Landfield 1977).

Kelly (1955: 155–56) described several kinds of thinking that do not permit the hierarchical superordination implied by the capacity for considering degrees of greater or lesser meaningfulness. Chi-square assesses this capacity to consider degrees of meaningfulness by measuring variations in rating-scale-point utilization. One way that chi-square appears to improve on New Ord, with which it correlates –.80, is that chi-square takes into consideration the zero point as well as the ratings of 1 through 6.

Chi-square assumes a rectangular distribution of ratings as the theoretical expectation for utilization of 13-point rating scales. Sidedness is disregarded in the chi-square analysis, so the 13-point scale is reduced to 7 points, ranging from 0 to 6. The theoretical or expected number of ratings for each scale point 1 to 6 will be equal on a Scaling Grid, since each point occurs twice on a construct scale. Since 0 occurs only once on each 13-point scale, the theoretical or expected number of 0 ratings will always be half that of the other numbers.

The chi-square program takes into account the number of opportunities to use different scale points on a particular Scaling Grid. The chi-square analysis for every column and row consists of subtracting from the theoretically expected number the observed number of times a particular scale point was used. This number is squared and divided by the theoretical expectation for each of the 7 scale points from 0 to 6. The row scores are averaged and added to the column average, yielding a total chi-square score for an individual Scaling Grid. The chi-square formula is described more fully in an article by Landfield and Schmittdiel (1983).

Our final measure of organization in hierarchy is the *Implicative String Level,* a score derived from the Change Grid. This computer string analysis begins with the first construct, then proceeds to the other constructs, noting what each construct, in turn, implies. Reciprocal implications to each construct are also noted. Then the upward search begins, starting with the construct or constructs (tied) with the most implications to other constructs. The question is asked, "What other constructs imply the starting implier construct that are not implied in return (reciprocated)?" If any of these are found, the computer asks the same question about these superordinate constructs. The question is asked continuously until (a) the top of the system has been reached, or (b) the quest leads to a circularity in which the top construct leads back to a lower-level construct, a lower-level construct that implies the upper-level construct. What initially might seem a simple procedure can become quite complex because of branching, upward strings. Thus, the starting construct of 3 might lead upward to 3–1–5, or 3–2–6, and so on.

Following the upward search, the computer begins a downward search. In this case the question is reversed: "What other constructs are implied by the starting construct that do not, in return, imply this construct?" Again, we locate many different downward pathways. The search along any one downward path stops when (a) a lower-level construct fails to imply further constructs, or (b) a circularity or backlooping occurs in which a lower-level construct loops back onto a higher-level construct. (Default limits are also embedded in the program.)

After all upward and downward branches are found from a starting construct or constructs, these strings are put together in all their variations. At this point, many of the constructs used on the Change Grid may be accounted for. In case they are not all accounted for, the computer can be directed to systematically search from the constructs not accounted for.

Note that a string can be just one independent construct (one level), or it can involve many constructs and many levels. In the assessment of string levels we count all constructs involved or contained within a circular logic or backlooping as only one level of hierarchy. Illustrating this point, imagine that a particular string search leads from starting construct 6, downward to the next construct subordinate to it, construct 4. Then construct 4 leads down to construct 3. Finally, construct 3 leads directly back in a unidirectional (not reciprocal) way to construct 6. In this illustration, all constructs caught up in this circularity of implications will be considered as being at the same level of the system. The computer would print out these constructs horizontally, rather than vertically (e.g., 6 4 3). This string relationship moves from left to right from 6, to 4, to 3, then back again to 6. If these three constructs did not form an implicative circle, they would be printed out vertically, with 6 at the top of the string and 3 at the bottom.

The horizontal string may have a second meaning. It is possible that the bookend constructs, 6 and 3, could relate to each other in a reciprocal way. Since all reciprocals are printed out, the reciprocal or backlooping nature of these constructs can be quickly checked. In either case, backlooping or reciprocity of relationship leads to treating constructs at the same level of organization.

With these restrictions on levels, the computer obtains the number of string levels for each of the many strings put together through the upward and downward searches. Of course, one can then obtain an average string level for the protocol, as well as information about the longest string and the most superordinate and subordinate constructs. Since the strings are laid out in vertical order, with the exception of backlooped constructs, the investigator can develop a hypothetical picture of how the person thinks, feels, values, and behaves in relation to his or her hierarchies.

Having introduced the Rep Test Scaling Grid (Scaling Grid), the Implications for Change Grid (Change Grid), and certain concepts and measurements, we now will orient the reader to what one may expect to see on the computer printouts.

COMPUTER ANALYSIS

THE SCALING GRID

The first information on the printout for the microcomputer program indicates that it may be used with any combination of rows and columns, from 5 x 5 to 30 x 30. Although your data matrix will be entered on the computer screen by rows defined as sequential ratings of elements or persons, the printout of the data matrix will reverse the meaning of columns and rows. Thus, columns will mean ratings of persons and rows the ratings on construct dimensions.

Next, the investigator's criteria for column relationships and for row relationships are separately listed. Separate listing is important when asymmetrical grids are used. Consider the example of a 10-element x 15 construct grid. Each of the 10 elements will be rated on 15 constructs. However, the 15 constructs will each be defined by the 10 elements.

The next display shows the matrix data broken down into a 3-point scale, where left-side ratings are scored as 1, right-side ratings as 2, and the mid-position as 0. The FIC is based on these data. The New Ord and chi-square measures are based on the first data display of 13 point scale ratings.

In the analyses shown later, remember that elements refer to columns and descriptive dimensions to rows. Further, note that the criterion inserted for row relationships refers to descriptive dimensions. The criterion for column relationships refers to persons or elements described.

The third major display is meaningful only when constructs have been systematically arranged by the investigator with regard to value preferences. For example, if all preferred poles are placed on the left side of the rating scales, or the data is recorded that way, then the number and percentage of left- and right-hand ratings become useful information. The printout indicates the number and percentage of positively, negatively, and neutrally (zero) rated elements, descriptive construct, and the totals for the grid.

The fourth and fifth displays show all relationship scores among all rows and among all columns. Remember that rows refer to descriptive constructs. Columns refer to elements described (e.g., people). As stated previously, the investigator determines his or her own criterion of minimal relatedness (e.g., 12/5 on a 15 x 15 matrix), where construct relations are determined across 15 acquaintances.

At the end of these two displays, CRES scores are shown. CRES means construct relationship saturation score. In other words, the number of related rows or columns are shown at each level of relationship. Accumulated relationships at a certain level and higher also are shown. One may answer such questions as: How many rows or columns are related for example, at the 15/15 level, the 14/15 level, the 13/15 level, and so on? Also, how many rows or columns on the grids are related at the 12/15 level and above?

The seventh display presents the most interrelating row or rows and the most interrelating column or columns. In other words, what row is most related to other rows? What column is most related to other columns at the minimal criterion level given by the investigator?

The eighth display shows each numbered row or each column, in sequence, followed by the rows or columns to which it is minimally related. Sign of relationship also is shown. This tree of relationships enters into the functionally independent construction (FIC) score. Finally, the FIC scores for constructs (FICc), for people described (FICp), and the total (FICt) are given.

The ninth display gives the New Ord scores for each row and column as well as the total extremity or polarization score for each row and column. The average New Ord scores for columns and for rows also are given together with the total of the column and row averages.

The tenth display presents the chi-square score for each row and each column, the mean of chi-squares for rows and for columns, and the total of all chi-squares. Note that low chi-square scores point to distributed ratings across the polarization scale of 0 to 6 points. However, New Ord scores point to the greater distribution of ratings across the polarization scale of 1 to 6 points.

THE CHANGE GRID

The first computer printout begins with a display of the input matrix. Each implication from an implier to an implied construct is given a score of 1 in the intersecting cell. The W and K designations, defined earlier, are punched as 1s for the computer data. At the right side of the matrix, total implications from each construct are summed.

The next display shows three columns. The first one, called General Role, refers to each construct number or construct pole number used. This column may be understood as the construct implier column. The second column, called Implications, lists each separate implication from each construct. For example, 1/2 means that construct 1 implied construct 2. The third column, called Reciprocal Status, shows whether the implied construct (number 2 in our example) reciprocally implies number 1. If so, an R is found in the third column.

The third display indicates which constructs, by rank and tied rank, imply most and least, and the number of times each construct implies other constructs. The fourth major section displays the constructs not found in the up and down searches for implications to or from the highest-ranked construct or cosntructs. Constructs not appearing in the main search can then be analyzed, sequentially, for implications to and from them.

In the next display, one finds the many combined strings from up and down searches for implications. These numbered strings do not show any repeated strings, although certain strings may seem very much alike. For example, the unidirectional string of constructs 5–8–1 could branch into 5–8–1–10; 5–8–1–3–7; and 5–8–1–2–10.

Not all constructs line up so nicely in unidirectional strings. For example, a seemingly lower-level implication may loop back and imply some construct higher in the system. Observe the situation in which 3 leads to 7, and 7 leads to 4, and 4 leads back to 3. This occurrence, not so infrequent, is associated with two possibilities. First, 4 is a one-way implier of 3. Second, 4 and 3 reciprocally imply one another. If the horizontal display shows 3–7–4–3, construct 3 does *not* also imply 4. However, in the display 3–7–4, all on the same line, 3 and 4 are reciprocals.

Printing constructs at the same *horizontal* level of the string means that these constructs, caught between and within reciprocals and backloops, are treated at the same level of hierarchical significance. Constructs printed at the top of the vertical strings are considered more superordinate. Constructs at the bottom of the string are subordinate. At the end of each string, string levels and number of constructs in the string are printed. For investigators who crave a total score, an average string level is shown for the protocol.

APPLICATIONS AND EXTENDED POSSIBILITIES

The concept of functionally independent construction (FIC) has been presented and the location of FIC scores on Scaling Grid printouts has been described. Since the development of the first FIC computer program, research applications of this organizational measure have encompassed a number of areas. Representative examples include Landfield's (1971) systematic study of therapist-client congruence in the therapeutic relationship. Among other hypotheses, Landfield hypothesized that a moderate discrepancy between FIC scores of therapist and client would contribute to a positive therapeutic outcome. It was hypothesized that this discrepancy would provide a stimulus for the client to reorganize experience in a different way. The hypothesis was confirmed. Clients showing the most improvement had FIC scores at the beginning of therapy that were moderately incongruent with the scores of their therapists. Greater congruence of FIC scores occurred over the course of therapy.

In an application of personal construct theory to the study of suicidal behavior, Landfield (1976) found very high FIC scores, reflecting disorganization, to be associated with serious suicidal actions. In another clinical study, Landfield (1977) found that alcoholics being treated in a detoxification center often obtained either very low or very high FIC scores. These scores suggest either tightly organized systems or systems in which constructs are unrelated, respectively.

Curtin's (1984) study of coronary heart disease and type A behavior is an example of how the application of organizational measures derived from personal construct theory may clarify research questions that have failed to yield clear results because of the lack of theoretical conceptualization in much psychological research. Curtin found structural differences, including FIC score differences, between type B individuals without coronary heart disease and other groups studied, including those with type A personalities suffering from coronary heart disease. Her results are interpreted to suggest a broader understanding of the psychological dimensions underlying the coronary-prone pattern.

Doster's (1985) study of marital violence also extends Scaling Grid measures into a new research area. In addition, he has extended the FIC score itself, deriving a related measure from the computer program called functionally equivalent persons (FEP). Doster found that husbands occupied an unusual position in the construct systems of abused wives, failing in most cases to cluster with an average or expected number of functionally equivalent persons. The FEP measure also showed significant relationships with a number of subscales from the Millon Behavioral Health Inventory.

Meaningfulness as assessed by rating scale polarization is another measure that can be derived from the Scaling Grid. Bonarius (1970, 1977) conducted a definitive series of investigations in which he showed how polarization increases when the person rates significant people on his or her own construct scales. Mitsos (1961) reported more polarized rating on semantic differential scales, which participants designated as most meaningful to themselves in thinking about people. Isaacson and Landfield (1965) found that participants gave more extreme self-ratings within their own personal construct language than within the more generalized language of Butler-Haigh Q Sort statements. In addition to supporting rating-scale polarization as a measure of meaningfulness, an additional finding of this study has important implications for psychotherapy. Personal construct items, even negative ones, were more acceptable in describing the self than Butler-Haigh items. The willingness of the therapist to utilize the client's language, especially when making a negative interpretation, may enable clients to feel more open and less resistant when dealing with the issues that brought them into therapy.

Two representative studies employing rating-scale polarization provide a glimpse of the type of information that can be generated when personal construct methodologies are applied to the study of interpersonal processes. Utilizing interpersonal transaction groups as their research format, Landfield and Rivers (1975) examined, among other issues, the individual's empathy for the rest of the group and the group's empathy for the individual. Group members were asked to enter the personal construct systems of other group members and to predict how the other person might rate him/herself in relation to his/her own personal constructs. Predictive accuracy scores were calculated for each individual in relation to the other group members and for the group as a whole in relation to the individual. It was found that individuals who attributed greater meaningfulness to other members were also more accurate in predicting how others would rate them. Conversely, greater attribution of meaningfulness to the individual by the group was accompanied by higher group predictive accuracy. Interpersonal meaningfulness appears to be related to predictive accuracy when prediction is defined as the ability to enter empathically the construct systems of other persons.

A recent study by Benesch (1985) also examines processes affecting the congruency of personality descriptions given by oneself and by one's peers. Target persons generated self-constructs, contexts for the constructs, and actions that might be expressive of the constructs. Close acquaintances responded to these descriptions. The most meaningful self-constructs as assessed by rating-scale polarization produced greater agreement between peers and the target person as to the manifestation of that self-construct in the target person's personality. Benesch pointed out that the convergence of self and peer perceptions on those self-constructs that are considered most meaningful has significance for the issue of cross-situational consistency of traits and behavior.

Interest in *construction in hierarchy* was stimulated by the clinical observation that some individuals with elevated FIC scores (high differentiation) did not appear fragmented, but seemed capable of making thoughtful and efficient choices. While a between-construct differentiation in type of meaning is reflected in the FIC measure, a within-construct measure with implications for the capacity to integrate hierarchically was needed. An early form of the New Ord measure was developed. With independent measures of differentiation (FIC) and integration (New Ord) now available, a quadrant approach to data analysis became possible, with four quadrants defined by high–low differentiation (FIC) on one axis and by high–low integration (New Ord) on the other. Hypotheses regarding the functioning of individuals whose scores would place them in one of the four quadrants were examined within the framework of the interpersonal transaction group (Landfield and Rivers 1975; Landfield 1977).

The question of greatest initial interest was how to distinguish between two hypothesized classes of highly differentiating or highly complex (high-FIC) people. Whereas high FIC initially was thought to point toward fragmentation, confusion, and maladjustment, some individuals with high FIC scores appeared to be well adjusted. The difference between these two hypothesized classes became apparent when their integration (New Ord) scores were examined. Individuals falling in quadrant 4 (high differentiation and high integration) were described primarily as healthy, mature people. However, individuals falling in quadrant 3 (high differentiation but low integration) were described as maladjusted, withdrawn, and unstable. Landfield (1977: 159) noted that "these data support the hypothesis that complexity which is uncorrelated with integrative processes will be found in the context of difficulties in social decision making."

Combining measures of differentiation and integration has extended possibilities for resolving controversies among those who study cognitive complexity. For example, in the area of impression formation, the relation between cognitive complexity–simplicity and change in impression formation is unclear. Contradictory findings in this area might be explained if more information were available on the integrative capacities of individuals.

Chi-square was developed in an effort to assess the capacity for individual hierarchical potential with greater mathematical precision. It appears to be a superior measure to New Ord in some respects, although it has a similar theoretical base. In a 1983 study of interpersonal prediction, Landfield and Schmittdiel found that other people were able to do a better job predicting those with high chi-square scores (reflecting organizational simplicity) than predicting those with low chi-square scores (reflecting organizational complexity). Also, the person who is organizationally simpler (high chi-square score) is less able to predict others accurately than the person who is organizationally complex (low chi-square score).

Our interest in hierarchical organization led to the idea of measuring how a construed change on one dimension might lead to construing change on some other dimension. The computer program developed for assessing Implicative String Levels is based on our own version of the Implications for Change Grid (Fransella and Bannister 1977). While using grid methodology somewhat different from our own, implications grids have been applied to the treatment of a number of problems, including stuttering (Fransella 1972) and weight change (Fransella and Crisp 1970). Bannister and Fransella (1980: 144) point out that "people are unlikely to 'give up' something that is an integral part of themselves unless they become aware of the personally meaningful implications of the alternative ('desired') behavior." They suggest applying the same basic approach used successfully with stutterers to other problems such as smoking.

Since our two grids, the Scaling Grid and the Implications for Change Grid, both get at construct organization, our own current research interest lies in studying the grids in tandem. Larry Leitner of Miami University, Oxford, Ohio, and the senior author have designed a study in which each subject will take both grids. We will observe how the independency of construction on the Scaling Grid relates to hierarchical organization on the Implications Grid. We will also observe the relation between the chi-square measure of variation in rating polarization on the Scaling Grid and levels of hierarchical stringing on the Implications for Change Grid.

APPENDIX

The two programs have been written in DOS for the microcomputer, specifically, for those computers compatible with the IBM PC having at least 256K memory capacity. The program and user manual for the Rep Test Grid can be obtained at a cost of $100; the Implications Grid program and manual for $200. At this time, the stated cost includes shipping charges. Checks or requests for information should be directed to: Kent Landfield, 7550 South Street, Lincoln, NE 68506, U.S.A. Information also may be obtained by writing to Al Landfield, Department of Psychology, University of Nebraska–Lincoln.

5 OMNIGRID: A Program for the Construction, Administration, and Analysis of Repertory Grids

John Mitterer and
Jack Adams-Webber

The Role Construct Repertory Grid Test, introduced by George Kelly (1955), has played an integral part in the development of Kelly's (1955, 1969, 1970, 1973) personal construct theory (summarized by Adams-Webber 1984a) as both a clinical assessment technique and a research instrument. This test, which is still widely used, was designed to elicit from each subject a representative sample of personal constructs (bipolar dimensions of judgment such as happy/sad), and to assess the relationships among these constructs as they are used by the subject in categorizing a list of personal acquaintances (Rigdon and Epting 1982). Thus, the repertory grid is a complex sorting task used for quantifying and statistically analyzing relationships between the cognitive dimensions used by people to understand or "construe" their social world (cf. Fransella and Bannister 1977).

More recently, many other investigators have devised a variety of repertory grid tests, all of which are variants on the original. In some, either a standard set of constructs is supplied to all subjects (Bannister and Fransella 1966), or some combination of elicited and supplied constructs is used (Adams-Webber and Benjafield 1976). A number of different grid formats have been developed in which people, objects, situations, or other kinds of elements are either classified, rated, or rank-ordered in terms of each construct. In all of these different types of grid, however, the data collected from each subject are entered into a separate two-dimensional table ("grid") with a row for every element and a column for every construct.

Similarly, a number of different mathematical procedures have been applied in the analysis and interpretation of individual repertory grids in both clinical settings and experimental research, including nonparametric factor analysis (Kelly 1955), principal component analysis (Slater 1976), multidimensional scaling (Rathod 1981), linkage analysis (Thomas and Harris-Augstein 1985), hierarchical cluster analysis (Smith and Leach 1972), and information statistics (Adams-Webber 1979). Related methods of analysis have been applied to the pooled repertory grid data elicited from groups of subjects (Slater 1972).

It is only comparatively recently that a number of interactive programs for the on-line administration and statistical analysis of repertory grids for use with microcomputers have been developed by Shaw (1980), Thomas (1985), and Space, Dingemans, and Cromwell (1983). These programs tend to reflect a particular approach to the automation of the repertory grid procedure, namely the creation of particular programs for particular variants of the grid technique. In contrast, OMNIGRID, the system to be described here, adopts a substantially different approach by offering a general tool for the design, administration, and analysis of repertory grids by microcomputer.

Today computers are an indispensable tool for both natural and social scientists alike. In spite of the fact that computers have now become quite inexpensive, many social scientists are still not using them to full advantage. This is partly because of a lack of programming knowledge and partly because of a scarcity of generally useful software. This state of affairs certainly characterizes the area of personal construct psychology, in that most data collection and analysis is still done by hand in spite of the fact that suitable software can speed up the process by at least an order of magnitude. While the savings of resources that can be achieved by automating data collection and analysis is impressive, it is the consequences of these savings that are most important. For example, the speed with which hypotheses can be tested with such an improved methodology can also be increased by an order of magnitude, resulting in a significant improvement in the rate at which personal construct psychology is theoretically elaborated. Further, the ease with which new practitioners can be trained can also increase. Therefore, it is argued that there is a need for general-use software in order to foster the spread of microcomputer technology in an area such as that of personal construct psychology.

In OMNIGRID, this generality has been achieved in several ways, all of which are offered as design criteria for others interested in creating similar software. First, OMNIGRID itself is a general, menu-driven program that allows the user to construct a wide variety of different repertory grid formats by selecting various combinations from the list of structural, content, and data analysis options outlined below. Once the desired grid format has been designed, this system can be employed to test subjects and analyze their data. Options were selected for inclusion in OMNIGRID based on their demonstrated breadth of use and experimental robustness. Second, OMNIGRID was explicitly written to be easy to modify as desired. To achieve this end, OMNIGRID was written in a dialect of BASIC (Applesoft Basic), a very common microcomputer language. Further, the source code for OMNIGRID and a description (or "map") of the structure (both data structures and subroutine structures) of the program are included with the program. Third, although OMNIGRID itself will run only with Apple II+, IIe, and IIc microcomputers, it was designed to be easily transported to other microcomputers running BASIC. In general, machine-specific commands (such as those relating to the Apple's high-resolution graphics pages) were avoided wherever possible, making translation to other types of microcomputer a feasible undertaking. Fourth, documentation of the program has been created. This documentation includes this chapter, which links the program with the literature on which it is based, a user's manual, and an extensive on-line help system that was designed to be especially useful for students. Finally, OMNIGRID, including the source code, help system, user's guide, and map of data and subroutine structures, has been placed in the public domain and is available from the authors on request. One of the reasons why automated data collection and analysis methods have been slow to spread in the area of personal construct psychology is that existing software has tended to be too expensive.

The remainder of this chapter illustrates the richness of the methodology of personal construct psychology by discussing the variety of methods OMNIGRID makes available for the design, administration, and analysis of repertory grids. As such, it does not provide sufficient information about the program to serve as an operational manual for the user. OMNIGRID is made up of three main interlinked programs, Configure, Collect, and Analyze. The most important of these is Configure, which takes the grid designer through questions that span the full range of issues involved in grid design. The help facility has been incorporated with Configure so that if the meaning of any particular question is unclear, simply pressing "H" will result in the display of relevant information. Answers to these questions are saved and subsequently used by the Collect and Analyze programs to determine the resulting data collection and analysis process. What follows is a discussion of the grid design options available in OMNIGRID.

CONTENT

ELEMENTS

OMNIGRID accepts any number of elements between 1 and 20 (a limit that can be overridden). There will be a separate row in the final grid matrix for every element. These elements can be elicited directly from each subject individually on the basis of a list of predefined role-titles (such as "mother," "boyfriend," and "boss") that have been input previously by the experimenter, as in Kelly's original procedure (Kelly 1955). The role titles are permanently stored as part of a configuration file from which they are recovered at the time of testing, and presented to all subjects in the same random order; or their order can be individually randomized for each subject during elicitation. If the experimenter wishes, subjects can also be instructed to specify the gender of every figure they nominate. Alternatively, the experimenter can supply the same set of elements of any description to all subjects alike, for example, the names of different nations (Lemon 1975). As a third option, it is possible to supply some of the elements and then elicit the rest of them using the procedures described above, for example, combining the elicited names of personal acquaintances and a supplied list of drugs (Leenaars 1981). The "ideal self" is an element that is often inserted into a list of elicited elements (Space, Dingemans, and Cromwell 1983).

CONSTRUCTS

Any number of constructs between 1 and 20 (again, this limit can be overridden) can be used by subjects to judge elements. Each of these constructs is represented by a separate column in the final grid. The experimenter may enter a standard list of constructs in either bipolar (e.g., happy/sad) or unipolar (e.g., warm) form that will be stored in the configuration file and later supplied to all subjects alike (Adams-Webber and Benjafield 1973). The experimenter can also elect to designate which is the positive pole of every standard construct at the time of input. On the other hand, a different set of constructs can be elicited from each subject individually, using variations of Kelly's (1955) original triad method, described below. A third option is to input some standard constructs, and then elicit additional constructs individually from each subject. For example, like-me/not like-me is a standard construct that is often inserted into a set of individually elicited constructs (Mair 1969).

OMNIGRID elicits constructs from subjects by presenting them with successive triads of previously stored elements (either elicited or supplied) and asking a paraphrase of Kelly's (1955: 273) question, "How are two of these alike in some important way in which they are different from the third?" After a subject indicates how two of them are alike (e.g., reserved), the opposite pole of this construct can be elicited by asking either of the following two questions at the discretion of the experimenter: (1) "How is the third one different?" (Kelly 1955), or (2) "What is the opposite of [for example] reserved?" (Space and Cromwell 1980). If the experimenter wishes, the subject will be asked to designate the "positive" pole of each elicited construct.

The list form of Kelly's (1955) Role Construct Repertory Test is complete as soon as a desired number of constructs have been elicited in this way. There is considerable evidence, reviewed by Adams-Webber (1979), that when Kelly's triad procedure is used to elicit constructs from the same subjects on different occasions, many of the same constructs are repeated. Hunt (1951) indicates that not many new constructs appear after about 20 to 30 triads have been presented. In fact, a highly reliable measure of individual differences in "cognitive complexity" (differentiation) is the number of different constructs that can be elicited from each subject with a certain number of presentations of different triads, say, for instance, 20 (Bieri and Blacker 1956).

The experimenter also has the choice of either preselecting specific triads and storing them in the configuration file for later testing, or instructing the computer to create a set of triads by randomly combining previously stored elements three at a time. The experimenter will have an opportunity to inspect the list of triads created in this manner and replace any of them with new ones that are either randomly generated or deliberately selected. Furthermore, the experimenter can choose to have a different set of triads created randomly for each subject individually. It is also possible to select one particular element (either elicited or supplied), for example, the "self" (Kelly 1955), to be included in every triad created, with the remaining two elements selected randomly from a previously stored list.

STRUCTURE

SEQUENCE

In administering any form of repertory grid test, subjects are required to judge all of the elements successively on the basis of every construct. If the experimenter decides to present subjects with both poles of the constructs during grid testing, their "positive" and "negative" poles (if these have been identified previously) can be "counterbalanced" with respect to their left-right location in the grid display. On the other hand, the experimenter can choose to present only their positive or negative poles, or to alternate randomly between the positive and negative poles of successive constructs.

Furthermore, the constructs can be presented to all subjects in the same random order or in a different random order for each subject. Alternatively, the constructs can be presented during grid testing in the exact order of their original elicitation from a particular subject. OMNIGRID allows various combinations of these basic options. For example, the experimenter may choose to randomize the order of constructs for each subject, and then relegate certain supplied constructs to the end of the list, behind all the constructs elicited from a particular subject.

Once the mode of construct presentation has been selected, subjects will judge all the elements on each construct in turn. At this stage, the elements can be prearranged in any desired order for all subjects, or in a different one for each subject. They also can be presented in the same random order for all constructs, or their order can be randomized repeatedly across constructs. As in the case of constructs, these basic options can be combined to establish patterns of elements that are partly random and partly systematic. For example, the figures previously nominated by a subject and stored in memory can be presented in a different random order for each construct, except that the "self" is always presented first.

DATA

Dichotomous classification. A number of options are available in OMNIGRID for structuring the subjects' grid responses. As in Kelly's (1955) original procedure, subjects may be instructed to simply classify the elements dichotomously with respect to the alternative poles of each construct without imposing any restrictions whatsoever in terms of how many elements can be assigned to either pole. Although this format is still used widely, it has been observed that the way in which subjects distribute elements between the positive and negative poles of constructs under these conditions tends to be markedly biased in favor of the positive poles (Adams-Webber and Benjafield 1973). This form of "construct lopsidedness" can lead to overestimation of the degree of interrelationship between constructs (Cochran 1976). Consequently, many grid users prefer to control lopsidedness by imposing some constraints on subjects with respect to the allocation of elements to the positive and negative poles of constructs. Therefore, OMNIGRID enables the user to implement Bannister's "split-half" technique, in which subjects are required to assign exactly half the elements to each pole of every construct (Bannister and Mair 1968).

Rating scales. OMNIGRID affords options that permit subjects to make finer discriminations among elements on any given construct. For instance, the experimenter can define Likert-type rating scales of any width between 1 and 11, with or without midpoints, for example, –3 to +3 (Bieri et al. 1966). Some of the sources of systematic variation in these kinds of rating grids have been clearly identified. For instance, it has been shown repeatedly that subjects rate themselves and others more extremely on elicited constructs than on supplied ones (Bonarius 1977). Moreover, within sets of supplied constructs, subjects rate themselves and others more extremely on those constructs that they regard as most meaningful (Adams-Webber and Benjafield 1973). In addition, subjects tend to rate highly familiar elements more extremely than less familiar ones (Bonarius 1970a, 1970b).

As Reid (1975) points out, however, the use of such scales implicitly assumes an equality of intervals, that is, that the distribution of the subjects' judgments meets the requirements of at least an interval scale of measurement. Experimenters may hesitate to accept this assumption on a priori grounds, and therefore they might wish to impose a known distribution with invariant statistical properties on subjects' responses. Perhaps the easiest way to accomplish this is to require subjects to rank-order the elements on each construct (Bannister and Fransella 1966). OMNIGRID includes several ranking options.

Rank-ordering. Subjects can rank the elements in terms of one pole of the construct only. It is possible to have subjects rank elements on just the positive poles or just their negative counterparts (Adams-Webber 1980), or randomly alternate between positive and negative poles across constructs (Bannister and Fransella 1967). Additionally, both the positive and negative poles of every construct can be displayed simultaneously as subjects rank the elements on a single continuum from the most positive (e.g., happy) to the most negative (e.g., sad).

ANALYSIS

OMNIGRID allows the experimenter to select from a wide range of different composite indices and summary statistics, tailored to the specific grid format options described above, including (among others) measures of construct interrelationship (Cochran 1976), element distances (Slater 1976), rating extremity (Bonarius 1977), and information statistics (Signell 1967). This section provides a summary of the methods of analysis available within OMNIGRID for each type of repertory grid format described in the previous section. Given the "decentralized" structure of this program, it is a relatively simple matter to add new statistical subroutines to meet specific experimental and clinical measurement requirements.

BINARY GRIDS (NOMINAL DATA)

Matching scores. When m elements have been categorized dichotomously on each of n constructs (regardless of whether any constraints have been imposed with respect to the number of elements that can be allocated to the alternative poles of constructs), each construct is represented by a single m-digit binary number that can be compared in terms of matches for 1 and 0 values with any other binary number of the same length. For example, if there were 10 elements, a given construct might be represented in the appropriate column of the grid as follows: 1101001010. Each 1 indicates that an element has been assigned to a particular pole of the construct (say, the positive one), and each 0 indicates that it has been assigned to the opposite pole. If either one or both of a pair of columns in the grid have been generated by a purely random process, such as tossing a coin, the expected match between columns will be $m/2$.

The experimenter can elect to compute and print out the absolute match between each construct and every other. There will be $n(n-1)/2$ matching scores for the grid as a whole. The average of these scores provides an estimate of the overall degree of relatedness among the n constructs that is analogous to Bannister and Fransella's (1966) "intensity score," which is interpreted as a measure of construct integration (see Intensity, under "Rating Grids," below). The overall pattern of matching scores serves as a reliable map of the linkages among constructs within the grid (Bannister 1962). Kelly (1955) provides a table containing the binomial probabilities of different degrees of match between any two constructs under the null hypothesis that at least one of them has been generated by a random process.

Deviation matching scores. Deviation matching scores also can be computed by subtracting the expected value of $m/2$ from the empirical match between each construct and every other, retaining the sign. Thus, the deviation matching score has both a magnitude indicating the extent to which the relation between two constructs exceeds what we should expect to find on the basis of the null hypothesis that either or both of them has been generated by a purely random process, and a sign indicating the direction of the relation between them (Fransella and Bannister 1977).

Positivity bias. Positivity bias is a measure of the relative frequency of usage of the positive poles of constructs in the grid (Benjafield and Adams-Webber 1976). There is considerable evidence that subjects apply the positive poles of constructs to themselves and others in repertory grids more frequently than their negative opposites (Adams-Webber 1982). It also has been found in several studies that clinically depressed subjects assign persons to the negative poles of constructs more frequently than normal or clinical controls (Space, Dingemans, and Cromwell 1983). The number of elements (excluding the self) assigned to the positive pole of each of n constructs is determined, and then these values are summed across the n constructs. This total is divided by $n(m)$ to yield the overall proportion of positive judgments in the grid (Adams-Webber 1982). There is evidence that individual differences in terms of this index are quite reliable in the grids of normal adults (Benjafield and Adams-Webber 1975; Adams-Webber and Rodney 1983). Findings presented by Bavelas et al. (1976) suggest that this index relates to the measures of construct matching (described above) and element distances and self–other differentiation (described below).

Uncertainty (H). This is a measure of the average amount of information in a binary grid matrix. Given an $m \times n$ binary grid, we can compute the value of $H = (-p \log_2 p) + (-q \log_2 q)$, where p is defined as the relative frequency of ones and q as the relative frequency of zeroes, and H represents the average amount of information expressed in "bits" (Attneave 1959; Adams-Webber 1979). In some grids, at the option of the experimenter (see above), 1 always indicates that the positive pole of the construct has been applied, and 0 the negative pole (Benjafield and Adams-Webber 1976). In other grids, the designation of construct poles in terms of 1 and 0 will be arbitrary (Adams-Webber, Schwenker, and Barbeau 1972). In general, *H* can be interpreted as essentially a measure of variability in nominal scale data that is comparable to the variance as an index of variability with interval scale data (Brody 1971).

Salience. The salience of any particular category of response can be defined operationally in terms of two of its characteristics: (a) its relative frequency of occurrence (i.e., *p*); and (b) its informational content (see above), defined as $-\log(2)p$. Salience (*S*) is defined as the product of these two terms, $S = -p\log(2)p$ (Frank 1964). *S* reaches its maximum value when $p = 1/e$, which works out to about .37 (Berlyne 1971). The experimenter can elect to compute the salience of either category of grid responses, 1 or 0, in any binary grid. For example, each zero may indicate that the negative pole of a construct has been applied to a given element. Thus, the value of *S* would serve as an estimate of the salience of negative judgments in the entire grid (Adams-Webber and Rodney 1983). It has been found consistently that normal adults assign figures to the negative poles of constructs, on average, approximately 37 percent of the time, suggesting that they organize their impressions in such a way that their negative judgments will stand out as maximally salient (Benjafield and Adams-Webber 1976). It also has been shown that subjects regard constructs on which about 37 percent of figures are assigned to the negative poles as the most useful ones for understanding people (Rigdon and Epting 1982).

Self–other differentiation. The grid row representing the self is compared in terms of binary matches with every other row in turn in order to determine how many figures were allotted to the same poles as the self across all constructs (columns). Then, the proportion of "unlike-self" judgments is computed for the entire matrix. Individual differences in this index have been found to be highly reliable (Adams-Webber 1985). This index has been found to average approximately .37 in the repertory grids of normal adults, suggesting that they structure their interpersonal judgments in such a way that differences between them and others will stand out as maximally salient, as operationally defined in the previous item (Adams-Webber and Davidson 1979). It also has been shown that this index increases gradually between the ages of eight and fifteen, when it stabilizes at approximately .37 (Adams-Webber 1985). It has been found to decrease with clinical depression (Space and Cromwell

1980) and agoraphobia (Frazer 1980), and to increase with hypomania (Ashworth et al. 1982), but to remain at .37 with schizophrenia (Kahgee, Pomeroy, and Miller 1982).

OMNIGRID will also print out the binary match between the self row and each of the other columns in the grid. This permits the experimenter to inspect for specific patterns of identification with parents and other significant figures. Pedersen (1958) presents data pertaining to the reliability of certain comparisons (e.g., self/mother).

Self-esteem. Two measures of self-esteem are available in OMNIGRID. The first of these is the number of constructs on which the self has been assigned to the positive pole divided by *n* (the total number of constructs). Normal adults tend to assign themselves to the positive poles of a majority of constructs (Adams-Webber and Rodney 1983), in contrast to clinically depressed patients (Space, Dingemans, and Cromwell 1983). This index can be computed whenever the self is one of the elements, and the positive poles of all the constructs have been identified by either the subject or the experimenter; it is fairly reliable (Adams-Webber and Rodney 1983). The second measure of self-esteem is the simple binary match between the row representing the self and that representing the "ideal self" (Space and Cromwell 1980). This only requires that both these figures be included in the list of element descriptions supplied by the experimenter.

Element distances. Each element (row) is compared with every other in terms of binary matches using the same procedure as employed in comparing constructs (columns), and all the same statistical assumptions apply (see "Matching Scores," above). The grid matrix as a whole can be viewed as giving the locations of *m* elements distributed in an *n*-dimensional (construct) hyperspace. Although this space is multidimensional, the distance between any pair of elements is, by definition, a straight line, and is consequently unidimensional. It can be calculated as $d = (SS_1 + SS_2 - 2SP)$^$1/2$, where SS_1 is the sum of squares for element 1, SS_2 is the sum of squares for element 2, and SP is the sum of their cross-products. The distances between each element and every other can be printed, together with their average. There will be $m(m - 1)$ distance scores, where *m* is the number of elements. The average distance is essentially a measure of the extent to which the elements have been differentiated from one another in terms of *n* constructs (Adams-Webber 1970).

The experimenter also may elect to express the distance between each pair of elements as the ratio of the empirical distance between them to the expected distance between any two elements in the grid selected at random. This "unit of expected distance" is computed as $[2V/(m - 1)]^{1/2}$, where V is the total sum of squared deviations of all entries in the grid around their respective construct (column) means (Slater 1977).

RATING GRIDS

Correlations between constructs. When the same m elements have been rated successively on n different constructs, regardless of the width of the scale, Pearson product correlation coefficients (r) can be used to estimate the degree of relationship between each construct and every other. OMNIGRID will print out all $n(n - 1)/2$ correlations in a symmetrical matrix. As with matching scores (see "Matching Scores," above), this information can be used to construct a reliable map of the pattern of linkages among constructs (Slater 1972).

We cannot directly apply arithmetic operations to these values of r; for example, we cannot average them. Such operations, however, can be carried out with angles. Thus, each value of r can be converted to an angle according to the general principle that the correlation between two constructs is equal to the cosine of their angle of separation (Slater 1964). For example, if two constructs are orthogonal (i.e., their correlation is 0), then they will be separated by an angle of 90°. OMNIGRID will print out the angular distances between all construct pairs as well as the average angular distance. The latter provides an index of the degree of mathematical complexity of the grid as a whole (Adams-Webber 1979). The standard deviation of these angular distances between constructs provides an operational definition of Radley's (1974) "variability of intensity" (see next section), which he interprets as a measure of the degree to which the structure of the grid is articulated into a complex pattern of differentially related constructs.

Intensity. OMNIGRID computes an Intensity score on the basis of Bannister and Fransella's (1966) formula. The correlations between each construct and every other are squared and multiplied by 100 to yield "variance-in-common" scores, which then are summed across pairs of constructs to yield a single index of the overall "intensity of construct relationships" within the grid. This score is interpreted as a measure of the degree of integration of an individual's construct system. It has been found consistently that thought-disordered schizophrenics exhibit lower-intensity scores than normals and other clinical populations (Bannister, Fransella, and Agnew 1971).

Interelement distances. These are computed and interpreted in the same way as element distances within a binary grid matrix, which have been explained above (see "Element Distances").

Self–other distances. In a rating grid, OMNIGRID computes the distance between self and any other figure with the following formula: $d = (SS_S + SS_O - 2SP)$^1/2; where SS_S is the sum of squares for the entries in the self column, SS_O is the sum of squares for the entries in the column pertaining to the other figure, and SP is the sum of the cross-products. As explained in "Self–other Differentiation" above, although the grid as a whole is usually more than two-dimensional, the distance between the self and any particular figure will be, by definition, a straight line. The average of these distances has been used as a measure of the differentiation of the self-concept (Space and Cromwell 1980). Sperlinger (1976) reports evidence that this measure is highly reliable ($r = .95$). Space, Dingemans, and Cromwell (1983), using this measure, found that a higher identification with the opposite-sex parent than with the same-sex parent relates to clinical depression and neurosis.

Rating extremity. This measure is available only with rating-type grids. When *m* elements have been rated successively on each of *n* constructs using scales that exceed the range 1 to 0 (e.g., from 0 to 6), OMNIGRID will compute the extremity of each rating as its absolute deviation from the midpoint of the scale; for instance, a rating of 1 on a scale of 0 to 6 would have an extremity score of $|1 - 3| = 2$ (Adams-Webber and Benjafield 1973). The experimenter can elect to print out the average rating extremity for both constructs and elements.

Rating extremity has been interpreted frequently as an indication of the importance or "meaningfulness" to the subject of a given construct or element (Bonarius 1977). Bonarius (1970a, 1970b) has shown that subjects rate their close associates (e.g., my best friend) more extremely than remote acquaintances (e.g., my doctor). There is considerable evidence, reviewed by Adams-Webber (1979), that subjects tend to rate themselves and others more extremely on elicited constructs than on supplied ones (see "Constructs," above). Rating extremity also correlates with personal judgments of the relative meaningfulness of supplied constructs (Adams-Webber and Benjafield 1973).

RANK-ORDER GRIDS

Correlations. When subjects have rank-ordered the same list of *m* elements on each of *n* constructs, there are two statistics that estimate the correlation between any two constructs: Spearman's Rho and Kendall's Tau. Although both indices are available in OMNIGRID, Rho is probably the more useful because it is linearly related to Pearson *r*. Thus, all of the measures based on Pearson *r* for rating grids (described under "Correlations between Constructs," above) can be calculated for rank-order grids, including the following: (a) the correlation between each construct and every other (Gathercole, Bromley, and Ashcroft 1970), (b) the angular distances between constructs (Slater 1972), (c) the Intensity score (Bannister and Fransella 1966), and (d) the average correlation between constructs (Agnew and Bannister 1973). (See "Correlations between Constructs: and "Intensity," above, for further discussion and interpretation of each of these indices of grid structure.)

Coefficient of concordance (W). In grids where the elements have been rank-ordered on the basis of constructs, *W* serves as an estimate of the overall level of agreement among the *n* sets of ranks (Adams-Webber and Mirc 1976). It is defined as the ratio of the variation between *m* elements to the total variation within an $m \times n$ matrix of ranks. Thus, its value can vary between 1 and 0. This is essentially a form of analysis of variance that indicates the extent to which all *m* elements have been ranked in the same order across all *n* constructs. Thus, it provides a convenient index of the mathematical complexity–simplicity of the grid matrix as a whole (Adams-Webber 1984b). In addition, an average Spearman's Rho (see the previous section) can be derived directly from the value of *W*.

Element deviations. When elements are rank-ordered on constructs, OMNIGRID will also compute a "deviation score" for each element in the following manner. Constructs (rows) are all compared two at a time and the rank for a given element on construct *x* is subtracted from its corresponding rank on construct *y*. All of these differences are then converted to absolute values and summed separately for each element in turn. This is basically a measure of the extent to which the profile of any given element tends to "fit" the specific pattern of intercorrelation among constructs within the grid as a whole (Adams-Webber 1979).

SUMMARY

OMNIGRID is an Applesoft BASIC program for designing, administering, and analyzing repertory grids with Apple II+, IIe, and IIc microcomputers. This program has been explicitly designed to be of general use. As such, it affords a variety of grid formats, including rating scales, nominal categorization (unconstrained or split half), and rank-order procedures. Elements can be elicited from subjects with predefined role titles supplied by the experimenter, or a combination of elicited and supplied elements can be used. Constructs are elicited from each subject individually, using variations of Kelly's (1955) triad method (random, preselected, self-comparison, etc.) or a standard list of constructs supplied by the experimenter, or elicited and supplied constructs can be combined.

In administering the grid, the orders of both elements and constructs can be either preselected or randomized. Another option allows either the experimenter or subjects to identify the positive and negative poles of constructs and counterbalances these in terms of location in the display and order of presentation. Following testing, the experimenter can select from a wide range of composite indices and summary statistics tailored to the specific format options, including, among others, construct relationships, element distances, rating extremity, information statistics, various ratios involving selected indices, and response latencies. Statistical procedures for analysis of completed grids can be carried out independently on each grid in real time, or on groups of grids stored on disk, such as a series of grids completed by the same subject. Results are displayed in a tabular format on the screen or a printer. More programs like APPLEGRID must become available if microcomputers are to achieve an appropriate role in the area of personal construct psychology.

APPENDIX

The Apple II version of OMNIGRID, complete with source code and documentation, has been placed in the public domain and is available from its authors for a nominal (cost-recovery) fee. IBM and MacIntosh versions are also available directly from the authors. Write to: John Mitterer *or* Jack Adams-Webber, Department of Psychology, Brock University, St. Catharines, Ontario L2S 3A1, Canada.

6 A Grid Tool for Eliciting Expert Knowledge

John H. Boose

EXPERT SYSTEMS AND KNOWLEDGE ENGINEERING

An *expert system* is a computer system that uses the experience of one or more experts in some problem domain and applies their problem-solving expertise to make useful inferences for the user of the system. This knowledge is typically gathered in the form of rules of thumb, or *heuristics*. Heuristics enable a human expert to make educated guesses when necessary, to recognize promising approaches to problems, and to deal effectively with incomplete or inconsistent data. Gathering, representing, and using such knowledge in working systems is referred to as *knowledge engineering*.

There are several ways to categorize expert system problems. Of particular interest is the distinction between *analytic* (or *structured selection*) problems and *synthetic* (or *generative*) problems. Analytic expert systems contain the complete set of possible solutions, while synthetic expert systems typically construct unique solutions built from component pieces. Diagnostic and classification problems are examples of analytic domains; design, configuration, and planning are examples of synthetic domains. It is generally easier to build analytic systems than synthetic systems. The methods discussed here apply mainly to analytic problem domains.

Acquiring knowledge from the expert is usually the central task in building an expert system. A long series of incremental interview, build, and test cycles is necessary before a system achieves expert performance. The time typically required to build an expert-level prototype is from 6 to 24 months (Buchanan et al. 1983; McDermott 1982, 1984). Currently, there are few formal techniques for acquiring this necessary knowledge.

Figure 6.1 shows a methodology for knowledge elicitation, testing, combination, and expert system delivery. Knowledge is *elicited* from *information sources* and placed into an *information base*. From there, it is *analyzed* and organized into *knowledge bases*, which are used directly with expert system shells. These shells are used for rapid prototyping and to extensively test the knowledge for *necessity* and *sufficiency*. Test case histories are collected as the knowledge base is incrementally refined. Individual knowledge bases are then combined into *knowledge networks*, where further testing occurs. Finally, *delivery systems* are *tailored* for efficiency, and on-the-job case records are kept to further improve the system.

The Expertise Transfer System (ETS) is an ongoing embodiment of the methodology in Figure 6.1. ETS interviews an expert, analyzes the information gathered, and produces production rule knowledge bases for several expert system shells (Boose 1984). It also contains several tools for refining and testing the resulting knowledge. Several experiments have been performed using ETS to combine expertise from different experts. The shaded, bold areas in Figure 6.1 represent the current capabilities of ETS.

ETS can significantly shorten the knowledge engineering process. To do this, ETS helps the expert construct and analyze an initial set of heuristics and parameters for the problem. Experts need no special training to use ETS; an initial 15-minute explanation of the basic theory and how to use the work station is usually all that is necessary.

The quality of the problem-solving information elicited from the expert in the early stages of the knowledge acquisition process is improved over manual methods. This is due to the fact that ETS provides the expert with knowledge analysis tools and mechanisms for exploring internal conflicts in the way that different problem cases are handled. *Consistency* is used conceptually to elaborate important aspects of the problem.

In addition to eliciting the initial knowledge and producing knowledge base reports and listings, ETS is capable of testing the problem-solving ability of the knowledge. ETS contains an inference engine that supports

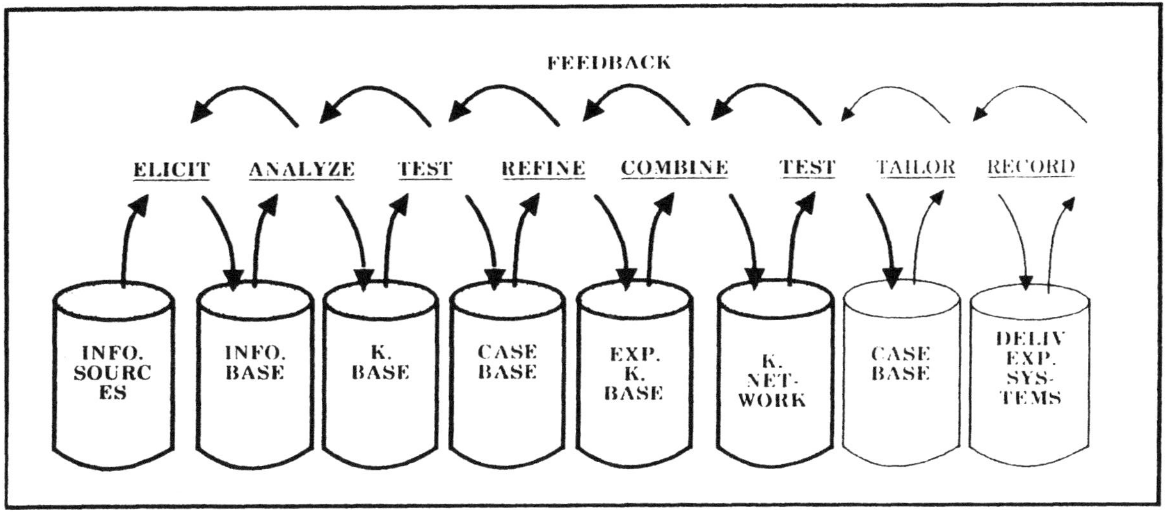

Fig. 6.1.
The Expertise Transfer System (ETS) embodies this framework for knowledge acquisition and expert system delivery.

end-user consultations by transforming the knowledge from the expert into production rules. ETS also produces knowledge bases for several expert system shells.

ETS can also combine rating grids into consultation systems for experts in the same and different domains (Boose 1985b).

In this chapter, aspects of the technology of personal construct psychology that are relevant to the Expertise Transfer System will be discussed. Next, the system itself is described, along with its relation to the knowledge engineering process. Finally, results and limitations of the methodology are discussed.

PERSONAL CONSTRUCT TECHNOLOGY

ETS employs clinical psychotherapeutic interviewing methods originally developed by George Kelly (1955) and extended by other researchers in recent years.

Elicitation and analysis of *repertory grids* has been made available through interactive computer programs (PLANET; Shaw 1980; Gaines and Shaw 1981; Shaw 1982). A variety of grid analysis techniques using distance-based measures between vectors (either rows or columns of the grid) have been used, where both elements and constructs may be graphically compared by the subject to find similarities and differences. Some of these techniques include principal components analysis (INGRID; Slater 1977), a Q-analysis of the grid in a cluster-analyzed hierarchical format (QARMS; Atkin 1974), and a linear cluster analysis (FOCUS; Shaw 1980).

A description of implication relationships that is based on logic is presented by Gaines and Shaw (1981, 1985). Instead of looking at grid rows and columns as vectors in space, Gaines looks at them as assignments of truth-values to logical predicates. In binary rating systems, such as those used in Kelly's original grid methodology, an "X" would simply mean true, and a blank would mean false. A grid, then, can be seen as a matrix of truth values. Gaines goes on to show a method of deriving implications from grids that uses rating scales rather than binary scales. The method is based on multivalued logics (Rescher 1969) using fuzzy set theory (Zadeh 1965). Using this method, the implication relation can be extended to include *implication strength* and *information* content. The program ENTAIL produces graphs that show implication relations among constructs and elements (Gaines and Shaw 1981, 1985). ETS incorporates a similar algorithm for the computation of these implication relationships.

A grid interviewing method known as *laddering* helps connect the constructs in their *superordinate* and *subordinate* relationships. For instance, the clinician might start with the construct "warm–cold" (as applied to people), and ask the patient, "Why is someone warm?" The patient might respond, "Because they're loving." Next, he or she might ask, "Why is someone loving?" and obtain the response, "Because they're good," and so on. Each "why" answer develops another *super*ordinate connection in the network hierarchy of constructs, in which "loving" is superordinate to "warm," and "good" is superordinate to "loving." To move in the *sub*ordinate direction in the grid, "how" questions are asked, such as, "How do you know that?" "What is your evidence for that?" or "What do you mean by that?" Moving in the superordinate direction uncovers constructs that are more general, while moving in the subordinate direction uncovers those that are more specific.

Another technique is useful in verifying those relationships that are inferred indirectly by the grid analysis. In this analysis, the examiner assumes that a statistical relationship between constructs reflects a conceptual relationship that may or may not be true. For example, if a "loving–harsh" construct is highly matched with the "answers questions–won't answer questions" construct, the examiner might attempt to verify this relationship by asking such questions as, "If you mean someone is loving, do you also mean that they are almost always willing to answer your questions?" and "If someone is always willing to answer your questions, are they almost always loving?" and so on.

Hinkle developed a taxonomy of implication types in construct hierarchies (Hinkle 1965) and described some of the possible implications between two constructs A–B and X–Y as follows (Fig. 6.2):

- *Parallel.* A implies X, and B implies Y (e.g., love–hate; pleasantness–unpleasantness).
- *Orthogonal.* A implies X, but B does not imply Y; also A implies X, and B implies X, but neither A nor B imply Y (e.g., employed–unemployed; has income–has no income).
- *Reciprocal.* A implies X, and B implies Y, and X implies A, and Y implies B (e.g., nervous–calm; tense–relaxed). Hinkle noted that a reciprocal relationship suggests a functional equivalence between the two label pairs.
- *Ambiguous.* A and B imply X, and B implies Y; also A implies X and Y, and B implies X and Y (realism–idealism; desirable– undesirable; in which the subject says that realism and idealism both implied desirable and undesirable aspects for him or her). Hinkle thought this situation may arise when: (1) a subject has an incomplete abstraction of the differences between the contexts in which the construct is used, or (2) a subject uses one construct label for two or more independent constructs. He also felt that the

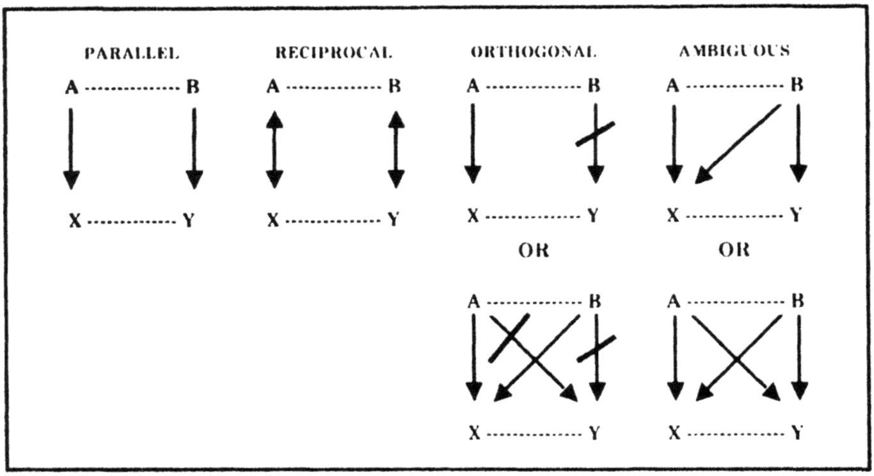

Fig. 6.2.
Implications that exist between two constructs (A–B and X–Y) can be used to help refine the knowledge base.

> processes of psychological movement, conflict resolution, and insight depend on locating such points of ambiguous implication, and then resolving them into parallel or orthogonal forms. As will be seen later, this can be a useful approach for resolving conflicts and inconsistencies during knowledge engineering. Laddering can be used to resolve ambiguous implications into parallel or orthogonal forms.

Hinkle was interested in psychological change, and developed a *resistance to change grid,* as well as an *implication grid* that were based on a subject's willingness to change relationships in the construct hierarchy. Such information was used to elicit the relative importance and stability of constructs.

Researchers have extended Kelly's original binary rating method ("X" or blank) to include rating scales. Thus, instead of simply deciding whether some left-hand part of a construct pair applies to an element, the subject rates the construct's applicability on a scale from 1 to 5, which allows expression of finer shades of distinction. Another rating technique goes beyond this, and allows subjects to use "N" (for "neither pole applies"), and "B" (for "both poles apply"), in addition to a 1-to-5 rating scale (Landfield 1976).

The Expertise Transfer System synthesizes many of the techniques described in this section, especially ideas used in PLANET. ETS extends this collection of techniques in several areas: (1) the creation of production rules, (2) interactive testing of the problem-solving ability of the knowledge contained in a grid, (3) production of knowledge bases for expert system shells, and (4) support of an interactive "test-bed" environment that helps experts expand and refine the grid in several ways.

DESCRIPTION OF THE EXPERTISE TRANSFER SYSTEM

SAMPLE SESSION: THE ORGANIZATION DEVELOPMENT ADVISOR

The Expertise Transfer System (ETS) applies grid techniques to knowledge acquisition for expert systems. The system is written in Interlisp-D and runs on the Xerox 1100 series Lisp Machines, using the high-resolution bitmap windows and mouse interaction capabilities provided. It is also available in a VAX-based version of Interlisp-10.

In the following example session, an expert will attempt to build a knowledge base for an Organization Development (OD) Intervention Advisor. The completed expert system would be able to advise an OD management consultant about which intervention technique to use for an organization in a particular situation.

Initially, the Expertise Transfer System elicits *conclusion items* (elements) from the expert. These are the set of recommendations that would be made by the proposed expert system: specific diseases, management decisions, diagnostic recommendations, and so on. In the following example case, the elements are the specific OD interventions that the expert would recommend (Fig. 6.3). The expert starts by listing nine interventions.

If the expert cannot verbalize the set of conclusion elements initially, ETS enters an incremental interview mode of operation based on a program called DYAD (Keen and Bell 1981), where elements are elicited one at a time, based on differences between and similarities to three initial elements.

After the expert has listed the intervention techniques to be considered, ETS asks him or her to compare successive groups of three techniques, and name an important trait and its opposite that distinguishes any two members of this triad from the third one (Fig. 6.4). The result is a list of elements to be classified and a list of classification parameters that were derived from the expert.

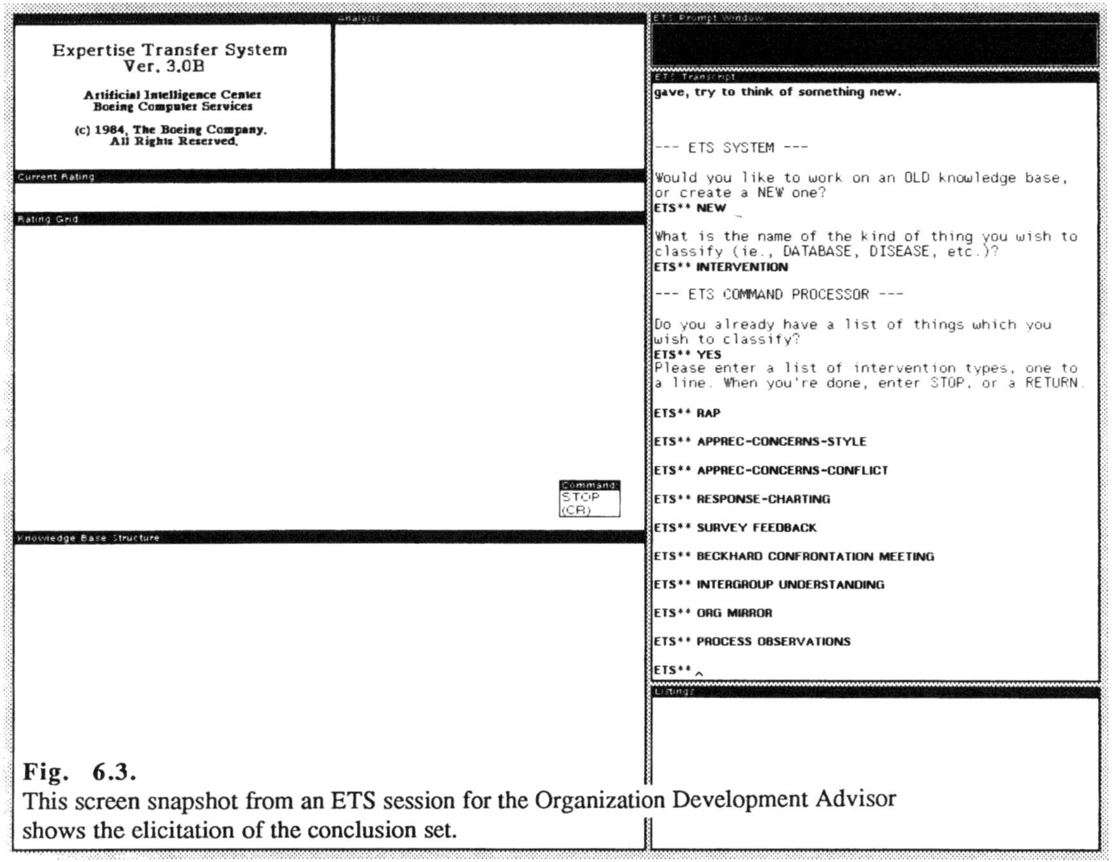

Fig. 6.3.
This screen snapshot from an ETS session for the Organization Development Advisor shows the elicitation of the conclusion set.

Think of an important characteristic that two of RAP, APPREC-CONCERNS-STYLE, and APPREC-CONCERNS-CONFLICT share, but that the other one does not. What is that characteristic?
ETS** **STYLE AND FEELINGS**

What is that characteristic's opposite as it applies in this case?
ETS** **ROLE EXPECTATIONS**

Think of an important trait that two of APPREC-CONCERNS-CONFLICT, RESPONSE-CHARTING, and SURVEY-FEEDBACK share, but that the other one does not. What is that trait?
ETS** **DECISION MAKING**

What is that trait's opposite as it applies in this case?
ETS** **AFFECT**

Think of an important characteristic that two of RESPONSE-CHARTING, SURVEY-FEEDBACK, and BECKHARD-CONFRONTATION-MEETING share, but that the other one does not. What is that characteristic?
ETS** **GROUP DATA GATHERING**

What is that characteristic's opposite as it applies in this case?
ETS** **INDIVIDUAL DATA GATHERING**

Think of an important attribute that two of SURVEY-FEEDBACK, BECKHARD-CONFRONTATION-MEETING, and INTERGROUP-UNDERSTANDING share, but that the other one does not. What is that attribute?
ETS** **SYSTEM-WIDE PROBLEMS**

What is that attribute's opposite as it applies in this case?
ETS** **INTERPERSONAL PROBLEMS**

Think of an important trait that two of BECKHARD-CONFRONTATION-MEETING, INTERGROUP-UNDERSTANDING, and ORG-MIRROR share, but that the other one does not. What is that trait?
ETS** **INTACT WORK GROUPS**

What is that trait's opposite as it applies in this case?
ETS** **REPRESENTATIVES**

:

Fig. 6.4.
ETS uses the conclusion set to elicit important discriminating traits from the expert.

The particular traits that are elicited depend on which elements are combined into triads. ETS builds these triads in the order in which the elements are given by the expert. This initial set of constructs will probably not be enough of a window into the expert's problem-solving construct system. However, the constructs elicited will tend to be significant, since they are based on discriminations among important conclusions. Later in the interviewing process, ETS uses other methods to help expand and refine the knowledge base.

Next, the system asks the expert to rate each element against each pair of traits (Fig. 6.5) forming a rating grid (Fig. 6.6). In addition to allowing numerically scaled ratings, ETS accepts the ratings "N" (neither trait applies) and "B" (both traits apply), as described by Landfield (1976).

GRID ANALYSIS METHODS

Once a rating grid is established, ETS invokes several analysis methods to structure the knowledge. First, the system builds an entailment graph of implication relationships using the method of ENTAIL. The expert may begin to see some structure and organization in the information. The entailment graph shows implication relationships between various poles of the constructs. For instance, "ad-hoc response" implies "interpersonal problems." This means that, given the examples in the rating grid, every intervention technique characterized by "ad-hoc response" is also characterized by "interpersonal problems." The thickness of the arrows representing the implication arcs shows the relative strength of each inductive generalization. The strengths are also listed numerically in the transcript window. These arcs should correspond with paths in the expert's superordinate and subordinate construct system. However, verbal representations do not necessarily correspond with a person's internal construct hierarchy. The "training examples" represented by the rating grid may contain errors and be inconsistent or incomplete. Typically, the expert is surprised at many of the relationships that are revealed by the graph. A mechanism for reviewing these relationships will be discussed later.

RULE GENERATION

After the entailment graph has been constructed, ETS generates two types of heuristic production rules: *conclusion rules* and *intermediate*

```
Please rate these things on a scale of 5 to 1, where 5 means more like STYLE AND FEELINGS and 1 means more like
ROLE EXPECTATIONS. If neither one seems to apply, enter N(either). If both seem to apply, enter a B(oth).
STYLE AND FEELINGS(5) ROLE EXPECTATIONS(1)
  (RAP) ** 1
  (APPREC-CONCERNS-STYLE) ** 5
  (APPREC-CONCERNS-CONFLICT) ** 5
  (RESPONSE-CHARTING) ** 2
  (SURVEY-FEEDBACK) ** N
  (BECKHARD-CONFRONTATION-MEETING) ** 3
  (INTERGROUP-UNDERSTANDING) ** 3
  (ORG-MIRROR) ** 2
  (PROCESS-OBSERVATIONS) ** 4
```

Fig. 6.5.
The expert rates each OD intervention technique against each pair of traits. This information is used to generate production rules.

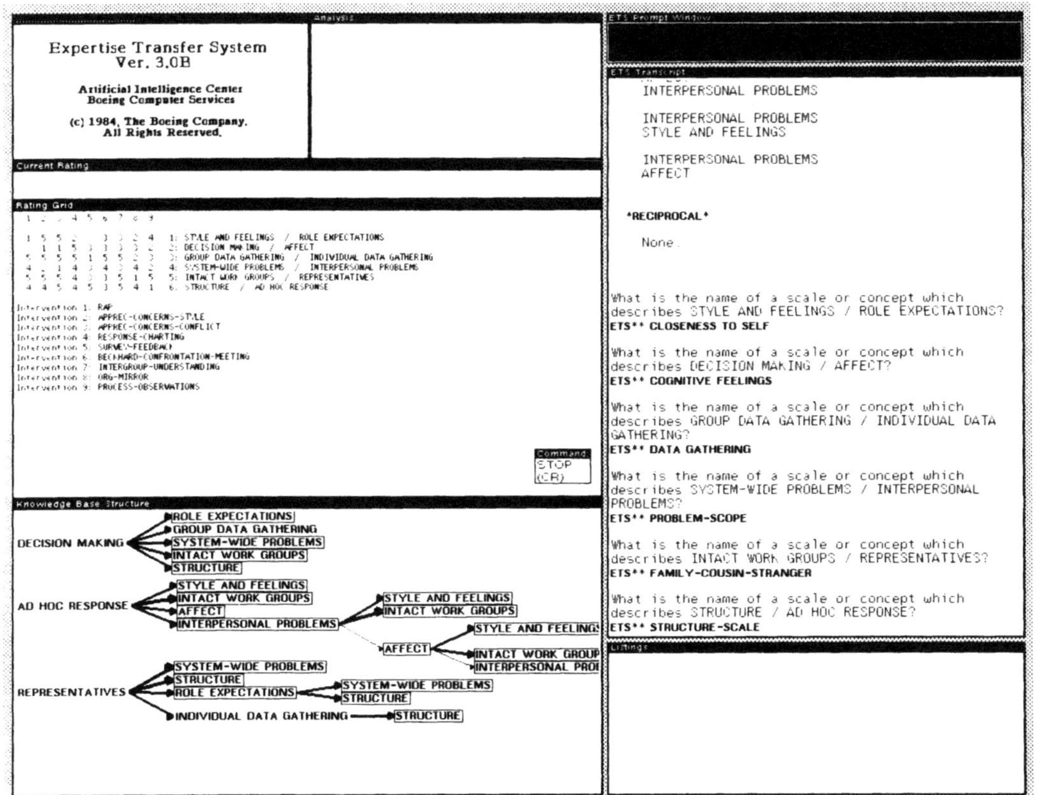

Fig. 6.6.
This screen snapshot of ETS shows the rating grid and entailment graph. The graph displays implication relationships between the traits. This information is used to further refine the knowledge base and produce production rules.

rules. Each production rule is generated with a belief strength or *certainty factor*. Certainty factors can represent slightly different concepts in different expert system building tools. In KS-300/EMYCIN, for example, certainty factors represent a *strength of belief* that the expert associates with the conclusion of the rule. This is the definition used by ETS.

Conclusion rules are created from individual ratings in the grid. Each rating has the potential for generating a rule. The expert is first asked to rate the relative importance of each construct in terms of its potential importance in solving the problem. Then ETS employs an empirical algorithm to generate certainty factors for each rule. The algorithm takes into account grid ratings, relative construct importance, and the certainty factor combination algorithm in the target expert system building tool (Boose 1985b). When employed, these conclusion rules will generate evidence that will be gathered by the expert system to point to specific intervention techniques.

Intermediate rules are based on relations in the entailment graph. For each entailment, one rule is generated. The strength of the rule's certainty factor is based on the relative strength of the entailment. These rules generate intermediate pieces of evidence at a higher conceptual level than those of conclusion rules.

After ETS generates conclusion rules and intermediate rules based on the current knowledge base (see the top of Figure 6.7), the expert may review the rules. Each rule represents a chunk of knowledge, with which the expert may agree or disagree. Although this knowledge is still logically equivalent to the knowledge in the rating grid and implication graph, seeing it in a new representation tends to help the expert consider the problem in another way. If the expert disagrees with particular rules, a rating examination and laddering process may be used to identify sources of potential conflict either in ETS's knowledge base, or between the knowledge base and the expert's internal constructs.

Allowing the expert to work with multiple forms of his or her stated problem-solving knowledge is an important aspect of ETS. Lenat (1982) argues that knowledge representations should shift as different needs arise. Each different representation method in ETS potentially helps the expert think about the problem in a new way, and tends to point out conflicts and inconsistencies over time. Rather than trying to force the expert to eradicate inconsistencies, or simply not allowing them to exist, ETS takes advantage of the important psychological and problem-solving aspects of such inconsistencies by helping the expert explore them. It was

```
Generating rules:

If: CLOSENESS-TO-SELF = ROLE EXPECTATIONS
Then: PROBLEM-SCOPE = SYSTEM-WIDE PROBLEMS (.89)
If: CLOSENESS-TO-SELF = ROLE EXPECTATIONS
Then: The intervention may be ORG-MIRROR (.22)
If: CLOSENESS-TO-SELF = ROLE EXPECTATIONS
Then: The intervention may be RAP (.44)

62 rules were generated.

Go, Edit, Fill-in, List, etc...
ETS** TEST

This will be case number 106.

What is the CLOSENESS-TO-SELF attribute for this case (STYLE-AND-FEELINGS ROLE-EXPECTATIONS)?
ETS** STYLE-AND-FEELINGS

What is the COGNITIVE-FEELINGS attribute for this case (DECISION-MAKING AFFECT)?
ETS** AFFECT

What is the DATA-GATHERING attribute for this case (GROUP-DATA-GATHERING INDIVIDUAL-DATA-GATHERING)?
ETS** GROUP-DATA-GATHERING

What is the PROBLEM-SCOPE attribute for this case (SYSTEM-WIDE-PROBLEMS INTERPERSONAL-PROBLEMS)?
ETS** SYSTEM-WIDE-PROBLEMS .9

What is the FAMILY-COUSIN STRANGER attribute for this case (INTACT-WORK-GROUPS REPRESENTATIVES)?
ETS** REPRESENTATIVES

What is the STRUCTURE SCALE attribute for this case (STRUCTURE AD-HOC-RESPONSE)?
ETS** STRUCTURE

Test results for case number 106:

1 : APPREC-CONCERNS-CONFLICT (.71)
2 : APPREC-CONCERNS-STYLE (.7)
3 : BECKHARD-CONFRONTATION-MEETING (.55)
4 : INTERGROUP-UNDERSTANDING (.44)
5 : ORG-MIRROR (.42)
6 : SURVEY-FEEDBACK (0.0)
7 : RESPONSE-CHARTING (-.02)
8 : RAP (-.09)
9 : PROCESS-OBSERVATIONS (-.58)

Do you agree with the order of the test results?
ETS** YES
```

Fig. 6.7.
This test consultation is based on a knowledge base that was produced by ETS after interviewing an expert for less than one hour. Responses to questions can be "UNKNOWN" and appended with certainty factors. ETS automatically produced knowledge base rules from the rating grid.

this same process that Kelly believed to be important in the clinical setting for bringing about critical psychological change (Kelly 1955).

TESTING: RAPID PROTOTYPING OF AN EXPERT SYSTEM

Once production rules have been generated, the expert can test the knowledge base. This may be done by generating a knowledge base for an expert system tool, or by using ETS's internal inference engine. In this session, the expert first used ETS's internal test facility and then generated an M.1 knowledge base.

A test case is run by asking the end user (here, the expert) to specify an application problem in terms of the traits in the rating grid (Fig. 6.7). The expert selects the appropriate responses from a pop-up menu, the rules are "fired," and ETS gives the consultation results. Here, the expert agreed with the order of the OD Advisor's recommendations. If enough test cases are eventually successful, this would give the expert and knowledge engineers an indication that the knowledge involved was useful, and approaching sufficiency. Later, a test case will be shown in which the expert disagreed with the system's recommendations.

FURTHER KNOWLEDGE BASE REFINEMENT

ETS computes matching scores between traits and elements (Fig. 6.8). The expert is asked questions to help separate traits or elements that are closely matched. This technique is based on a method used in PEGASUS (Shaw 1980), a part of the PLANET system of programs (Shaw 1982).

ETS can also help the expert review the implications shown in the entailment graph. Since the implications are all "logically true" given the information on the rating grid, one of several things could be true if the expert disagrees with an implication: (1) one or more ratings are wrong, (2) there are important elements that the expert omitted that would have generated exceptions to the implication, thereby creating a different graph if they had been included, (3) the expert is inconsistent in the way the trait is applied to each element, or (4) the implication really *was* sound, and the expert just never considered the information in that way before.

ETS helps the expert track down suspicious implications by allowing him or her to review each one in a structured manner (Fig. 6.9). The expert may edit the ratings that led to the implication. If this does not correct the perceived problem shown by the graph, the expert can specify a new element that would be an exception to the implication. If the expert can think of an exception, then that element is added to the knowledge base, rated against all the constructs, and the implication graph is regenerated. If this still does not correct the problem, ETS asks the expert if he or she would like to "refine" the constructs involved in the implication relation by checking their consistency. This involves breaking up a suspect trait pair into two or more new trait pairs. To do this, a simple laddering method is used that asks "Why?" and "How?" questions about the constructs. Any new constructs are added to the knowledge base, and the rating grid and implication graph are then regenerated.

```
Go, Edit, Fill-in, List, etc...
ETS** ANALYZE-MATCHES

The two pairs
 SYSTEM-WIDE PROBLEMS / INTERPERSONAL PROBLEMS
and  DECISION MAKING / AFFECT
 are matched at the 72% level. This means that
most of the time you are saying
 SYSTEM-WIDE PROBLEMS, you are also saving
 DECISION MAKING, and that most of the time you are saying
 INTERPERSONAL PROBLEMS, you are also saving  AFFECT.
 Try and think of another INTERVENTION which is either SYSTEM-WIDE PROBLEMS and AFFECT or
INTERPERSONAL PROBLEMS and DECISION MAKING. Can you do this?
ETS** YES

What is the new INTEVENTION?
ETS**
              :
```

Fig. 6.8.
ETS asks the expert to make a new distinction between similar traits and elements.

```
Go, Edit, Fill-in, List, etc...
ETS** REVIEW-GRAPH

Review All-Pairs, Ambiguities, or Selected-Pairs?
ETS** SELECTED-PAIRS

1 DECISION MAKING -> STRUCTURE
2 DECISION MAKING -> INTACT WORK GROUPS
3 DECISION MAKING -> SYSTEM-WIDE PROBLEMS
4 DECISION MAKING -> GROUP DATA GATHERING
5 DECISION MAKING -> ROLE EXPECTATIONS
6 STYLE AND FEELINGS -> INTACT WORK GROUPS
7 STYLE AND FEELINGS -> INTERPERSONAL PROBLEMS
8 STYLE AND FEELINGS -> AFFECT
9 AD HOC RESPONSE -> INTERPERSONAL PROBLEMS
10 AD HOC RESPONSE -> AFFECT
11 AD HOC RESPONSE -> INTACT WORK GROUPS
12 AD HOC RESPONSE -> STYLE AND FEELINGS
13 REPRESENTATIVES -> INDIVIDUAL DATA GATHERING
14 REPRESENTATIVES -> ROLE EXPECTATIONS
15 REPRESENTATIVES -> STRUCTURE
16 REPRESENTATIVES -> SYSTEM-WIDE PROBLEMS
17 INTERPERSONAL PROBLEMS -> AFFECT
18 INTERPERSONAL PROBLEMS -> INTACT WORK GROUPS
19 INTERPERSONAL PROBLEMS -> STYLE AND FEELINGS
20 INDIVIDUAL DATA GATHERING -> STRUCTURE
21 AFFECT -> INTERPERSONAL PROBLEMS
22 AFFECT -> INTACT WORK GROUPS
23 AFFECT -> STYLE AND FEELINGS
24 ROLE EXPECTATIONS -> STRUCTURE
25 ROLE EXPECTATIONS -> SYSTEM-WIDE PROBLEMS

Which implication pair would you like to review
(enter its number)?
ETS** 11

11 AD HOC RESPONSE -> INTACT WORK GROUPS

Do you AGREE with implication? If not, would you like to REVIEW the ratings which led to this implication, add an
EXCEPTION ELEMENT, or CHECK your consistency in the use of these traits?
ETS** EXECPTION-ELEMENT

What is the new intervention which is an exception to the implication?
ETS**
```

Fig. 6.9.
ETS helps the expert review perceived problems in the implications in a structured manner.

If the implication still exists on the graph after this exploration process, the expert may indeed agree that the implication relationship is sound, and that he or she just never thought about the problem in that way before. In this way, ETS helps the expert structure the problem-solving knowledge based on his or her own operative internal construct network. On the other hand, if the implication relationship still exists, and the expert still disagrees with it, then this represents an important inconsistency in the way the expert thinks about the problem. What has happened, in effect, is that ETS has captured an important internal conflict in the expert's construct hierarchy.

Ambiguous construct relations (see the above section on Hinkle) also point out internal conflicts. When the expert is finished correcting implication arcs, ETS searches for and lists ambiguous relations. Laddering may again be used to refine these points of conflict into parallel or orthogonal forms.

Both types of conflict points (ambiguous relations and relations with which the expert disagrees) are important points in the expert's problem-solving methods. The process of resolving these conflicts (either with ETS or in later discussions between the knowledge engineer and the expert) involves "psychological movement, conflict resolution, and insight" (Hinkle 1965). These are the points where further exploration is necessary, both in producing the expert system, and in refining the expert's own problem-solving processes. Transcripts are kept of all the interactions with ETS, and a set of conflict points is generated as part of the knowledge base report listings.

ETS also employs a *consultation review* mechanism. In a later test case, the expert does *not* agree with the order of the test results (Fig. 6.10), and ETS tries to help the expert improve the knowledge base. First, the expert compares his or her expected rank-ordering to the ordering produced by ETS. Spearman's coefficient of rank correlation provides a measure of the difference between the two ordered lists. A correlation of 1.0 means that the lists are identical; a correlation of –1.0 means the lists are exactly reversed; a correlation of 0.0 means that the lists are "randomly" ordered with respect to each other. ETS also notes whether a high positive correlation is statistically significant at the 5 percent or 1 percent levels. The expert may use the rank correlation scores to measure progress while refining the knowledge base. Here ETS matched his or her expectations at the 1 percent level of significance.

The expert then names the element that he or she feels is most out of order, and tells ETS where it *should* fall in the list for this test case. ETS uses this information to try to elicit a new pair of traits. Theoretically, including these new traits during another consultation will make the named intervention technique closer to where the expert thought it should have been in the recommendation list. After adding the trait, the expert can regenerate the rules and retest the knowledge.

In addition to the methods already mentioned, the knowledge base in ETS may be expanded in several other ways:

- Information (elements and traits) may be volunteered by the expert.
- Elements and traits may be directly edited.

Test results for case number 109:

1 : APPREC-CONCERNS-CONFLICT (.9)
2 : APPREC-CONCERNS-STYLE (.81)
3 : SURVEY-FEEDBACK (.69)
4 : PROCESS-OBSERVATIONS (.53)
5 : INTERGROUP-UNDERSTANDING (.44)
6 : RAP (-.43)
7 : ORG-MIRROR (-.43)
8 : BECKHARD-CONFRONTATION-MEETING (-.55)
9 : RESPONSE-CHARTING (-.68)

Do you agree with the order of the test results?
ETS** **NO**

Would you like to compare the way the results were ranked with the way you would rank the results?
ETS** **YES**

How would you rank the elements (list them in order on the same line)?
ETS** **APPREC-CONCERNS-CONFLICT APPREC-CONCERNS-STYLE SURVEY-FEEDBACK ORG-MIRROR PROCESS-OBSERVATIONS INTERGROUP-UNDERSTANDING RAP BECKHARD-CONFRONTATION-MEETING RESPONSE-CHARTING**

The correlation .9 between your expectations
and the actual results is significant at the .01 level.

Which intervention on the recommendation list do you think is most out of place?
ETS** **ORG-MIRROR**

Where SHOULD it be (give your answer in the form: BEFORE / AFTER <intervention>)?
ETS** **AFTER SURVEY-FEEDBACK**

What trait do ORG-MIRROR and SURVEY-FEEDBACK share that make it different from BECKHARD-CONFRONTATION-MEETING?
ETS**

Fig. 6.10.
Test case feedback provides a measure of system performance as well as a method for adding specific problem-solving traits. All responses are selected from pop-up menus with a mouse.

- The expert can ask ETS to begin an incremental interviewing dialogue to expand the knowledge base.
- ETS can combine more elements together to form new triads for comparison by the expert.
- Laddering can be invoked on any portion of the implication graph to expand the hierarchy of constructs.

GENERATING KNOWLEDGE BASES FOR EXPERT SYSTEM SHELLS

Currently, ETS can generate knowledge bases for KS-300/EMYCIN, M.1, S.1 (expert system tools from Teknowledge, Inc., of Palo Alto, California), OPS5 (Forgy 1981), LOOPS (Xerox, Inc.), MRS (Stanford University) and Prolog (the POP11 system). In this session, the expert generated a knowledge base for M.1 (Figure 6.11). A sample transcript

```
Go, Edit, Fill-in, List, etc...
ETS** BUILD-EXPERT

Build an expert system for AUREA, KS-300, LOOPS, M1, MRS, OPS5, PROLOG, or S1?
ETS** M1

Writing to file {DSK}INTERVENTION.M1;1
```

Fig. 6.11.
ETS can generate knowledge bases for a number of expert system shells by converting its internal rules to the appropriate format and adding appropriate control and dialogue information.

```
S.1 SYSTEM TRANSCRIPT
This case will be Case 17.
AI-TOOL Consultant, created by ETS.

1: What is the AI-TOOL.expert attribute of this AI-TOOL (EXPERT.1 EXPERT.2 EXPERT.3 EXPERT.4)?
1 > EXPERT.1 EXPERT.2 EXPERT.3 EXPERT.4
2: What is the SUPPORT attribute of this AI-TOOL (NOT.WELL.SUPPORTED WELL.SUPPORTED)?
2 > WELL.SUPPORTED
3: What is the MULTI.REP attribute of this AI-TOOL (SINGLE.REPRESENTATION MULTIPLE.REPRESENTATIONS)?
3 > SINGLE.REPRESENTATION <.9>
                    :
        The consensus value of the TAI-OOL is
    tool8 <1.0>,
    tool2 <.98>,
    tool9 <.94>,        [Consensus opinion.]
    tool6 <.89>,
    tool4 <.24>,
    tool1 < -.62>,
    tool7 < -.79>,
    tool5 < -.9>, or
    tool3 < -.99>

    The most different value of the AI-TOOL is
    tool8 <.59>,
    tool6 <.54>,
    tool2 <.41>,        [Dissenting opinion.]
    tool8 <.27>,
    tool5 < -.07>,
    tool4 < -.07>,
    tool1 < -.1>,
    tool7 < -.4>, or
    tool3 < -.63>
```

Fig. 6.12.
Consultation systems built by ETS present a *dissenting opinion* by finding which combination of experts disagrees most with the consensus opinion. The user then employs the expert system shell (in this case, S.1) to examine the justifications for each opinion.

from an S.1 consultation system (from an AI-Tool Advisor produced by ETS) is shown in Figure 6.12.

REPORTS AND LISTINGS

ETS generates reports and listings of the knowledge from each session, in addition to session transcripts and screen hardcopy "snapshots." When reviewing these reports later, the expert tends to think of new traits and elements and finds more inconsistencies and other pints for further exploration. The expert may then rerun ETS with his or her existing knowledge base and revise it.

Occasionally, the expert may wish to start over again with a different set of conclusion elements, or with a different level of abstraction in mind for producing trait pairs. Using current manual interviewing techniques, this would probably mean a major revision to the knowledge base. For instance, a new abstraction of knowledge may be needed to overcome some perceived limitations in the current abstraction. With ETS, however, new abstractions may be tentatively explored without major resource expenditures. By modifying the knowledge base in these ways the expert starts his or her own knowledge refinement cycles.

The listings and reports are also helpful in later manual interviewing phases of the knowledge engineering process. The knowledge engineering team does not need to begin from scratch when starting discussions with the expert. They have in hand basic vocabulary, important problem traits, implication hierarchies of these traits, areas of conflict where discussions may begin, a prototype expert system, and test case histories. This has been an invaluable aid in streamlining the knowledge acquisition process in building several expert systems at Boeing Computer Services. Knowledge engineers may also use associated interviewing techniques from personal construct methodology, such as laddering and the resolution of ambiguous construct relationships.

EXPERT-LEVEL PERFORMANCE

An expert system that performs at an expert level still needs to evolve through the human interview–test–modify process with the expert, at least at this time. It is not suggested that the initially generated knowledge base will necessarily be similar in structure to the "final" one. However, fast prototyping is a helpful feedback mechanism, in that it can help demonstrate project feasibility in a matter of hours, and establishes a basis for communication between the knowledge engineering team and the expert.

The expert system tool itself can also be used to refine the knowledge base. However, this means that the expert needs to be trained in the use of the tool, sometimes extensively. KS-300/EMYCIN contains knowledge base editors, for example, that check for syntactic and semantic consistency in the rule base. It also incorporates TEIRESIAS, a tool for incrementally adding to and debugging an existing knowledge base (Davis and Lenat 1982).

OTHER EFFORTS IN DEVELOPING KNOWLEDGE ACQUISITION SYSTEMS

ETS could be used in combination with any of the knowledge acquisition tool families described below as a front-end processor to elicit initial traits and heuristics.

TEIRESIAS (Davis and Lenat 1982) is a subsystem of EMYCIN, which aids the expert and knowledge engineers when they attempt to refine an existing knowledge base. ETS can be used to supply the initial knowledge base, since TEIRESIAS is not capable of eliciting such information on its own.

META-DENDRAL (Buchanan and Feigenbaum 1978) and AQ11 (Michalski 1980) both perform classification analyses of training examples from their respective knowledge bases to produce generalized rules using inductive inference strategies. META-DENDRAL learns rules that predict how classes of compounds fragment in a mass spectrometer, and AQ11 formulates rules from traits and test cases. Both of these systems need an initial set of problem traits before classification can begin. It is up to the expert and knowledge engineer to produce the initial list of applicable traits and relevant training examples. Again, ETS's methods could be used as a front-end for these systems to elicit the problem characteristics.

NANOKLAUS (Hass and Hendrix 1983) attempts to elicit a classification hierarchy from an expert through a natural language dialogue. The information is then used for certain classes of deductive data retrieval. The expert uses NANOKLAUS to enter *IS*-A hierarchy relations and object descriptions. The expert needs to have such a hierarchy developed in mind before using NANOKLAUS. ETS's methods could be combined with this system to help elicit initial relevant concepts about constructs derived from objects and to produce heuristic rules.

DISCUSSION

KNOWLEDGE ARTICULATION

It is almost always difficult for the expert to articulate problem-solving knowledge in terms that are ready for expert system use. Human interviewing processes elicit knowledge that is imprecise, incomplete, and inconsistent. The knowledge is often subconscious, and the expert usually has not needed to be precisely introspective about his/her work. In addition, the expert must come to trust the interviewer enough to overcome any fears or insecurities felt about the expert system building process, especially at the outset of the project. The expert may feel insecure about losing his/her job, or feel threatened by the encroachment of computers into his/her private domain, or not want to expose his problem-solving methods to the scrutiny of other experts or the general public. These problems inevitably lead to difficulties in all phases of knowledge acquisition. During conceptualization, it is difficult to isolate an appropriate set of concepts, which eventually leads to incorrectly and incompletely stated knowledge in the program. With the use of ETS, the expert usually becomes interested and enthusiastic about the project, and understands the kind of knowledge that is expected of him/her. The expert tends to look on the knowledge engineer as an assistant rather than as an encroacher in his/her private domain.

ETS AND TRADITIONAL KNOWLEDGE ENGINEERING

Eventually, the expert will feel that he/she needs help beyond ETS to further expand and refine the knowledge base. At this point the manual knowledge engineering process starts, and the knowledge engineering team uses the results of the ETS sessions as a starting point.

The use of ETS has been of key importance in streamlining and assisting manual interviewing methods during the *expert system life cycle* (Fig. 6.13):

- *Identification.* Initially, ETS helps the expert organize his/her thoughts. This can be useful before describing and defining the formal problem scope, since many tentative ideas can be quickly tested. ETS helps identify what class of

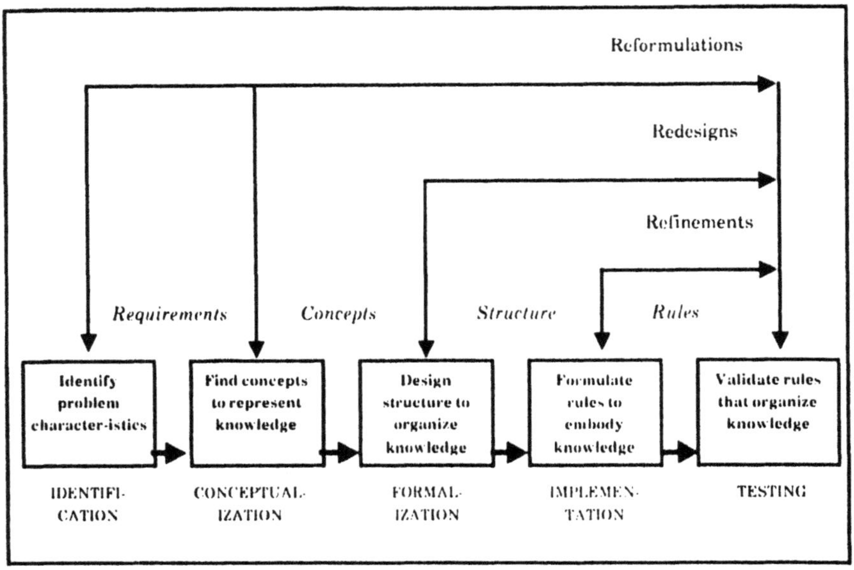

Fig. 6.13.
ETS can significantly shorten the traditional knowledge engineering life cycle (Buchanan et al. 1983).

problem can be solved, and how these problems are characterized. The system helps partition the problem by helping to structure the problem-solving knowledge into a construct hierarchy. Much of the data, important terms, and their interrelations are identified. Problem solution sets are described. Some essential aspects of the necessary human expertise are identified.

- *Conceptualization.* This stage is initially minimized, since ETS helps the expert explore key concepts and relationships needed to describe the problem-solving process.
- *Formalization.* ETS automatically maps the key concepts into several representations that can immediately be used for automatic rapid prototyping.
- *Implementation.* ETS automatically "implements" an initial expert system, by building a knowledge base to construct a target production rule expert system.
- *Testing.* Several tools and techniques are provided for incrementally improving ETS's knowledge base, using knowledge expansion methods and feedback from the prototype expert system.

APPLICATIONS

ETS has significantly reduced the knowledge acquisition time for many expert system projects. Knowledge engineers feel that ETS can save at least two months of project calendar time. This estimate is made by comparing the time taken for knowledge acquisition for similar projects. The reduction in time results in savings of both the expert's time and the knowledge engineers' time. Some of the prototype knowledge-based systems that have been built with ETS are shown in Figure 6.14. So far over 300 such systems have been built.

It took the expert less than two hours to complete the example Organization Development Intervention Technique ETS session.

Due to ETS's rapid prototyping capability, project feasibility is being demonstrated in several areas that otherwise may not have received consideration. Consequently, a large number of these small prototypes are being accrued, giving resource managers a concrete basis for comparing potential applications and sets of applications. For instance, the feasibility of supplying a software engineering work station with several small, communicating expert systems is being studied. These would help the software engineering team with resource allocation decisions, personnel management, requirements and specifications production, testing, debugging, documentation production, and configuration management. Rapid simulation of the components of such an environment may be greatly facilitated by using ETS.

USE OF ETS

The quality of the problem-solving information elicited from the expert in the early stages is improved over manual methods, because ETS provides the expert with knowledge analysis methods and a mechanism for exploring internal conflicts in the way that he/she handles different problem cases. Consistency is used conceptually to elaborate important problem aspects and not as a set of criteria for rejecting "bad" heuristics.

Experts and their managers have been enthusiastic about ETS's knowledge elicitation process. Gaining the confidence of the expert early in the knowledge acquisition phase is important, as discussed above.

Multiple representation strategies and analysis methods are available to the expert that enable the knowledge to be viewed and modified in several interrelated ways.

Age Guesser (by facial features)
AI Book Advisor
AI Library Advisor
AI Tools Advisor
Aircraft Identifier
Aircraft Fault Isolator
Airplane Configuration Mass Property Estimation Risk Analyzer
Airplane Design Flutter Analyzer
Alphanumeric Character Recognizer (by feature)
Animal Identification Advisor
Artificial Intelligence Citation Tutor
Automated Numerical Control - Cutter Consultant
Automatic Flight Controls Diagnostic Aid
ATLAS Structural Analysis Advisor
AXOTL Software Advisor
Bank Examiner
Bar-Tender's Assistant
Bicycle Selector
Bond Durability Consultant
Business Computing Needs Advisor
Business Graphics Package Consultant
Car Engine Diagnostic Aid
Character Recognizer
Car Horn Diagnostic Aid
Chair Selector
Climbing Gear Advisor
Cloud Identifier
Composite Materials - Design Optimization
Composite Materials - Design Retrieval
Composite Materials - Materials Retrieval
Composite Materials - Process Planning
Computer Communications System Bug Advisor
Computer Languages Consultant
Conflict of Interest Advisor
Curriculum Advisor
Database Management System Consultant
Documentation Update Consultant
Energy Control System Model Evaluator
Expert System Application Advisor
Expert System Tools Advisor
Failure Modes and Effects Analyzer
Fast Food Advisor
Finish Advisor for Design Engineers
Finish and Corrosion Control Consultant
Flight Controls Human Factors Assistant
Flight Mode Manager
Furniture Workstation System Consultant
Geology Analyzer
Graphics Package Advisor
GT-STRUDL Structural Analysis Advisor
Houseplant Disease Identifier
Ice Cream Flavor Selector
Japanese Restaurant Advisor (for Seattle)
Jet Engine Diagnostic Aid
Jet Engine Fault Isolator
Jet Engine Manual Advisor
Materials Technology Advisor / Database Pilot
Meal Advisor
Mental Health Diagnostic Aid
Micro Computer - Needs Analysis
Micro Computer - System Recommendations Consultant
Micro Computer - Workstation Configuration Advisor
Molded Rubber Seal Advisor
Motorcycle Selector
MugWump Political Advisor
Newspaper Selection Consultant
Office Automation System Advisor
Office Automation Workstation Advisor
Organization Development Intervention Consultant
Personality Factor Advisor
Personnel Resource Management Decision Aid
Pet Locator
Palo Alto Restaurant Advisor
PAN AIR Aerodynamic Analysis Software - Geometry Advisor
PAN AIR Aerodynamic Analysis Software - Front End Advisor
PAN AIR Aerodynamic Analysis Software - Back End Analyzer
Portfolio Management Aid
Program Bug Advisor (FORTRAN)
Programming Language Advisor
Programming Language Applications Advisor
Programming Language Evaluator and Selector
Propulsion System Advisor
Radio Diagnostician
Rapid Software Prototyping Aid
Relational Database Construction Advisor
Resin Advisor for Composite Parts
Reporting Assignment Advisor
Rivet Selector
Robotic System Application Advisor
Software Bug Diagnosis and Prescription Consultant
Software Management Consultant
Software Release Advisor
Software Services Advisor
Statistics Package Use Advisor
Structural Analysis Software Selector
Tax Regulation Consultant
Technical Sales and Services Consultant
Telephone Feature Selection Consultant
Transport Airplane Configuration Initial Selection Advisor
Travel Agent for Domestic Cities
Travel Agent for Foreign Cities
Velocity Analysis Advisor
Visual Target Identifier
Wine Advisor
Wood Identifier
Word Processing System Consultant

Fig. 6.14.
Some of the rapid prototype knowledge bases built using ETS.

Much attention has been paid to the development of a friendly user interface. As in all computer systems, interfaces must be engineered with end-user acceptance in mind. Commands may be entered from pop-up menus with the system mouse, or simply keyed in. Interlisp's spelling completion and correction facilities are used to manage user interaction when appropriate. This interface has been critical in gaining the acceptance of experts who use ETS.

COMBINING EXPERTISE FROM MULTIPLE EXPERTS

As mentioned in Slater (1981) and Gaines and Shaw (1981), methods are being developed to combine psychological information captured as rating grids from several subjects. These techniques may help to overcome a serious practical problem with building consultation expert systems — combining knowledge from many experts. Two experts, for example, may attempt to solve a problem, using similar or dissimilar methods, and may or may not achieve the same results. Trying to capture this type of information in one coherent expert system has proven to be difficult.

By letting several experts build grids independently and then combining them together into one consultation system, the refine-and-test cycles can be shortened. This is because more specialized and diverse special case knowledge will be uncovered earlier in the knowledge acquisition process. Promising experiments have been performed using ETS to combine expertise from several experts. For instance, ETS produced knowledge bases from four experts for an Artificial Intelligence Tool Advisor, which were combined to produce one large consultation system. The end-user could then select the expertise of any subset of experts during the consultation, and receive *consensus* and *dissenting* opinions (Boose 1985b; see Figure 6.12). The "dissenting opinion" mechanism tends to preserve expertise about special cases and exceptions. Negotiating techniques based on grid analyses presented by Slater (1977) and Gaines and Shaw (1981) have also been used successfully.

LIMITATIONS AND FUTURE DEVELOPMENTS

SYSTEM LIMITATIONS

There are some fundamental limitations to the use of ETS for knowledge acquisition:

> Kelly's grid method is best suited for *analysis* class problems (debugging, diagnosis, interpretation, classification) whose solutions may be enumerated ahead of time. The system cannot readily handle *synthesis* class problems where unique solutions are built up from components (design and planning), or problems that require a combination of analysis and synthesis (control, monitoring, prediction, repair). However, ETS can handle the analytic portions of these problems, and it should be noted that many planning and design problems involve synthesizing the results of several analytic components (for instance, R1 in McDermott 1980a, 1980b). These components may be investigated with ETS.
>
> It is difficult to apply grid methods to elicit "deep" *causal* knowledge, *procedural* knowledge, or *strategic* knowledge. ETS elicits traits and builds relationships, but does not find out much about *how* or *when* this information is used in the problem-solving process. Some of this information could be gathered by modifying ETS to ask for more specific constructs during the interview process. For instance, to elicit procedural knowledge, ETS could ask, "Think of a procedure, or part of a procedure, that would be useful for concluding about two of 'a,' 'b,' and 'c,' but not the other. What is that procedure?" This has been tried in manual interviewing following the initial use of ETS, but the results have been mixed. The process depends on the ability of the expert to think about the problem at a useful level of abstraction. Similarly, ETS could ask about strategic knowledge. Causal knowledge could only be elicited by breaking down analysis problems into smaller subproblems, and breaking these down into smaller problems, and so on, asking questions about how the problem components work together as a system. This is much more difficult for the expert, since he/she needs to keep global relationships in mind continuously, as well as the specific aspect of the problem he/she is focusing on. The interview process would also be much more difficult to control. Another interviewing technique is being applied to this problem in MDIS, a maintenance and diagnostic and information elicitation system (Antonelli 1983). It may be possible to tie these two techniques together in one knowledge acquisition system.
>
> It is sometimes difficult for the expert to identify conclusion sets that are at similar, useful levels of granularity. For instance, in a maintenance system, the expert may include the elements "engine" and "ignition coil." This can lead to problems when constructs are elicited, since those applied to the engine will be at a different level of abstraction (more general) than those applied to the ignition coil. However, once the expert understands how the elements and constructs

work together to build rules, consistent levels of abstraction can usually be identified at the next ETS session, starting over from scratch. At most the expert will have "wasted" a few hours in coming to grips with a more consistent abstraction of his/her knowledge.

Methods are also being examined to allow the expert to combine several ETS knowledge bases at varying levels of abstraction (Saaty 1980). This paradigm is based on Clancey's description of generic structured selection (analytic) problem solving (Clancey 1984).

All constructs are bipolar; they may only take on two values. It may be more convenient to describe a single trait that could take on any number of discrete values rather than just two values. This becomes particularly awkward when the construct is numerical, and there are many critical points on the scale. Currently, all such points (and their "negations") must be represented as individual pairs of traits.

These are some of the limitations of grid methodology reviewed by Kelly (1955):

Representative elements. The assumption is that the elicited set of elements will be a sufficient representation of the problem conclusion set. It must be assumed that the expert knows what these conclusions are, or that the relevant set will be built with ETS knowledge expansion methods or later manual interviewing.

Representative constructs. It is more difficult to verify that a sufficient set of constructs has been elicited. Inappropriate constructs are easier to weed out of the system (see the discussion of construct types above), but errors of omission are harder to detect. Some important constructs that are missing may be elicited using ETS's knowledge expansion techniques, but there is no guarantee that a sufficient set will be found. This is a problem with knowledge acquisition in general. Expert-level performance of the final expert system is critically dependent on obtaining and effectively using a sufficient set of problem-solving knowledge.

Several limitations exist in the prototype expert systems that are built by ETS:

It is difficult to make minor corrections directly based on the final recommendation set, since the constructs and elements that produced the rules are so interrelated. The methodologies mentioned above that compare the expert's expectations with consultation results can be used to circumvent this problem to some extent.

Individual certainty factors associated with rules may have little meaning when examined by the expert. Each factor has significance only when compared with all the other factors in the system. Thus, some loss of system transparency is incurred.

OTHER FUTURE WORK

ETS is being expanded in many areas to improve its utility:

Implement some of the manual methods described above to try to elicit procedural, strategic, and causal knowledge.

Add principal components analysis to detect interdependent parameters and compute the strength of the interdependence.

Implement an element preference analysis to assist in certainty factor generation and relative element importance analysis. Produce resistance to change grids that would provide other measures of the relative importance of constructs in the expert's hierarchy. Create implication grids that provide an additional method of analyzing the relationships in the expert's construct hierarchy (Hinkle 1965).

Continue to experiment with methods for combining expertise from many experts.

In spite of the limitations of ETS, it has been an invaluable aid to the knowledge engineering process. Especially in situations where analysis problems can be represented using production rules, ETS dramatically streamlines the knowledge acquisition process.

ACKNOWLEDGMENTS

Thanks to the OD expert, Dr. Wendell French, an OD consultant and member of the University of Washington School of Management who participated in the example session; also to Ray Allis, Roger Beeman, Miro Benda, Jeff Bradshaw, Keith Butler, Wendell French, Brian Gaines, Alistair Holden, Earl Hunt, Ted Jardine, Cathy Kitto, Janusz Kowalik, Art Nagai, Mildred Shaw, Steve Tanimoto, Lisle Tinglof-Boose, Steve White, and Bruce Wilson for their contributions and support. This work was performed at the Artificial Intelligence Center of Boeing Computer Services in Seattle, Washington.

APPENDIX

Expert Transfer System (ETS) is now available for internal use at Boeing Company. It is expected that ETS will be offered outside of Boeing in the future.

7 Idiothetic Methods for the Analysis of Behavioral Decision Making: Computer Applications

James Jaccard, Choi K. Wan, and Gregory Wood

Considerable research has been conducted on the development of expert systems as aids for decision making and problem solving. The majority of this research focuses on the professional decision maker, such as medical doctors, electricians, business managers and psychiatrists. In contrast, relatively little research has explored the development of decision aids for the "nonexpert" decision maker. Individuals in everyday life frequently face a wide range of major decisions (e.g., what type of car to buy, what method of birth control to use, what career to pursue). This chapter describes a methodology that can be used to analyze how individuals orient themselves toward important decisions. The approach does *not* provide an "expert" system that can make a decision for the individual. Rather, the focus is on computerized methods for clarifying for the individual the perceptions and orientations he or she has in addressing the decision topic. The approach has been applied to such areas as choice of birth control methods, pregnancy resolution decisions in teenagers, consumer choice decisions of products to purchase, career decisions, and decisions to continue infertility treatment.

PRELIMINARY CONSIDERATIONS

IDIOGRAPHIC VERSUS NOMOTHETIC PERSPECTIVES

The decision framework described can be applied at either the idiographic or nomothetic level. The approach will illuminate decision orientations of either a single individual or groups of individuals. We will discuss in each section the relevant issues involved in idiographic versus nomothetic applications. Some general issues are noted here.

For purposes of aggregate (nomothetic)-level analyses, one must consider two classes of cautionary issues. The first concerns the use of rating scales, a major tool in the present approach. When an individual is asked to make a judgment about an object on a dimension, he/she first derives a judgment through some cognitive process. The investigator then seeks to obtain a representation of that judgment by asking the individual to translate the judgment onto a rating scale. Two individuals might make the same cognitive judgment, but differ in their observed ratings, if they translate that judgment differently onto the rating scale. At issue is whether group (e.g., mean) differences reflect differences in the true underlying judgment, or whether they reflect differences in the ways the groups use the rating scale. Research in psychophysics (e.g., Wegner 1982; Upshaw 1962) suggests that the problem of response translation may be more serious than applied researchers realize. Traditional nomothetic methods typically assume a common response language across individuals. In contrast, the methods to be described do not assume that any two individuals use a scale in the same fashion. The measures of interest are derived within individuals such that this assumption is unnecessary even for many of the proposed aggregate-level analyses. The primary assumptions are that a given individual will interpret a scale in the same fashion when rating different stimuli (e.g., the individual will interpret an unfavorable–favorable scale in the same fashion when rating each of the decision options), and that the ratings will have approximately interval-level properties.

Independent of the issue of response language is the fact that aggregate-level analysis can suggest misleading inferences about individuals or subgroups of individuals vis-à-vis the nature of between- and within-group variability. A classic example with correlation coefficients involves Simpson's paradox and is illustrated in Figure 7.1. There are three subgroups of individuals (e.g., lower class, middle class, and upper class), each of which exhibits a strong negative correlation between variables x and y. If a correlation is computed ignoring subgroups, a strong positive correlation between x and y results. One might infer from the across-group analysis that positive changes in x will yield positive changes in y, when exactly the opposite would occur, as revealed by the within-group analyses. The methods we propose cannot circumvent potential problems such as the above, as they are inherent in aggregate-level analysis. Appropriate cautions in interpretation are required (see Jaccard and Wood 1986 for a detailed discussion of misleading aggregation for means, correlations, and proportions).

ACTIVITIES IN BEHAVIORAL DECISION MAKING

There are at least eight types of psychological activities that an individual can engage in during active decision making. First, the individual recognizes that a problem exists and that a decision is required. Second, the individual specifies the purpose of the decision. That is, the person derives from his or her cognitive system the ideal outcome of the decision. Third, the person engages in option identification. That is, the

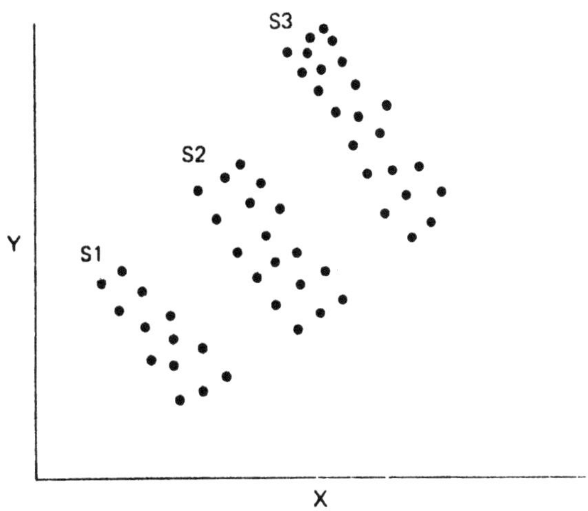

Fig. 7.1.
Relationship between x and y for three socioeconomic groups.

S1, Low socioeconomic-status subjects; S2, middle socioeconomic-status subjects; S3, high socioeconomic-status subjects.

individual retrieves from his/her cognitive system potential alternative solutions to the problem at hand. Fourth, the person engages in information search, in which he or she seeks information, either about additional available options or about properties of one or more of the options under consideration. Fifth, the individual considers the information he or she has about different decision options and forms a preference structure. The term "information" is used in a general sense and refers to any anticipated consequence or concept subjectively associated with a given decision option. A *preference structure* refers to a general feeling of favorableness or unfavorableness (i.e., an attitude) toward each decision option. Given *p* decision options, a preference structure refers to the set of *p* attitudes. Sixth, the individual chooses one of the decision options for purposes of future behavioral enactment. The choice will be some function of the individual's preference structure. Seventh, the individual translates the decision into overt behavior. Finally, a post-decision evaluation takes place. The individual reflects on the decision after the option has been enacted and evaluates the decision process in light of the outcomes that have resulted.

A decision maker does not necessarily perform all of the above activities. Nor must the process follow the sequence described. Each activity forms the basis of our theory of behavioral decision making. Unfortunately, space limitations do not permit consideration of each activity in this chapter.

OVERVIEW

The remainder of this chapter describes three major facets of our theoretical approach. First, we develop methods for characterizing a person's construction system with respect to different decision options. The focus of analysis is a *perceptual structure matrix,* which is a representation of the different types of information an individual has about the decision options. Second, the major role of the preference structure in the decision process is discussed. We describe methods for measuring and analyzing preference structures to better understand an individual's choice of a given option. Finally, we link the above two facets by describing a methodology that reveals how the individual uses information in forming preferences. Thus, the theoretical connections between the perceptual structure matrix and the preference structure are explicitly addressed.

ANALYSIS OF PERCEPTUAL STRUCTURES

A perceptual structure is characterized by an $m \times p$ matrix of p options and m informational dimensions along which an individual evaluates each option (see Table 7.1). For example, the options might be different birth control methods that an individual is considering using (e.g., the pill, the IUD) and the informational dimensions (or properties) might be factors such as cost and effectiveness. The content of the options and dimensions are elicited from individuals by asking them (1) to name all of the options they can think of (e.g., name all of the available birth control methods you can think of), and (2) to name all of the factors they would consider when evaluating the options. The individuals then rank-order the dimensions in terms of their importance in evaluating options, and rate each dimension on a 21-point importance scale (ranging from 0 to 100 in five-unit increments with adverbs "not at all, slightly, quite, and extremely" appropriately spaced). Finally, the individuals are asked to rate each option on each dimension in terms of its "standing" on that dimension (e.g., is it "good," "neutral," or "bad" in terms of cost). These ratings use a special format that is central to later procedures and analyses. The individuals are told to assign a letter rating such that an A means the option is good on the dimension, a B means the option is neutral on the dimension, and a C means the option is bad on the dimension. The individuals can make finer distinctions if they desire by assigning a plus or a minus to a letter (e.g., A+, B–). This yields a nine-point scale, scored from 1 (C–) to 9 (A+).

Table 7.1
Perceptual Structure Matrix

	Options				
Dimensions	*1*	*2*	*3*	....	*p*
1	R_{11}	R_{12}	R_{13}	....	R_{1p}
2	R_{21}	R_{22}	R_{23}	....	R_{2p}
3	R_{31}	R_{32}	R_{33}	....	R_{3p}
.	.	.	.	....	.
.	.	.	.	....	.
.	.	.	.	....	.
.	.	.	.	....	.
m	R_{m1}	R_{m2}	R_{m3}	....	R_{mp}

Source: Compiled by the authors.

ANALYSIS OF OPTION SIMILARITY

The perceptual structure matrix reflects how the individual construes the decision options on different informational dimensions. Social scientists are frequently interested in describing similarities between options across informational dimensions. For example, a counselor might want to identify careers that an individual perceives as similar when making a career choice. A consumer researcher (who is planning an advertising campaign to market a microcomputer) might want to identify other brands that are perceived as similar to his or her brand as well as brands that are perceived as being different. A psychologist working with couples who are infertile might be interested in social support mechanisms that people use in confronting the infertility problem. Different sources will be perceived by the client as offering support or nonsupport on different dimensions (e.g., emotional support, financial support, providing useful information, etc.). The psychologist might want to identify which sources are similar in the kinds of support they have to offer and which sources are different.

The perceptual structure matrix can be analyzed to determine similarities between options. Similarity, in this case, reflects the common perceptions of the options across different informational dimensions. The analysis is based on an option dissimilarity matrix consisting of Euclidean distance scores. Given p options, the matrix is a symmetric $p \times p$ matrix, with the dissimilarity between any two options, i and j, defined as

$$d_{ij} = 1/m \sum_{k=1}^{m} (R_{ki} - R_{kj})^2 \qquad (7.1)$$

where d_{ij} refers to the dissimilarity between options i and j, R_{ki} is the rating of option i on dimension k, R_{kj} is the rating of option j on dimension k, and m refers to the number of dimensions. By subjecting the matrix of dissimilarity measures to cluster analysis or multidimensional scaling analysis, one can identify clusters of options that have similar profiles across dimensions.

DECOMPOSITION OF DISSIMILARITY SCORES

Three or more options may be dissimilar, but for quite different reasons. It will often be instructive to explore specific features of the data that contribute to option dissimilarity. We have found the following approach to be useful: The distance score between any two options can be conceptualized as a function of three factors, elevation, scatter, and shape. *Elevation* refers to the mean difference between options collapsing across dimensions. Table 7.2 illustrates two options that differ in elevation. Note that the options have identical patterns of scores across dimensions, except that the respondent has consistently rated the second option 2 units higher than option 1. In this case, the nonzero distance score results from differences in the elevation of ratings. *Scatter* refers to the standard deviation of ratings for a given option across dimensions. Table 7.2 presents two options that differ in scatter. In this case, the nonzero distance score derives, in part, from differences in the standard deviations of the ratings of options. *Shape* refers to the correlation between dimensional ratings assigned to the two options. Shape reflects a common pattern of ratings across dimensions. The correlation between options 1 and 2 in Table 7.2 is 1.00, indicating an identical "shape" (pattern) of ratings.

The distance score in Equation 7.1 can be expressed in terms of elevation, scatter, and shape as follows:

$$d_{ij} = (M_i - M_j)^2 + (s_i - s_j)^2 + 2s_is_j(1 - r) \qquad (7.2)$$

where M is the mean rating for a given option across dimensions, s is the standard deviation for a given option across dimensions, and r is the correlation between ratings across dimensions for the two options in question. The first component of the right side of Equation 7.2 reflects elevation, the second component represents scatter, and the third reflects

Table 7.2
Example of Elevation and Scatter

	Difference in elevation		*Difference in scatter*	
Dimension	*Option 1*	*Option 2*	*Option 3*	*Option 4*
1	3	5	3	2
2	4	6	4	3
3	6	8	4	4
4	5	7	4	5
5	1	3	5	6

Source: Compiled by the authors.

a scatter by shape interaction. The relative contributions of these three components to any given distance score can be computed as follows:

$$C_{e} = (m_i - m_j)^2 / d_{ij} \quad (7.3)$$

$$C_{sc} = (s_i - s_j)^2 / d_{ij} \quad (7.4)$$

$$C_{sh.sc} = (2 s_i s_j (1 - r)) / d_{ij} \quad (7.5)$$

where C_e is the contribution of elevation, C_{sc} is the contribution of scatter, and $C_{sh.sc}$ is the contribution of the shape by scatter interaction. The three contribution indices will sum to 1, and when multiplied by 100 can be interpreted as percentages.

We have found it useful to calculate a matrix of C_e scores, with cells corresponding to those of the original matrix of dissimilarity scores. One may readily observe the contribution of elevation to any given dissimilarity score. In addition, summary statistics in the form of the lowest C_e score, the highest C_e score, the average C_e score, and the standard deviation of C_e scores help to provide perspectives on the impact of elevation on option similarity. Similar matrices can be computed for the C_{sc} scores and the $C_{sh.sc}$ scores.

A cluster analysis of option dissimilarity matrices can also be performed so as to distinguish the three components. A three-step strategy is required. First, options are clustered on the basis of shape. This requires standardizing scores for each option relative to the mean and standard deviation (across dimensions) for that option. One would then calculate distance measures (using Equation 7.1) based on these standard scores. The standardization of scores removes the effects of both elevation and scatter, and the resultant distance score will reflect only the influence of shape. A cluster analysis is then applied to the matrix of distance scores. At a second stage, one performs a cluster analysis on options *within* each of the resultant "shape" clusters, having defined a new set of distance scores to reflect only scatter. A scatter distance score is formed by substituting deviation scores for the raw scores before applying Equation 7.1. A deviation score is defined as the relevant raw score minus the mean rating for the option across dimensions. A cluster analysis is then applied to this matrix of dissimilarity scores. Finally, at a third stage, options in each of these subgroups would be cluster-analyzed using distance scores that reflect only the influence of elevation. One can index the elevation distance between options A and B by calculating the squared difference of the respective mean ratings of the two options across dimensions (see Morrison's [1976] treatment of profile analysis of independent groups via the Hotelling T^2 statistic for a complementary approach).

The theoretical and practical significance of decomposition of distance scores will depend on the area of application. As an example from the consumer area, several researchers (Holbrook and Huber 1979; Huber and Holbrook 1979; Kafrey, Jacobs, and Zedeck 1979) have proposed that perceptual distortions, called "halo effects," can bias respondent ratings and create "artificial" correlations between options (e.g., different types of microcomputers). The assumption is that a respondent's overall evaluation (positive or negative) of the option distorts the ratings in the direction of the evaluation. Such distortion would increase the correspondence between dimensional ratings for options that share common evaluations. Investigators have treated halo effects as artifacts, despite the fact that they represent a valid psychological process. A researcher might wish to examine the correspondence between ratings of two options, with halo effects removed from the data (Dillon, Mulani, and Frederick 1984). Halo effects in the dissimilarity scores defined by Equation 7.1 would manifest themselves in the elevation component. Thus, the C_e index would reflect the relative contribution of halo effects (as well as other response biases and true mean differences between options) to the similarity/dissimilarity of any two options. The effects of halo biases can be removed from option similarity analysis by using the three-stage cluster analytic strategy discussed above.

CLUSTER DIFFERENCES

Once clusters of options have been identified for an individual, it is useful to document informational dimensions that distinguish the clusters. We will illustrate the issues involved in isolating the differences at the individual level, using an example of a consumer deciding on which brand of a product class to purchase. We will focus on isolating cluster differences on a single dimension, cost.

At the simplest level, one would first calculate the mean cost rating across options for each cluster. If brands 1, 2, and 3 define a cluster, then the mean cost rating across brands would be based on $n = 3$. The mean differences between clusters would then be examined informally, identifying relatively "large" and "small" differences.[1] This approach is reasonable but ignores measurement error. One solution is as follows. The perceptual structure matrix ratings are obtained at three (or more) points in time, using a test–retest reliability design. The mean cost rating of a given option across the three sessions is an estimate of the "true" score for that option (Cronbach et al. 1974).[2] The variability of ratings across sessions is an estimate of random measurement error. If replicates are the ratings in each session, contrast coefficients can be defined that formally compare one set of grouped options to another by means of an F test (Kirk 1968: 74). In this case, the mean square between reflects the size of the difference in the true scores between the clusters, and the mean square within reflects measurement error. The traditional F test applies if session differences reflect only random error.

There are two limitations to this approach. First, if the number of options is small, the test may lack statistical power. This can be offset by increasing the number of test–retest sessions. Second, when a large number of contrasts are made across many attribute dimensions, the probability of a Type I error increases. Despite these limitations, the approach explicitly takes into consideration measurement error and is preferable to the alternative of ignoring measurement error. The researcher will have increased confidence in a between-cluster mean difference if it is substantially larger than what one would expect on the basis of random error.

RELATIVE SCORE MATRIX

The perceptual structure matrix can be transformed to a *relative score* matrix to provide further insights into option–dimension perceptions. The relative score matrix involves calculating a mean rating for each dimension across options and a standard deviation for ratings within dimensions and across options (Table 7.3). The scores within a row are then standardized relative to this mean and standard deviation. The mean score for a given row indicates the tendency for the individual to view options, on the average, as positive (large scores) or negative (low scores). The standard deviation reflects variability in options across the dimension. A small standard deviation would indicate that options tend to be perceived as the same on the dimension. Finally, the within-cell standard scores indicate how "unique" an option is on the dimension (relative to the mean and standard deviation).

In sum, the perceptual structure matrix for an individual can be analyzed to reveal clusters of options that are perceived as similar or

Table 7.3
Relative Score Matrix

	Options						
Dimensions	*1*	2	*3*	....	*p*	*Mean*	*SD*
1	Z_{11}	Z_{12}	Z_{13}	....	Z_{1p}	—	—
2	Z_{21}	Z_{22}	Z_{23}	....	Z_{2p}	—	—
3	Z_{31}	Z_{32}	Z_{33}	....	Z_{3p}	—	—
.	.	.	.	....	.	.	.
.	.	.	.	....	.	.	.
.	.	.	.	....	.	.	.
m	Z_{m1}	Z_{m2}	Z_{m3}	....	Z_{mp}	—	—

Source: Compiled by the authors.

different across dimensions. It is possible to identify these clusters, controlling for the effects of elevation, shape, and/or scatter. Once clusters are identified, it is possible to isolate attribute dimensions that contribute most to option dissimilarity. Finally, the relative score matrix indicates those informational dimensions along which options are perceived by the individual to exhibit little variability or considerable variability. The matrix also indicates the "uniqueness" of an option, given this variability.

ANALYSIS OF DIMENSION SIMILARITY

The above discussion focused on the analysis of option similarity. The perceptual structure matrix can also be analyzed to determine similarities among dimensions across options. This would involve calculating a dimension dissimilarity matrix consisting of Euclidean distance scores. Given m dimensions, the matrix will be a symmetric $m \times m$ matrix. The dissimilarity between any two dimensions, i and j, is defined as

$$d_{ij} = 1/p \sum_{q=1}^{p} (R_{iq} - R_{jq})^2 \qquad (7.6)$$

where d_{ij} is the dissimilarity between dimensions i and j, R_{iq} is the rating of dimension i on option q, R_{jq} is the rating of dimension j on option q, and p is the number of options. All of the notions developed in the analysis of option similarity can be applied to a dimension dissimilarity matrix.[3]

NOMOTHETIC PERSPECTIVES

Thus far, a single individual's responses have formed the basis of analysis. One can also aggregate individually derived indices to perform group comparisons. For example, it would be possible to compare two or more groups on the mean number of option clusters, the mean number of dimension clusters, the mean contributions of shape, elevation, or scatter to a given distance score, and the content of cluster categories (Jaccard and Wan 1985). None of these comparisons requires the measurement assumptions detailed at the outset of this chapter. The idiothetic nature of the approach differs from factor analytic and regression approaches in that the latter methodologies make strong measurement assumptions about a common across-subject response language, and/or they assume homogeneous perceptual structures across individuals.

In our research, where we have studied decision making at the aggregate level, we have found one deviation from a purely idiothetic approach to be useful. This deviation involves measuring the perceptual structure matrix for a common set of investigator-provided options and dimensions. This facilitates aggregate-level analyses in which a specific set of options or dimensions is of interest. There are two potential limitations to this practice. First, we may exclude an option/dimension from those presented that the individual would otherwise consider. Second, we might include options/dimensions that the individual would not normally consider. To minimize these possibilities, we typically conduct a pretest in which we ask a representative sample to list relevant options and dimensions. A content analysis of items elicited determines the list of options/dimensions used (with a criterion that at least 10 percent of the sample must mention the option/dimension for it to be included). In addition, when the list of options/dimensions is presented, we include an "other: please specify ________" category. The individual can then write in an option/dimension if an important one has been omitted. Finally, by introducing importance weights into the calculation of dissimilarity indices (see Note 1), an investigator can further reduce the possibility of including irrelevant dimensions. Although none of these practices guarantees the integrity of the representation of the individual's construction system, we have found them to be effective in research applications where our focus is on aggregate-level descriptions.

If the researcher is willing to make the assumption that individuals use rating scales with the same response language, then the cluster analytic strategy described above can be augmented with a useful nomothetic strategy that permits clustering of individuals as well as the clustering of options and dimensions. Consider a study with 50 subjects, each of whom has responded to the same 8 (dimensions) x 10 (options) matrix of stimuli. For any given pair of subjects, A and B, one can calculate a dissimilarity score as follows: (1) subtract the rating of subject A from the rating of subject B for each cell of the matrix; (2) sum the squared differences across all cells. A 50 x 50 matrix of dissimilarity scores can be formed for all possible pairs of subjects. A cluster analysis of the 50 x 50 matrix would identify clusters of individuals who tend to rate the options in a similar fashion across the dimensions. Mean rating scores for the 8 x 10 dimension-by-option matrix can be computed for each cluster of subjects, and the resulting matrices subjected to the analyses discussed above.[4] The subgroups can then be compared on the measures detailed earlier, as well as on relevant background and individual difference variables. It is also possible to differentiate clusters of subjects in terms of elevation, shape, and scatter.

PREFERENCE STRUCTURES

This section focuses on the nature of preference structures. An individual's preference structure refers to his or her attitude toward each of the decision options. The preference structure is a key concept in our theoretical framework, since a person's choice is conceptualized, in large part, as a function of the preference structure. As discussed later, the preference structure is linked to the individual's perceptual structure matrix (i.e., the way he or she construes the options on the informational dimensions).

PREFERENCE STRUCTURE ANALYSIS AND CHOICE

An attitude is conceptualized in very restricted terms in our framework. It refers to the extent to which an individual feels favorable or unfavorable toward enacting a given behavioral option. A preference structure is measured by asking the individual to rate each decision option on a –10 to +10 unfavorable–favorable scale. Consistent with subjective expected utility (SEU) theory, it can be argued that an individual will choose to perform that option toward which the most positive attitude is held, or that option toward which he or she feels most favorable. Empirical support for this proposition is presented in four studies reported in Jaccard (1981) and Jaccard and Becker (1985). (However, see Jaccard and Wood [1986] for a discussion of instances where the principle does not hold.)

Preference structure analysis involves measuring an individual's judgments of favorableness/unfavorableness about each decision option, and then analyzing the distribution of attitudes across the options. As noted above, the option toward which the individual feels most favorable is the one that he or she will likely choose for behavioral performance. A large discrepancy between the attitude ratings for the most favorable option and the second most favorable option usually implies that the individual will have little difficulty in making a choice. We also find that the decision as to what to do is relatively stable over time. In contrast, when the discrepancy of ratings between the most favorable option and the other options is relatively small, the choice will usually be perceived as difficult, and the decision is less stable over time, everything else being equal. Preference structure analysis reveals to the social scientist those options that the individual feels most inclined to choose (namely, those options that are close in favorableness to the most positively evaluated option) and those options that the individual feels uninclined to choose (namely, those options that are highly discrepant from the most favorable option).

CHANGING DECISIONS

The concept of a preference structure implies that a social scientist can change an individual's choice by changing his or her preference structure. For example, suppose an individual chooses to use an over-the-counter headache remedy, brand A, to treat headaches. A marketing psychologist who wishes to change this behavior can alter the individual's choice (so that he or she will use brand B) by changing the preference structure (and making brand B the most positively evaluated option). Methods for changing preferences, by changing how the individual construes the options vis-à-vis the perceptual structure matrix, are discussed in the next section.

Preference structures also imply that a choice can be stable, even though attitudes and perceptions of the options change. For example, an individual may come to believe that brand B is effective in treating headaches, whereas previously he or she thought it was not. Because of this, the individual might revise his or her overall evaluation of brand B to be more positive. However, unless this revision is large enough to make brand B the most positively evaluated option, the chosen option will not change.

ERROR THEORY FOR PREFERENCE STRUCTURE ANALYSIS

The comparison of attitudes across options for a single individual must address the problem of measurement error. In our research, we typically obtain ratings of attitudes on three separate occasions, and use the mean attitude score as an index of the "true" score. Differences between means for any two options are then evaluated relative to an index of the average unreliability across options. This is accomplished using a one-way analysis of variance model, in which the different options define the levels of the analysis, and replicates are the ratings in each session. The mean square within constitutes the index of unreliability, and all between-option differences are evaluated relative to this mean square by an F ratio. This strategy is similar to the error theory of functional measurement (Anderson 1981, 1982). The major assumption is that within-cell variation reflects only random measurement error. The approach is problematic if the number of options is small, since the statistical test may lack power. This can be offset, however, by increasing the number of repeated assessments.

NOMOTHETIC ANALYSES

One can conduct nomothetic (mean)-level analyses on preference structures with minimal assumptions about a common response language, if the mean comparisons are between two or more decision options (i.e., between "repeated measures" means). The necessary assumption is one of a common scale unit across individuals (the origin being irrelevant). This assumption will probably be met if the measurement practices discussed earlier are effected. Subgroup comparisons can also be made without recourse to common origin assumptions, if the focus is on group differences in the differences between means (e.g., the difference in mean attitude scores between options A and B for upper-class individuals as compared with the difference between mean attitude scores for options A and B for lower-class individuals).

PERCEPTIONS UNDERLYING PREFERENCE STRUCTURES

This section integrates the previous material on perceptual structures and preference structures. We consider the problem of identifying why an individual feels favorable or unfavorable toward a given option. A major factor underlying judgments of favorableness/unfavorableness is how the individual construes the options on specific informational dimensions. We present a methodology for isolating how an individual uses perceptions of an option on different informational dimensions to form an overall judgment of favorableness or unfavorableness about that option. We refer to this as the "integration process," since it reflects how an individual integrates the positive and negative features of an option into a global judgment of favorableness/unfavorableness. The methodology also yields indices of how changes in perceptions will impact on the attitudes comprising the preference structure. We refer to these indices as the *perceptual implications* of a perception for an attitude.

The assessment of perceptual implications and integration processes is problematic, since verbal reports of these phenomena by the individual are of questionable validity. Research has shown that individuals have difficulty in accurately characterizing these complex mental processes (McGuire 1976). For example, individuals tend to overestimate the amount of information they consider and to report using more complex integration processes than appears to be the case (Wiggins 1972; see also Nisbett and Wilson 1977). The present approach uses an indirect assessment procedure that does not require individuals to report complex mental processes. The strategy is to describe to individuals a set of *hypothetical* options that are rated in terms of how favorable or unfavorable he/she would feel about choosing each one. The options are defined so that the ratings of favorableness or unfavorableness provided by the individual will allow one to *infer* the implications of different perceptions for attitude and to *infer* plausible integration processes that might be operative. A procedure for assessing the external validity of the inferences is then applied.

INTEGRATION RULES

Psychologists have expended considerable research effort on the analysis of integration rules used by individuals. Two general classes of rules can be distinguished. *Compensatory* rules are those in which negative features of an option can be offset by positive features of the option. In essence, the positive qualities "compensate" for the negative qualities in the formation of a judgment of favorableness/unfavorableness of an option. *Noncompensatory* rules are those in which positive qualities do not offset negative qualities. The occurrence of a negative feature on a given dimension may lead to a negative attitude (i.e., judgment of unfavorableness), independent of the positive features of that option on other dimensions. One prominent approach to conceptualizing compensatory tradeoff processes has been Anderson's (1981) information integration theory. Integration theory states that an attitude toward a behavioral alternative is a function of information that the individual has with respect to that alternative. One common variant of integration theory suggests that the individual integrates information by means of an averaging process; the positive and negative features of an option are psychologically "tallied" (with the positive features offsetting the negative features), and the attitude is formed accordingly. An averaging model can be represented mathematically as follows:

$$A_p = \sum_{i=1}^{N} s_i / N \qquad (7.7)$$

where A is the attitude toward option p, s is how positive or negative the individual judges a given piece of information to be (we will call this judgment a *scale value*), and N is the number of pieces of information. For example, suppose an individual is evaluating a birth control method and perceives it as ineffective in preventing pregnancy. The individual might think that "ineffectiveness" is a very negative quality. If asked to judge how negative "ineffectiveness" is on a –10 to +10 negative–positive scale, the individual might assign a rating of –8. Suppose the individual also believes the method is inexpensive to use. He or she believes this is a positive quality and assigns "inexpensive to use" a rating of +4. Equation 7.7 would state that a rating of how favorable or unfavorable the individual feels about the birth control method in general should correspond to the average of the ratings assigned to the individual pieces of information: (–8 + 4)/2 = –2. The highly negative quality is compensated for, in part, by the positive quality, reflecting an averaging-based compensatory integration process. Anderson (1982) recognized that different types of qualities may be more important to an individual than other types (e.g., effectiveness in preventing pregnancy might be more important to the individual than the cost of using a birth control method), and that some qualities may be attended to more so than others. He therefore introduced an importance weight for each perception, yielding the following modification of Equation 7.7

$$A = \sum_{i=1}^{N} w_i s_i / \sum_{i=1}^{N} w_i \qquad (7.8)$$

where w is a weighting coefficient reflecting the importance of a given piece of information. Equation 7.8 represents an averaging-based compensatory integration process in which the perceptual implication of a piece of information for an attitude is reflected by the values of w and s. Other types of integration rules are discussed in Jaccard and Becker (1985), Lynch (1985), and Anderson (1982). Our methodology permits a test of the viability of Equation 7.8 as well as other integration strategies that the individual might employ. It also yields estimates of the weighted scale value (ws) of a given perception.

FUNCTIONAL MEASUREMENT

The methodology used in our framework is based on Anderson's (1980, 1981) functional measurement approach. The following strategy would be used in the case of a birth control decision: First, the investigator develops descriptions of hypothetical birth control methods based on a set of specific informational dimensions. For example, a hypothetical method might be described to an individual as follows: "The method is 98 percent effective in preventing pregnancy, has no side effects, does not impact adversely on sexual pleasure, and is relatively inexpensive to use." The individual would then be asked to rate how favorable or unfavorable he or she would feel about using such a method. This description presents information with respect to four dimensions, effectiveness, side effects, impact on sexual pleasure, and cost. A second hypothetical contraceptive method would then be described using the same informational dimensions, but altering the "values" of some. For example, a method might be described as only 75 percent effective, with no side effects, as having a light negative impact on sexual pleasure, and as inexpensive to use. The individual would then rate how favorable or unfavorable he or she would feel toward using this method. The process is continued for a series of hypothetical methods. The descriptions of the methods, however, are designed so that an analysis of the ratings of each method will reveal integration processes that the individual is using and perceptual implications of different pieces of information.

The most informative way to structure the hypothetical descriptions is by means of a factorial manipulation of the informational dimensions of interest. If one were interested in assessing the perceptual implications of effectiveness, cost, and side effects information, one would develop descriptions by factorially manipulating these three dimensions. A rationale is needed for determining what informational dimensions to manipulate and how to manipulate them in forming the descriptions. We will now consider these issues.

SPECIFICATION OF AMOUNT AND TYPE OF INFORMATION

Our preliminary research on birth control suggests at least nine types of informational dimensions may underlie a given attitude. These are: (1) health risks, (2) effectiveness in preventing pregnancy, (3) negative impact on sexual pleasure (e.g., interrupting the sex act, reducing spontaneity), (4) cost, (5) minor side effects (e.g., weight gain), (6) requires doctor's attention, (7) reliance on male/female, (8) convenience in using, and (9) partner's reaction. Obviously, it is not feasible to manipulate orthogonally all nine informational dimensions. Using three levels per factor would yield 19,693 hypothetical methods, a prohibitively large number. The number of descriptions can be dramatically reduced by assuming an additive integration rule and using a fractional factorial design. However, this is unsatisfactory because the nature of the integration rule must be assumed and not empirically tested. In addition, individuals would be forced to consider simultaneously nine distinct items of information for a given hypothetical method, a task that could prove to be confusing and difficult. (We will discuss fractional factorial designs in more detail, shortly.)

One solution to the above problem is to manipulate only a small number of informational dimensions. In the present approach, three dimensions are manipulated with three levels per factor. The dimensions can differ for each individual studied and are selected by presenting to the individual a list of the nine types of information. The individual rank-orders the dimensions from most important to least important, and the three highest-ranked dimensions are used to construct descriptions of 27 (3 x 3 x 3) hypothetical birth control methods. Thus, each individual responds to the same stimuli in the sense that the three most subjectively important dimensions in his or her perceptual matrix are manipulated, although the actual content of the dimensions might differ between individuals.

MANIPULATION OF INFORMATION

Given that one has identified the dimensions to be manipulated, the selection of the values that will be used to manipulate a dimension is of primary importance. For example, if "cost of method" is being manipulated with two levels, one could choose the values $1 versus $5, or $1 versus $100, or $5 versus $25, and so on. The selection of a particular set of values can influence the outcome of the study, both in terms of the integration rule used by the subject and estimates of $w_i s_i$. To the extent that the values are arbitrarily selected, the results of the analysis will also be arbitrary.

The method of manipulation we use is designed to complement the ratings of existing methods of birth control obtained when the individual completes the perceptual structure rating task described in the first part of this chapter. Recall that the individual rated each option in terms of how "good" or "bad" it was on a specific informational dimension using an A–B–C rating scale. For example, if an individual thought that the pill was "good" in terms of its effectiveness, he or she would give the pill an "A" rating on this dimension. If he or she thought the pill was "bad" in terms of cost, he or she would give it a "C" rating on this informational dimension. And so on. Each rating can be further qualified with a plus or a minus. We describe a given hypothetical method in terms of the A–B–C rating scale. For example, we might describe a hypothetical method as having an "A" on effectiveness, a "B" on side effects, and an "A" on cost. The individual is then asked to rate how favorable or unfavorable he or she would feel toward using such a method. We typically manipulate a given dimension using three levels, A versus B versus C. For three informational dimensions, this yields 27 hypothetical methods in accord with a 3 x 3 x 3 factorial design. The advantages of using this form of manipulation will be apparent shortly.

MEASUREMENT ERROR

Our approach formally recognizes that the ratings of favorability of each of the hypothetical methods may be subject to measurement error. Thus, differences in favorability ratings between two hypothetical methods could reflect the effects of measurement error rather than true differences in judgments. This must be taken into consideration. We typically ask individuals to rate each hypothetical method on three separate occasions for purposes of reliability analysis. As will be discussed shortly, these multiple ratings are used to define a formal error theory for the analysis of integration processes.

METHOD OF ANALYSIS

The overall favorableness–unfavorableness ratings of the hypothetical methods are analyzed by means of a 3 x 3 x 3 analysis of variance. Replicates are the three ratings of a given method made in the reliability sessions. Consider the results of an analysis in Tables 7.4 and 7.5 for an individual in one of our experiments. This individual rated each of the 27 hypothetical methods on a 21-point (–10 to +10) unfavorable–favorable scale, as described earlier. The first issue is to evaluate different integration processes that could be operating in making judgments of favorableness–unfavorableness about the hypothetical methods. It can be shown (Anderson 1981, 1982) that compensatory processes will yield only main effects in the analysis and that no interaction effects should be apparent. In contrast, noncompensatory processes predict the existence of interaction effects. Thus, if interaction effects are present, this would suggest that the individual is using a noncompensatory integration process. If no interactions are present, this would suggest that the

Table 7.4
Summary Table for Factorial Analysis of Variance

Source	*SS*	*df*	*MS*	*F*
Effectiveness (E)	176.49	2	88.24	152.15
Health risks (H)	103.35	2	51.68	89.09
Sexual pleasure (S)	31.74	2	16.37	28.22
E x H	3.50	4	.88	1.51
E x S	2.50	4	.63	1.07
H x S	2.00	4	.50	.85
E x H x S	2.00	8	.25	.43
Error	31.42	54	.58	—

Source: Compiled by the authors.

Table 7.5
Main Effect Means for Analysis of Variance

	A	*B*	*C*
Efffectiveness	8.34	.33	–2.00
Health risks	7.00	.17	–0.50
Sexual pleasure	3.65	3.45	–0.43

Source: Compiled by the authors.

individual is using a compensatory integration process. The *F* ratios in Table 7.4 evaluate mean differences in ratings of methods relative to the mean square error. In this case, the mean square error is an index of unreliability of the ratings, and hence measurement error is formally taken into account. For this individual, no interaction effects were apparent in the data that couldn't simply be attributed to measurement error. Thus, the data suggest the individual is using some type of compensatory integration process (for a discussion of different types of compensatory processes and how to differentiate them, see Anderson 1981, 1982).

The analysis of variance also yielded the following eta squares (proportion of explained variance) for the main effects: the most important dimension (effectiveness) = .50, the second most important dimension (health risks) = .30, and the third most important dimension (impact on sexual pleasure) = .08. The total amount of explained variance for a main-effects-only model was .88, indicating a good level of model fit. An examination of mean scores associated with the main effects reveals the perceptual implications of each piece of information (Table 7.5). For example, for effectiveness, the difference between the categories "A (or good) on effectiveness" and "B (or neutral) on effectiveness" is 8.34 – .33 = 8.01. The effect of a perception changing from "good" to "neutral" on this dimension is to decrease the attitude by approximately eight scale points (on a 21-point scale). Thus, the table of means can be used to project the effects of changes in perceptions on a specific informational dimension on overall judgments of favorability.

VALIDATION OF APPROACH

The above approach is subject to the criticism that it focuses entirely on hypothetical birth control methods. A validational procedure is required that relates the analysis to preferences for existing birth control methods. We use the following approach: An attitude toward using each of seven existing methods of birth control is measured on a 21-point unfavorable–favorable scale. As noted earlier, the attitude measures represent the *observed* preference structure. Each existing method is also rated using the A–B–C grading system on the nine informational dimensions identified above. These A–B–C ratings are used to determine that cell in the 3 x 3 x 3 factorial design that a given existing method is perceived to occupy. A predicted attitude score based on the analysis of hypothetical methods is computed by summing the grand mean and the relevant treatment effects for each of the statistically significant effects in the analysis of variance.[5] This is done for each existing method. The seven observed attitudes are then correlated with the seven predicted attitudes. To the extent that the approach suggested is valid, the predicted and observed preference structures should be comparable. To the extent that any one aspect of the approach is inappropriate or invalid, the fit between the predicted and observed preference structure will be adversely affected. For example, if using only the three most highly ranked informational dimensions in defining the hypothetical methods of birth control is inappropriate (because individuals actually use more than three dimensions), then the ability to predict the existing preference structure from the resulting model will be decreased accordingly. For the individual described earlier, the correlation between predicted and observed preference structures was .94. This is a good level of fit and gives the investigator increased confidence in the validity of the analysis.

ADDITIONAL CONSIDERATIONS

This section addresses selected issues relevant to integration analysis. They are discussed in greater detail in Jaccard and Wood (1986) and Jaccard and Becker (1985).

QUALITATIVE VARIABLES

The present approach can incorporate qualitative variables into the analysis of integration processes, using a conceptualization that is distinct from most functional measurement applications. If a qualitative variable involves up to four levels, the convention has been to include all levels in the description of the hypothetical options. However, when the number of levels is large, the number of hypothetical options to be rated can become unwieldy. Usually the investigator resorts to arbitrary selection of a subset of levels to include, or uses an external criterion to eliminate levels (e.g., a marketer might exclude those that are not cost-effective in the market).

In the present approach, qualitative variables with any number of levels can be incorporated, using the same A–B–C rating scheme applied to quantitative variables. If the informational dimension is "type of radio," then a hypothetical car might be described as having an "A" on this dimension (i.e., the car is "good" in terms of the type of radio it has). The question of which types of radios are perceived as "good" or "bad" is a separate issue that can be addressed outside the context of analysis of the integration process. Note that this conceptualization also permits the inclusion of qualitative variables in the analysis of perceptual structures.

FRACTIONAL FACTORIAL DESIGNS AND RELATED APPROACHES

A problem faced by functional measurement approaches is to limit to a reasonable number the hypothetical options that an individual must rate. This chapter advocates a procedure that restricts analysis to the three most important informational dimensions (conceivably, four or five could be manipulated, if judgments are spread over multiple sessions). This approach has the advantage of providing the greatest insight into the integration process, but suffers from the fact that only a limited number of information dimensions can be investigated. Contributions to the consumer literature make frequent use of fractional factorial designs, in which one prespecifies one or more integration rules that will be evaluated, and then selects a smaller set of hypothetical options that will permit evaluation of those rules. For example, Green, Carroll, and Carmone (1978) specify designs by which one can assess the impact of all main effects and selected interactions, yet still retain multiple (e.g., 7 or 8) informational dimensions. These procedures are appropriate for the present approach, given that one can specify a priori the set of viable integration rules an individual might use. If the set excludes the true integration rule employed by the individual, then inferences are subject to error.

Lynch (1985) and others (Lerman and Louviere 1984) have suggested a strategy in which pilot studies are conducted to isolate potentially relevant integration rules. Fractional factorial designs are then used in the main investigation to permit testing of the viable rules suggested by the pretests. This strategy is reasonable, given that the pilot studies accurately identify all viable integration rules for individuals in the main investigation.

Space limitations do not permit a discussion of other strategies applicable to the problem of defining hypothetical options. Interested readers are referred to Green and Srinivasa 1978; Johnson 1974; Pekelman and Sen 1979; Lerman and Louviere 1978; Green 1974; Green, Carroll, and Carmone 1978; and Lynch 1984.

A related issue for fractional factorial designs is that individuals can find the presentation of large numbers of information dimensions confusing and complicated. This can be alleviated, in part, by the use of nested designs, with a corresponding tradeoff of decreasing the number of integration rules that can be tested. Alternatively, a strategy of selecting only the *n* most important dimensions can be used.

FACTORIAL VERSUS REPRESENTATIVE DESIGNS

The definition of hypothetical options using factorial designs can be criticized, because hypothetical options that have no basis in reality may be presented to the individual to rate (e.g., a birth control method that is 99 percent effective and has no side effects). This criticism is minimized with the proposed A–B–C scheme, although it is still possible to define nonmeaningful hypothetical options. In such instances, the nonmeaningful options can be omitted, without necessarily disrupting the estimation of the integration rule or the estimation of perceptual implications. The consequences of omitting the nonmeaningful option will depend on the nature of the research question.

LACK OF INFORMATION AND PSYCHOLOGICAL IMPUTATIONS

When evaluating a set of options, an individual will sometimes have incomplete information about selected options. For example, when evaluating a set of banks, the individual may have no idea what the interest rate is at banks he/she is less familiar with. Of psychological interest is how individuals deal with "missing data." We have been investigating five processes. First, the individual could impute the "average" value of all other banks on the dimension of interest, and form an attitude accordingly. Second, the individual could simply ignore the dimension when evaluating the option for which there is missing information. Third, the individual could "downgrade" the option on the dimension, equating no information with a "bad" standing. Fourth, the individual might "downgrade" the option entirely, and eliminate it from consideration (thus forming a very negative attitude toward it). Finally, the individual might infer the missing value based on other options that are related to the option in question or other dimensions that are related to the dimension in question. Our preliminary research suggests that individuals tend to impute an average value and form attitudes accordingly.

When rating existing options, we instruct individuals to guess whenever they are not sure. This encourages them to impute a value on whatever basis they prefer, and is probably representative of what they would do in everyday life (i.e., we have found little support for the process of "downgrading" the option entirely). Given this procedure, application of our framework is straightforward for the case of "missing data."

NOMOTHETIC ANALYSES

The above analysis of the relationship between perceptual structures and preference structures focused on the single individual. It is possible to use the approach at the nomothetic level to characterize groups of individuals, although some complications arise. The major problem focuses on the fact that the *content* of the dimensions manipulated in the analysis of hypothetical options may differ across individuals. This would occur if there is within-group variability in the ranking of the three most important dimensions. If this variability is minimal, then content is, for all intent and purposes, constant across individuals and nomothetic analyses are straightforward. When within-group variability in the ranking of the top three dimensions is large, an alternative strategy can be used. This strategy would involve imposing the same three dimensions on all individuals. The dimensions can be selected either because they are of interest in their own right or on the basis of an empirical criterion (e.g., the three dimensions with the highest modal rank). The imposition of dimensions on individuals will have the effect of decreasing the fit between observed and predicted preference structures and will bias the investigator toward missing the perceptions underlying an attitude. However, it does permit an analysis of the effects of specific dimensions on attitudes toward behavioral options. An alternative strategy for dealing with this issue is discussed in Jaccard and Wan (1986).

Given a common set of dimensions across individuals, group-level analysis of variance can be performed in the 3 x 3 x 3 design. One can also include grouping factors in the analysis (e.g., males versus females). Minimal assumptions (common scale unit) of uniform response language are in effect, as long as the focus is on differences between "repeated measure" means or on how differences between means are different in the various subgroups (e.g., for males, the difference between a "good" and "neutral" rating on the dimension of price is 4.12 units, whereas the corresponding difference for females is only .13 units).

A nomothetic issue that has arisen in our research is that of identifying groups of individuals with similar integration rules and perceptual implications. One approach is to use cluster analysis, in which individuals are grouped empirically. This involves the following: For a given individual, calculate the mean score for each cell of the factorial design. Subtract the grand mean from each score to eliminate effects of the origin. Form a distance score between individuals A and B, by subtracting the score in a given cell for individual A from the corresponding cell for individual B, and summing the squared differences of all cells. This is repeated for all possible pairs of individuals, and the resulting N x N matrix of dissimilarity scores is then subjected to cluster analysis, using the methods discussed earlier. This approach requires the assumption of a common scale unit. The resulting clusters of individuals can then be subjected to functional measurement analysis. An alternative approach would be to retain the effects of the grand mean, thereby discriminating individuals with distinct origins.

DECISION AIDS

We have adapted the above framework to help individuals in making major decisions. The decision aid is designed to reveal to the individual the structure of his or her perceptions about different options (via the analysis of the perceptual structure matrix) and to reveal the nature of the tradeoffs he or she makes between dimensions (via the analysis of hypothetical options). Frequently, the individual is surprised at the nature of the tradeoff rule he or she appears to be using. The individual is permitted to readjust the attitudinal ratings of the hypothetical options to reflect better the tradeoff policy he or she thinks is desirable. From these final ratings, an equation based on the sum of the grand mean and relevant treatment effects for statistically significant main effects and interactions is isolated. The equation is a mathematical representation of the tradeoff model the individual wishes to apply in evaluating options. The ratings of the existing options from the perceptual structure matrix are then substituted into the math model to generate what the individual's preference structure *should* be, given the desired tradeoff process. The option that has the highest generated attitude score is the recommended option. Our empirical research has demonstrated that individuals who use this decision aid tend to be more satisfied with their decisions than individuals who do not. When applied to birth control decisions, we have found the aid to increase the probability that the individual will consistently and accurately use birth control, thus decreasing the probability of an undesired pregnancy.

COMPUTER PROGRAMS

This section describes the computer programs used in our research program.

PERCEPTUAL STRUCTURE COMPUTER PROGRAMS

Three coordinated programs have been developed for perceptual structure analysis. OPTION ELICIT elicits from individuals the options that they perceive as relevant for the topic in question. DIMENSION ELICIT elicits the relevant informational dimensions. PSM MEASURE assesses the perceptions for the cells of the perceptual structure matrix, using the A–B–C rating scheme. The program is coordinated with OPTION ELICIT and DIMENSION ELICIT to permit either individual-generated or experimenter-generated options and dimensions. A statistical program, OPTION ANALYSIS, performs cluster analysis on the option dissimilarity scores. The average link hierarchical clustering method is used. In addition, the program provides indices of skewedness and elongation for the distance scores. One can use these indices to diagnose the appropriateness of cluster analysis versus multidimensional scaling for the analysis of distance scores (Pruzansky, Tversky, and Carroll 1982). If the diagnosis calls for multidimensional scaling, we recommend INDSCAL. OPTION ANALYSIS generates matrices that decompose dissimilarity scores into the contributions of elevation, shape, and the shape–scatter interaction. In addition, the program serially produces cluster analyses on the traditional Euclidean distance scores, and then on scores defined to isolate shape, scatter, and elevation. OPTION ANALYSIS also provides the option of applying principal components analysis to the individual-based correlation matrix of option relationships. DIMENSION ANALYSIS parallels OPTION ANALYSIS, but focuses on the analysis of dimension similarity. Another statistical program, SUBJECT CLUSTER, produces a clustering of individuals with similar perceptual structure matrices.

PREFERENCE STRUCTURE COMPUTER PROGRAMS

PREFERENCE MEASURE is a computer program designed to measure an individual's preference structure using the rating scales discussed earlier. The program is coordinated with OPTION ELICIT and permits the researcher to assess a preference structure using either subject-generated options or experimenter-imposed options. PREFERENCE ANALYSIS is a statistical program that applies the analysis-of-variance error model to preference structure analysis for multiple-session data. Output includes the mean attitude score for each option, the standard deviation of scores for each option, a test of homogeneity of variance of the attitude scores for each option, the analysis-of-variance summary table for purposes of reliability analysis, and a critical difference (CD) statistic (based on Tukey's hsd test; see Jaccard, Becker, and Wood 1984), which indicates the magnitude that a mean difference between any two options must achieve in order to be statistically significant (i.e., reliable). The latter statistic assumes all possible pairs of options are of interest, and hence is a conservative index. PREFERENCE CLUSTER is a nomothetic-based program that clusters individuals within similar preference structures, using the same principles as SUBJECT CLUSTER.

INTEGRATION ANALYSIS COMPUTER PROGRAMS

INTEGRATION MEASURE is a computer program designed to assess attitudes toward hypothetical options for purposes of functional measurement analysis. The program is coordinated with DIMENSION SELECT so that either individual-generated or experimenter-generated informational dimensions can be used. INTEGRATION ANALYSIS is a statistical program that performs the basic analyses of functional measurement. It is an analysis-of-variance–based program with the following output: a summary table for the analysis (note: if only one assessment session is used, the analysis is based on one observation per cell, yielding no error term. In this case, evaluation of the significance of effects would focus on eta squares); cell and marginal mean scores; the grand mean; and all relevant treatment effects. In addition, the program contains a number of options for testing specific forms of interactions (e.g., the bilinear component), which are useful in distinguishing certain classes of integration rules (Anderson 1981, 1982).

VALIDATE is a program to perform tests of the correspondence between observed and predicted preference structures. Output includes the predicted values (PV) and the observed values (OV), the discrepancy between each PV and OV, the correlation (and associated significance tests and standard errors) between PV and OV, the regression equation for predicting OV from PV, and the form of the model used to generate the PV. INTEGRATION CLUSTER is a nomothetic-based program designed to cluster-analyze individuals with similar integration rules and perceptual implications. It has the option of retaining the effects of the grand mean or removing it. Finally, FRACTIONAL DESIGN is a program that generates the content of hypothetical options for fractional factorial designs, to aid in the design of experiments that can impose certain integration rules.

CONCLUDING REMARKS

This chapter has described a set of procedures and computer programs designed to measure and analyze selected aspects of the decision-making process of the nonexpert. This includes the analysis of perceptual structures, the analysis of preference structures, and a methodology for linking perceptual structures to preference structures. The approach can be applied to one individual or nomothetically. We have found it useful in counseling situations as well as for designing educational and advertising efforts. Decision making is a complex phenomenon, and we have been able to describe only a small subset of analyses necessary to gain insights into how individuals make decisions. We hope this chapter will stimulate other computer applications in this regard.

APPENDIX

All of the programs described in this chapter are available from James Jaccard, Department of Psychology, State University of New York at Albany, Albany, New York. The programs are available in either FORTRAN (for mainframes) or BASIC (for IBM-compatible microcomputers). A nominal fee will be charged to cover costs of tape and/or diskettes.

NOTES

1. Formal definitions of what constitutes a "large" or "small" difference, as with any statistical comparison, is a function of substantive criteria within the domain of interest. In the absence of guidelines, Cohen's (1977) definition of small, medium, and large effect sizes can be used in the context of the *d* coefficient, using the square root of the error term (identified below) in the denominator of the statistic.

2. These estimated true scores would be used in defining the dissimilarity scores in the original cluster analysis.

3. Our discussion of Euclidean distance scores has omitted consideration of several important issues, such as the use of importance weights, the reliability of measures, and the use of principle components analysis instead of cluster analysis. See Jaccard and Wood (1986) for a discussion of these topics in our framework.

4. For the analysis of informational dimensions that distinguishes clusters, one would use traditional multivariate analyses instead of those presented earlier.

5. Predicted scores were further modified to take into account the "plus" and "minus" distinctions the individual used in rating existing banks. For example, if the individual assigned a bank a B+, then the treatment effect for the B category was increased by one-third the difference between means of the A and B categories. This procedure assumes the individual uses the pluses and minuses in a fashion that approximates equal intervals. A similar approach has been used by Pekelman and Sen (1979) and Green, Carroll, and Goldberg (1981) in the context of conjoint measurement.

8 The Galileo System: A Theory and Method for Analyzing Cognitive Processes

Joseph Woelfel

INTRODUCTION AND BACKGROUND

Grid-theoretic approaches to the study of cognitive processes share in common the notion that cognitive structures may be represented by (generally) rectangular arrays of numbers, or grids. In general, these grids represent a set of constructs used by an individual or set of individuals in some situation, and the relation of the individual or group to those constructs.

Grid models differ primarily in the way data are collected (Fransella and Bannister 1977) and in the way the data are analyzed (Slater 1972; Pope and Keen 1981; Shaw 1981). Regardless of the methods by which data are collected or analyzed, however, most methods share the goal of determining some underlying structure from the data.

The Galileo model (Woelfel and Fink 1980), in contrast, has as its primary goal the analysis of cognitive processes. Process may be thought of as change of structure over time, and Galileo is specifically designed to measure changes in cognitive structure over time.

The analysis of change data inherently involves the measurement of differences and quotients. Any change, of course, represents a difference between a structure at one time and the same structure later. If we consider the rate at which a structure is changing, we must divide the amount of change by the elapsed time, and so, at the minimum, any analysis of rate of change involves examining ratios of differences. As we move toward more sophisticated analyses of change, such as changes in the rate of change, or accelerations, we must consider even more complicated mathematical transformations of the raw data.

Since the (random) error component around a difference score is the sum of the individual errors, and since the error component around a quotient is the product of the errors of its components, the error around a rate of change (a "velocity") may be seen to be the product of the sums of the original error components. For this reason, the Galileo model places extraordinary emphasis on measurement precision. For the same reason, Galileo's mathematical model and computational software place a great premium on preservation of information present in the original data to an extent that is unusual in the analysis of cognitive data.

Finally, since large amounts of data are required to attain sufficient precision to perform meaningful analysis of time series, Galileo researchers have been intensive users of computer-based data collection and analysis systems for two decades, and current versions of Galileo methods are heavily computerized.

Galileo differs from other grid models, then, because it has a goal different from that of most other methods, and this (the analysis of cognitive processes) imposes unique measurement and analysis requirements on the Galileo researcher.

DESCRIPTION OF THE TECHNIQUE

The Galileo system is both a theory of cognitive processes and a set of computer software that implements the theory. The software is best understood in the light of its underlying theory.

THEORY

Galileo theory represents the domain of cognition as a multidimensional Riemann space. Every point in this space is considered to have a meaning. Points that are "close" to each other in the space have similar meanings, and points that are "far" from each other differ in meaning in proportion to their distance from each other. Since the space of cognition is assumed to be continuous everywhere, the Galileo model is noncategorical, and may be thought of as a "fuzzy-logic" model (Zadeh 1977).

THE CULTURAL SPACE

Some of these points are sufficiently salient to a given culture to be given a name or label, which consists of a word or symbol or a combination of words and symbols. These "labeled points" are called "landmarks" in Galileo theory, and serve as points of reference for measuring or "surveying" the space.

As already mentioned, every point in the space has meaning, not just the labeled points. Thus, in the neighborhood of the space that represents colors, we may find the label "red" and the label "white." A point midway between the two might be labeled "pink"; a point between the two but closer to red than white might be called "reddish pink," and so on. One may designate the meaning of any point in the space more or less accurately by a judicious combination of nouns, adjectives, adverbs ("slightly more red than pink") and other parts of speech.

In general, any *n* labels may be seen to form a geometric figure. The geometric center of that figure is the point whose meaning is given by that combination of labels. Thus, for example, if an object were completely defined as "large, heavy, and black," it would be located at the geometric center of the triangle that had "large," "heavy," and "black" as its three vertices.

Entire regions of the space may themselves be labeled, so that one might identify the neighborhood in which one finds terms like "red," "green," "blue," and the like as "colors." These higher-level constructs may themselves be grouped and named, so that the (large) region including colors, sounds, tastes, and so on may be labeled as "attributes." Thus, while the Galileo model is infinitely "fuzzy," it is also capable of representing hierarchical structures as well.

INDIVIDUAL REPRESENTATIONS

Clearly, the potential complexity of such a space is beyond what could be held in attention at any moment by any individual, and, indeed, Galileo theory generally holds that the space is a property of the culture rather than the individual, with each individual holding a partial representation of the entire cultural space in his or her own cognition. These individual spaces may differ, perhaps even substantially, from the "average" or aggregate cognitive space. (Galileo software provides quantitative estimates of the degree to which any individual's space differs from the general cultural space, which may serve as measures of "cognitive deviance.")

Even the less complex representation of the cultural space resident in any individual is still far too complex to be held in attention at once, and so Galileo theory assumes individuals represent only selected neighborhoods in consciousness at a given moment.

THE SELF CONCEPT

Within each of these neighborhoods, each individual may label a point or subregion as "him/herself." Like any point in the space, the self has a meaning that is given entirely by its location in the space — that is, by its distance relations with the other points or constructs. We expect that individuals will locate their self point close to those concepts they believe describe them well, and far from those concepts they believe describe them poorly or not at all.

Within the theory, an attitude is defined as the distance relation between the self-point and any other point; a belief is defined as the distance relation between any two points. Thus all attitudes are beliefs — that is, beliefs about the self. The self concept may be defined as the set of all attitudes.

Since the entire space is never held in attention at once, it is assumed that the self may be defined differently in different neighborhoods. Thus, within the Galileo theory, the self is thought to have a relative and situational definition.

The location of the self point relative to other "objects" or constructs in the space is assumed to have behavioral significance. Any behavior, of course, may be represented as a point or region in the space, and behaviors are assumed to be performed with a frequency inversely proportional to their distance from the self point. Product market share is inversely proportional to distances of the products from the average self of a market, and so on.

INCONSISTENCY

Galileo theory does not assume that either individuals or whole cultures need to obey Euclidean geometric rules in their definitions of the distance relations among the objects. Persons and cultures may, for example, define two points as "close" to a common third point, but not close to each other. For example, people may place "blue" close to themselves since it is a large part of their daily life, and also place "food" close to themselves for the same reasons. But they may place "blue" and "food" far apart, because foods are virtually never blue. Or, for example, people may place themselves close to "hot tea" and close to "iced tea," since they drink both, but relatively farther from "tepid tea," which, of course, must lie "between" hot and iced tea, an impossibility on a flat Euclidean plane.

Triangles made of these distances will not in general satisfy the "triangle inequalities" constraints and hence do not lie in a Euclidean space. They can, however, fit without distortion into a Riemann space. Galileo software is generally Riemannian, and will accommodate any pattern of distance relations. Should they prove empirically to be Euclidean, Galileo software will automatically accommodate itself and produce a Euclidean solution, but does not constrain the solution to be Euclidean (Woelfel and Barnett 1982).

It is important to note that the Galileo theory does not ascribe any special significance to the dimensions or axes of this space, since every point in the space is considered meaningful. The axes or dimensions are simply mathematical constructions that provide a convenient mathematical description of the locations of the points.

COGNITIVE PROCESSES

Once the notion of the cognitive space has been understood, it is simple to define cognitive processes as "changes" in the structure of this space over time. In general, any pattern of motions one can define for space in general can be applied to the Galileo model. We will discuss some of the main concepts and processes here: cognitive development, attitude and belief change, inertial mass, and planned intervention.

COGNITIVE DEVELOPMENT

The space of the newborn infant might be expected to be relatively empty and undifferentiated. Few points in the space are labeled, and few distinct neighborhoods could be distinguished. Galileo theory represents development as an expansion of the space, and an increase in the number of points that are labeled. Forgetting, similarly, is represented as a shrinking of the space.

ATTITUDE AND BELIEF CHANGE

Since beliefs are defined as the distance relations among points in the space, and attitudes are defined as distance relations between the self and other points, changes in beliefs and attitudes may be represented as motions of the points relative to one another. Rates of change may be described by the relative velocities of the points' motions, and changes in the rate of change as accelerations of the objects. These processes are well defined mathematically by straightforward generalizations of the equations of relativity physics, which also describes physical motion with equations defined on a multidimensional Riemann surface.

INERTIAL MASS

The theory, following Woelfel and Haller (1971), assumes that any point in the space has coordinates that are the average of the coordinates of all those proposed to the individual by his or her experience. Put another way, different experiences, such as the information received from various other persons ("significant others"), or from direct observations, may suggest at one time or another that a given object is located in different places. The Galileo theory posits that the location actually established in an individual (or cultural) space will be the arithmetic mean (the geometric center) of those proposed locations.

If this is so, then it follows that objects whose location has been established on the basis of a great deal of information will be harder to "move" than will those whose location was established on the basis of only a few inputs, just as a student's grade point average will be harder to change in senior year than in freshman year. This property of resistance to acceleration is defined in the Galileo theory as the "inertial mass" of a concept.

PLANNED INTERVENTION

Since the Galileo theory has a well-defined mathematical model for predicting the meaning of any combination of words or phrases, it is possible to form hypotheses about the likely effects of any combination of such words and phrases on the cognitive structure of an individual or culture. Specifically, Galileo hypothesizes that any two concepts associated in some "message" (e.g., "A is B"), will approach their common center in the space. Similarly, any *n* concepts associated in a message are expected to approach their common geometric center.

Alternative hypotheses exist in the Galileo literature as to whether the concepts should approach the geometric center of the figure or some "weighted" center (such as their center of mass), but the practical differences among these versions of the theory are as yet usually too small to be measured precisely by data currently available.

THE COMPUTER MODEL

Since the process by which the Galileo theory is operationalized is so extensively computerized, it is useful to describe the measurement model in the context of the software by which measurement is implemented. The Galileo model is implemented in four phases, all computer-assisted: identification of the landmarks (constructs) to be included in the neighborhood being surveyed; measurement of the distance relations among the landmarks; calculating the coordinates of the points for each of the time periods available and measuring their trajectories; and, finally, interactive display of the data.

IDENTIFYING THE LANDMARKS (CONSTRUCTS) IN THE NEIGHBORHOOD

The definition of any object whatever of cognition is given in the Galileo system by its location in space. One measures its location in space by measuring or "surveying" its distance relations among the set of other landmarks or constructs that lie in its neighborhood. The first step, therefore, in constructing a Galileo "map" of the neighborhood of an object or concept is to determine what other concepts lie in that neighborhood.

Although several methods are used by Galileo researchers, most commonly this is done by interviewing the subject or subjects in question. A computer program, Galileo*INTERVIEW, asks subjects to list the main attributes of the object to be defined. After several subjects have been interviewed, or after one subject has answered several questions, the data are passed to another set of programs, Galileo*CATPAC (category package). CATPAC is a linked set of programs that parses the text of the interviews, strips off punctuation, articles, prepositions and the like, counts the frequency of occurrence of each word in response to each question, subject, or "episode," and constructs a words x episodes occurrence matrix.

CATPAC then postmultiplies this matrix by its transpose to produce a words x words co-occurrence matrix, which in turn provides the input to a diameter-method cluster-analysis program. The clustering program provides dendograms instantly on the computer screen. These clusters are then expected to form the list of underlying concepts that populate the neighborhood of the object to be defined.

CATPAC is very fast, accomplishing in a few minutes what ordinarily takes several weeks of effort by several people using conventional methods.

MEASURING THE DISTANCES AMONG THE CLUSTERS (CONSTRUCTS)

The clusters output by CATPAC are then named (usually using one of the most frequently occurring words in each cluster as the name of that cluster), and entered into another interactive program, Galileo*AQM (automated questionnaire maker). These questionnaires are then administered either in person, by telephone, or by computer using another interactive program, Galileo*SPED (simplified process for entering data), which automatically inputs the data to an appropriate file.

The Galileo measurement model is particularly precise, asking respondents to estimate the differences in meaning between each of the $k (k - 1)/2$ possible pairs of the k landmarks or constructs on a ratio-level scale. Extensive research has shown this scaling procedure typically produces between one and two orders of magnitude more precision than do typical rating scales or categorical scales (Barnett 1972; Gillham and Woelfel 1977; Cary 1985).

After these data have been gathered (or while they are being gathered, in many instances), they are passed through another series of Galileo programs that find the coordinates of the constructs or landmark objects in the Riemann space. Since precision is so important to a time-series model, all analysis conducted by these programs is distance-preserving. This means that the original raw distances can always be recovered from the Riemann coordinates without error.

Technically, the Galileo software calculates the centroid scalar products matrix B* following Torgerson (1958), then extracts all the eigenvectors, including the imaginary eigenvectors, from this B* matrix.

For time-series data, this step is carried out for each time point in the series, then each set in the time series is rotated to a least-squares best fit to its immediate predecessor in time. These rotations can be constrained when additional data are available, so that any subset of landmarks can be held stable and serve as a reference frame against which the relative motion of the remaining landmarks may be gauged.

Galileo provides too many options to describe in the remaining space, but the main hardcopy output for a typical analysis might include

- A list of the job parameters
- A list of all errors identified in the raw data
- A list of all numbers higher than a given value
- A list of all values deleted from the raw data (if any)
- Statistics for each time period or data set, including the mean distances for each pair, their standard deviation, standard error, variance, skewedness, kurtosis, sample size, maximum value, and percentage relative error
- Largest distance and smallest distance in each data set
- Matrix of mean distances and sample sizes for each pair
- Principal axes of the space for each data set
- Eigenvalues for each data set
- Warp factor (degree of departure from Euclidean space) for each set
- Rotated ("matched") coordinates in Riemann space
- Distance moved by each concept across each interval of time
- Correlations among position vectors of the concepts across each time interval
- Correlations among dimensions across each time interval

If the user wished to determine a strategy for changing any belief or attitude in any way and thus chose the Message Generator option, additional hardcopy outputs would be available:

- A list of every combination of concepts that could serve to produce the desired effect
- Quantitative information about the effectiveness of each combination of concepts in producing the desired effect, including the distance to the goal before implementing the strategy, the distance remaining if the strategy had its theoretically maximum effect, and the ratio of these two values expressed as a percentage

If the strategy had already been applied, say, in an experiment, message effectiveness outputs would be available:

- For each interval in the time series, the correlation between the predicted trajectory and the observed trajectory
- For each interval in the time series, the angle between the predicted trajectory and the observed trajectory
- For each interval, the predicted distance moved and the distance actually observed

INTERACTIVE DISPLAY

In addition to this hardcopy output, Galileo*STRATEGY provides a powerful interactive visual display (Fig. 8.1). The first three dimensions of the Riemann space are presented on the screen, with each object or construct represented as a sphere. The radius of each sphere represents the standard error around the location of the concept, so that there is a 68 percent likelihood that the concept's actual location is within the sphere.

In the initial display, the brightness of each sphere is inversely proportional to the square of the distance between the sphere and the

Fig. 8.1.
Galileo*STRATEGY display on the DEC PRO 350.

viewer's eye, so that objects distant from the viewer glow more dimly than those that are closer.

The viewer can interact with the display in many ways. One can either zoom or dolly toward or away from the display, rotate the space in any direction by any amount, brighten or darken the spheres, expand or shrink the spheres, or ask for numerical readouts of the distances between any two concepts or between any subset and any other subset of concepts. Similarly, the user may inquire about the likely effects of any given strategy and receive an instant response that would include the current distance to the goal, the distance remaining after the hypothetical strategy was enacted, and the ratio of these numbers expressed as a percentage.

When a picture on the screen is particularly desirable, the user may dump it either to hardcopy on a graphics printer, (see Fig. 8.2), or to black and white (Fig. 8.3), color print, or color slide on a graphics imaging device (not illustrated).

APPLICATIONS

Galileo is a highly general model, both theoretically and computationally, and so has broad potential application across many fields. In fact, several hundred applications are already known, far too many to report in this space. Barnett (1985), however, has maintained a fairly complete bibliography of Galileo applications, which are available directly from him.

Although Galileo can be used quite generally wherever other grid-theoretic approaches are appropriate, Galileo may be particularly suitable:

- When high levels of precision are needed or desired
- When deliberate intervention to change cognitive structure is planned
- When multiple structures are to be compared
- When changes in cognitive structure are an object of study

Furthermore, since CATPAC provides a fast and convenient way to identify underlying attributes or constructs, Galileo may be particularly useful when the investigator does not have a firm idea of what constructs are to be included in the grid. Commercial applications usually require high levels of precision, since a single percentage of market share may often amount to several hundred million dollars. Commercial applications often involve deliberate manipulations of cognitive structures as well.

Figures 8.2 and 8.3 display the output of the programs. Figure 8.2 shows an elementary commercial application in the alcoholic beverages market. It was produced by the Digital LA 100 printer from the Galileo*STRATEGY display.

Figure 8.2a shows the Strategy Selection Form superimposed over the display, and requests the user to specify a goal or "target." In this case (as is typical), the user has selected "YOURSELF" as goal, since research shows a very substantial negative correlation (usually about –.95) of the distance between products and the self point with their market share. Next (not shown) the user is asked what concept(s) he/she wishes to move to that target, and is asked to select a potential combination of constructs to test.

Figure 8.2b shows that Heublein (the product to be marketed with this campaign) is currently 96.25 units from the target, and that the strategy that uses the themes or attributes "smooth," "distinctive," and "authentic" can reduce this distance by over 82 percent, which makes it a very good strategy.

Figure 8.2c shows that a strategy that relied on the concepts "elegant," "subtle," and "flavor" would be much less effective, since it has the potential to reduce the distance by only slightly more than 26 percent.

This example is about as simple a commercial application as can be found, and most cases are much more complex, involving both multiple samples or market segments and multiple strategies.

COMPARISON OF SPACES

Since Galileo is specifically designed to model time series, it has a powerful capacity to compare data sets. Figure 8.3a shows the beliefs and attitudes of a group of students of the State University of New York about SUNY. Figure 8.3b shows the beliefs and attitudes of a group of parents of SUNY students about SUNY. These figures were produced by Galileo*STRATEGY, implemented on a Digital Pro/350 and imaged by a Polaroid Pallette.

Comparison of these two spaces is not as simple a matter as it may first appear, since the orientations of both spaces are essentially arbitrary; one may turn out to be "upside down" with regard to the other, for example, although, most likely, they will simply be rotated an arbitrary amount relative to each other.

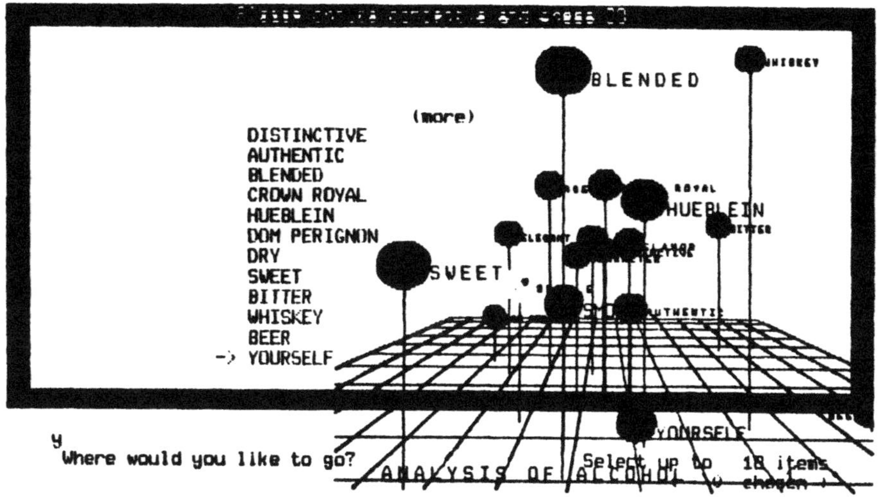
BLENDED
WHISKEY
(more)
DISTINCTIVE
AUTHENTIC
BLENDED
CROWN ROYAL
HUEBLEIN
DOM PERIGNON
DRY
SWEET
BITTER
WHISKEY
BEER
-> YOURSELF
ROYAL
HUEBLEIN
SWEET
YOURSELF
Where would you like to go?
ANALYSIS OF ALCOHOL
Select up to
items

Fig. 8.2a.

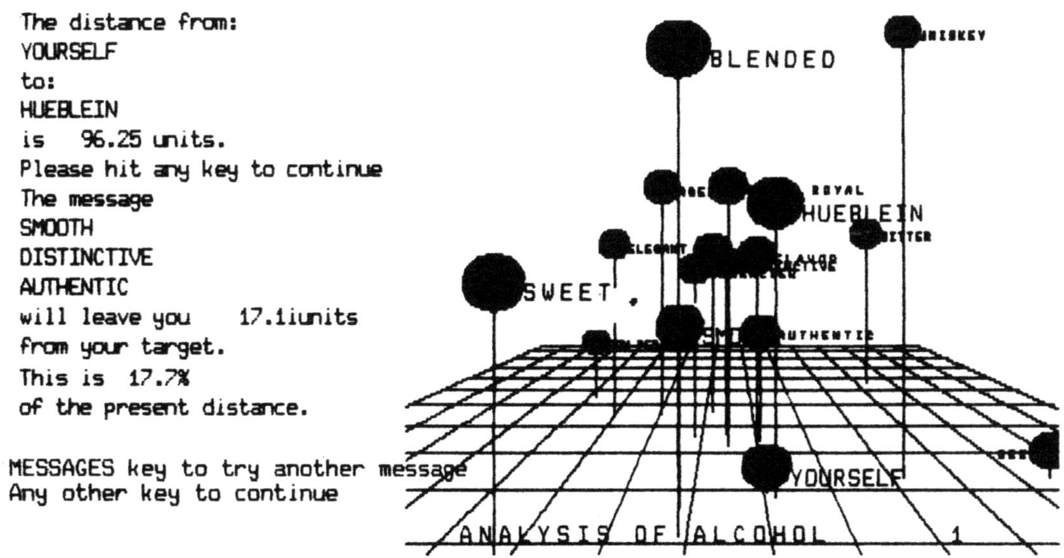
The distance from:
YOURSELF
to:
HUEBLEIN
is 96.25 units.
Please hit any key to continue
The message
SMOOTH
DISTINCTIVE
AUTHENTIC
will leave you 17.1iunits
from your target.
This is 17.7%
of the present distance.
MESSAGES key to try another message
Any other key to continue
BLENDED
ROYAL
HUEBLEIN
SWEET
YOURSELF
ANALYSIS OF ALCOHOL 1

Fig. 8.2b.

The message
ELEGANT
SUBTLE
FLAVOR
will leave you   70.7 units
from your target.
This is 73.5%
of the present distance.

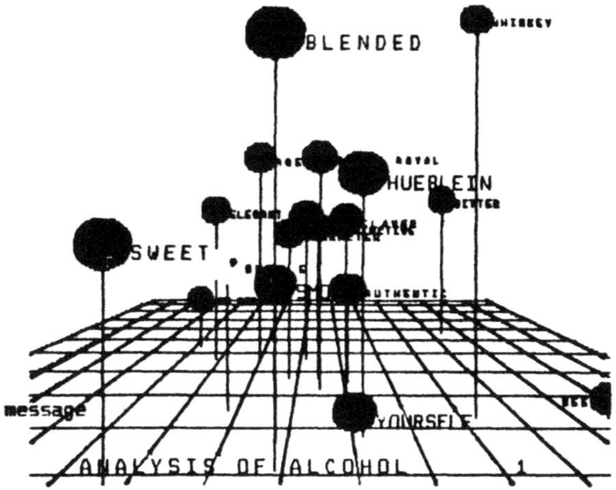

MESSAGES key to try another message
Any other key to continue

Fig. 8.2c.

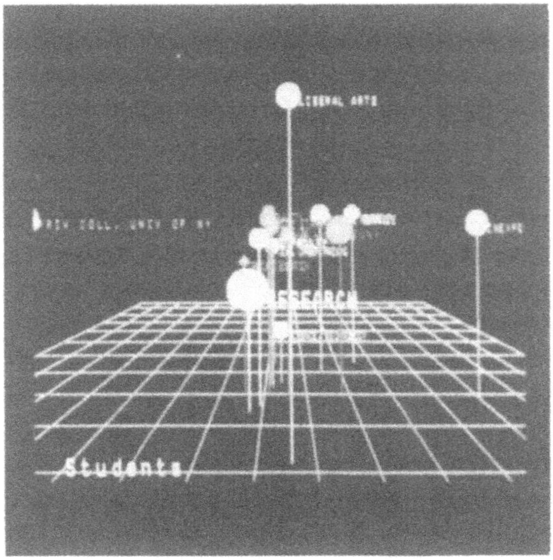

Fig. 8.3.
Perceptions of the State University of New York.

3a. Students' perceptions.

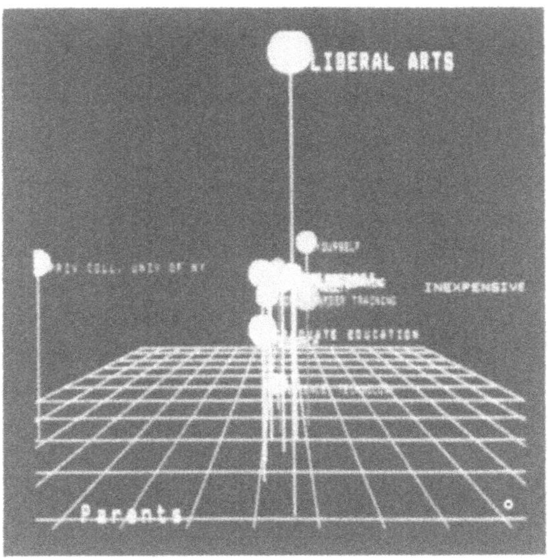

3b. Parents' perceptions.

In Figure 8.3, the space of the students has been rotated as a rigid body to a least-squares best fit against the space of the parents. This rotation process does not affect the measured distances at all, but does remove artifactual differences due solely to arbitrary differences of orientation between the spaces.

Table 8.1 shows the distance between each concept in the space of the parents and the same concept in the space of the students. Since the Galileo program is designed to be a time-series program, the labeling of the output implies motion, but the comparison is appropriate in any case. Also, since the space is Riemannian, some of the distances are imaginary, which is represented in the table by minus signs. Only the magnitudes need be considered for the comparisons, however, with smaller numbers meaning greater agreement between the samples being compared. The overall difference between the two spaces taken as a whole is given at the bottom of Table 8.1 (12.689 units).

These numbers are all expressed on the original scale of measurement, and may be treated as ratios. Thus students and parents

Table 8.1
Differences between Parents and Students

Distances moved in the interval between time 1 and time 2		
CONCEPT 1 (SUNY	) Moved	22.544 Units
CONCEPT 2 (Priv coll, Univ of NY	) Moved	37.202 Units
CONCEPT 3 (Good	) Moved	4.717 Units
CONCEPT 4 (Quality	) Moved	4.528 Units
CONCEPT 5 (High standards	) Moved	–9.011 Units
CONCEPT 6 (Inexpensive	) Moved	23.675 Units
CONCEPT 7 (Good students	) Moved	13.690 Units
CONCEPT 8 (Jobs, career training	) Moved	–8.495 Units
CONCEPT 9 (Liberal arts	) Moved	18.974 Units
CONCEPT 10 (Science, technology	) Moved	6.768 Units
CONCEPT 11 (Good faculty	) Moved	22.522 Units
CONCEPT 12 (Research	) Moved	6.653 Units
CONCEPT 13 (Public service	) Moved	26.940 Units
CONCEPT 14 (Lifelong learning	) Moved	19.371 Units
CONCEPT 15 (Graduate education	) Moved	31.078 Units
CONCEPT 16 (Yourself	) Moved	–18.133 Units

Note: The mean distance between all points in space 1 and their counterparts in space 2 is 12.689.

Source: Compiled by the author.

disagree about the location ("meaning") of Good Students by about 13 units, and disagree about the location of Public Service by about 26 units, or about twice as much.

Table 8.2 shows the lengths ("magnitude") of the position vectors of each construct for the parents (T1) and the students (T2), the scalar product of the two position vectors, the correlation between them, and the angle included between them. If the magnitudes are the same (the correlation 1.0 and the angle 0°), the position vectors are identical and the two constructs are in exactly the same place.

Once again, since the space is Riemannian, correlations can exceed 1.0, and should be evaluated in terms of their distance from 1.0. Thus the first correlation in Table 8.2, 1.008764, is nearly perfect, indicating that Concept 1 (SUNY) lies at virtually the identical orientation in the space of both students and parents, but is nearly twice as far from the center of the space for the students (57.67 units) as it is for the parents (34.36).

Table 8.2
Correlations between Position Vectors of Constructs for Parents and Students — Row Vector Correlations between Time 1 and Time 2

Concept	*T1 Magnitude*	*T2 Magnitude*	*Scalar Product*	*Corrleation*	*Angle*[1]
1	34.36	57.67	1998.86	1.008764	*****
2	88.99	119.18	10357.34	.976533	12.4
3	15.80	13.84	186.12	851120	31.7
4	11.91	12.38	104.82	.710750	44.7
5	20.77	30.94	521.32	.811193	35.8
6	93.51	107.85	9868.47	.978500	11.9
7	10.65	19.73	156.06	.742714	42.0
8	28.24	47.47	1271.01	.948140	18.5
9	56.50	64.69	3504.93	.958870	16.5
10	39.78	53.14	1986.79	.939775	20.0
11	5.60	35.06	314.86	1.602701	*****
12	26.13	45.53	1331.18	1.118782	*****
13	28.66	58.23	1598.61	.957737	16.7
14	13.93	35.97	549.24	1.096251	*****
15	24.56	35.17	424.27	.491298	60.6
16	27.47	68.72	1959.28	1.037952	*****

Source: Compiled by the author.

[1]Angle size is indicated in degrees

Table 8.3
Comparison between Dimensions of Parents' and Children's Conceptions of SUNY — Col Vector Correlations between Time 1 and Time 2

Concept	*T1 Magnitude*	*T2 Magnitude*	*Scalar Product*	*Correlation*	*Angle*[1]
1	131.30	172.88	21686.41	.955397	17.2
2	87.21	94.33	7918.92	.962605	15.7
3	47.93	67.58	2492.52	.769552	39.7
4	42.06	81.74	2847.65	.828239	34.1
5	34.73	53.85	1358.79	.726488	43.4
6	28.25	38.08	983.00	.913775	24.0
7	25.49	57.70	1137.09	.773126	39.4
8	21.88	38.75	763.95	.900997	25.7
9	20.17	56.16	864.17	.762753	40.3
10	8.73	28.43	152.97	.616230	52.0
11	.00	8.83	.00	1.000000	.0
12	.37	.00	.00	1.000000	.0
13	10.28	33.64	107.01	.309454	72.0
14	17.23	32.23	331.40	.596879	53.4
15	33.26	46.24	487.94	.317234	71.5
16	59.81	69.89	3145.95	.752582	41.2

Source: Compiled by the author.

[1]Angle size is indicated in degrees

Table 8.3 shows the relationships among the dimensions of the spaces of the parents and students. The first row, for example, shows that the first dimension of the parents' space is somewhat shorter (131.30 units) than the first dimension of the students' space (172.88 units), but that those dimensions are aligned fairly closely, lying at an angle of 17.2° from parallel.

These outputs provide fairly complete information for comparison of the samples, both globally and with regard to particular elements, although, of course, the numbers become more meaningful as one gains experience with them in different contexts.

TIME SERIES

Figures 8.4a–8.4g represent the perceptions of 421 randomly selected telephone subscribers in the Capital District (Albany, Schenectady, and Troy, NY) about the days of the week and common activities related to

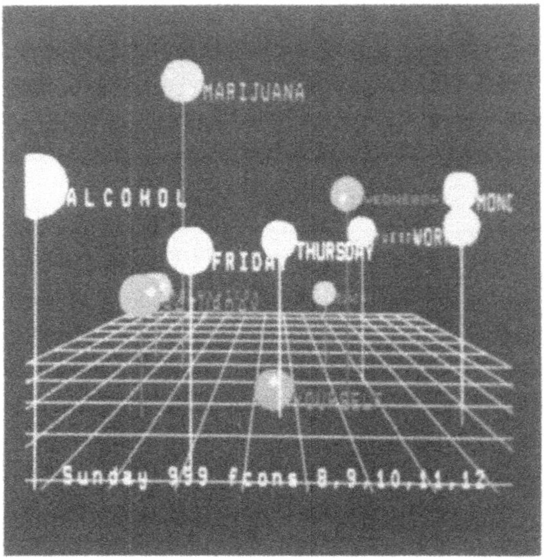

Fig. 8.4a.
Locations of work/relaxation concepts as extracted from responses of 421 respondents: Sunday responses.

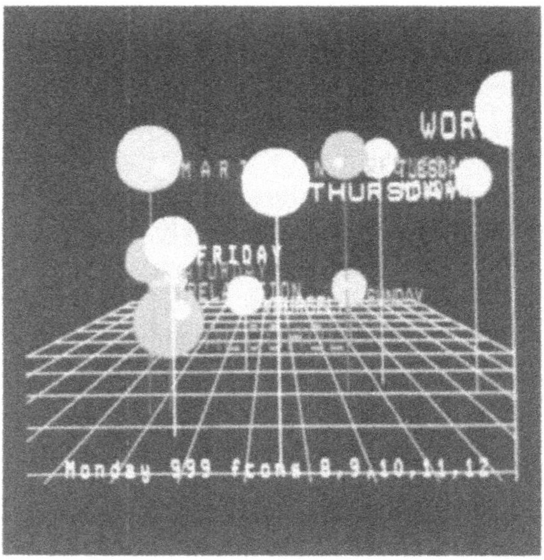

Fig. 8.4b.
Monday responses.

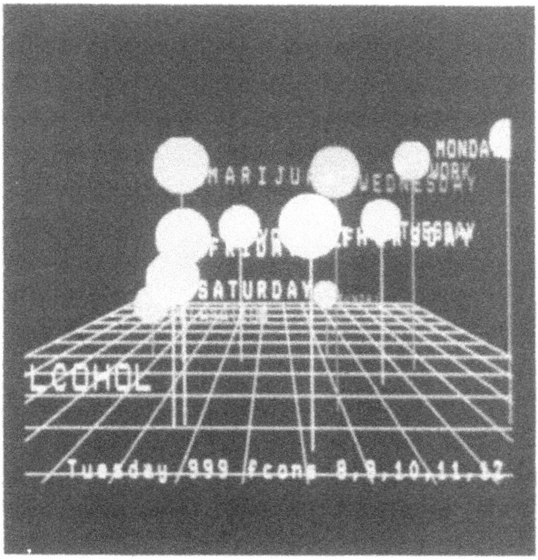

Fig. 8.4c.
Tuesday responses.

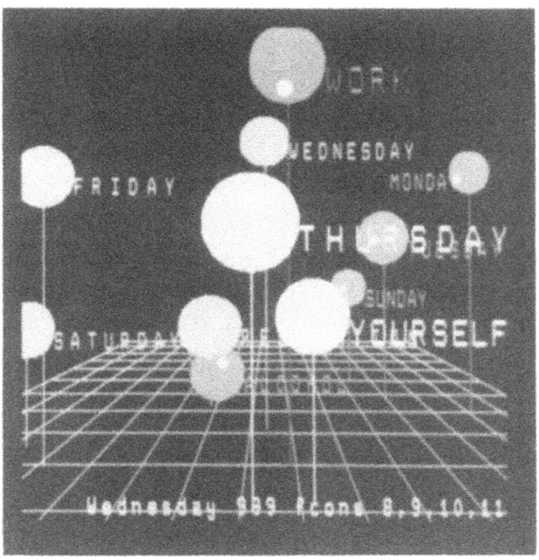

Fig. 8.4d.
Wednesday responses.

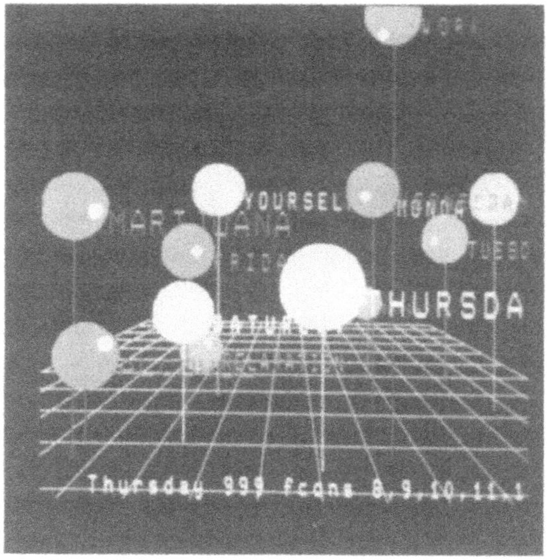

Fig. 8.4e.
Thursday responses.

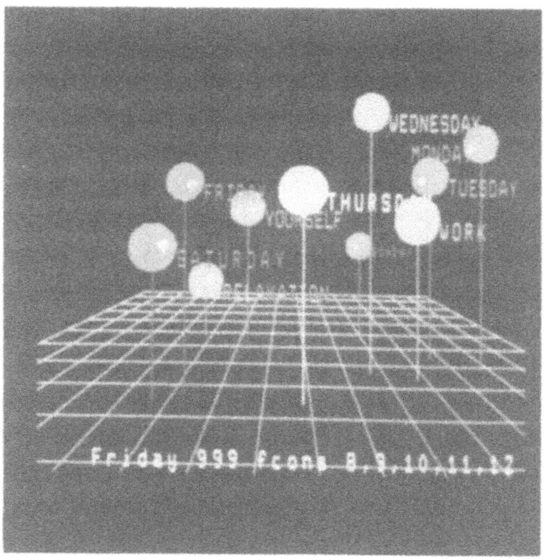

Fig. 8.4f.
Friday responses.

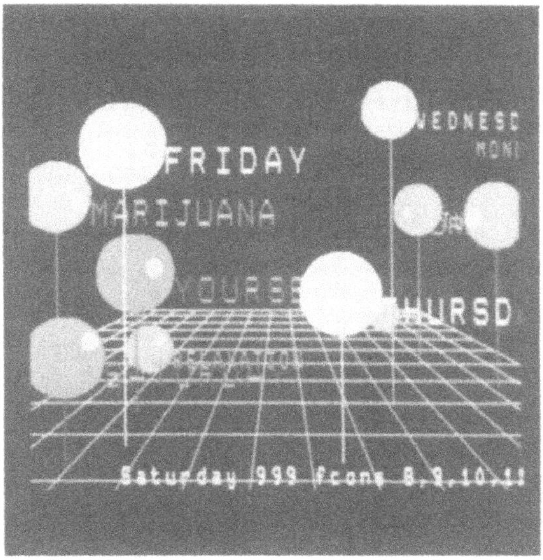

Fig. 8.4g.
Saturday responses.

work and relaxation. Figure 8.4a represents all such calls that were conducted on Sunday; Figure 8.4b represents all those calls that were made on Monday, and so on. Thus, the seven pictures in Figure 8.4 represent seven frames of a "movie" about the way people's concepts about the week, work, and relaxation change as the week progresses.

Within any frame of this movie, the days of the week form a distorted elliptical figure. Figure 8.4 represents the shape of this figure by its shadow on the floor of the space. This makes it somewhat easier to see that Monday is displaced to the right front of the ellipse. As the shadow makes clear, this distorted ellipse is in fact quite stable across the week.

While more is happening in this movie than can be described here, we will concentrate only on the motions of the concept "work." Notice that, on Sunday (Fig. 8.4a), "work" is quite close to "Monday." On Monday, "work" is still close to "Monday." By Tuesday, "work" has moved to lie a bit closer to "Tuesday" than to "Monday." On Wednesday, "work" has moved to be closest to "Wednesday."

By Thursday, however, "work" begins to recede from the week (although it is relatively closer to "Thursday" than previously). By Friday, "work" has moved back to a position nearly between

"Monday" and "Tuesday," and, by Saturday, it is closest to "Monday" again.

This process should be expected to repeat itself week after week, and describe a periodic function in the cognitive structure, which indeed coincides well with common understanding about the actual working behavior of individuals on a day-to-day basis.

CLINICAL USES

As yet we are aware of no actual clinical uses of the Galileo procedures, although such applications are easy to visualize. Figure 8.5 shows the space of the emotions of several dozen undergraduate students at the State University of New York at Albany. Notice that the self point ("Yourself") lies quite close to "Happiness" in this space. Motions of the self point in the emotions space could serve as a useful measure of emotional condition in the normal person, and, perhaps substantial deviations from the normal configurations of the emotions might indicate psychological or emotional abnormalities in an individual. In any event, Figure 8.5 shows that Galileo can be used to represent even fairly abstract emotional conditions with some precision.

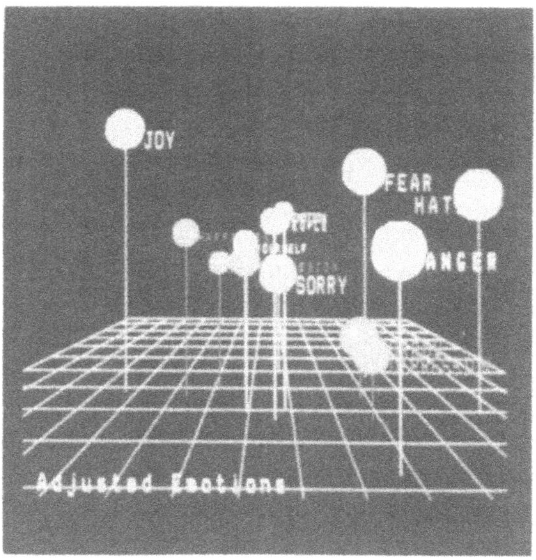

Fig. 8.5.
Location of self in relation to emotion concepts as extracted from college students.

The use of the strategic repositioning options of the Galileo program might prove particularly useful in therapeutic situations, especially if the therapist has a good idea as to what kind of cognitive structure is normal or healthy.

EXTENDED POSSIBILITIES

A clear goal for Galileo analysis is the operation on a continuing basis of a system for real-time monitoring of cognitive processes. Although real-time monitoring of the cognitive processes of an individual would require rather extraordinary efforts with current technologies, monitoring the cognitive processes of large populations in real time is not difficult for Galileo technology.

APPENDIX

Galileo software is the property of the Galileo Company, 5903 Johnston Road, Slingerlands, New York 12159. Commercial use of Galileo software, except under written license from the Galileo Company, is strictly prohibited. The Galileo Company has supplied versions of Galileo software to about 30 universities in the United States and abroad for scientific and educational use; check with your computer center concerning availability in your area.

All Galileo software can be accessed via telecommunication through terminal and modem to the Galileo Company computing facilities on a fee basis. The Galileo Company offers a limited number of grants and other forms of support to research scientists without other sources of funding. Proposals for use of Galileo computing facilities or other forms of Galileo Company support should be directed to Robert Zimmelman, Director of Research Services, at the Galileo Company.

Galileo, Telegal, AQM, SPED, CATS, STRATEGY, and Automatic Message Generator are trademarks of the Galileo Company.

9 Characters in Search of an Author: The Self as a Narrative Structure

Richard Lehrer

> It's a mixing up of the parts, according to which you who act your own part become the puppet of yourself.
>
> — Pirandello

Popular accounts of self consistently tie the experience of a unique existence to the structure of memory. For example, in one science fiction film, an artificially intelligent robot construes herself as possessing an identity because she recalls episodes of interaction with other members of her "family." The continuity among these episodes of her past validates her conception of herself as an author — a creator of a script to integrate these diverse elements of her experience. That these past experiences were implanted by her creators in no way detracts epistemologically from her construction of a unique existence, for while the memories are "theirs," the story relating the episodes is hers. On the contrary, the very integratedness of these created memories serves to convince other characters in the film that she, like them, is unique.

Popularizations of the self such as that described above share much in common with earlier presentations by dramatists such as Pirandello and by social psychologists such as James (1890) and Mead (1932, 1934). In many of these presentations, self derives from a resolution of the dialectic between experience and existence (Broughton 1980). To illustrate, both Mead and James distinguished between "me" and "I" components of self, in order to separate the data of self-experiences ("me") from the processes ("I") that impute meaning to these experiences. Applying this distinction to the film described above, distinctive episodes of experience, such as interacting with members of a family, constitute separate "me's" according to which the protagonist infers the nature of her uniqueness.

"I" and "me." The "me" entails presentation of a variety of characters to fit each occasion (Gergen 1977; Goffman 1959), which has prompted dramatists as historically disparate as Shakespeare and Pirandello to liken the self to a part played on a stage. In contrast, "I" processes limit the inherent entropy of the "me's," acting to create an integrated existence through knowledge of the rules that transform one "me" into another (Mead 1932). In this tradition, Markus (1977) defines self-schema (schema-based accounts of self are elaborated later in this chapter) as "cognitive generalizations about the self [the "I"], derived from past experience [the "me's"], that organize and guide the processing of self-related information" (p. 63). Mead and James both noted, however, the difficulty of reporting or reflecting on the constituents of "I," prompting the latter to designate "I" as the proper study of philosophy, not psychology. To reconcile "I" with "me," this essay develops the self as a text (Mancuso and Sarbin 1983) that is simultaneously written and read. Reading parts from this text corresponds to "me" and the writer of the text to "I." Before detailing the ways in which the self may be likened to a text, "I" versus "me" perspectives are developed further with respect to contemporary principles of cognitive science.

THE TWO SIDES OF THE "I"

Study of "I" often confounds two senses of "I." First, "I" refers to one's existence or sense of self as an *author* (or playwright). In this regard, "I" transcends particular events and may be derived from participation in them (Markus 1977; Mead 1934). Correlatively, Mancuso and Sarbin (1983) suggest that "I" (existence) emerges from "me" (experience) as one distinguishes between the *self-as-cause,* "I," and the self-as-caused, "me." In a second sense, "I" refers to an *authoring system* that simultaneously creates characters and infers the author (itself) from these characters. In this regard, "I" denotes programs or processes, but "me" entails data acted on by these programs (Greenwald and Pratkanis 1984). See Figure 9.1 for a display of relationships between

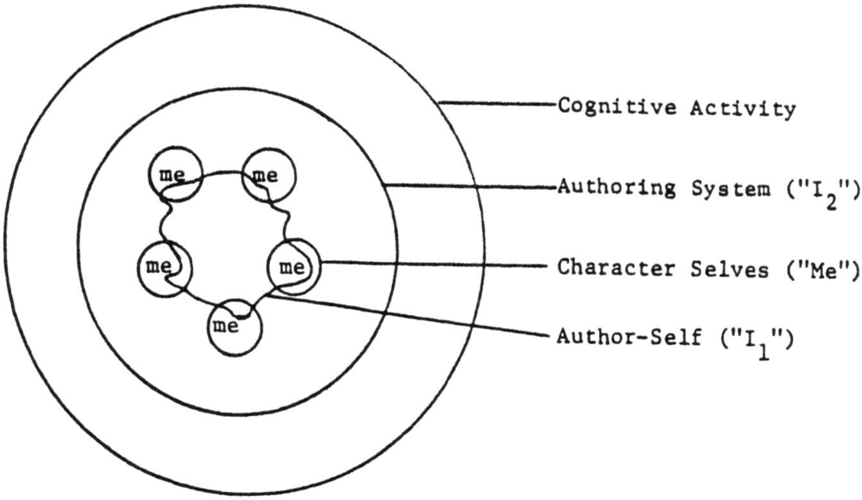

Fig. 9.1.
The self system.

these two senses of "I" and "me." Note that the "I"-authoring system is not isomorphic with all of cognitive processing, nor is the author-"I" merely a superset of distinctive "me's." Indeed, some components of each "me" may have little to do with the author-"I"; they contribute instead by making "me's" complete and coherent in some sense. For example, elements of one's interactions with a specific acquaintance such as a "wide smile" may have few implications for the definition of "I." Nonetheless, smiling may facilitate one's interaction with an acquaintance and thereby contribute to the coherency of this "me."

PROBLEM SOLVING AND SELF-UNDERSTANDING

As noted previously, Mead (1932, 1938) linked "I" with knowledge of rules that enable transitions between "me's." This association shares much in common with contemporary study of problem-solving processes. For instance, current frameworks for problem solving often represent a problem solution as an application of operators (rules) that enable transitions between problem states (Newell and Simon 1972). Extending this description to study of the self, states correspond to "me's" and operators to "I." In addition, studies of differences between expert and novice problem-solving performances in a wide variety of domains indicate a predominant role for knowledge organization in limiting the search among problem states. In essence, experts and novices in a domain represent problems differently, thus accounting for experts' more efficient performance (Chi, Glaser, and Rees 1982; Larkin et al. 1980). Most studies suggest that experts represent knowledge in multiple, well-integrated levels of understanding, whereas novices tend to encode information at a single level of detail. Accordingly, in further explorations of the influence of knowledge on performance, Eylon and Reif (1984) noted a comparative increase in students' ability to understand physics problems when experimental manipulations induced students to represent physics concepts hierarchically rather than at a single level of detail.

Further study of principles of cognitive science indicates that one learns by doing (Anazi and Simon 1979). What one learns by doing entails creation of mental structures that represent relations among specific instances of experience. For example, Anderson (1983) describes a composition mechanism that creates a new mental structure from previous structures that share the same goal. In this way, two (or more) different structures representing distinctive components of experience coalesce into one. Recasting the existence–experience dialectic in this framework, existence ("I") requires the creation of new mental structures that integrate those structures developed previously to interpret specific experiences ("me"). Stated another way, "I" emerges as a construction that specifies relations among character-"me's." Accordingly, the self emerges from structures created while characters search for an author.

The self-schema. In summary, application of problem-solving metaphors to self-understanding mandates study of the organization of knowledge about the self. Accordingly, the remainder of this chapter develops schema-based accounts of the self, because schema theories consider both process and structure in the development of knowledge (Brewer and Nakamura 1984). Narrative schemata occupy a central position in this chapter, since they provide a plausible metaphor in the self-as-a-storyteller (Mancuso and Sarbin 1983; Mancuso 1986). Stated another way, characters' search for an author takes the form of a narrative. Moreover, narrative frameworks underscore the key organizational role played by causal networks for understanding text (van den Broek and Trabasso 1986). Considering the self as a text then implies analyzing the self as a system of cause.

Earlier sections of this chapter develop applications of schema theory to elucidate the study of self, whereas later sections present schema-based measures of self-organization. Thus, the first section contains an overview of principles of schema theory. These principles are extended in the second section to illustrate how a theory of episodic processing may serve as an adequate framework for the study of self. In the third section, a theory of analogical processing is proposed as a means for developing knowledge of the "rules of relation" among components of various role enactments. Thus, analogical processes form the cornerstone of the development of a self. Accordingly, a specific analogical mechanism elaborates previous suggestions (Mancuso and Sarbin 1983; Mead 1934) about how persons can infer an author and consequently an existence from particular experiences. This section also includes exploration of the potential role of analogical processing for developing self-understanding and for understanding others. The remaining sections develop narrative measures of self-structure. Thus, two computer-assisted, interactive measures of self-organization are presented in the fourth section, and the fifth section contains a survey of analytic techniques to elucidate this organization. Results obtained from an empirical study of social self-structure are presented in the last section to illustrate how the proposed measures illuminate the self-as-author.

SELF AS SCHEMA

Although self-related experiences may be fragmented, the self nonetheless is experienced as coherent. Recalling the previous discussion of "I" and "me," we see that the self also knows and is known to itself. In the following sections, schema-based accounts of self explicate these and related qualities of self-description (Carver and Scheier 1981; Cantor and Mischel 1979; Greenwald and Pratkanis 1984; Kihlstrom and Cantor 1984; Mancuso and Ceeley 1980; Markus and Sentis 1982; Showers and Cantor 1985). Most contemporary schema-based accounts of self rely on Bartlett's (1932) original description and its recent representational amplifications, such as *node-link* (Woods 1975), *prototype* (Rosch 1975), and *script* (Abelson 1981; Schank and Abelson 1977) models. Setting aside these variations for the moment, Brewer and Nakamura (1984) advance the following general propositions concerning schemata: (1) they influence attention, (2) they structure incoming information, integrating the new with the old, (3) they guide retrieval, and (4) they influence retention, biasing it toward generic information and away from retention of specific propositions. These propositions serve to explicate everyday observations about the self as follows.

Self-coherency. From a schema perspective, self-coherency derives from the development of a self-schema that guides processing in the manner described above. For instance, a variety of studies suggest an association between performance and the degree of self-reference of stimuli presented to participants (Greenwald and Pratkanis 1984). To illustrate, Bower and Gilligan (1979) presented episodes (e.g., a boring lecture) to subjects and discovered better recall for episodes judged in reference to oneself (e.g., decide whether the episode refers to a specific personal experience) rather than for those judged for meaning (e.g., decide whether the episode refers to an interpersonal interaction) or for sound (e.g., decide whether the words contain more than two occurrences of the letter *e*). Because recall from a schema perspective depends on relating inputs to a well-differentiated memory structure, superior recall under the self-reference condition indicated an elaborate structure concerning the self, a self-schema.

"I" versus "me." Schema-based approaches also provide a process framework for distinguishing "I" from "me" (Greenwald and Pratkanis 1984). The everyday activity of the authoring system (the second sense of "I" noted previously) generally proceeds without conscious awareness, which suggests an automatic process. Recall that "once learned, an automatic process is difficult to suppress, to modify, or to ignore" (Schneider and Shiffrin 1977: 2). Consequently, self-related enactments proceed "naturally." In contrast, self-report or self-reflection entails a controlled process that is a limited-capacity process available for consciousness. Hence, reports of episodes of self–other interactions ("me") or of generalizations thereof (the author-"I") are necessarily schema-guided summarizations of consciously available data, in part because complete reports would overwhelm a limited-capacity processor. The measures presented later in this chapter overcome some of these limited-capacity constraints on self-understanding in that persons respond to specific experiences (stories) from which their organizational framework (the author-schema) is inferred.

The two sides of "I": Schema availability versus accessibility. A distinction between available and accessible schemata (Rabinowitz and Chi 1987) serves to distinguish heuristically between the authoring-"I" and the author-"I". Available self-schemata refer to components of self-knowledge structures that guide further self-processing in the manner proscribed in points (1)–(4) above. Not all schemata, then, are self-schemata. The accessibility of a self-related schema, in turn, is governed by the type and strength of associations among its constituents. For example, in a node-link format for self-schemata (Mancuso and Ceeley 1980), the self-descriptive node of "warm" may be highly associated (a high "link" strength) with "thoughtful" and be less highly associated (a lower link strength) with "intelligent." Consequently, when asked to choose which is a better self-description, "warm and thoughtful" or "warm and intelligent," the former's superior accessibility results in its selection as the appropriate response for the individual. Alternatively, contextual cues may activate the "thoughtful" node, enhancing the retrieval (the accessibility) of its associates in preference to other potentially activated components of the self-schema (Anderson 1983; Kihlstrom and Cantor 1984; Mancuso and Ceeley 1980). In sum, accessible portions of the self-schema (the authoring system) delineate the author-"I." In this way, associating the self-as-author with accessibility distinguishes between the "voice" of the writer and that of the general system of self-composition. Note that this voice will change in response to varying patterns of spreading activation (Collins and Loftus 1975) and corresponding changes in accessible components of the self-schema. For example, Scheier and Carver (1983) observe that environmental cues such as a camera often result in self-reports biased toward public presentation. In this instance, the perception of a camera presumably activates portions of self-schemata associated with public presentation, making these public elements more accessible for report (especially considering working memory limitations). In contrast, an environmental cue of a mirror tends to produce a self-reporting "voice" that reflects private components of self-understanding (Scheier and Carver 1983).

In summary, schema-based approaches to the study of self provide an adequate framework for understanding variegated aspects of "I" and "me." Existence evolves from experience as a person constructs a self-schema as a mental model regulating self–other interactions. The distinction between available and accessible components of self-schemata resolves the paradox of a self that is simultaneously coherent and multiple, linking coherency with availability and multiplicity (e.g., public and private selves) with accessibility. In the next section, theories of event or episodic memory further elaborate the "I"–"me" dialectic by providing an integrative framework that interweaves phenomenal experience and schema-based existence.

SELF-STRUCTURE AND EPISODIC STRUCTURE

Early theories of self included axiomatic stipulations of interpenetration between social and temporal structure. For example, Mead (1932) underscored the importance of past and future selves for self-regulation in the present. Paraphrasing Mead, the development of the self-as-author entails simultaneous projection of oneself into the future and the extension of oneself into the past. For instance, Markus (1983) notes the proclivity of persons to use a future-self as a fulcrum for self-enactment in the present. More recently, Mancuso (1986) advocates "emplotment" as a fundamental characteristic of social cognition. In his view, when confronted with novel inputs, persons tend to create stories about these events, thereby making them coherent (Freeman 1985). Among schema theories, episodic representations uniquely represent temporal features of events (Nelson and Gruendel 1979, 1981). Moreover, as observed previously, treating the self as an event structure integrates phenomenal experience ("me") with schema-based existence ("I"). Consequently, the following sections develop self in terms of Schank's (1980) general theory of event representation.

SCHANK'S THEORY OF EVENT MEMORY

Schank (1980) proposes a four-tiered hierarchy for event memory. The lowest level, *event memory,* represents specific sequences of actions, such as "I talked with my friend Joan yesterday about her match with Bob." The second level, *general event memory,* denotes information that usually applies to specific components of memory represented at the first level. For example, common features of my interactions with Joan (e.g., "visits with Joan include discussion of her tennis game") could be abstracted at this level.

Situational memory. Generalizing interactions with Joan to interactions with other friends as well leads to a third level of event representation, situational memory. At this level, stereotypical event sequences or "scripts" (Schank and Abelson 1977) guide interactions with friends in which interaction with Joan represents one potential instantiation. For example, one portion of a "friend" script could include "begin by inquiring how :X feels today," where :X would be replaced by Joan in general event memory.

Memory organization packets. Schemata are strategic units because they are organized according to the purposes for which they are intended

(Kelly 1955; Kintsch and van Dijk 1983). Therefore, Schank (1980) proposes that script application in situational memory occurs "as needed," a reconstructive process that shares much with Neisser's (1967) proposal of "analysis-by-synthesis." In brief, situation memory guides comprehension by constructing parts of scripts or "memory organization packets" (MOPs) according to the goals of the individual in the situation. MOPs are constructed from portions of general event memories that are similar according to the intentions of the individual interacting in the situation. Similarity among strands in general event memory is circumscribed by intention, or, stated another way, intention governs the construction of similarity. For example, interactions with two friends at different times may share events in common that are represented as a MOP. This MOP regulates future interactions with friends by establishing pointers between itself and specific friend-related events represented at lower levels. However, two MOPs may share common strands yet remain distinctive in that they point to different events at the lower two levels.

Intentional memory. The number of MOPs accessible for processing is governed by the fourth and highest level of intentional memory. Intentional memory contains the goal structure of an event and directs understanding to the highest level of structure available to explain an input event (Carver and Scheier 1981; Mancuso and Lehrer 1985; Powers 1973). To illustrate, consider Table 9.1, which represents an interaction with a friend (capital letters denote higher-level structures). At the highest level, the intention to interact with a person is represented as a simple story with expectations of an initiating event, some type of input, and a terminating event. Understanding in this instance depends on this structure because the remaining levels are increasingly more specific instantiations of this intention. Note also that the lowest level contains the most detailed information, but not all of this information is represented in succeeding levels.

EVENT MEMORY AND SELF

"I" and "me." Application of Schank's model for event memory to the study of self provides an adequate framework to represent self-process and self-structure. The authoring-self is represented by all available intentions and goal structures that a person utilizes to anticipate social interactions. Metaphorically, the organization of memory at this level delineates a system of composition. However, particular goals and

Table 9.1
Interacting with a Friend from the Perspective of Event Memory

Level	*Representation*
IM	INTERACTING WITH OTHERS = CONTACT + LISTEN + RESPOND
SM	INTERACTING WITH A FRIEND = GREET WARMLY + LISTEN WITH A SMILE + INQUIRE ABOUT RECENT EVENTS
GEM	Interactions with Joan = Say hello + listen to her cheerful response + ask about her most recent tennis match + eat something that she has just finished baking.
EM	I visited with Joan last week. We talked about her match with Bob. Bob put a lot of top-spin on the ball, so Joan had difficulty dealing with his serve. Joan shared some chocolate-chip cookies with me.

Source: Compiled by the author.

intentions activated and accessible within a context of social interaction (Showers and Cantor 1985) — the strategies of the "I" — circumscribe the self-as-author. Consequently, a variety of authors exist in association with varying intentions. Intentional memory encompasses both senses of "I" in that self-related goals delineate the authoring system, but accessible goals within a particular context define the author. Situational memory, in contrast, contains MOPs concerning a variety of character selves (the "me's") subordinate to the "I." These MOPs regulate interactions in specific situations by means of the pointers to the lower two levels of memory noted previously. Because "me" MOPs are regulated in turn by higher levels (the "I"), qualities of the author-self may be inferred from pointers connecting MOPs to self-related goals. Consequently, an "I" MOP denoting similarities among character-"me's" may be constructed and experienced by the individual as self-understanding. Recall that construction of any MOP relies on detecting similarities among event-strands linked by identical goal structures. Hence, the degree to which character-"me" MOPs share strands determines the relative coherency of self-understanding or the "I" MOP. For example, a "parenting" MOP could share strands of "caring" and "concerned" with a MOP for "child-care professional." Consequently, self-understanding could include such generalizations as "caring" and "concerned." Later in this essay, analogical processes provide constraints for the degree of such generalizations. Recall, however, that even though two MOPs may share strands, nevertheless each may point to different events at the lower two levels. Consequently, some aspects of each "me" may remain distinctive, as was suggested earlier in reference to Figure 9.1.

Self-reflexiveness. How can you who act become the puppet of yourself? The predicament referred to by Pirandello finds contemporary expression as a concern for how mental structures process information and how, in turn, mental processes structure information (Glaser 1984). Applied to self, how can the self take itself as an object and consequently influence further self-related processing? Resolving this dilemma, Schank (1980) proposes that the same structure used to represent information also serves to process information. This isomorphy between structure and process indicates a general reflexivity of thought of which self-reflexiveness is but one manifestation. Thus, when understanding a new experience, old memories are accessed because "the structures we are using to process this new experience are the same structures that we are using to organize memory" (p. 267). Schank advances the phenomenon of reminding as a prototype for the inherent reflexivity of thought (see also Ross 1984). For example, aspects of interacting with a child while engaged in the role of child-care professional may remind one of similar experiences with a child as a parent. That is, these MOPs share strands. The nature of this reminding can then change current processing by including intentions associated with parenting and not originally associated with the "me" of the child-care professional. In contrast, the absence of reminding may also serve to alter processing. To illustrate, a person whose self-understanding includes "not easily angered" may attribute his or her display of anger in a situation to a random fluctuation in processing or to extreme provocation: "that wasn't the real me." One might expect future processing in similar situations directed toward the goal of minimizing discrepancy between the self-standard regulating anger and inputs received during interactions with others (Averill 1982; Carver and Scheier 1981; Mancuso and Lehrer 1985). For instance, the person may decide to try to be more understanding of others in the future.

Although commonplace attributions concerning the self are represented adequately by the model of event memory outlined here, the model fails to constrain adequately the development of self-understanding. For example, studies of the development of self-understanding indicate an evolutionary progression from infancy through adulthood, which in principle must be accounted for by a schema theory of self (Broughton 1978; Damon and Hart 1982; Harter 1983; Livesley and Bromley 1973; Selman 1980). In the next section, a general analogical mechanism is presented to elucidate how self-understanding evolves.

THE SELF AS AN ANALOGICAL PROCESS

A FRAMEWORK FOR ANALOGY

An analogy is an assertion that a relational structure normally applied in one domain can be applied in another (Gentner 1983; Rumelhart and Norman 1981; Van Lehn and Brown 1980). The assertion entails mapping elements from one domain (the base) onto a second, target domain. For example, "an atom is like a solar system" constitutes an analogy in which the solar system is the base domain and the relations mapped include attractive force and orbits.

Gentner (1983) proposes a formalization to describe analogy that I have adopted. First, she assumes a node-link format for long-term memory wherein predicates express propositions about concept nodes. Similarly, we proceed by assuming that event structures are encoded as predicates. Next, Gentner distinguishes between *relations* and *object-attributes*. Relations are predicates with multiple arguments such as LOVE (Sally, Joseph). In contrast, predicates with single arguments, as in BROWN EYES (Sally), denote attributes. Finally, predicates may be ordered. For example, MEET (Sally, Alice) and GREET [MEET (Sally, Alice) TALK (Sally, Alice)] are first- and second-order predicates, respectively. Note that causal structures generally will entail highly ordered predicates, because causal sequences often contain multiple sets of relations (Gentner 1983).

Appearance, similarity, analogy. Using the formalization depicted above, Gentner (1983) contrasts three types of mappings between base and target domains. The first, an *appearance match,* occurs whenever domains share object-attributes but not relations. For example, Sally and Alice may share "brown eyes" or "went to the concert." In contrast, *literal similarity* results from mappings that include both attributes and relations. For example, Sally and Alice may share attributes of "brown eyes" and "short stature" as well as the relational structure denoted by "altruistic motives." Completing the continuum, *analogies* rely on mappings between relational structures in conjunction with few mappings based on attributes. For example, Gentner (1983) notes that 2:6::4:12 depends on a relation between numbers and not on literal attributes of the numerals. To further illustrate, "he's another Alice" derives its power from relational mappings, perhaps concerning conversational style, and not from literal attributes such as gender. In summary, appearance matches, literal similarity, and analogy are anchor points of a continuum.

Motivational principles and the power of analogy. According to a motivational perspective that emphasizes the role of the reduction of discrepancy between inputs and memory structures to maintain equilibration of the person-perceiving system (Carver and Scheier 1981; Mancuso and Adams-Webber 1982b; Mancuso and Lehrer 1985), analogies constitute a potentially powerful means for reducing discrepancy, whereas appearance or literal similarity matches are less likely to achieve this goal. For example, we confidently predict a person's future actions knowing his or her motives. Such predictions involve mapping a relational structure (e.g., motives) that applies in the present to the target domain of the future. Knowledge of a person's facial features, in contrast, usually results in less confident prediction. In most instances, relational structures are superior predictors when contrasted with structures constituted by object-attributes. More generally, relational mappings subsume a wider range of events; they have a greater "range of convenience" (Kelly 1955; Mancuso and Eimer 1982). Consequently, analogies extend prediction by highlighting relevant dimensions and values of events. Within this framework, matches based on literal similarity occupy an intermediate position. Although these mappings contain relational structures useful for prediction, they also contain literal features that may be less useful for anticipating events. Assuming a limited-capacity processor, literal similarity may simply overwhelm the system by providing a wealth of information, only some of which is useful for anticipating events.

ANALOGY AND THE "I"

Relational mappings between character-selves constitute the base structure of the author-"I." Thus, analogical processes result in the development of self-understanding. For example, one might report, "I am a kind person," because a relation of "kindness" applies when I interact with a friend and when I interact with a disliked other. These interactions constitute separate "me's," but the kindness relation applies in both interactions. Hence, "I" am kind. To further illustrate, one could "get angry" when provoked by one associate, Robert, and enact the same anger-MOP when similarly provoked by a second associate, Linda. In this instance, a self-as-author description includes "I get angry whenever :X does K" because the relational structure of anger (Averill 1982) applies across more than one character-"me." Hence, analogical processing limits the inherent entropy of the cornucopia of "me's" to the degree to which mappings between "me's" are successful. On the other hand, self-fragmentation (Kelly 1955) ineluctably results from the comparatively small number of relational structures that apply across many "me's" when contrasted with the total set of relational structures that comprise the authoring system. For example, many components of an interaction with a friend apply only to that friend, and are represented at the level of event or general event memory without pointers to MOPs at the higher level of situational memory.

Predicate order and the structure of the "I." In accordance with the hierarchical model for events and the motivational perspective presented previously, self-mappings occur at the highest possible level of relation. As Schank (1980) notes: "[A]n intelligent understander stores his experiences as generally as possible so as to be able to learn from them, i.e., so as to make them available for use as often as possible or in as many situations as possible" (p. 268). Gentner (1983) specifies this processing bias as a "systematicity principle" which during mapping preserves the highest-order predicate relation constructed by the person. In practice, application of this principle preserves predicates belonging to a system of mutually connecting relationships. Considering the self as a text, motives and other causal structures comprise the most important exemplars of highly ordered predicates. As a result of the utility of personal-causal relations for inferring appropriate self-related actions in contexts, the self emerges as a causal structure. More generally, a schema perspective assigns a central role to inference — the fitting of new information into a context that explains it and predicts other facts that follow from it (Schank 1980). In theories of text processing, causal structures play a key role in such inference (Kintsch and van Dijk 1978, 1983; Rumelhart 1975; Schank 1980; van den Broeck and Trabasso 1986). Moreover, older persons usually summarize self-understanding in terms of causal structures such as intentions, motives, and life themes. Hence, the "I" is biased toward relational structures that encode cause.

Constraints on the "I." Although a large number of mappings among "me's" are available, the set of mappings that contribute to self-definition is more limited. First, analogical processes involve working memory. If the system attempts to match a complex relational structure between "me's," such as a cause for an interpersonal interaction, the probability of a successful match diminishes with increases in predicate order. Highly ordered predicates are most likely to invoke working memory failure, because activation of nodes within a system decays rapidly (Anderson 1983) and such decay decreases the accessibility of components of complex structures. Although lower-order predicates are more easily mapped, they are also less powerful according to the motivational principle enunciated previously. In this way, the self-system's bias toward higher-order predicates reduces the set of mappings defining the "I." A second constraint on the range of the "I" also results from the motivational perspective presented previously. Recall that the authoring system's construction of self-intentions guides future processing. But sometimes self-related intentions are not validated by significant others, and the "looking glass" (Cooley [1902] 1964) becomes a fun-house mirror. Hence, procedures associated with invalidated intentions may lose "strength" (Anderson 1983) because the authoring system maintains structures that remain useful as guides to the future and correspondingly diminishes those that serve poorly (Mancuso and Adams-Webber 1982b).

Analogy and self-reflexiveness. Although analogical construction of self-understanding entails mappings among character-"me's," analogical processes apply equally to the author-self. To illustrate, one could meet a new person, enact a role with respect to that person, and then reflect on the quality of the interaction from the perspective of the author-self: "Was that really me?" If several relational mappings between the author-MOP and the character-MOP are not successful, one could conclude "that wasn't the real me." Future interactions with this person could be altered to reduce the discrepancy between the "real me" and specific components of the interaction. In this way, you who act your own part become the puppet of yourself. Alternatively, one could reexamine the discrepancy between the "real me" and one's behaviors, perhaps by enlarging the sampling to include other character-"me's" (see Grossberg 1980, for a discussion of transitions among cognitive codes). Such reflection could prompt reorganization of the "I" MOP to share new strands with character-"me's." In this way, one might conclude that "I guess I really am that way" because the relational structure maps successfully between this specific interaction and previous interactions with others. While these relational mappings may have been available previously, perhaps they were not accessible. In this instance, the discrepancy between actual and anticipated behavior activates reflective strategies to resolve the difference between inputs and an "I" standard. Recalling the previous discussion of spreading activation and accessibility, the author-self emerges only from accessible portions of the authoring-system because the analogical processes that serve to create and maintain the author require working (accessible) memory.

Intersubjectivity. Sharing the self occurs whenever the authoring-system treats the predicates of another person as self-predicates. Consequently, mappings may be established between the base domain of the author-self and the target domain of the character-self of the other person. The likelihood of successful mappings depends on the exchange of relatively simple relations. For example, Freyd (1983) refers to "shareability constraints" and notes the enhancement of communication when the message can be encoded by a small dimensional structure with few values on each dimension. Hence, intersubjectivity can never be total, just as the author-"I" can never encompass the totality of the character-"me's." Moreover, sharing the self need not be symmetrical. Perhaps one can apply a relational system but the other person cannot. Consequently, one may enact a role of understanding successfully that is not available in the same way to the other person (Kelly 1955; Selman 1980).

DEVELOPMENTAL TRENDS IN SELF-UNDERSTANDING

Studies of self-understanding suggest a developmental progression beginning with very simple causal relations (the self as an agent) and solitary trait descriptors (I have brown eyes) which evolve into complex causal structures (motives, thoughts, feelings, differentiations between real and ideal selves, etc.) and networks of trait descriptors (Barenboim 1977, 1981; Bannister and Agnew 1977; Damon and Hart 1982; Harter 1983; Livesley and Bromley 1973; Selman 1980). Mancuso (1986) suggests the metaphor of transitions in text grammar to account for these changes in self-understanding. He proposes that persons develop better stories about themselves as they get older. Initial stories may be confined merely to designating the self by the semantic category of agent, but stories told later in development will reflect increasingly sophisticated text devices such as voice and a narrative deep structure. *Deep structure* refers to the organization of a story by functional features, such as causal relations, in preference to surface characteristics, such as time of day or setting.

The transition between surface and deep structures in the self-narrative corresponds to changes expected from application of the systematicity principle previously presented. Recall that systematicity biases the self-system toward representing mappings between domains using the most highly ordered predicates available to it. In addition, systematicity biases the processor toward analogical mappings due to their wider range of potential application across settings. The quality of early self-reports suggests mappings anchored by appearance matches. For example, "I have brown eyes. I am a boy" reflects invariant mappings of object-attributes across character-"me's" by a young child (Livesley and Bromley 1973). By middle childhood, these mappings tend to include relational structures as well. For example, Secord and Peeves (1974) and Ruble et al. (1980) report third- and fourth-grade self-descriptions that compare the self with classmates. Similarly, Barenboim (1981) describes a progression of self-understanding from middle childhood to adolescence that encompasses a transition in description from behavioral characteristics to networks of relations among traits. The increased incidence of relational structures in these self-descriptions, particularly those concerning causal mechanisms such as motives, intentions, and the placement of self within a broader cosmology (see also Damon and Hart 1982; Selman 1980), suggests an increasing bias with age toward mappings that preserve relational structure and which relegate attributes to a lesser predictive status. In short, self-mappings appear to progress toward the analogical pole and away from literal similarity or appearance. Stated another way, components of self-understanding at any point in the developmental cycle may include matches based on appearance, literal similarity, or analogy. Developmental trends shift the fulcrum away from appearance matches and toward analogical matches. According to the motivational principle suggested previously, this progression toward analogical mappings enables the self to tell a better story — one characterized by a deep structure.

In summary, I propose a general analogical mechanism as the cornerstone of the author-"I." The mechanism constructs the "I" by attempting to map elements from one "me" onto a second "me." Commonalities that result from this process are stored as an "I" MOP which in turn may serve as a base domain for future mappings. The motive principle enunciated during the course of this discussion biases the mapping process toward the preservation of relations of the highest order. Consequently, the self evolves as a system of cause, since causal relations prototypically consist of highly embedded relational systems.

Correlatively, the story describing self-understanding begins with simple structures, such as the self as an agent with a certain appearance, and concludes with a deep structure governing a system of personal cause.

In the next sections, computer-assisted measures are presented to aid a researcher or therapist (or oneself) in the search for an author among the characters of self-related role enactments. The first measure, MYSCRIPT, encapsulates the narrative metaphor directly through interactive solicitation of stories about typical interactions of a respondent with significant others. The stories are told in the first-person. The second measure of self-role enactment (SRA) assesses narrative structure indirectly and follows in the role repertory tradition of personal construct psychology (Adams-Webber 1979; Gaines and Shaw 1981; Slater 1977). Both self-elicitation programs rely on a respondent's judgments of associations among role enactments in order to infer the structure of the author-"I." A survey of statistical models to "uncover" the pattern of associations among responses to MYSCRIPT and SRA follows. The final section traces the authoring-structure of the social self as adults differentiate between friendship, love, and acquaintance. This last section illustrates prototypical applications of the MYSCRIPT and SRA programs.

ELICITING THE STRUCTURE OF THE AUTHOR

THE NARRATIVE METAPHOR

Considering the self as a storyteller constrains the measurement of the self in several ways. First, stories comprise a subset of events. Accordingly, the range of potential action structures is circumscribed to include only those that can be related as stories. Thus, story structure plays a role in data reduction. In addition, narratives contain conventionalized semantic and pragmatic constraints that create a normative basis for idiographic measure. Stated another way, although stories vary in content, their structure remains invariant from one telling to another (Kintsch and van Dijk 1983).

MYSCRIPT

General description. MYSCRIPT is an interactive program that takes a respondent's stories about herself as input. For instance, a person keys in a story about a typical interaction with a friend or describes a significant life event (Kihlstrom and Cantor 1984), such as a marriage or divorce. The elicitation occurs at whatever level of social specificity best serves intended purposes and is set in advance by the researcher/therapist. For example, subjects relate stories about friends and acquaintances in an empirical study that I will present later.

A text editor allows the respondent to modify her story as she types it. After telling each story, the subject responds to a series of questions concerning the narrator's motives, the motives of the other characters in the story, and other constituents of the tale. After all stories have been told and all questions have been responded to, the participant judges the degree of association between each story and all the other stories. This is accomplished by means of ratings concerning the degree to which each constituent of a story fits into the remaining stories. For example, a motive generated in a story about a friend may also apply somewhat to a story about an acquaintance. The final product of the program is a rectangular matrix of ratings for which columns represent motives, settings, and the like and for which rows represent specific persons (or life events, etc.). Before elucidating how such outputs reveal the self as an author, other features of the program are presented in greater detail.

Story structure. Stories relating self-interactions are decomposed as a canonical text grammar containing macropropositions and micropropositions (Kintsch and van Dijk 1983). Macropropositions refer to thematic frames whereas micropropositions denote specific episodes. Analysis of text in MYSCRIPT follows Thorndyke's (1977) macropropositionally oriented text grammar, because this grammar is especially simple and because schema theory suggests retrieval of self-related enactments by macropropositional structure rather than by individual episodes. Consequently, interactive questioning concerning stories written by respondents follows the categories of Thorndyke's (1977) grammar, which decomposes text into a setting, theme, plot, and resolution. Thus, respondents provide information about the goals of characters (motives of self and others), complications, and methods of resolving complications.

Operation of MYSCRIPT. The interactive cycle is listed next.

1. Responding to a list of role titles (Gara and Rosenberg 1979), such as best friend or most disliked person you know well, the participant instantiates each title with a specific person. For example, Bob is a best friend. The list of instantiations may be reviewed and edited at any time. This component of the program may be bypassed when the

inquiry concerns major life events or other aspects of social interaction where it may not be necessary.

2. For each person listed in (1), the participant writes a story about a typical interaction with that person from the point of view of the "I." The program notifies participants that stories need not be "real" with respect to real-time (different times may be blended) or factual characterizations (the "backbone" of the script is of interest, not literal qualities of interactions). An interactive editor with a mouse input device facilitates word processing.

3. After writing each story, an interactive questioning mode elicits the narrative structure of the story following the categories of Thorndyke's (1977) grammar. (Other types of text analysis could be substituted and may prove more useful in the future.) The respondent places answers in an "answer box" (a rectangular border placed in the lower portion of the screen) and may use the mouse to place segments of the story in the box. Thus, additional typing is minimized.

4. After all stories have been written and all questions have been answered, the participant rates the degree to which each element of each story (e.g., each theme of each story, each motive of each story, etc.) applies to each person listed in (1). For example, the main idea of one story about a best friend, Frank, could be "I try to solve problems by talking them through." The respondent then rates how well such a theme fits her interactions with all the other persons listed in (1).

Ratings consist of moving the cursor to the desired position along a continuum defined by the anchor points of "fits extremely well" and "does not fit at all." Although the scale appears continuous to the user, it contains 51 points (0 to 10 in .2 increments). In this way, a rectangular matrix of ratings emerges in which rows correspond to the persons listed in (1), and columns to the elements of each story. To illustrate, if a participant writes stories about five different people and answers six questions for each story concerning main idea, motives, and so on, the matrix of ratings would contain 5 rows and 30 columns.

5. The matrix of ratings is converted to distances among row elements or to distances among column elements. These distances are subsequently analyzed with techniques described later to elucidate the structure of the author-"I." Before describing how ratings are converted to distances, I present a role-repertory approach to self.

SELF ROLE ANALYSIS

General description. A second elicitation procedure represents the self-as-author by delineating the respondent's implicit personality theory of the self. Self role analysis (SRA) consists of a modification of a procedure developed by Gara and Rosenberg (1979). In Gara and Rosenberg's protocol, a person lists several ways in which another person feels toward, thinks about, or acts toward her. This process is repeated for many people in the person's life, and relationships among these features of one's perceptions of others are used to uncover the structure of one's implicit personality theory. Heerdt (1982) and Kihlstrom and Cantor (1984) suggest the simple expediency of changing the point of view of the protocol so that a person lists ways in which she feels toward or thinks about others. The operation of SRA follows this prescription and is described next.

Operations of SRA. The cycle of interaction is listed next.

1. As in (1) above, a participant instantiates a list of role titles. This list may be edited by the respondent.
2. For each person (presented randomly), the participant describes a way in which she usually acts toward, thinks about, or feels about that person. This interactive cycle continues until the participant responds a total of 50 times or until the respondent's recall of descriptors is exhausted. As in (1), the participant may edit the list of descriptions and add to it at any time during this phase of program execution. Error trapping prevents repetition of nonunique descriptors.
3. The user rates each person named in (1) with respect to how well each descriptor applies to that person. The rating scale is identical to that described previously for MYSCRIPT. In this way, a rectangular matrix of ratings emerges in which rows correspond to persons and columns to descriptors.
4. As in MYSCRIPT, the ratings are converted to distances among persons (rows) or to distances among descriptors (columns). Models are then fitted to these distances following procedures outlined in the following section.

In summary, two methods of self role elicitation have been presented. The first, MYSCRIPT, directly employs the self-as-narrative metaphor and represents self-structure with categories of a text grammar. The second, SRA, tacitly acknowledges a narrative metaphor by emphasizing the features of self role enactment for a variety of self–other interactions.

CHARACTERIZING THE STRUCTURE OF THE AUTHOR AS A SEMANTIC SPACE

This section contains a survey of some methods that provide models of association among elements of self-structure. These models provide a basis for interpreting the pattern of composition that integrates the stories written by the respondent. In this way, the author-"I" emerges from specific stories concerning self–other interactions. Before proceeding to formal models, I sketch preliminary explorations of the data generated by the interactive programs. In most cases, I confine my remarks to MYSCRIPT, but most of what follows applies equally to results obtained from SRA.

QUALITATIVE ANALYSIS

Following completion of MYSCRIPT, descriptive data analysis includes summaries of the types of motives respondents attribute to themselves and to others, enumeration of major life themes, and perceptions of typical conflicts and of typical methods for resolving these conflicts. Considering each story grammatical category (e.g., main idea, motives, setting) as a category of self-structure, one could examine the degree of differentiation within each category and the degree of differentiation when elements in one category are compared with those in another. For example, does the respondent differentiate between her own motives and those of others, or does a common set of motives govern both the self and others? A second interactive software package, STATSCRIPT, lists all answers to each question to facilitate this type of exploration. STATSCRIPT also prints "defining features" for each role title, which consist of all story constituents rated as highly applicable to the role figure by the respondent. For example, motives such as "Bob loves to play, so he was trying to engage me" and "She appreciates the wilderness, so we hike together" might both be rated as highly applicable to a third person, "Al." Consequently, both would appear as defining features of the respondent's interactions with Al. Selection of these features is not intended to denote an all-or-none (classical) model of categorization (Smith and Medin 1981). Instead, this selection provides a preliminary heuristic for examination of the constructs employed by the author-"I."

CALCULATION OF MEASURES OF ASSOCIATION

Spatial proximity among the constituents of self stories underlies application of a class of methods that display the self as a semantic space. Rather than directly eliciting subjects' judgments of pairwise "distances" between role figures, distance between role figures is inferred mathematically through commonalities in categories of text. For instance, two stories concerning interactions with two different friends could share common motives and main ideas. Consequently, the respondent's pattern of ratings concerning how well varying constituents of the text grammar (motives and main ideas) fit her interaction with each friend should be highly similar. Thus, these two friends are perhaps less distant than either friend and a third person. Conversely, distances among narrative constituents could be derived from commonalities with respect to role enactments. For example, the respondent could rate each of two themes as highly applicable to her interactions with most people, but a third theme only appears to apply to one person. In this instance, the first two themes are proximate and simultaneously distant from the third.

A variety of metrics may represent distances among role figures or among constituents of the stories written by respondents, including simple Euclidean distance, the correlation coefficient, and the delta measure discussed by Mancuso in this volume (Rosenberg 1977; Slater 1977). However, the analyses reported later in this chapter employ a comparative distance metric as a measure of association.

The comparative distance model. The comparative distance model (Reed 1972; Palmer 1978) represents pairwise similarity between two objects, *i* and *j*, as the ratio of their pairwise proximity and the average proximity between members of the pair and all contrasting objects. As a result, proximity between two objects depends not only on the absolute distance between them, but also on the context — the field defined by the remaining objects.

Comparative distances index the degree of prototypicality of objects in that these distances are regulated by family resemblance (Rosch 1975). In this instance, objects that are most proximate pairwise also maximize the distance between themselves and other objects. In this sense, they constitute the core of the self. Unlike measures of profile, such as the correlation coefficient, comparative distance reflects both the pattern of ratings for each object and the value of these ratings. For example, the profile of ratings 2, 4, 4 for object *i* and 4, 8, 8 for object *j* would ensure a correlation of 1.0 despite the large differences in rated values. The comparative distance model, however, would index a less-than perfect proximity between these objects, which can be confirmed by inspection of Equation (9.1). The variable d_{ij} refers to the Euclidean distance between objects i and j, d_i denotes the average Euclidean distance between object i and all other objects except j, and d_j represents the average Euclidean distance between object j and all other objects except i.

$$\Delta(ij) = \frac{2d_{ij}}{(d_i + d_j)} \tag{9.1}$$

FITTING MODELS TO MEASURES OF ASSOCIATION

After calculation of measures of association among objects (persons or story constituents), a variety of models may be fitted to these data to "uncover" their pattern. Two families of models, network and dimensional, are outlined below (Shepard 1980). Pruzansky, Tversky, and Carroll (1982) provide guidelines for choosing which model may best apply to a particular data set.

Network models. Network models represent role figures or story constituents (motives, main ideas, etc.) as nodes in a connected graph, usually a tree. Distances between nodes correspond to observed proximities among objects. Classes of network models may be distinguished by consideration of the types of constraints they impose on the data. For example, hierarchical clustering restricts objects so that every triplet of objects is treated as if the objects form an isosceles or an equilateral triangle (Johnson 1967). Clusters developed by such a procedure define a strict hierarchy where objects either are or are not members of a cluster. On the other hand, other clustering procedures are less restrictive, allowing an object to have partial membership in more than one cluster. Additive clustering has this property insofar as intra-cluster distances may exceed inter-cluster distances (Sattath and Tversky 1977). In the additive tree, the distance between nodes (e.g., role figures) is equal to the length of the path that joins them. STATSCRIPT provides options for both types of clustering. Additive trees are constructed in this research with a microcomputer version of ADDTREE/P (Corter 1982) with enhanced interactive capabilities.

Dimensional models. Dimensional models locate objects in an n-dimensional space so that metric distances between points reflect observed proximities between objects. Multidimensional scaling (MDS) procedures (Schiffman, Reynolds, and Young 1981) observed proximities to a dimensional configuration that minimizes departure of the data from the *n*-dimensional model. Some forms of MDS involve the construction of two spaces (Carroll and Chang 1970), one for objects such as role figures and a second for individuals (or occasions or experimental conditions, etc.). In the second space, each individual has a weight for each dimension of the object (stimulus) space. The weight represents the salience of the dimension for the individual. If the weight is large, the dimension is perceived as important by the individual. A computer program, INDSCAL (Carroll and Chang 1970), implements a weighted MDS. The degree to which the self is shared may be discerned by applying the INDSCAL model to the proximities generated by MYSCRIPT. In this instance, given a common set of objects such as role titles (a best friend, a valued acquaintance, etc.), the weights for each person reflect individual differences. Hence, similar weighting of dimensions may be typical of friends, and interpretation of the nature of the dimensions may suggest the basis for the intersubjectivity modeled in this way. However, the INDSCAL model also assumes a common frame of reference for individuals. Individual differences, then, are a matter of stretching or shrinking common dimensions and do not entail the development of new dimensions of thought.

In summary, associations among role figures or among constituents of self stories may be represented as a tree or as an *n*-dimensional space. Different types of trees result from application of more or less restrictive constraints for relations among objects. Dimensional structures are typically obtained from unweighted or weighted MDS procedures. The latter provide a (restricted) model for intersubjectivity when applied to self-structure. The next section contains illustrations of the application of these analytic models to the study of the social self.

AN ILLUSTRATIVE EXAMPLE FOR THE MEASUREMENT OF SELF

Taking multiple selves as a starting point (Shavelson and Bolus 1982), a small empirical study examined the social world of the self. Operationally, subjects were provided a list of 12 role titles depicting friends, lovers, acquaintances, and disliked others as follows: most liked person met in the last six months, most disliked person met in the last six months, good friend –1, –2, –3, casual friend or acquaintance –1, –2, –3, someone you love (like a spouse or lover), someone you loved (past lover or spouse), disliked person you know well –1, –2. Participants then interacted with MYSCRIPT or with SRA.

The role titles presented to subjects were a sampling of occasions for common social role enactments ("me's"). Because a relatively simple structure anchored by like and dislike poles was expected, responses to these other-person role titles provided a simple test of the recovery of structure when MYSCRIPT or SRA is employed to elicit self-understanding. Moreover, the contrast between liking and loving role figures could lead to a deeper understanding of the basis for the everyday differentiation between the two. For example, is loving construed simply as an amplification of liking? In terms of a dimensional representation, loving role figures might then anchor one end of a contrast defined by love–dislike. With respect to a tree representation, one might expect to find loved and liked role figures as members of the same (tight) cluster.

Four female and two male adults ranging in age from 24 to 37 years participated in the study. All participants completed the SRA program. One week later, two of these subjects (one male, one female) interacted with MYSCRIPT. For each elicitation procedure, each subject's rectangular matrix of ratings was converted into two symmetric proximity matrices with STATSCRIPT. The first matrix contained the comparative distances among the 12 roles and the second the comparative distances among the story constituents (or the descriptors in the SRA case). Due to space limitations, truncated results are presented next.

TREE REPRESENTATIONS

Relations among role figures. An additive clustering solution obtained from one participant's responses to SRA is displayed in Figure 9.2 (the solution obtained from this subject's responses to MYSCRIPT also reflected this structure). The root of this tree minimizes the variance of the distances among the (external) nodes (Sattath and Tversky 1977). Other roots could be chosen to induce different hierarchies of partitions or clusters without changing distances among nodes, just as the selection of a coordinate system in many forms of MDS does not change the configuration of points, only their interpretation. The vertical dimension of the tree displayed in Figure 9.2 appears to divide others into those central (significant) and those peripheral to the self. For instance, casual friends are located near the bottom of the tree. Each arc defines a cluster that consists of all objects that follow from it and is labeled in lower-case letters to facilitate interpretation. Accordingly, significant others are further partitioned into those regarded positively and those regarded negatively. The length of each arc measures the distinctiveness of the respective cluster. Note, then, the length of the arc leading to persons

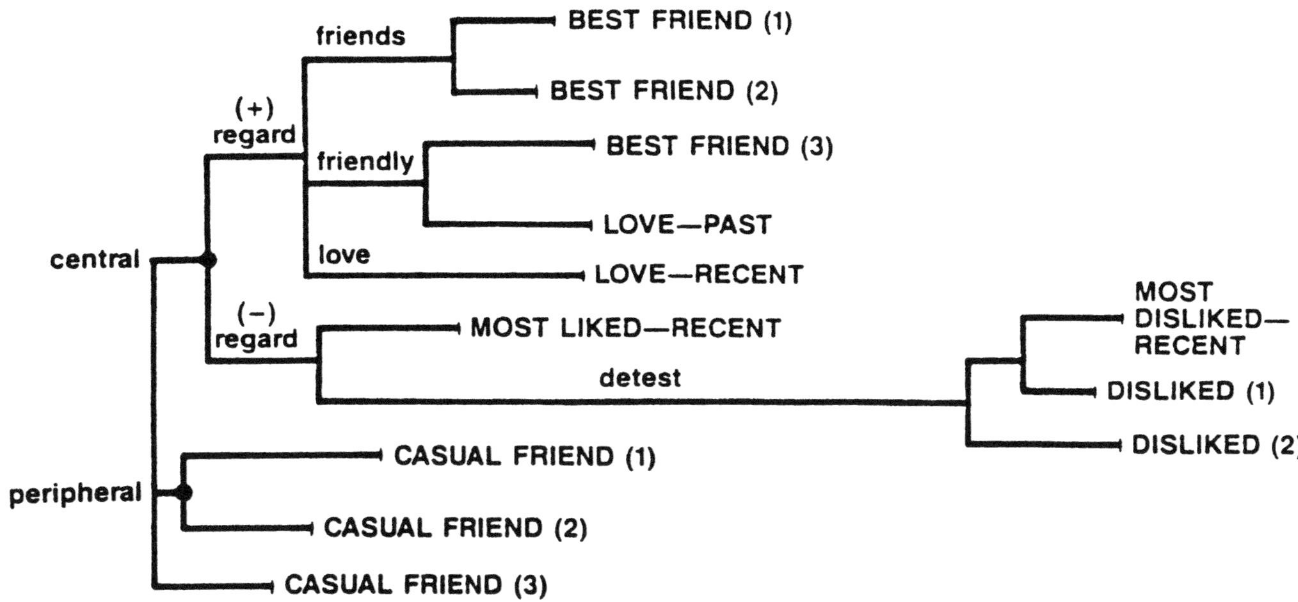

Fig. 9.2.
Additive trees representation of the social self.

who this respondent evidently detests. In this way, interactions with highly disliked others differ significantly from all other interactions. The association of a recently met person with the cluster of disliked others reveals ambiguous feelings toward this person, which were confirmed in a follow-up interview with the respondent. Furthermore, the arcs connecting this person to liked others is shorter than those connecting with a disliked person whom the respondent also has met recently. Such joint membership could not be represented in a tree derived from hierarchical cluster analysis. Returning to the positive-regard portion of the tree, although a past love has been reconstructed as a friendly remembrance, a contemporary love occupies a distinctive cluster. Hence, love and friendship are structured as distinct components of positive regard.

Relations among story constituents. Additive clustering solutions also describe relations among constituents of the stories elicited during subjects' interactions with MYSCRIPT. Tree representations depicting relations among descriptors resulting from subjects' interactions with SRA were also obtained, but the MYSCRIPT model suggested a more coherent framework for analysis. For example, recalling the perspective of the self as a cause, do subjects differentiate between their motives and those of others? Does this differentiation vary substantially with each role figure? Further, what are the relations between various types of conflicts the respondent encounters and the strategies s/he uses to resolve these conflicts? Are multiple strategies evident, or despite labeling differences, are there few strategies from a functional point of view? These questions and others like them evolve from consideration of the self as a text. Hence, MYSCRIPT provides a quantitative framework for asking new types of questions about the organization of the self. STATSCRIPT simplifies the process by allowing the user to specify subsets of text categories for further analysis. To illustrate, rather than considering all story constituents simultaneously, a user may decide to select interactively just those concerning motives. STATSCRIPT then computes comparative distances among motives excluding all other categories and recomputes distances among role figures to reflect respondents' judgments with regard to motives only.

The top half of Figure 9.3 (Subject A) contains a condensed portion of one subject's tree depicting the motives of the self and the motives of others when interacting with positively regarded others. *S* denotes a motive attributed to the self and *O* a motive attributed to a significant other. The numbers displayed refer to particular role titles, presented either in the context of questions concerning self-motives (role titles 1–12) or in the context of questions concerning other-motives (role titles

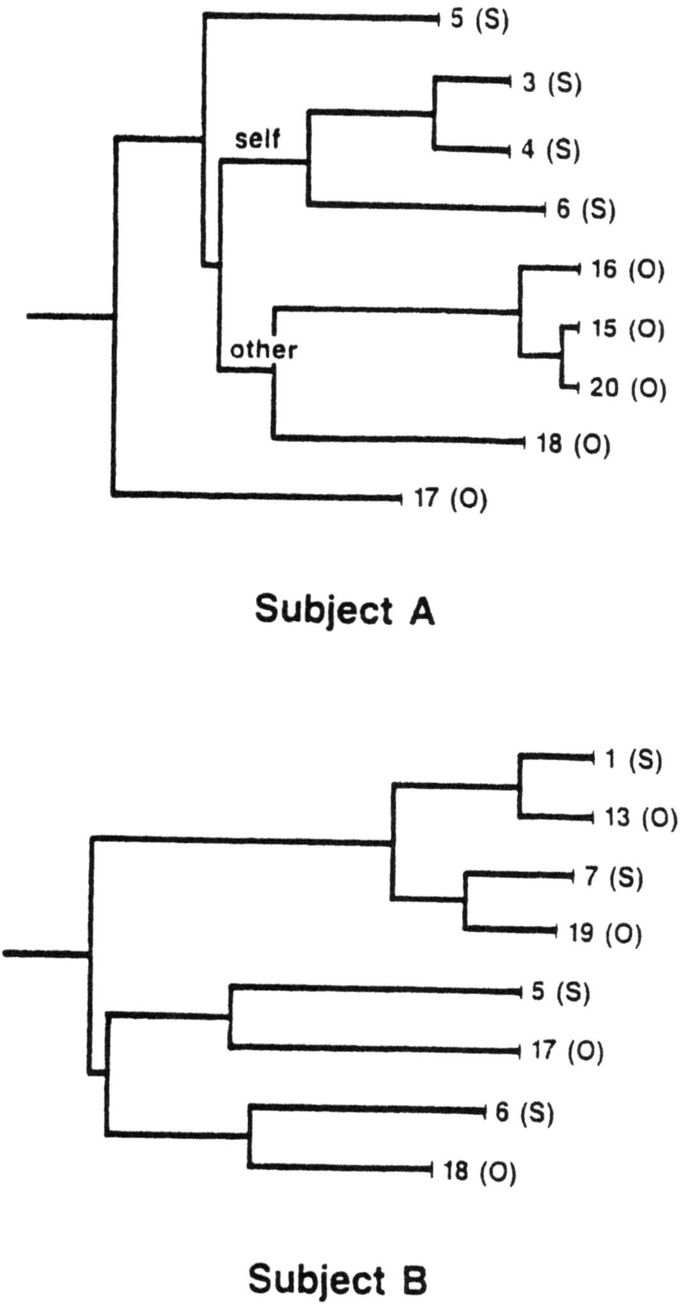

Fig. 9.3.
Relative congruence of self- and other-motives for two subjects.

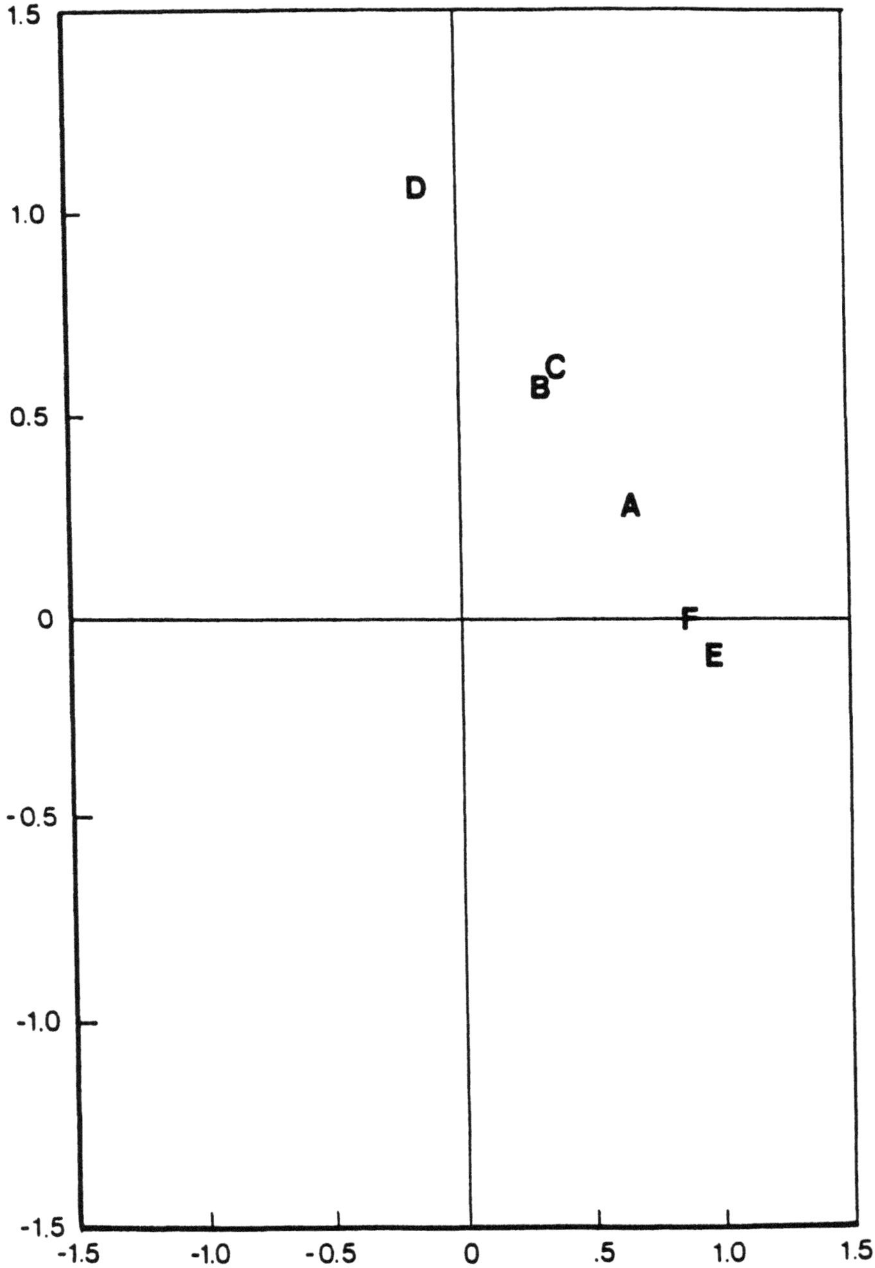

Fig. 9.4.
Location of subjects in interpersonal space: INDSCAL solution.

13–24). The counterparts of role titles for self-motives (e.g., 1) are obtained for other motives by adding 12. For instance, 1 and 13 refer to the same role title, the most liked person the subject has met in the last six months. Other details for these role titles may be ignored for this analysis. Note the clear differentiation for subject A between self- and other-motives, although both sets of motives are perceived as similar for interactions with friends. This similarity decreased sharply when disliked others were considered (not displayed). In contrast, in the lower half of Figure 9.3, a condensed portion of another subject's tree representation for motives when interacting with positively regarded others displays a near isomorphy between the motives of others and the motives of the self.

DIMENSIONAL REPRESENTATIONS

Comparative distances among role figures obtained from the six subjects who interacted with SRA were analyzed with INDSCAL. A two-dimensional solution accounted for 82 percent of the total variance. A like–dislike contrast defined the first dimension, anchored by best friends at one pole and by disliked others at the second pole, with acquaintances near the midpoint of the dimension. A second correlated dimension denoted a commitment–alienation dichotomy, contrasting loved ones to casual acquaintances and disliked others. This second dimension indicates loving is not simply an amplification of liking; rather, loving entails a conjunction of commitment and positive regard. Subject weights for each dimension of the INDSCAL solution measured individual differences in the social self. Note the person space displayed in Figure 9.4 as a measure of the degree of intersubjectivity among persons. Location of each person with respect to each dimension is determined by the subject weight for that dimension. In this instance, the subject weight denotes the contribution of that dimension to the person's self-structure. Interviews afterward indicated that subjects B, C and E, F define two friendship dyads; subject A shares an office or has frequent contact with all subjects except D. Hence, with regard to this reference group, subject D occupies an isolated position.

In summary, both tree and dimensional representations elucidate aspects of self-structure. In this instance, both dimensional and tree models of representation appeared to recover the major features of self-structure expected from the choice of role figures. Moreover, both MYSCRIPT and SRA provided an interactive environment for elicitation of self-related events far superior to their paper-and-pencil equivalents.

With regard to treating the self as a text, the structure of the "I" was elaborated by analysis of relationships among categories of text obtained from participants' interactions with MYSCRIPT. The structure of self and other motives illustrated this potential of the MYSCRIPT model. Although not presented, different "voices" of the authoring system may be illuminated by choosing different roots for additive clustering. For example, one could choose one theme as a root and trace its connections with other story constituents.

CONCLUDING REMARKS

The self as an episodic structure interleaves phenomenal experience and schema-based existence. Within this framework, "I" processes regulate lower-order "me's" by setting goals and intentions that govern the accessibility of particular "me" MOPs. The distinction between schema availability and accessibility resolves the apparent paradox of a self that is both coherent and multiple. Reflexive qualities of the self result from two related properties of the episodic system. First, the structure used for storing information is also used for processing information. Hence, process and structure reciprocally influence each other. Second, qualities of the authoring system common to several "me's" emerge as an "I" MOP that can then serve as a standard for future processing. Commonalities among "me's" develop as the self-system maps relations across "me's" through the proposed action of a general analogical mechanism. Episodic self-structure receives further elaboration and additional constraint by treating the self as a text. In this way, self-related episodes are interpreted as narratives with a deep structure akin to that delineated by text grammars.

Following Kaplan's (1964) suggested interpenetration between theoretical constructs and measurement operations, the metaphor of the self-as-a-storyteller is elaborated through a set of interactive computer programs that elucidates characters and reveal their author. Several illustrative examples concerning responses by participants to MYSCRIPT and to SRA support their utility as measures of self-concept. For instance, participants' responses to these software packages revealed dimensions of self-understanding for a broad spectrum of significant others. Further, shared understanding among subjects (intersubjectivity) was represented by subject weights in an INDSCAL-derived interpersonal space. In addition to providing an integrative framework for measurement and theory, the self-as-text model offers an opportunity to reassess continuity and change in the development of self-understanding.

The changing nature of the self. Most developmental studies that rely on some variety of self-report invariably conclude that persons' conceptions of self evolve during the life span (Broughton 1980; Damon and Hart 1982; Selman 1980). However, the measurement of self from a more psychometric tradition appears to indicate the opposite; self-structures are stable over considerable developmental spans (Marsh et al. 1984). Similarly, recent investigation of functional self-knowledge also indicates developmental invariance (Pullybank et al. 1985). In this latter instance, children from seven to eleven years of age were presented with adjectives preceded by either a semantic encoding question (does this word mean the same as X?) or a self-reference encoding question (does this word describe you today?). Like most self-reference studies (see "Self-coherency" in the beginning of this chapter), the self-reference condition resulted in superior free recall of the adjectives. However, younger children showed roughly the same degree of enhancement as older children in the retention of these trait descriptors under the self-reference condition.

To reconcile the contradictory results described above, consider self-structure as a network of labeled relations among concepts. Typical self-concept inventories in the psychometric tradition then appear to emphasize two relations: subset of and member of. For example, "I like to read" may be interpreted as requesting a value for the relation: member of, reading. Similarly, self-reference studies apparently also emphasize this type of relation. For example, "Is this word like you?" suggests a member-of relation. In contrast, interviews with people in the developmental tradition emphasize the connection of member-of and other relations to more complex relational structures, including those concerning epistemological knowledge and knowledge of the dynamics of self. Stated another way, developmental interviews appear to focus on knowledge encoded by highly ordered predicates. Damon and Hart (1982) suggest that relatively early in development a broad differentiation of the self into social, academic, and other selves occurs. Consequently, administration of self-concept inventories constructed in the traditional psychometric tradition to different age groups confirms the stability of this differentiation by emphasizing the member-of relation (e.g., "I like mathematics"). Developmental interviews, however, emphasize more complex relations, such as how a self can be both real and not real, and these apparently change during the life span.

To reconcile the psychometric and developmental traditions concerning a self-understanding, consider the self as a text with a deep structure that reflects a system of cause. One might then expect developmental invariance for comparatively static relations, such as member-of, and developmental transition for dynamic causal relations, such as those concerning motives. Thus, the empirical disagreement between the psychometric and developmental traditions over the evolution of self-understanding results from a focus on different categories of the narrative. Recall that MYSCRIPT emphasizes the dynamics of a storytelling self, a self-as-cause. Although subjects' responses to MYSCRIPT are less constrained when compared with traditional self-concept inventories (and hence are more like those obtained from interviews), the structure of responses to MYSCRIPT may be modeled mathematically, an option that pure interviews preclude. Consequently, treatment of the self as a text with the MYSCRIPT measurement model may serve to integrate the precision of the psychometric tradition with the scope of the developmental tradition for the study of self. Recalling Kaplan, future research could be guided by treating the self as a text, and future theories concerning the self-as-text could be constrained by empirical findings obtained within this framework.

ACKNOWLEDGMENTS

Parts of this work were supported by a grant to the author by the University of Wisconsin Graduate School and by grant no. NIE-84-0008 to the Wisconsin Center for Education Research from the National Institute of Education. The usual disclaimers apply. James C. Mancuso played a critical and constructive role in the development of this chapter. Thanks to the people who volunteered to participate in the empirical portion of this work; their critical comments were invaluable. Thanks also to James Corter, who generously provided ADDTREE/P, to Paul C. Smith, who modified ADDTREE/P for the IBM PC, and to Tom Guckenberg, who wrote portions of the STATSCRIPT program. Herbert Van DeVenter implemented the code for MYSCRIPT and contributed much to its development. Cheryl Hogue carefully typed this manuscript.

APPENDIX

All computer programs described in this chapter are available upon request. Write to Richard Lehrer, Cognitive Science, Department of Educational Psychology, 1025 West Johnson Street, Madison, Wisconsin 53706.

10 Analyzing Cognitive Structures: An Application to Parent Role Systems

James C. Mancuso

After having observed a young child's reaction to a variety of environmentally regulated inputs, an investigator can readily classify the child as a *difficult* child or as an *easy* child. Such classifications follow from a system based on carefully collected data and well-formulated principles (Kagan et al. 1984; Thomas, Chess, and Birch 1968). A difficult child, in contrast to an easy child, negatively responds to novel stimuli, adapts slowly to changes, reacts predominantly with intense reactions, and so forth. The investigator then can confidently predict patterns of behavior that the classified child will show as it develops psychologically. Among other outcomes, an infant classed as difficult, relative to an infant classed as easy, will more probably develop behaviors that will lead its parents to seek professional psychological consultation.

Although these findings easily induce some commentators to speak of *temperament* as "cause," one can claim that the difficult child's psychological development intricately involves not only an elemental characteristic of the infant, but also cognitive organizations that guide the parents' behaviors. Anecdotal (Brazleton 1961; Thomas, Chess, and Birch 1968) and more formal data (Prechtl 1963; Thomas and Chess 1977) document the high variability in the parental response to difficult infants and in developmental outcomes (Kagan et al. 1984). Such variability, one can assume, has a base in the ways in which parents variously construe their parent roles.

What concepts usefully explain the variability of parent behavior and the associated variation in the psychological development of difficult children? Consider the following constructivist formulation of parent/child interactions. The difficult child's functioning highly involves the infant's reactions to situations wherein he or she cannot apply constructions that would successfully anticipate the flow of input (see Mancuso and Adams-Webber 1982b; Mancuso and Hunter 1983, for elaboration of the concept *successful anticipation*). That is, the behaviors that differentiate difficult and easy children occur in discrepancy situations. A discrepancy occurs when the child's acquired, input-integrating cognitive organizations do not readily match the sensory patterns deriving from event-associated, sensory-affecting energies. Infants, like all persons, undergo mobilization reactions in such discrepancy situations. Mobilization states would affect sensory systems located within the infant's body. The resulting mobilization-associated input would also become a source of nonintegratable input patterns. Eventually the infant will "know" those inputs as *emotions* — anger, fear, guilt, and so forth. Until that "knowledge" is acquired, such input (arousal input) would necessarily function as "free-floating," nonintegratable input. Arousal input would enter a positive feedback loop that would perpetuate and raise the mobilization state occasioned by the initial distal nonintegratable events. One could summarize in familiar terms: Novelty generates mobilization. Mobilization changes body functions. Those changes register at sensory endings. To an infant, intense mobilization inputs also are novel; and, thus, they augment the novelty/arousal cycle.

Now reconsider the varied growth-inducing practices of the caretakers of difficult children. First note that some of Thomas, Chess, and Birch's (1968) initially identified *difficult* children did not develop problematic behaviors. Other difficult infants persisted in, and even enlarged on, their difficult-to-manage behaviors. Apparently, parents who had successfully managed their difficult children had been guided by their parent-role construing systems to set up controlled routines for the difficult children. They had regulated the input given the children to minimize the novel, nonintegratable input that generates mobilization reactions. Additionally, they had assisted the infants in "understanding" and regulating their arousal inputs. In short, these parents of children who evolved from *difficult* to *manageable* had implemented those attachment-building parent/infant interactions described by Sroufe (1979).

One could conclude that contrasting constructions of parent/child interactions had guided the parenting practices of the parents of difficult infants who were later classed as problematic children (Brazleton 1961; Thomas and Chess 1977). Inevitably these latter parents construed their parent/child interactions in terms of *control* and *regulation,* while paradoxically creating environments described as "disorganized," "unstructured," and "highly variable." These parents commonly supplied coercive reprimands, including spanking or shaking their toddlers, shouting at them, and social isolation, any of which would augment the nonintegratable input entering the toddler's psychological system. The parents of difficult children who become problem children, then, appear to provide to their children those inputs that coercively divert the children from those novel, mobilization-inducing events that first generate the infants' "difficult" behaviors. The child, then, cannot build a cognitive system that can satisfactorily anticipate the original novel and arousing input. These parents also fail to prompt the child to build a useful understanding of mobilization-associated arousal inputs. As Thomas and Chess (1977) observed, "In all these cases, whether the parents are threatened, resentful, or intimidated, they can hardly provide the patient, gradual repeated exposures to new situations and demands that such a child requires to make a positive adaptation" (p. 71). Furthermore, rather than leading the infant toward building solid parent/child attachments, these parents alienate themselves from their children so that they commonly report "frustration," "anger," "guilt," and otherwise "displeasure" with their parent role functioning.

In summary, then, the outcome of parenting efforts unavoidably involves the constructions that a parent can recall to process the input provided by the infant's actions. The parent's construction system guides the processing of his or her self-defining parenting roles relative to the child's behaviors. The same system guides the construing of the infant's response-to-novelty and arousal actions. In turn, the parent's enactments provide input that must be integrated into the infant's developing construction systems. Inputs from parent behaviors regulate the building of the self-construing systems that the child will use as he or she defines his or her interpersonal roles, particularly in relationships with people who engage in parenting-type behaviors. It follows that the parent who can successfully regulate his or her difficult infant's unusual mobilization reactions will lead that child to construe the possibilities of advantageous attachments to adults. On the other hand, the "temperamentally difficult" child who has not been helped to acquire the means by which to moderate his or her varied mobilization states will repeatedly engage in negatively valued behaviors.

Such theory, in that it gives a focus to the organized cognitive processing system that a person brings to parenting activity, directs an investigator to consider the generality of descriptions of the operations of construing systems. If one can deem it advisable to search out and define an "intelligent system" for solving problems of medical diagnoses, for example, then one may equally justify the search for and definition of an intelligent parenting–problem-solving system. Further, those methods that an investigator would find useful for laying out one particular cognitive system should work equally well for mapping out another organized construing system.

THE DEVELOPMENT OF A PARENT ROLE REPERTORY ANALYSIS TECHNIQUE

Developmental psychologists have not characteristically used paradigms that would prompt a search for technologies by which to lay out quantitative representations of organized parent role construing systems. Some have, however, recognized the utility of techniques for assessing parent belief systems (Schaefer 1971; Sigel 1985a). Studies (for example, Feldman and Nash 1978; Sigel 1985b) using self-report of parental beliefs have proved moderately helpful in clarifying relationships between parental constructions, parental behaviors, and child development outcomes. Investigators have noted the limited scope of such efforts, and continue to explore innovative approaches to modeling parental belief systems. Sameroff and Feil (1985), for example, concur with the general view that "the way a parent interprets the behavior of his or her child is related to the parent's complexity of developmental thought" (p. 89), and they tried to assess the complexity of the system of thought that parents bring to their roles. By use of a Concepts of Development Questionnaire, they sought to lay out "the stages in the parent's construction of the child at four levels analogous to Piaget's sensorimotor, preoperational, concrete operations, and formal operational. These were the symbiotic, the categorical, the compensating, and the perspectivistic" (p. 86). Clearly, Sameroff and Feil envisioned greater informational gain from assessment of a parent's general orientation toward child rearing than from a cataloguing of beliefs about specific parental actions. A similar deemphasis of the specific content of parent belief systems led Mancuso and Handin (1980, 1983) to adapt Kelly's (1955) Role Repertory Grid method (see also Adams-Webber 1979; Fransella and Bannister 1977) as a method for assessing an individual's parent role construing system.

A ROLE REPERTORY APPROACH TO ASSESSING PARENT ROLE CONSTRUCTIONS

It appears theoretically and mathematically logical to expect considerable good from appropriate structural analysis of the psychological systems that a person uses to integrate "domain-specific" input. (Quotation marks are placed around the term *domain* in order to alert readers to a view that guided the writing of this chapter, a view that contests the advisability of defining domains, in terms of an extant, "out-there," system. *Domains,* one here assumes, refers to inputs that conveniently fall within the range of one or another of a construer's hierarchically ordered construct networks.) Theoretically one should profit, for example, from techniques that map out the ways in which categorizing dimensions are hierarchically linked, the extent to which two or more categories are used similarly, the number of subordinate categories that one may apply to a domain, and so forth.

This chapter contains a description of a protracted effort to explore the utility of attempting structural analyses of an individual's parent role construing system. The techniques used here have been borrowed from statisticians, other psychologists, and other role repertory grid analysts.

During the first phase of the conduct of a Parent Role Repertory Analysis (ParRep) a participant produces data to fill in a 16 x 14 matrix. In that matrix, a statement of a belief about a parenting practice stands as the label of each of the 16 rows of the matrix. Each of the 14 columns in the matrix would be labeled by a description of a parent role. Figure 10.1 displays a permuted ParRep matrix that has been completed by one of the 15-year-old males (JOEP) who participated in Kanner's (1985) study. The parent roles and the belief statements were clustered to reflect this participant's judgments as he responded to the task. The permutations of the original data matrix brought the roles (vertical axis) and the belief statements (horizontal axis) into proximity, as defined by the cluster analysis. (Examples of the roles and the belief statements, along with their acronymic titles, are presented in Table 10.1. Figure 10.1 also shows a dendrograph that would represent the

Table 10.1
Selected Examples of Parent Role Descriptions and Parent-Practice Belief Statements

Selected Parent Role Descriptions

4. Helen Bruno really loves her child. She wants her child to be a happy child. (LUVNHAPY)

6. Three or four couples are at a gathering. They are talking about their young children, talking about how to raise the children. How hard would it be for these couples to believe this statement? (GROUPCONS)

7. Bob Wilson has really tried to raise his children so that they do things the first time they are asked to do them. (CHCOMPLY)

9. Ruth Kramer is a mother who knows the best thing to do when children get upset. (CALMWELL)

11. Barbara Moore has a child who can't stand being in new situations. Barbara just hasn't helped her child to put up with anything new — new food, new places, new people. Barbara's child really fusses whenever the family tries something different or new. (CH-NOVEL)

14. John Powers is a man who is known to be very fair with his children. John's friends, and all the other kids always say, "John Powers is fair in whatever he asks his children to do." (FAIR)

Selected Parent-Practice Belief Statements

1. A child who learns to do what his parents says to do will grow up to be a person who won't get into trouble. (OBEYPARS)

3. A child should settle down whenever he's told to settle down. (SETLDOWN)

4. Whenever a child has done something that a parent doesn't like, talking to the child works better than punishing the child. (TALK-PUN)

8. There are a lot of children who will end up causing trouble, even though the parents are really good parents. (SOMEBAD)

13. If you are trying to teach a child something, like how to put on his shoes, let him work it out his own way. (LRNBYDNG)

14. A parent makes it clear to his children that they will be punished whenever they do something stupid. (PUNISCLR)

Source: Compiled by the authors.

hierarchical arrangement of the clusters. The dendrograph will be discussed at a later point.)

Mancuso and Handin composed the parent roles and the belief statements by considering a constructivist theory of parenting like that outlined above. The roles and statements provide the stimulus base that should evoke a person's constructions of parenting practices. The investigators had a special theoretical interest in a respondent's understanding of processes by which parents consider and work with a child's constructions of events.

The participant, seated before a microcomputer display screen (see the appendix at the end of this chapter), first sees a simple explanation of the process. He or she then answers a set of questions about his or her understanding of and possible previous progress with the Par Rep data collection process. The actual data gathering begins when the respondent sees on the screen the first parent role description, which the computer has selected randomly from among the 14 role descriptions. Initial instructions prepare the participant to try very hard to develop a thorough impression of the parent defined by the role description. He or she is urged to continue to respond to the role description in terms of that thorough impression. Directly beneath a role description there then appears one of the belief statements, which also has been selected randomly from among the 16 belief statements. Following the earlier instructions, the respondent considers and then makes a judgment: To what extent would the person filling the displayed role description agree with the displayed parenting belief statement? By pressing the 1, the 2, or the 3 key, the respondent registers the judgment that the displayed role parent "Wouldn't believe it at all," "Might believe it," or "Would believe it completely," respectively. The participant's response is then sent to a memory location that represents the row/column (role/belief statement) intersect of the data matrix.

After a participant has recorded an estimate of the first-presented role occupant's level of agreement with each of the 16 belief statements, there appears a second randomly chosen role descriptor. The belief statements, having been reordered randomly, are again presented serially in conjunction with the second role description. The participant repeats the process of judging the extent to which a person who fills the second role description would agree or disagree with each of the 16 belief statements. Under the microcomputer's guidance the respondent continues this process, ultimately registering his or her judgments about the beliefs of each of the 14 persons described by the role descriptors.

The program then transfers the participant's completed Par Rep matrix to the microcomputer's data disc. The investigator may then submit the recorded grid to any number of multidimensional analysis programs that are available on the microcomputer, or he or she may use the microcomputer as a terminal to transfer the grids for analysis by another computer. Programs that transpose the response matrix allow an investigator to perform complementary analyses on the structures of both the belief statements and the role descriptions.

One may now (using programs for a TRS-80, Model III microcomputer, in BASIC language) obtain (1) a principal components analysis, (2) a varimax rotation of components, (3) a cluster analysis and cluster displays that parallel those developed by Rosenberg (1977) and his colleagues (Rosenberg and Jones 1972), and (4) a prototype analysis adapted from the work of Gara and Rosenberg (1979).

THE THEORETICAL AND QUANTITATIVE LINKAGES IN ParRep ANALYSES

By initiating the appropriate program, an investigator may submit the data matrix — either in its "beliefs as rows" orientation or in its "roles as rows" orientation — to the appropriate program to obtain printouts of descriptive statistics, correlation coefficients, principal components analysis, and a varimax rotation of components. The clustering analysis program, on the other hand, sends to the printer the matrix of distance measures, which, like the correlation coefficients, provide an index of the relationships between roles and the relationships between beliefs.

One can assume that the quantified relationships displayed by the computer output (product moment correlations or distance measures) reflect in some way the relationships that are embedded in the respondent's parent role repertory construing system. Following that general assumption, an investigator schooled to think about principal components analyses and factor analyses would readily find uses for the indices of the ways in which belief statements and parent roles relate to each other and to the "major themes" that run through the raw data supplied by a person who has completed the ParRep. Many readily available sources provide explications of the results of factor analytic techniques built into the ParRep analyses (see, for example, Slater 1977; Pruzek, this volume). Rather than providing a focus on those analyses, the ensuing sections will contain a discussion of the linkages between indices extracted from the clustering analysis, or from the prototype analysis, and the tenets of personal construct theory (Kelly 1955). A brief discussion of categorization processes can facilitate the discourse.

QUANTITATIVE REPRESENTATION, CATEGORIZATION PROCESSES, AND ParRep ANALYSES

Kelly (1955) succinctly tied categorization theory to his general theory in his Range Corollary. He expressed the Range Corollary in the following terms: "A construct is convenient for the anticipation of a finite range of events only" (p. 68). Close analysis can reveal dense linkages between the Range Corollary and theories of cognitive functioning, particularly by noting the corollary's relation to personal construct theory's fundamental postulate (see Mancuso and Eimer 1982 for an extensive discussion of those linkages). One assumes that a person places an event at one or the other end of an idiosyncratic, acquired, two-poled construct in order to anticipate successfully the flow of event-related inputs. To a firm constructivist, category placement culminates as the process of locating an input-associated event at one or the other end of bipolar personal constructs, such as *arbitrary–fair* or *excites–calms*.

By this formulation, personal construct theory assimilates investigations of the concept of *prototypicality* in the categorization process. Category assignment completes the process of fitting an event to one or another end of a bipolar construct. One speaks of a "prototype" when referring to the clearest case of category membership. A prototype event would be that event which best fits at the extreme end of a construct. Thus, to anticipate an event successfully, one's cognitive processes should lead to locating any input *qua* event as an instance of its most proximate prototype. A theorist might hedge at accepting a concept of *approximate prototypicality,* since the prefix *proto-* drives one's cognitive processes toward the categories *first, unique,* and so forth. As Rosch (1978) points out, however, "to speak of a prototype is simply a convenient grammatical fiction; what is really referred to are judgments of degree of prototypicality" (p. 40). In practice, no event would be taken as an absolute exemplar of a prototype. A prototypically *easy* parent would exist as a "fictional" category pole that some "real" parents might approach, but no parent would fit decisively into that slot.

Prototypical parent types, then, serve a crucial function. Prototypes within a personal parent-construing system provide a person with a *standard* against which to contrast others and self during enactment of parent roles. As a person observes a person (his or her self, as well as others) acting as a parent, he or she anticipates that the ensuing flow of input will match his or her assembled construction of an internally represented prototypical parent. When inputs fail to match that standard, the person would enter into a mobilization state. He or she would be motivated either to reconstrue or to alter the input so that an input-to-standard match can be achieved.

In sum, anticipatory construction can proceed by locating an event in a category (placing it at one or another end of a construct) through assessing the extent to which the event shares with a construction of a prototype an overlapping set of probabilistically assigned features. Not all members of a category can be taken as equally representative of the category's prototype. One best regards exemplars of a category as members of a "fuzzy set." An input-associated event exemplifies one or another end of a construct when it "fuzzily" shares with a prototype an overlapping set of assigned features. (It should be noted here that the concept *features* must also bee explicated. Such explication is offered by Mancuso and Eimer [1982: 134], for example, who propose that feature assignment is one subexemplar of the general process of category assignment. That is, feature assignment processes involve locating an event on one of a person's set of invented constructs.) In short, the prototypes that a person can retrieve can facilitate the anticipation of a continued flow of input patterning that would validate that event's category placement.

Tversky (1977), parts of whose feature analysis model of categorization and contrast underlie the foregoing discussion, shows that clustering analysis proceeds from a metric that indicates the judged similarity (or dissimilarity) of two events. Indices of (dis)similarity quantitatively express a respondent's judgments of the extent to which two events share common features which, at the same time, are not shared with other events in the set of events under consideration. (See Shaw 1980, pp. 155–67, for further discussion of [dis]similarity indices.) In common practice, the mathematical process of assessing the (dis)similarity of every event to every other event in a set of events yields an $N \times N$ symmetrical matrix of distance measures. An investigator can then use this symmetrical matrix as input into an algorithm that produces a representation of clusters of events that a respondent has judged to be similar. Additionally, the output of the procedures allows one to represent the patterning of the hierarchic relationships among the events that a respondent has categorized.

The propositions embedded in the foregoing discussion of categorizing processes may be linked to the ParRep analysis in the following manner. To begin, take the parent roles as events that are to be construed, that is, as events that are to be categorized — to be anticipated conveniently through their assignment at one or the other end of one of a person's two-poled construct. Take the belief statements as the "features" that may be assigned to roles.

Within the construing system of the respondent who is completing the ParRep, a parent role (for example, role 9 CALMWELL) would be attributed with holding certain beliefs. One may say that while judging whether or not the CALMWELL parent would endorse the belief statements embedded in the ParRep, the respondent had attributed certain features (a set of beliefs) to the CALMWELL parent. Similarly, persons who enact other roles, such as role 7 (CHCOMPLY), would be described in terms of the features (the beliefs) that the respondent has attributed to them.

The distance measures, which become the basis for the clustering analysis, index the extent to which a participant has judged two contrasted parent role figures to have the same features. That is, the algorithm that produces the distance measures yields indices of the respondent's judgments about the shared features of the two role figures that are compared to produce the distance measure. The distance measure indicates the respondent's estimate of the extent to which two role figures share the parenting practice beliefs.

The basic output of the prototype analysis (the implications phi), on the other hand, can be taken as an index of the extent to which a role figure represents a "pure type" of parent. The implications phi (Φ_{imP}) algorithm (Francis 1961, adapted from Gara and Rosenberg 1979) indicates the extent to which an event (in this case, a parent role) has been assigned distinctive features that are not shared by other elements in the subset to which it belongs, while having many of the features that are shared by other elements in the subset.

The CALMWELL parent, for example, could emerge as a prototype in a particular respondent's ParRep grid. In that case, the respondent who has produced the grid of raw scores has indicated that CALMWELL holds all the beliefs held by other parents in the cluster in which CALMWELL is located. Additionally, CALMWELL holds more of the beliefs held by other members of the set than do any of those other parent role figures. In short, CALMWELL can be taken to be "more prototypical" of the clustered role category than is any other member of the cluster of roles. In other words, one could say that the most prototypic member of the cluster best represents the superordinating master term for the cluster.

In sum, by use of the clustering analysis algorithm, coupled with the implications phi analysis, one may survey two broad, quantified structural features of each respondent's ParRep grid: (1) the pattern of hierarchical relationships among the parent role figures that the respondent has imposed implicitly, through having judged the extent to which each parent role endorses or rejects the beliefs; and (2) the extent to which one or another parent role stands, in the respondent's parent role construing system, as a prototype of the superordinate category into which that parent role falls. Similar analyses may also be applied to belief statements as elements.

HIERARCHICAL CLUSTERING ANALYSIS OF ParRep GRIDS

The hierarchical clustering analysis algorithm was adapted for grids analysis by Rosenberg and Jones (1972), following the procedures devised by Johnson (1967). The program first extracts distance measures that index the dissimilarity of each pair of parent roles (or child-rearing beliefs). The distance measure used here takes into account both direct and indirect co-occurrence. (See Rosenberg and Jones 1972 for an extended discussion of this δ-measure.) This δ-measure appears to satisfy a rationale based on the assumption that the level of judged similarity of two events (for example, parent roles) depends on the differentiation a person can impose as he or she cognizes all parent roles. The algorithm used in these programs computes δ-measures that take into account contrasts between each of two directly contrasted roles (or beliefs), *i* and *j*, as well as the contrast between those roles and every other role in the matrix. The δ for any two roles (or beliefs), then, represents not only the direct comparison of those two roles with each other, but also represents the comparison of every other role with the two roles that are of main concern in the calculation. By this latter procedure one builds indirect co-occurrence into the dissimilarity index.

The programmed clustering routines output schematic figures that display separate role clusterings and separate belief clusterings. Figure 10.1 illustrates a facsimile of the output of a ParRep analysis by displaying a two-way permutation of role clusters (on the columns) and the belief clusters (on the rows). This display resulted from running the routines on the ParRep grid of JOEP, a 15-year-old adolescent, who participated in Kanner's (1985) study. The dendrographs connect clusters

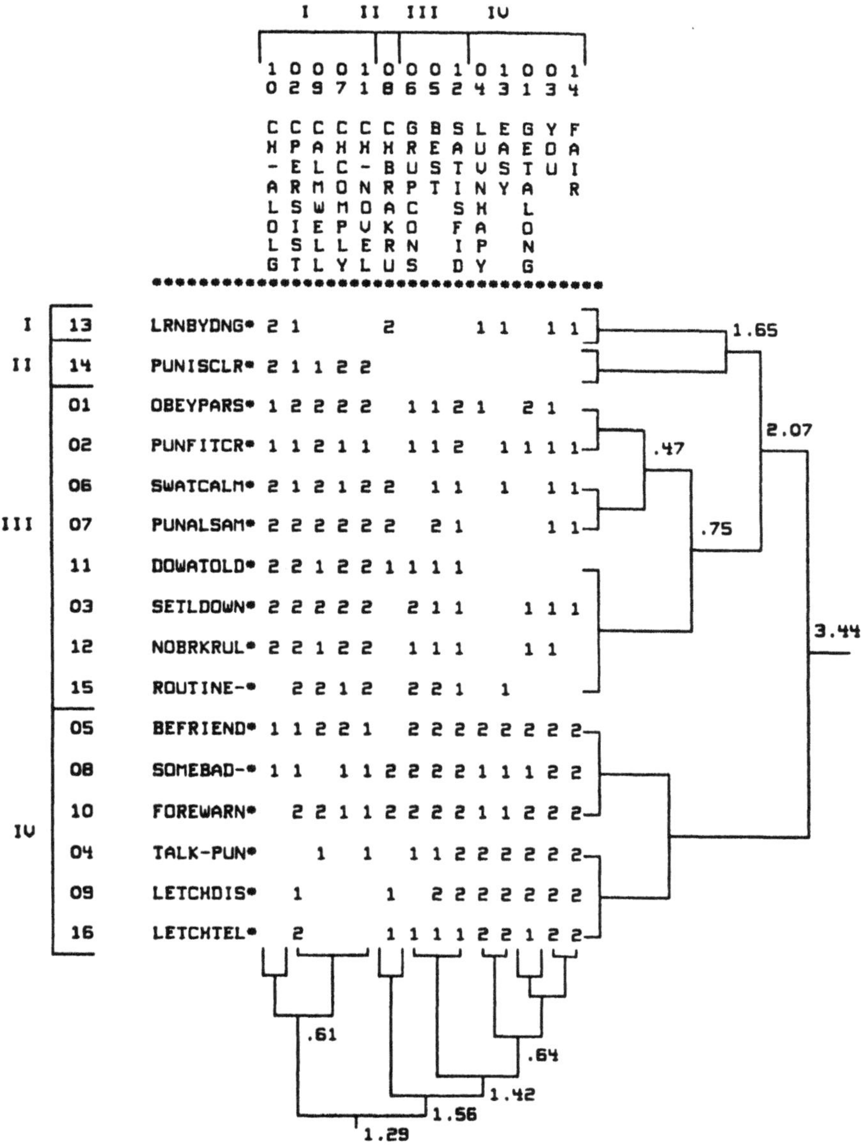

Fig. 10.1.

Permuted, two-way display of cluster-analyzed role and beliefs from ParRep matrix of JOEP. Four major clusters of beliefs (on the rows) are labeled on the left. Four major clusters of roles (on the columns) are labeled on the top. The tree diagrams on the bottom and on the right side trace through the clustering process, with the numbers at the stems indicating the δ–measure between those events that come together at that joining. Blank cells indicate that JOEP had indicated that the parent role in the column would not believe the statement on the cell row, whereas the number 2 indicates that JOEP ascribed a strong belief to the parent role.

and "outliers." The numbers at stems indicate the δ-measures that connect the roles that are joined to form the clusters created at that point.

The microcomputer programs that are now available also produce a bar-graph-like layout that indicates the δ-measure level at which the joining of two roles (beliefs) occurs. A quick inspection of the display would inform an investigator of the shape of the clustering pattern extracted from the respondent's matrix of judgments. From the bar graph one may draw out the information needed to plot the tree diagrams shown in Figure 10.1.

The hierarchical clustering routines that yield the two-way permutation of the clusters (a complete linkage routine) proceeds by a "diameter method"; and in this way it produces hierarchically arranged clusters — a previously formed cluster may become a subset of a subsequently formed "supercluster." One thinks of the δ-measure as a diameter. The routine first searches out the smallest "diameter." The parent roles that JOEP construes to be most similar (least dissimilar) were roles 11 (CH-NOVEL) and 7 (CHCOMPLY), $\delta = .034$. The routine establishes these roles as the first cluster. The routine then chooses "the next higher diameter." JOEP's grid yields a δ-measure of .069 between roles 3 (YOU) and 14 (FAIR). This pair of roles becomes a second cluster. The search for the third smallest diameter in JOEP's grid could result (1) in the roles associated with that diameter forming yet a third incipient cluster; or (2) one of the two roles that produced the third smallest diameter joining to a role that already stands in one of the two previously formed clusters, thus adding a third role to an existing cluster. Although the production of clusters and the program's graphic display continues until every role is linked to a cluster, any one of the roles in any particular grid could be taken as a single role in a "cluster" (an outlier) when the δ-measure between that role and any other role is sufficiently large. For example, in JOEP's grid the beliefs 13 (LRNBYDNG) and 14 (PUNISCLR) stand as outliers. Those beliefs, when contrasted to each other, yield a dissimilarity index of 1.650, and both of them differ from all other beliefs to the extent of yielding δ-measures of 2.078 or more.

Clustering analysis, while having an immediate face validity, has not yielded to the kinds of statistical analyses that are based on error theory. One must proceed cautiously, then, to explore the logically appealing hypotheses that the number of "meaningful" clusters that emerge from a respondent's grid would offer one index of the adequacy of that person's parent role construing system. One could build a nomological net around a hypothesis about quantity of meaningful clusters by adopting the following strategy. One would first ask, How many independent clusters would have been formed if the clustering routine were to stop when "the next highest diameter" reaches a certain level — let us say, 1.0? For example, if the clustering of parent roles in JOEP's grid were to have stopped when the routine reached the δ-measure of 1.0, three clusters would remain independent of each other and one outlier would have not yet been incorporated into the three independent clusters. (Note, on the dendrograph at the bottom of Figure 10.1, that four joinings of role clusters occur after the joining indicated by the branch labeled .649.) If the "cutoff" point of 1.0 were exercised in the analysis of JOEP's parent belief judgments, there would have been formed two independent clusters, with two beliefs remaining as outliers. (Note, at the side of Figure 10.1, the three joinings of belief subclusters, which take place above the joining indicated by the branch labeled .754.)

Having followed the first part of the suggested strategy one could then compare samples in terms of variables such as (1) the number of independent clusters, (2) the number of outliers, (3) the average number of belief (or roles) in each cluster, and so forth. The problems with the use of these techniques center around the determination of an appropriate δ-measure (see Aldenderfer and Blashfield 1984; Smith and Leach 1972, for a discussion of this point). One would also want to decide whether or not to treat outliers as separate clusters, as has been done in JOEP's case in Figure 10.1.

Ultimately, the validity of this approach will be determined by the adequacy of the nomological network that results from planned investigations. Such a gain would derive, for example, from supporting the hypothesis that respondents who produce grids with "optimum" numbers of roles (beliefs) would have achieved "optimally" differentiated parent role construing systems, and that such respondents would function most adequately as parents.

Another research strategy, which has been used by Rosenberg and his co-workers (Rosenberg 1977; Gara and Rosenberg 1979) and by Mascolo and Mancuso (1985), proceeds through the following steps. First, determine an appropriate cutoff distance measure and block off all role clusters and outliers that remain independent when the algorithm reaches that "diameter." One can then determine the mean level of commitment that the respondent has ascribed to occupants of that block, relative to any single belief or to any cluster of beliefs.

For example, observe that JOEP ascribes to Role Cluster IV very strong adherence to the parent beliefs that make up Belief Cluster IV. The parent type that makes up this cluster of parent roles, according to JOEP, would accept all the "soft" statements about parent role enactments. Parent roles that occupy JOEP's Role Cluster I, on the other hand, tend to reject the beliefs in Belief Cluster IV; and they, JOEP believes, endorse the beliefs in Belief Cluster III. Neither Role Cluster III nor Role Cluster I, however, incorporates the best satisfied or socially validated parent role. According to JOEP's construing of parent roles, these latter roles, which make up Role Cluster III, would hold strongly to the beliefs brought together in Belief Cluster IV, hold moderately to the parenting beliefs in Belief Cluster III, and reject the beliefs in Belief Clusters I and II.

This cluster-blocking procedure can be adapted to specific research strategies. Selected samples of persons can complete the grid. As they do so, the respondents also would rate each parent role on a variety of dimensions, such as, "Would rear a child who, at age 15, would be judged to be totally successful in school and in the community," or "Would regret ever having had a family." Then cluster-analyze a grid filled with the mean of the sample's judged level of the adherence of each role to each belief. The mean dimension ratings assigned to each role cluster category are then extracted. By appropriate statistical tests an investigator may then answer questions such as: (1) What is the mean level of success that would be ascribed to persons who strongly hold the beliefs in Belief Cluster I, II, or III? (2) Do the respondents expect that occupants of Role Cluster I, to whom they ascribe strong adherence to the beliefs comprising Belief Cluster III, will regret having taken on the parenting role? Furthermore, by permuting the grids from two separate samples so that they are similarly arrayed, one can test theory-based hypotheses about the similarities and differences between two parent role systems of two separate samples.

A clinician can readily see that the kinds of information extracted from ParRep analysis and discussed in the previous section can serve to construct the implicit "self stories" (see Mancuso 1986, for a discussion of the concept of *self stories*) that a respondent might compose to guide his or her own parenting practices, as well as those of other parents. The array of blocks of role-types x belief-types (see Figure 10.1), then, can serve a powerful function in generating discussions with students of parenting behavior or with parents who are in consultation about their own parenting techniques.

To illustrate, inspect JOEP's matrix of clustered and permuted roles and beliefs. Consider the three distinct role clusters, relative to the two distinct belief clusters (along with outlying roles and beliefs). If we listened to this 15-year-old adolescent's stories about parents, we would expect to hear something like the following:

> There are four types of parents: nice people [Role Cluster IV] who don't get on their kids' backs; parents [Cluster III] who tend to be somewhat "tougher," but who ultimately are more satisfied with the job they have done and who get social approval for their parenting activity; and parents [Cluster I] who tend to be very tough on their kids, but these parents haven't reared kids whom one would call happy, well-adjusted kids. A fourth type of person generally ignores his or her children, except to bomb down on them; and it shows, because he'll produce a real hell-raiser.
>
> I would be like the people in Cluster IV, but I'm a little ambivalent about it. I would want to be a good parent, even though I would want to be fair. I just couldn't insist that my kids should jump when I say "jump," even though that's what good parents would do.
>
> The main thing, though, is that parents can be sharply differentiated on one big dimension — *tough–considerate* [Belief Cluster III versus IV]. I just can't see any other useful way to categorize parenting beliefs.

THE PROTOTYPICALITY MEASURE

Gara and Rosenberg (1979) introduced the use of Francis's (1961) implications phi as a measure of the extent to which a role would stand as prototypical of a cluster. The algorithm that is followed by the computer program solves the equation:

$$\Phi_{\text{Imp}} = ad - bc \,/\, (a + c)\,(c + d) \tag{10.1}$$

where *a, b, c,* and *d* represent the number of tallies in the cells of a matrix displayed as follows:

	Role B	
Role A	*yes*	*no*
yes	*a*	*b*
no	*c*	*d*

A tally is placed in cell *a,* for example, if the respondent indicates that one parent role being considered, Role A, holds the belief, Belief Z, while the other parent role under consideration, Role B, also holds Belief Z. Similarly, a tally goes into cell *b* when parent Role A holds the Belief Z whereas parent Role B does not hold the belief, and so forth, for the 16 beliefs. Inspection of Equation 10.1 will show that Φ_{Imp} is asymmetrical, in that when, for example, Role B is located on the vertical axis of the diagrammed matrix whereas Role A is on the horizontal axis, the value of Φ_{Imp} would alter sharply.

Since the Φ_{Imp} is asymmetrical, the calculation of all Φ_{Imp}s extracted from a completed ParRep will produce a full matrix of Φ_{Imp}s. (See Figure 10.2 for the Φ_{Imp} matrix displaying the superordination pattern of parent roles which were extracted from JOEP's ParRep grid.) A Φ_{Imp} matrix may be subjected to the same clustering algorithms to which raw data scores had been subjected. In this way, one can observe the patterns of similarities and dissimilarities between the ways in which sets of parent-role persons "superordinate" other role persons in a respondent's system. One can see, for example, that in JOEP's Φ_{Imp} matrix the parent roles 9 (CALMWELL) and 7 (CHCOMPLY) tend to superordinate other roles, both in the negative and in the positive directions, to a high degree. Inspect the entry in the row at role 9, under column 11 (CH-NOVEL) — a Φ_{Imp} of 1.0. One can conclude that if JOEP were to meet a parent who can calm his or her child well, he would immediately construe him or her as a parent of a child who cannot tolerate novelty. Concurrently, the high and negative Φ_{Imp} at the intersect of the CALMWELL row and the column labeled LUVNHAPPY suggests that JOEP would believe that the parent who calms well would *not* be a parent who loves his/her child and wants his/her child to be happy. Note also that the CALMWELL and CHCOMPLY parent roles stand as clear prototypes in JOEP's parent construing system. One can see, by comparing the CHCOMPLY and the CALMWELL rows in his Φ_{Imp} matrix, that those roles have the same superordinating pattern, relative to all other roles. Three other roles, 11 (CH-NOVEL), 3 (YOU), and 14 (FAIR), also tend to be superordinating in JOEP's system. By looking at their distance from each other in the permuted display, one concludes that those roles tend to have independence as prototypes. If JOEP knows that a person enacts the role of a fair parent (FAIR), for example, he will believe that that person will tend to be the parent who gets along well with his/her children (GETALONG) and who is easy (EASY) on them. He would tend to believe the opposite about a person whom he has judged to be the parent of a child who can't stand novelty (CHI-NOVEL); this latter parent wouldn't get along well with his/her child and would not be easy on the child.

	08 CHBRAKRU	10 CH-ALONG	04 LUVNHAPY	02 CPERSIST	11 CH-NOVEL	03 YOU	09 CALMWELL	01 GETALONG	05 BEST	06 GRUPCONS	07 CHCOMPLY	12 SATISFYD	13 EASY	14 FAIR
11 CH-NOVEL*		8	H	4	*	F	6	B		2	8		E	H
04 LUVNHAPY*	A	A	*		C	4	B	2		A	A		6	5
02 CPERSIST*		7	H	*	7	C	5	B		3	7	A	B	E
08 CHBRAKRU*	*	3	A					B	2	1	A		B	1
10 CH-ALONG*	4	*	E	3	6	B	3	C		1	4	C	C	D
07 CHCOMPLY*	D	5	G	4	8	D	6	1	3	5	*	1	B	F
09 CALMWELL*		7	H	5	*	F	*	1	3	7	*	1	G	H
01 GETALONG*	C	B	3			5	1	*	3	2	1	5	3	4
03 YOU.....*		C	*	A	F	*	C	7	3	2	D	4	7	*
05 BEST....*	3		B			3	2	4	*	8	3	6	1	2
06 GRUPCONS*	1	1	E	1	2	2	3	2	6	*	4	5		1
12 SATISFYD*	B	E		A		5	1	*	8	7	2	*	3	4
13 EASY....*	C	B	*		B	5	A	3	1			2	*	6
14 FAIR....*	1	D	*	A	F	8	C	5	2	1	D	3	8	*

Fig. 10.2.
Permuted, two-way display of cluster-analyzed Φ_{Imp} matrix extracted from analysis of the role relationships in the ParRep matrix of JOEP. Φ_{Imp}s shown represent roundings to the nearest level of .1, .2, .3, etc. Φ_{Imp}s of 1.0 are indexed by an asterisk (*). Negative Φ_{Imp}s, –.1, –.2, –.3, etc., are indexed by the letters A, B, C, etc., respectively. Blank cells indicate Φ_{Imp}s of 0.

PROTOTYPES AND PARENT ROLE CONSTRUING

In that the Organization Corollary of PCT would lead to the assumption that a construing system's higher-level constructs are heavily implicated in successful construing, one would expect that prototypes are central to any construing process. Prototypes should be instantiated early in the course of building a multifaceted construction. The progress of the process will depend on the structural relationships between the prototypical constructs and other available constructs. Constructions that maintain more intricate implicative tie with prototypes will be more readily instantiated to anticipate the event-related sensory input.

When a person has access to only a single prototype, the system would have a restricted range of flexibility in the generation of alternative constructions. Further, greater numbers of prototypes provide the possibility of flexible generation of alternative constructions *only* if prototypes are differentiated with respect to their pattern of implication across other constructs. Two constructs within the system can stand as prototypical, but both imply other constructs to the same extent and in the same patterns, as do CALMWELL and CHCOMPLY in JOEP's system. Those prototypes, one would hypothesize, cannot serve to generate alternative constructions of parenting situations.

A clinician or an investigator will find it useful to review the clustering of the original data matrix with the information extracted from the matrix of Φ_{Imp}s. One can then observe the contrasting patterns of beliefs attributed to the prototype parent in contrast to beliefs attributed to other parent roles. One can observe the cluster locations of the prototype roles. One can then see that the respondent tended to attribute to prototype parent roles all of the beliefs that are attributed to other parent roles in the cluster containing the prototype, yet while seeing it as a role that is characterized by its own idiosyncratic beliefs. One can directly assess whether there appears within each extracted cluster a particular parent role whose Φ_{Imp}s are high as a result of having set that role in contrast to the other roles in the matrix. Although this kind of inspection does not provide a statistically manipulable index of role prototype independence, such inspection can offer another view of the integration of a respondent's parent role construing system. For example, three of JOEP's prototypes show up in Role Cluster I. On seeing this, one might predict that his prototypes are not as useful as they could be if each superordinated a different cluster.

SOME VALIDATING RESULTS OF ParRep ANALYSIS

Some validation of the ParRep analysis has been achieved by relating the ParRep structural indices to measures of people's concepts about reprimanding children. Mancuso (1979; Mancuso and Lehrer 1985) has expanded a theory of reprimand from which one would think of all reprimand situations as a source of input that disrupts the anticipatory constructions of the target of the reprimand — for example, a transgressing child. Thus, to demonstrate links between the structure of a person's parent role construing system and his or her views of the crucial parental activity of reprimanding would enhance a constructivist theory of parenting.

Kanner (1985) asked 20 participants of middle-adolescent age (13–16 years) to complete the ParRep grid. She also had the participants respond to Eimer's (1981) interview for analyzing a person's cognitions relative to the functions and purposes of reprimand. Eimer developed a reprimand interview scaling instrument by following a set of assumptions which specify that a person in our culture progresses through a prespecified series of levels. At each level he or she can use observably different constructions for conceptualizing the purposes and effects of reprimand. For example, in the last stages of this progression, Level II-A, a person can understand that a reprimand will have no effect on forestalling future transgressions unless that reprimand is directed toward and effects change in the transgressor's way of construing the transgression situation. That is, persons who develop Level II-A thinking about reprimand know that a reprimand will make no difference, relative to the transgressor's future behavior, unless the reprimander has done something to feed directly into the transgressor's understanding of events.

Kanner's participants were easily and reliably assigned to stages by the use of Eimer's techniques. Precisely half of the adolescents were classed at Level II-A status, whereas the remaining participants were classed at Level I-A or I-B.

An assessment of the participant's use of prototypes showed that independent prototypical roles reliably emerged more clearly from the ParRep grids of the adolescents who used "more sophisticated" constructions of reprimand (Level II-A) than from the grids of the "less sophisticated" participants. While two prototypes, on average, emerged from the grids of Level II participants, ParRep grids of Level I participants yielded, on average, but one prototype. A chi-square analysis showed that the number of prototypical roles produced by the Level II participants differed reliably from the number produced by the Level I participants ($\chi^2 = 10.76$; $df = 1$; $p < .01$).

Such initial results prompt continued exploration of the use of the above-described methods of quantifying the construction systems that are implicated in the processing of parent role information. The completed work leaves no doubt that the data collection processes and the analyses, which are immensely facilitated by the ready accessibility of computing hardware and software, can lead to understandable and meaningful representations of the content and the structure of parent role construing systems. Additionally, the scattering of results from the validating studies indicates the promise of these techniques as a method of differentiating the construction systems of people with adaptable parent construing systems from those people who have developed less adaptable parent role construing systems.

CONCLUSIONS

The work presented here represents a concerted effort to derive a method of representing a person's system for construing that portion of his or her world that one might label with the term *parenting activity*. Work on the Parent Repertory Analysis has proceeded from the premise that the greatest information gain will derive from laying out the *structural* properties of construing systems. This premise follows from the assumption that efficient psychological functioning depends primarily on the organizational properties of the system through which input is channeled.

A strict adherence to this assumption could lead one to make the claim that such organization is essentially "content-free." One could claim, for example, that the organization of a person's parent construing system would emerge from the ParRep Analysis, regardless of the content of the parent role descriptor or the belief items of which the grid is constructed. That is, one could propose that so long as the material is related to parent role enactments, the respondent will impose his or her organization on that input; and that organization, in turn, will be extracted by the analyses that have been described here.

This line of reasoning leads to the belief that the methodology described above would be applicable to any domain of input-producing events. One could proceed, then, to fill the role descriptor slots with any kind of role-describing events while filling in the belief statements with any kind of material that would provide input to the persons exemplified by the role descriptors. The respondent would then be required to make a judgment of the extent to which the imagined role occupant would react to the input illustrated by the situation written into the program by the investigator. When the respondent has completed his or her roles x situations matrix, that matrix could be subjected to the above-described analysis to extract representations of the participant's organized system of roles relative to the topic under study.

Mascolo and Mancuso's (1985) analysis of "anger" roles exemplifies this suggested extension of the analyses used in the ParRep work. They presented respondents with 17 role descriptions. After encouraging the respondent to fix that role person firmly in mind, the respondent then assessed the extent to which that person would *feel* angry in each of 15 potentially anger-evoking situations. In a repetition of the administration, the participants were asked to indicate the extent to which the role person would *act* angrily. Additionally, the participants rated each of the role types on 10 different scales, such as, "is in control of his/her life" and "is sociable." This study's clear results led Mascolo and Mancuso to propose that repertory analysis methods of representing "emotion-construing" systems will shed light on the usefulness of the prevailing theories of emotion. These methods will aid in strengthening the proposition, laid out by Mancuso and Hunter (1983, 1985), that "emotions," like any other human reaction, must be treated as context-embedded constructions. Mascolo and Mancuso's early results show that individuals do construe *anger* in self and in others in terms of the context surrounding a person's failure to anticipate. Furthermore, in that the method can quantify an individual's "emotion-construing system," it promises to be useful in clinical situations wherein there is an effort to prompt persons to develop more adequate constructions of their emotional reactions.

In the end, then, the above-described efforts to provide overt mappings of a person's parent role construing systems can serve as an exemplar of a total technique for laying out a quantitative configuration of a construing system. The exploration of these methodologies allows one to confront, rather than to discount and avoid, those events (the internal working of a psychological system) that have proved elusive to theorists, investigators, and practitioners who work with psychological science concepts. We believe that continued improvement of the computing methodologies and measurement techniques, in conjunction with the imaginative contributions of collaborating behavioral scientists, will allow for more facile ways of displaying the inner representations that a person brings to the processing of input deriving from those events that impinge on one or another part of his or her sensory systems.

APPENDIX

A series of programs that complete all processes described in this chapter has been written in BASIC language, for Tandy Radio Shack, Model III microcomputers (TRS-80, Model III). Any investigator may acquire these programs, along with documentation and instructions, by addressing an inquiry to the author. These programs will be given without charge to investigators who agree to supply the author with copies of any working modifications that are made on the ParRep programs.

11 Computer-Assessed Cognition in Psychiatric Settings: An Examination of the Issues

Richard M. Ashbrook,
Will Spaulding, and
Rue L. Cromwell

This chapter presents an assessment approach to the study of cognition in psychiatric settings. The rationale of this approach originates in cognitive models of psychopathology that rely on information-processing theory. The research strategy calls for the assessment of individuals across a broad spectrum of cognitive tasks. The use of multiple measures leads to a consideration of measurement issues peculiar to the multiple-task approach.

THE COGNITIVE APPROACH TO ASSESSMENT

Cognitive psychology attempts to understand human higher mental processes (Lachman, Lachman, and Butterfield 1979). Most contemporary approaches to cognitive psychology utilize the information-processing paradigm.

Basically, this approach emphasizes the collection, storage, modification, and interpretation of information. Each of these complex skills can be decomposed into simpler constituent skills. This involves specification of increasingly discrete components of the human processing system. An assumption underlying this approach asserts that the acquisition of precise knowledge of the functional components of this system will lead to a more useful understanding of the entire range of individual ability. The importance of this approach to the study of psychopathology is based on the association between behavior disorders and information-processing differences. Some of these differences may be specific and symptom-linked. Others may be nonspecific to symptoms yet associated with certain diagnostic groupings (i.e., they may be vulnerability-linked). Thus, a cognitive assessment system that identifies discrete components of cognition that can be operationalized by experimental measures is desirable.

COMPONENTS OF THE PROCESSING SYSTEM

The theoretical underpinning of the assessment system is derived from several decades of research in cognitive experimental psychology. As psychopathologists, we have borrowed from this vast literature many of the methods, paradigms, and theories that have guided investigation into human higher mental processes. Space does not permit a comprehensive discussion of the models, techniques, or debates in cognitive psychology. The interested reader is referred to Lachman, Lachman, and Butterfield's (1979) text, *Cognitive Psychology and Information Processing,* for a supplemental background.

Figure 11.1 presents the domain of cognitive assessment in which we are interested. The terms and constructs within this domain may be unfamiliar. Consequently, a brief description of several components of the human processing system is presented. As the name implies, the processing system is divided into stages that represent specific cognitive functions. Earlier research in cognitive psychology placed great emphasis on specification of these stages (Atkinson and Shiffrin 1968; Broadbent 1958; Sternberg 1969). Later research challenged the stage approach, since cognitive functions cannot always be easily fit into stages with fixed and invariant characteristics through which information flows serially (Craik and Lockhart 1972; Thomson and Tulving 1970). Convenience determined our adoption of a stages processing model. For the purpose of description and discussion, a stagewise organization more easily distinguishes between classes of cognitive functions. Nonserial models of functions are sometimes relevant and deserve discussion. By necessity, we must briefly and incompletely describe these components. Hopefully, some familiarization with them will be rapid by a clearer conception of what the psychopathologist intends to measure.

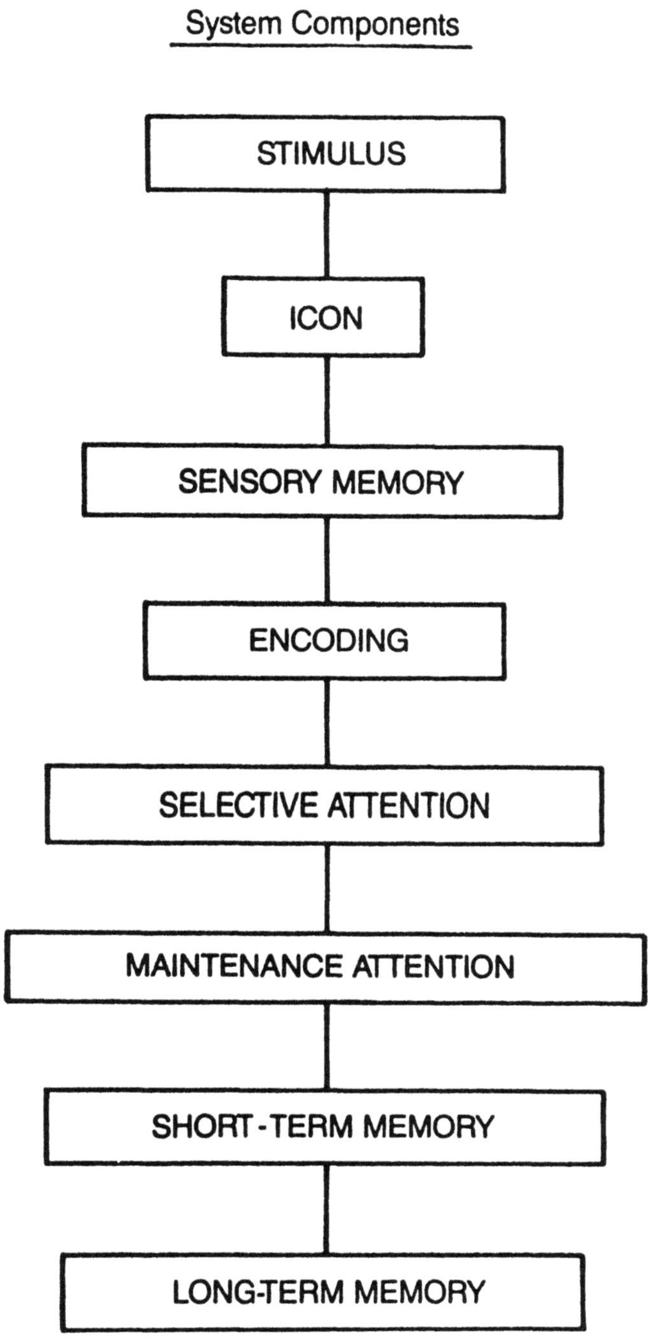

Fig. 11.1.
Schematic of human information processing system.

SENSORY MEMORY

Environmental stimuli enter the human processing system in a sensory form. Thus, the environmental stimuli convert to an internal representation through a sensory-perceptual or psychophysical transformation. In the visual modality, the resulting image or icon lasts from 10 to 1000 msec, depending on experimental conditions. This nearly literal record of external stimuli is lost in one of two ways. Either it spontaneously decays or new sensory input replaces it.

Purely perceptual events comprise iconic storage, the sensory memory for visual stimuli (Neisser 1967; Sperling 1960). It is generally presumed to be fairly independent of "meaning," to be simply a literal registration of a stimulus. The sensory store preserves incoming information long enough for it to be selectively transmitted to other processing stages where "meaning" is discerned.

ENCODING

A concept closely related but not identical to the iconic store is span of apprehension. The rate at which information can be processed from the iconic image defines the span of apprehension (Sperling 1960). Properties of the sensory store have been extensively studied using a backward masking technique (Neisser 1967; Kahneman 1968; Lefton 1973). Basically, impairment in recall following the presentation of subsequent, and temporally close, stimuli measures this effect.

Neisser (1967) posited two processes involved in the encoding of information, preattentive processing and focal attention. Preattentive processing produces an initial discrimination of information into holistic parts. It discriminates a form that is separated from the field for further analysis. In the transfer from preattentive to focal attention, the processing provides "image enhancement" by operating on and emphasizing contrast boundaries. As a focal level of attention is achieved, the encoded object is given a neural representation that matches a representation from one or more previous events. This may be described as a symbolic representation in that the original literal sensory properties are no longer retained. Also this stage may be described as the "conceptual" or "constructural" joining of the perceptual representation. Finally, the "conceptual" or symbolic representation allows a link with related remembered events (i.e., other stored symbolic representations).

Shiffrin and Schneider (1977) offered a theory of perceptual learning which, while distinct from the Neisser model, complements it for the purposes of our assessment model. They empirically demonstrated the operation of what they labeled automatic and controlled processing. Controlled search demands attentional capacity. It is dependent on load, usually serial with a limited comparison rate, and is easily established, altered, and even reversed. Automatic detection demands attention only when a target appears. It is parallel and difficult to alter, to ignore, or to suppress once learned. It is virtually unaffected by load (Shiffrin and Schneider 1977).

SELECTIVE ATTENTION

Selective attention involves the separation of relevant from irrelevant simultaneous stimuli. Irrelevant information within a task distracts in the sense that it obscures the critical stimulus dimensions. Selective attention relates to encoding, since input available to the processing system always exceeds the capacity of the system. Also, it typically operates within a preattentional stage of processing.

MAINTENANCE ATTENTION

Selective aspects of attention can be distinguished from other aspects of attention. Maintenance attention, for example, extends an attentional focus over time after completing selection of a focus. Vigilance tasks operationalize maintenance attention. Vigilance is the capacity for responding to changes in stimulus events over relatively long periods of observation. This dimension of attention was once referred to as "set" or "mental set" (Rodnick and Shakow 1940).

SHORT-TERM MEMORY

Short-term memory implies a relatively small period of time between acquisition and retrieval of information. For information to be maintained in the short-term store, it must be given constant attention. Once attention shifts away from information, it begins to decay, and will be gone completely in 15 to 30 seconds (Sternberg 1969). Maintenance rehearsal (i.e., simply repeating the information) preserves the contents of the short-term store without necessarily increasing its accessibility from long-term memory (Craik and Watkins 1973). Other forms of rehearsal may also be applied, although these likely involve the transfer of information to the long-term store. Elaborative rehearsal involves recoding by a mnemonic or by forming imagery. Since maintenance of information in the short-term store demands attention, the capacity of the store is limited. The short-term store maintains from two to twenty items. By "chunking" during elaborative rehearsal, a person may combine several items into a unitary code, and can thereby better process the contents of the short-term store.

LONG-TERM MEMORY

Long-term memory, as the name implies, retains information indefinitely. The study of long-term memory can be approached from different vantages. For instance, the effects of repetition, interference, and forgetting can be examined. One facet that seems to hold promise for the study of psychopathology is the role of organization in memory. Organization in memory determines recall ability. While different theoretical models have been advanced to account for this effect (Cohen 1963; Kelly 1955; Sternberg and Bower 1974), the experimental data clearly document that subjects employ some form of organization.

Organization effects are assessed with multitrial free recall. In a typical multitrial free-recall task, the subject views a list of words and attempts to recall them. The subject recalls the words in any order, and the same set of words is shown on a series of successive trials. In the course of multitrial free recall, the number of words recalled increases over trials, and the order of words recalled becomes increasingly stereotyped. The increasing organization of words over trials reflects the private and sometimes idiosyncratic manner in which an individual organizes the world.

Another method for examining the idiosyncratic and personal organization of information is the Kelly (1955) repertory grid technique. Organization of cognitive structures is assessed along dimensions generated and used by the subject. This technique is extensively discussed in this volume. Consequently, we will forgo further discussion here.

COGNITIVE ASSESSMENT BATTERIES

The above constructs describing the information processing system merely represent an arbitrary conceptual framework. It allows scientists to think about human cognition. Not all the aforementioned constructs (preattentive versus focal attention, iconic versus short-term memory) are mutually exclusive, and certainly not all-inclusive of the events to be studied. Other hypothesized components of this system exist. Since our interest here is mainly one of applications, further discussion about theoretical components of the system will be set aside. We now turn to the way cognitive assessment is operationalized in a computer-administered testing battery.

THE OHIO BATTERY

The first battery to be discussed is being developed at the Ohio State University in the laboratory of Peter Magaro (Magaro and Ashbrook 1984). A subset of this battery has been designed for use with children by Richard Ashbrook (1985). The battery was designed for use on the Commodore 64 microcomputer. The system consists of 64K of RAM, a Commodore VIC-1541 single disk drive, a Commodore 1526 printer, and a Commodore 1701 color video monitor. This equipment can be purchased for approximately U.S. $1000 at the time of this publication. Software uses CBM BASIC, except for response collection routines that utilize CBM machine code. Standardization for the entire Ohio battery is currently under way.

The Color Distraction Test. The Color Distraction Test is a refinement of the Stroop Color and Word Test (Stroop 1935). The Stroop procedure has been extensively employed in research on personality, psychopathology, and neuropsychology (Golden 1978). The central task involves naming the color of print of a word that designates yet a different color. For example, the letters *RED* might appear in a green-colored display, and the subject responds verbally to the color; in this case the subject says "green." Difficulty in naming the color of a discrepant color-word is the result of interference in verbal processing prior to response organization (Wheeler 1977). In condition 1 (Color Naming), subjects name color patches (red, green, yellow, blue) singly presented on the video monitor. In condition 2 (Color Reading), subjects read color words. For each condition, 6 practice trials and 20 experimental trials are administered. Stimulus presentation activates a timer that is deactivated by the experimenter when the subject emits a response. Duration of the stimulus presentation is contingent on the subject's response, and a 0.5-second inter-trial interval is employed. In the crucial condition 3 (Ignore Word), subjects name the color of a discrepant color word. In condition 4 (Ignore Color), subjects read a color word that is painted in a discrepant color. For each condition, 6 practice trials and 40 experimental trials are administered.

Response data is stored on magnetic floppy disk. Raw data and summary statistics can then be printed. Conditions 3 and 4 are divided into halves, that is, the first 20 trials and the last 20 trials. These are analyzed separately to yield a maintenance attention deterioration index. An interference index is also calculated for each subject by subtracting performance variables on condition 1 from condition 3, and condition 2 from condition 4.

Semantic Categorization Test. The Semantic Categorization Test is derived from a feature comparison model of semantic memory (Smith, Shoben, and Rips 1974). Semantic categorization may require two distinct comparison stages, depending on the nature of the categorization task. An intuitive example demonstrates the actions of the two-stage model. Given the category name *birds,* a subject may be required to respond with a "true" or "false" to whether the word *robin* is an instance of the category. The first stage compares the features of the instance–category pair. No consideration is given here as to whether the similar features are defining or only characteristic. If the featural similarity is very high or very low, one can decide immediately whether or not the instance is subsumed in the category. Thus, decisions of this type are generally quick, and can be construed as holistic or intuitive.

If the featural similarity is intermediate (as in the case of the word *chicken* or *bat*), use of the second stage is required. When the second stage is executed, it isolates the more defining features of the instance and the category. If all the defining features match (chicken and bird), the subject responds with "true," whereas if they do not match (bat and bird), the subject responds with "false." The second stage generally requires a longer time to make a decision. It is construed as logical and analytic in that it considers only defining features.

In this test, 80 instance–category trials are administered. A category name appears on the monitor, and ten instance trials are given for each of eight categories. Words are chosen on the basis of a normative sample's response to naming instances of categories. Of these ten trials, two are true high-frequency words (high likelihood of being an instance), two are true low-frequency words, two are false high-frequency (from another category) words, two are false low-frequency words, one is a semantically related word, and another is a semantically unrelated word.

Dependent measures of this test are the number of correct and incorrect responses and the response times for each type of instance.

Categorized Recall Test. The Categorized Recall Test assesses organization in long-term memory with a multitrial free recall paradigm. The subject views five trials of a 20-word list. The words appear for a duration of 2 seconds in the center of the viewing screen with an inter-trial interval of 1 second. Four categories each containing five words sampled across five levels of production frequency comprise the word list. No word appears in any one serial position more than once, and no two words are adjacent more than once. Immediately after each trial, subjects are given 30 seconds to recall the words aloud. The examiner records on paper the words recalled.

Dependent measures of this test are words correctly recalled by trial, repetitions (words repeated two or more times in a single recall), commission errors (words recalled that were never presented), words recalled by segment of the presentation list (serial order in recall), words recalled within a specific category, and words recalled by production frequency level. In addition, bidirectional inter-trial repetition measure is calculated on each pair of recall trials (Bousfield and Bousfield 1966). This is a measure of subjective organization in memory. The printout also produces a cluster plot for each individual, so that the amount of clustering is easily observed graphically (Table 11.1).

Preattentional processing test. This task follows a forced choice span of apprehension paradigm. In condition 1, 64 visual arrays are created by allocating the letter T or F to one position of an imaginary square matrix of 16 characters. Each target letter, T or F, appears once on two separate arrays in each of the 16 possible matrix positions, yielding a total of 32 T arrays and 32 F arrays. In condition 2, a second set of 64 arrays, 32 with T and 32 with F, contain the target letter plus 7 additional noise letters. In this set of stimulus displays, a target letter appears in one of the possible 16 positions, and then 7 different consonant letters are randomly selected without replacement and randomly allocated to 7 of the 15 remaining positions in the matrix. Subjects view the stimulus for 0.5 seconds, at which time they depress one of two response keys depending on whether a T or an F was displayed. Reaction time and accuracy are recorded.

Encoding style test. This task distinguishes between automatic and controlled visual processing. It is a variation of the Neisser (1963) procedure. Subjects search arrays consisting of 25 five-letter rows for a predesignated target letter. Letters in the array are upper-case character script and appear within a 5 x 25 character matrix. Each row in the

Table 11.1
Output of Analysis of Categorized Recall Test

Categorized Recall Test
(Version 2.2-R. Ashbrook)

Subject Ident.: 12345 Date Tested: 12/11/84
Subject Name: Sample Examiner: Ashbrook

**********SUMMARY DATA**********

TRI	REC	REP	COM	SER1	SER2	SER3	SER4
1	5	0	0	2	0	3	0
2	5	2	1	0	2	1	2
3	7	0	0	1	3	2	1
4	8	0	0	2	2	1	3
5	14	3	0	3	4	4	3

TRI	CAT1	CAT2	CAT3	CAT4	PFR1	PFR2	PFR3	PFR4	PFR5
1	5	0	0	0	1	1	1	1	1
2	5	0	0	0	1	1	1	1	1
3	4	1	1	1	0	4	1	1	1
4	3	1	1	3	3	1	1	2	1
5	4	4	3	3	2	2	4	3	3

**********LEGEND**********

TRI - Recall trial
REC - Number correctly recalled
REP - Repetition errors
COM - Commission errors
SER1 - Serial position 1-5
SER2 - Serial position 5-10
SER3 - Serial position 11-15
SER4 - Serial position 16-20
PFR1 - Number recalled from production frequency level
PFR2 - Number recalled from production frequency level
PFR3 - Number recalled from production frequency level
PFR4 - Number recalled from production frequency level
PFR5 - Number recalled from production frequency level

**********RECALL DATA**********

Trial 1	Trial 2	Trial 3	Trial 4	Trial 5	
Mountain	Mountain	Hill	Mountain	Mountain	
Hill	Hill	Lawyer	Cave	Lake	
Lake	Lake	Ruler	Ditch	Ditch	
Cave	Cave	Wind	Lawyer	Lake	
Ditch	Ditch	Lake	Hammer	Cave	
	Com. Err.*	Cave	Rain	Lawyer	
	Cave	Ditch	Cold	Teacher	
	Ditch		Fog	Nurse	
				Fog	
				Warm	
				Ruler	
				Pencil	Fog
				Glue	Doctor
				Cold	Lawyer

**********PAIR FREQUENCY**********

Trial 1 + 2	2.400
Trial 2 + 3	.285
Trial 3 + 4	.785
Trial 4 + 5	.535-

Table 11.1, Continued

**********CLUSTER PLOT**********

	01	02	03	04	05	06	07	08	09	10	11	12	13	14	15	16	17	18	19	20
1	0	0	1	0	0	0	0	0	0	0	0	0	0	0	0	0	0	0	0	0
2	0	0	0	0	0	0	0	0	0	0	0	0	0	0	0	0	0	0	0	0
3	1	0	0	0	0	0	0	0	0	0	0	0	0	0	0	0	0	0	0	0
4	0	0	0	0	0	0	1	0	0	0	0	0	0	0	0	0	0	0	0	0
5	0	0	1	0	0	0	0	0	0	0	0	0	0	0	0	0	0	0	0	0
6	0	0	0	0	0	0	0	0	0	0	0	0	0	0	0	0	0	0	0	0
7	0	0	0	1	0	0	0	1	0	0	0	0	0	0	0	0	0	0	0	0
8	0	0	0	0	0	0	1	0	1	0	0	0	0	0	0	0	0	0	0	0
9	0	0	0	0	0	0	0	1	0	0	0	0	0	0	0	0	0	0	1	0
10	0	0	0	0	0	0	0	0	0	0	0	0	0	0	0	0	0	0	0	0
11	0	0	0	0	0	0	0	0	0	0	0	0	0	0	0	0	0	0	0	0
12	0	0	0	0	0	0	0	0	0	0	0	0	1	0	0	0	0	0	0	1
13	0	0	0	0	0	0	0	0	0	0	0	1	0	0	1	0	0	0	0	0
14	0	0	0	0	0	0	0	0	0	0	0	0	0	0	0	0	0	0	0	0
15	0	0	0	0	0	0	0	0	0	0	0	0	1	0	0	0	0	1	0	0
16	0	0	0	0	0	0	0	0	0	0	0	0	0	0	0	0	0	0	0	0
17	0	0	0	0	0	0	0	0	0	0	0	0	0	0	0	0	0	0	0	0
18	0	0	0	0	0	0	0	0	0	0	0	0	0	0	1	0	0	0	0	0
19	0	0	0	0	0	0	0	0	1	0	0	0	0	0	0	0	0	0	0	0
20	0	0	0	0	0	0	0	0	0	0	0	1	0	0	0	0	0	0	1	0

25-row array is chosen by first randomly selecting 12 possible target positions. Then, for each successive block of 12 trials, the position of the target is determined by randomly selecting without replacement from the set of 12 positions. Subjects view a total of four trial blocks, or 48 trials. Two types of arrays are used. The target letter is always the letter K. As indicated in Table 11.2, the distractor or context letters can be either rounded (O, C, G, S, Q) or straight-lined (E, V, N, L, I). Subjects depress a response switch upon detecting the target letter.

Each trial block yields a slope statistic, defined as the linear regression between reaction time and position of the target letter in the array. Generally, steeper slopes reflect more serial processing. A second measure is the intercept indicating the overall time required to respond to the task. The rounded distractors encourage an automatic search, whereas the straight-lined distractors encourage a controlled search.

Continuous performance test. This version of the continuous performance test (CPT) is basically the same task as that employed by Erlenmeyer-Kimling and Cornblatt (1978). Unlike the conventional CPT, processing of two stimulus dimensions (suit and number of a playing card) is required. There is a relative rather than an absolute target criterion, and successive matching-to-sample operations must be performed. Thus there is an increased memory load requirement and a degree of complexity not characteristically found in other versions of the CPT. Of interest to us here is the separation of signal discriminability from response bias components of responding. These measures are derived through signal detection theory. Also of interest are the types of errors, such as errors of commission versus errors of omission.

Eighteen array files are constructed, each on an imaginary 3 x 3 character matrix. One numeral between 1 and 9 appears in the upper-right- and lower-left-hand corners of the matrix, and either a graphic character heart or diamond appears in both the upper-left- and lower-right-hand corners of the matrix. Thus, 18 arrays partially resemble a deck of playing cards with numeral values between 1 and 9, across two suits, hearts and diamonds. Subjects view three blocks of 59 trials (or 60 matrices). In 15 trials, the playing card face is identical to that of the previous stimulus marking a target (signal) trial. In another 15 positions, the card face resembles the previous one in number but not in suit, designating a nontarget (noise) trial. The remaining presentations differ in number and in suit from the previous array.

Immediate memory test. This task is a variation of the Sternberg (1966) procedure designed to access short-term memory ability. Briefly,

Table 11.2
Encoding Style Test

Detection of the letter 'K' among rounded distractors encourages automatic processing	Detection of the letter 'K' among straight-lined distractors encourages controlled processing
OUSCQ	LVMZX
UCSOQ	VMZXL
QSCOU	XMZLV
USOQC	VLMZX
CSUQO	ZMLVX
QUSCO	VMXLV
SOQUS	MZLVX
CQSUO	LZVXM
UQOSC	MXZVL
OUSCQ	LVMZX
UCSOQ	VMZXL
QSCOU	XMZLV
UOSQC	VLMKX
CSUQO	ZMLVX
QUSCO	VMXLV
SOQUS	MZLVX
CQSUO	LZVXM
UQOSC	MXZVL
CQSUO	LZVXM
UQOSC	MXZVL
OUSCQ	LVMZX
UCSOQ	VMZXL
QSCKU	XMZLV
UOSQC	VLMZX
CSUQO	ZMKVX
QUSCO	VMXLV
SOQUS	MZLVX
CQSUO	LZVXM
UQOSC	MXZVL
OUSCQ	LVMZX

Source: Compiled by the authors.

the task involves a set of detection trials in which subjects view a 1- to 6-digit array of letters for .5 seconds, followed by a 1.5-second blank screen, after which a box appears that is immediately filled with one target numeral. The subject responds if the target numeral appeared in the original list of digits. Accuracy and reaction time are recorded. A slope measure assesses the performance effects of increasing memory load. An intercept is also calculated to reflect the combination of decision making, response organization, and stimulus encoding.

Recall and recognition tests. A series of other tasks has been developed that assesses recall and recognition ability. These tasks follow a general procedure that involves the appearance of a word list presented at a 2-second viewing rate, followed by a period for free recall or for recognition of the words from a computer-administered list. Recall and recognition require different cognitive operations. While no single cognitive process has been widely accepted to explain this difference (Crowder 1976), several hypotheses have been offered (Anderson and Bower 1973; Tulving and Thomson 1973). In addition to recall and recognition scores, this data can be analyzed using hierarchical clustering techniques to estimate the organization patterns of information in the long-term memory store. Initial work has begun on constructing recall lists in which the content is differentially recalled as a function of diagnostic type. For example, depressives recall more words of depressive content.

Reaction time test. A standard reaction time task is also included in the Ohio Battery. Discussion of this type of task is deferred, since the next section elaborates this measure.

THE NEBRASKA BATTERY

The second battery, known as COGLAB, is being developed at the University of Nebraska–Lincoln in the laboratory of Will Spaulding. early conceptions basic to such a battery were developed at the University of Rochester in the laboratory of Rue Cromwell (Cromwell and Spaulding 1979; Huntzinger and Space 1979; Space 1975; Space and Cromwell 1978; Space and Huntzinger 1979; Spaulding et al. 1981; Spaulding and Space 1979). Standardization data for the COGLAB battery has been collected for nonclinical subjects and severely disordered psychiatric patients (Spaulding and Dras 1985). The battery was designed for use on the Apple II+ or IIe computers. The system consists of 48K RAM, an Apple serial interface card, an Apple language card, an Apple clock (Mountain Hardware), a printer, two Apple disk drives and interface card, a Micromodem (D.C. Hays), a 12-inch black-and-white monitor (Leedex, Inc.), a 19-inch color TV (Sony, Inc.), and a custom-built interface. The total cost of the system is approximately U.S. $6000 at the time of this publication. Two modifications were made to the computer. One of these allows the computer to blank or unblank video displays under program control. The other modification monitors the video synchronization pulse to permit accurate timing of very brief video display presentations. Together, these modifications permit the system to function as a tachistoscope. In addition, a special interface box is connected to the internal Apple II game connector. This interface controls a multifunction subject response console. The technical requirements for these modifications are detailed elsewhere (Spaulding et al. 1981).

Span of apprehension and vigilance test. Span of apprehension and vigilance are measured in COGLAB with a hybridization of the familiar continuous performance test (Kornetsky and Orzack 1978) and a more traditional span paradigm (Neale 1971). The subject watches the monitor for a specified target digit among other digits, and presses a button when it appears. Target and distractor digits appear for 240 msec at the rate of one per second, with a distractor ratio of 4 to 1. In condition 1, targets and distractors are presented one digit at a time. In condition 2, an array of eight digits is presented that may or may not contain the target. In condition 3, the eight-digit arrays are again presented, but the subject responds to a new target digit and ignores the old one. There are ten target digits in each condition. The computer scores hits and false alarms (errors of commission).

Vigilance is defined as the number of hits in condition 1. Span of apprehension is typically defined as the number of hits in condition 2, although general deficit and vigilance effects can be subtracted from span of apprehension by defining span as hits in condition 1 divided by hits in condition 2. Thus, span of apprehension is assumed to reflect the degree to which scanning a multi-element array impairs performance, compared to the one-element array.

Backward masking test. Backward masking, like span of apprehension, is another method for examining preattentional processes or sensory memory. Backward masking is measured in COGLAB by presenting pairs of digits for 32 msec on the video monitor. They are followed by a patterned mask (two *X*'s) of equal duration, with onset asynchronies (SOAs) of 48 or 96 msec. There are 30 stimulus presentations, ten each of the long-SOA mask, the short-SOA mask, and no mask. Apprehension of each digit in the pair is scored separately. The index of backward masking is defined as the degree to which the short-SOA mask decreases performance from the mask condition.

Reaction time test. A single reaction time protocol of 85 trials yields several cognitive measures. These include measures on noninformational distraction, reaction time crossover, reaction time variance, and reaction time anticipatory errors. Noninformational distraction is similar to a time-linked distraction impairment studied by Steffy and Galbraith (1975). A distracting stimulus is presented at the beginning of the preparatory interval (PI) of selected trials. The distractor is a border of *X*'s around the "Get ready" message on the monitor. It occurs on trials whose PI length is 3, 5, or 8 seconds (there are also nondistraction trials for each of these PI lengths). Noninformational distraction is defined as the degree to which reaction time is impaired by the distractor on 8-second PI trials.

Reaction time crossover is measured in COGLAB with a procedure similar to that used by Steffy and Galbraith (1974, 1980). A series of four isotemporal-PI trials of 7 seconds are embedded in the protocol, whose PI lengths otherwise vary randomly. There are five sets of isotemporal-PI trials. Reaction time crossover is defined as the difference in reaction time between the first trials of the sets and the average of the subsequent three trials. Reaction time variance is simply the statistical variance across trials. Anticipatory reaction time errors are those in which the subject lifts his/her finger from the button before the imperative signal.

Concept processing test. The concept processing test in COGLAB is derived from an adaptation of the Wisconsin Card Sorting Test (Fey 1952). The test demands that the subject discern through trial and error three sorting parameters (color, number, and shape). Subjects receive feedback on accuracy for each stimulus sorted. The relevant sorting parameter changes after five correct sorts. Subjects must apprehend the change and modulate sorting strategy.

The test yields two measures of conceptual processing — concept attainment and concept modulation. Concept attainment is defined as the number of errors required to finish the test. Concept modulation is the number of errors attributable to perseverative sorting by a parameter that is no longer the correct one. For example, when the correct parameter changes from color to shape, subsequent sorts using color increment the concept modulation score.

Size estimation test. Size estimation is measured with an adaptation of the traditional size estimation task (Cromwell 1975). Subjects view a figure for 3 seconds, followed 5 seconds later by two comparison figures of different sizes. Subjects indicate by pressing a button which of the figures appears closest in size to the first. The comparison figures are actually equidistant in size from the first, so the task reflects purely the subject's judgment bias. Ten trials are administered. The size estimation index is the number of overestimations minus the number of underestimations.

Mueller-Lyer test. The Mueller-Lyer effect is assessed using the familiar arrow figure. Subjects adjust the familiar arrow figure on the monitor until the arrow shafts appear equal in length. Normal control subjects commit constant errors in this adjustment because they process irrelevant information from the angles of the arrow heads. The measure of the effect is the amount of error produced by the illusion.

COGNITIVE DIFFERENCES IN PSYCHIATRIC GROUPS

Up to this point, we have mainly been interested in establishing a context in which to view the role of cognitive assessment. In the preceding section, two rather comprehensive computer-administered systems for cognitive assessment were described. The critical question, however, has yet to be considered: Can microcomputer-administered cognitive assessment be beneficially applied to clinical psychology and psychiatry? To answer this question, we will now describe some studies that have revealed differences among clinical groups that are important to the conceptual understanding of psychological disorders. These studies are not intended to provide a comprehensive review of cognitive differences among the psychiatric population. Rather, a sample of studies is presented that is mainly from our laboratories where the computerized assessment systems, or their partially automated forerunners, have been used. Thus, by reviewing differences in cognitive functioning across a broad range of clinical psychopathologies, we hope to demonstrate the benefit of the cognitive assessment approach.

DIFFERENCES AMONG PERSONALITY STYLES

College students who endorsed the compulsive and the hysteric personality styles were discriminated on the basis of their performance on the encoding style test (Magaro, Smith, and Ashbrook 1983). Hysterics had greater difficulty performing the search task than did compulsive or control subjects. They took a longer time to detect and process a target and missed the target more often, even though they processed the stimulus field in a careful and serial fashion. Hysterics seemed to have great difficulty focusing on specific elements in a stimulus field, even though they attempted a careful search. These results supported the clinical observation of Shapiro (1965) and Horowitz (1976), who described the cognitive process of the hysteric as impressionistic and lacking in sharp focus of attention.

The encoding style test was also employed in a group of criminal offenders who endorsed the psychopathic personality style (Ashbrook 1982). Primary psychopaths (those who are characterized by low anxiety and guilt) preferred the serial approach even when task conditions encouraged a more automatic or global strategy, thereby supporting the observations of others who find these individuals inflexible with changing task demands (Gorenstein 1982; Painting 1961).

Schizotypal college students, who were administered the complete COGLAB battery, revealed three types of information-processing deficits (Spaulding and Dras 1985). Controls included psychiatric patients and nonschizotypal students with elevations on other symptom scales. One type of deficit, measured by the backward masking test, indicated that schizotypal subjects' rate of sensory translation was slow, or that the presence of a mask disrupted further processing. This replicates the findings of several independent studies (Balogh and Merritt 1985). Schizotypal subjects' performance on other preattentional measures was not impaired. This suggested a fairly isolated deficit, possibly one that is a marker of some other factor, such as neurophysiological deficit. Schizotypal individuals also made more anticipatory errors and more errors of commission on the stress condition of the reaction time test. In signal detection terms, they appeared to use an overly sensitive response bias, as if compensating for their preattentional deficit. A third type of deficit in schizotypes was concept formation on the concept-processing test. It seemed that the concept deficit in this group resulted from a relatively specific concept manipulation problem without generalized performance deficit.

DIFFERENCES AMONG PSYCHIATRIC DISORDERS

A series of investigations by Peter Magaro (Chamrad 1982; Magaro and Chamrad 1983; Pic'l, Magaro, and Wade 1979) have emphasized information-processing strategies, rather than cognitive deficits, in paranoid and nonparanoid schizophrenics. One of these using the encoding style test demonstrated that nonparanoids prefer global, parallel, and automatic search strategies. In contrast, paranoid schizophrenics prefer serial, controlled, and sequential encoding (Chamrad 1982). This line of research has led to the specification of cognitive style in these two disorders and the relation of this style to symptom expression, psychosis, and hemispheric laterality (Magaro 1980, 1984).

The cognitive assessment battery has also been applied to childhood psychopathology. Ashbrook (1985), using the color distraction test, the semantic categorization test, and the categorized recall test, studied groups of hyperactive (attention deficit disorder), aggressive, and combined hyperactive/aggressive children. Only the purely hyperactive group exhibited a selective attention deficit, as assessed by errors on the color distraction test. Thus, there was evidence of an information-processing difference between the three groups, which was mainly distinguishable on the basis of a particular cognitive function. A recall deficit was found on the categorized recall test. Only the combined hyperactive/aggressive children exhibited this deficit, which seemed related to a problem in rehearsal strategies. The important point here is that the multi-task battery permitted the discovery of particular cognitive processing deficits that were unique to each group studied.

THE PSYCHOPATHOLOGY LABORATORY IN A PSYCHIATRIC SETTING

Over the past five years the Nebraska group has introduced working cognitive psychopathology laboratories into psychiatric inpatient and outpatient settings. The technological aspects of this endeavor have been discussed elsewhere (Spaulding et al. 1981; Spaulding, Crinean, and Martin 1983), as have its theoretical foundations and relation to treatment and rehabilitation (Spaulding, in press; Spaulding et al. 1986). Discussion here will focus on the conceptual and practical prerequisites of establishing such laboratories.

Guiding the development of the projects were three potential benefits of broad-scale applied psychopathology. These benefits are: (1) treatment and other services within a service system can be more systematically planned, coordinated, and delivered; (2) applied psychopathology promotes objectivity and accountability in service systems, at both clinical and administrative levels; and (3) systematic data collection and analysis help to identify gaps in psychosocial services programs, and they promote development of new services, new methods, and new ideas about psychopathology.

To realize these benefits, a broad view of the psychiatric patient was taken. Such a view calls for the integration of information across the spectrum of psychiatric services. Likewise, input is necessary from nearly every professional and paraprofessional discipline. To accommodate this need, the Nebraska group conceptualized the patient within a five-fold framework of functioning. Among these are psychophysiological, perceptual-attentional, cognitive, microsocial, and macrosocial functioning. This chapter has focused nearly exclusively on perceptual-attentional and cognitive functioning, and by now the reader is hopefully assured of their potential in psychiatric assessment.

The assumption of this multilevel analysis is that different levels of functioning bidirectionally influence others (Fig. 11.2). Consequently, it is necessary to consider an individual across several domains of functioning. The psychophysiological domain includes any directly measurable activity of the central or autonomic nervous system. The microsocial level includes behaviors observable in social settings. Psychiatric symptoms are among the most prominent behaviors at this level of analysis. Macrosocial behaviors are those occurring in the larger context of society and social relations. Vocational, social, or educational skills are examples of these. The relationship among levels of functioning, disciplines, and interventions is diagrammatically represented in Figure 11.2. Recommendations across levels of functioning are generated according to a set of intervention priorities.

The potential power of this rehabilitation model can be attributed to three factors. First, assessment occurs across all levels of functioning. Second, these data can be easily managed by a central computerized data file from which multidisciplinary treatment teams can generate interventions. And third, the system permits feedback on interventions and assessments to guide future treatments and research.

INTERPRETING COGNITIVE DEFICITS AS PSYCHOPATHOLOGY

At a time when computers are being applied to measure cognitive deficits in psychopathology, it is especially important to be aware of issues in interpreting the data of these batteries. As the field of psychopathology has moved ahead — certainly not in close relationship with the advances in cognitive measures — the issues are many.

Consider the simplest case. Consider the measurement of a single variable that is found to be deviant in a given pathological group as compared with other groups. For example, assume a particular cognitive

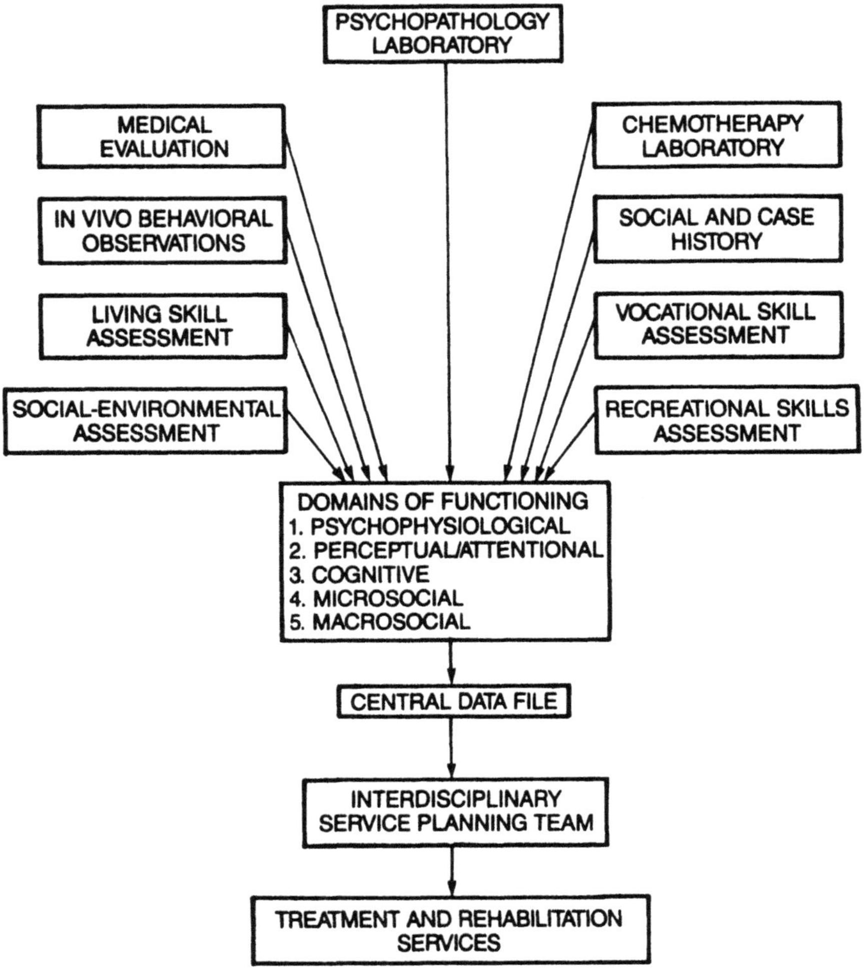

Fig. 11.2.
Multilevel analysis and the multidisciplinary team.

deficit has been found in schizophrenics. One impulse is to assume immediately that if such a difference is found, a characteristic of that pathological group has been identified — but not so fast!

Maher (1974) has emphasized that a deficit on a given task does not necessarily mean that a deficit in cognitive ability has been identified. Most tasks are readily assumed to be multiply determined. Thus, a profile of performance on multiple measures is ordinarily necessary. This permits the exploration of a differential deficit that is a greater loss in one ability than in one or more other abilities.

A major contribution in recent years has been the methodological elaboration by Chapman and Chapman (1973, 1978) in separating specific (differential) deficits from generalized deficits. They emphasized the artifactual effect of inferring specific deficit from performance on tasks that have been unmatched for discriminating power. The degree of inferiority of a performance score depends, among other things, on the specific deficit in the individual, the generalized deficit that is not unique to the specific pathology in question, and the psychometric properties of the task measure. Tasks that are unmatched with respect to the true score variance can lead to erroneous conclusions about a differential deficit. If a group of pathological subjects are equally inferior to normal subjects on two tasks, and if the tests to measure these two abilities differ in discriminating power, then the artifact described by the Chapmans is best illustrated. A greater performance deficit will be measured on the more discriminating of the two tasks.

Having described the issues of separating specific from generalized deficit, we now turn to some of the instances where one can go overboard in applying them. The first instance is when the psychopathological group is so poorly defined that the precise work of separating specific from generalized deficits is of questionable value. This especially applies to the differential deficits attributable to schizophrenia as opposed to the other functional psychotic disorders. While the advances in operational definition with DSM-III have greatly increased reliable interobserver discrimination of schizophrenia from many other disorders, its separation in particular from affective psychosis remains problematic. The activity of separating specific from generalized deficit under these conditions of vague diagnostic constructs would therefore seem of questionable value. The major problem presently is in refining of constructs used for grouping rather than in applying sophisticated criteria to comparisons after tenuous groups have been formed. This does not imply a shortcoming in the Chapman and Chapman contribution;

indeed, it implies that the Chapman and Chapman contribution is ahead of its time.

Knight (1984) proposed four research strategies that may be exempt from the Chapmans' psychometric artifact problem. The first strategy seeks to demonstrate the adequacy of a pathological group's abilities in particular stages or processes. Both pathological and control groups are required to achieve a predicted pattern of performance, either across the levels of a well-validated task or across a number of theoretically integrated tasks that have been demonstrated to measure various aspects of a process. If both groups perform according to specific predictions of the model, the argument for adequate functioning on the cognitive function is strengthened.

The second strategy calls for the design of experiments in which the deficiency of a clinical group's processing predicts their superiority of performance on a task relative to the performance of a nonclinical group. When superior performance of the pathological group is demonstrated relative to decremental performance of a control group, the effect then cannot be easily explained by generalized deficit or unmatched discriminating power. Knight's third strategy, a variation of the procedure just described, requires relative rather than absolute performance superiority by a clinical group. Relative superiority is still susceptible to a psychometric artifact. An understanding of a particular cognitive function in terms of the effects of task variations on performance can produce, across studies, a pattern of relatively superior or inferior performance that would be inconsistent with a general deficit.

A fourth strategy proposed that the predicted cognitive deficit would be observable across paradigms. In this way, the likelihood is reduced that the particular pattern of results predicted by the specific deficit model across paradigms will coincide with differential task or condition discriminability. The multiparadigmatic approach can be buttressed by choosing reliable tasks, in that the performance of a psychopathological population closely replicates the predicted performance pattern commonly observed on the task.

It will be noted that Knight's four instances are all focused on the testing of hypothetically deduced models not concerned with ability constructs, specific or generalized. That this latter distinction is important in certain research questions and not in others is the next matter to be addressed here.

Another research area that enjoys immunity from the generalized deficit problem is the study of task strategy. Task strategy refers to the plan used to solve a task or achieve a given goal. It is assumed that more than one alternative strategy usually exists. Choice of strategy may be limited by the ability structure, but strategies do not lend themselves to a simple dimension of correct/incorrect. Some strategies are better for some purposes; others are better for other purposes. Task strategies of paranoid and nonparanoid schizophrenic individuals have been extensively studied by Magaro and his co-workers (Magaro 1980, 1981, 1984). Construing task strategy in terms of specific versus generalized deficit appears to be unfounded.

DESCRIPTIVE PSYCHOPATHOLOGY VERSUS PSYCHOPATHOGENESIS

A major thrust of the present commentary is that research to advance knowledge about psychopathology falls into two natural categories: (1) to describe precisely the characteristics of pathological groups one from the other, and from normally functioning individuals, and (2) to describe the course and the influences on the course of a disorder. The former depends primarily on a group comparisons approach; the latter depends primarily on a predictive approach. The former concerns the accurate description of a specific pathology to the exclusion of both normals and other pathologies. The latter concerns pathogenesis within a single population regardless of whether this same pathogenesis occurs to any degree in other populations. Also, the latter depends more heavily on correlational techniques to study a singly defined parent population. Clearly, some research designs incorporate both purposes, but the problem of separating one purpose from the other is trivial. A major problem in the application of the Chapman and Chapman criteria (1973) has been the failure to recognize (a) that these two purposes are separate, (b) that the variables relevant to descriptive psychopathology are not necessarily the same as those relevant to pathogenesis, and (c) that the Chapman and Chapman criteria apply only to the problems of descriptive psychopathology.

APPENDIX

Additional information on the COGLAB computer programs can be obtained from Will Spaulding, Department of Psychology, University of Nebraska–Lincoln, 209 Burnett Hall, University of Nebraska, Lincoln, NE 68588-0308. Additional information on the Ohio Battery can be obtained from Richard M. Ashbrook, Department of Psychology, Capital University, Columbus, OH 43209-2394; or from Peter A. Magaro, Department of Psychology, 1885 Neil Hall, Ohio State University, Columbus, OH 43210-110. The corresponding address of Rue L. Cromwell is University of Rochester, 300 Crittendon Boulevard, Rochester, NY 14842.

12 Latent Variable Methods for Analyzing Grid Structures

Robert M. Pruzek

During the past 20 years, a wide variety of methods have been employed for analyzing rep grid data structures. All of the standard multivariate methods have been used, including multidimensional scaling, cluster analysis, principal component analysis, and common factor analysis (Adams-Webber and Mancuso 1983; Shaw 1981). With the exception of common factor analysis, however, the most frequently used methods are not model-based; that is, from the point of view of specialists in multivariate analysis, they are purely descriptive methods, mostly of an ad hoc nature. Although common factor analysis is a latent variable, model-based method, it appears to be the least used method of all in rep grid research.

George Kelly's central thesis was that a person may be viewed as a scientist, with his or her own (subjective) theories, hypotheses, evidence, and interpretations. Repertory grid methods were developed initially by Kelly, as a means "to examine and bring into awareness the conceptual system built and held by an individual" (Shaw 1981: 9). Thus grids were intended chiefly by Kelly to make inferences about personal construct systems from which individuals seek to predict or control the events with which they are involved. Given the central role of "science" in this theoretical system, it is especially unharmonious that the most frequently used methods for analysis of rep grids do not evolve from the most fully developed scientific methods for inference and prediction. To the extent to which rep grid methods — or their underlying assumptions — are inadequate (or unexamined) for their intended purposes, their use is likely to distort or misrepresent the underlying constructs the grid is intended to illuminate.

Rep grid researchers often acknowledge the handicaps posed by the limitations of using ad hoc structural analytic methods. Yet, there seems to be a widespread, though mostly tacit belief among such researchers that model-based multivariate methods are either inappropriate or impractical for analysis of the small and complex arrays that usually arise in rep grid applications. Although there are indeed reasons for skepticism, depending on the context of application, it is a major premise of this chapter that formal, latent variable methods for structural analysis can be viable for rep grid research, and that their use could offer numerous benefits, compared with the most frequently used methods.

The major purpose of this chapter is to demonstrate and discuss latent variable methods for structural analysis of rep grids, methods that provide both concepts and mechanisms for inference. The primary focus is on specialized methods of common factor analysis that are appropriate for small sample applications. Although it is widely believed that factor analysis cannot or should not be applied when sample sizes are small, recent work has shown this assessment to be overly pessimistic. Examples and simulation results are used to demonstrate the possible virtues of using common factor methods for small sample analyses, even when the number of variables exceeds the number of individuals.

In the following sections we shall examine a number of issues: First, the basic assumptions underlying use of exploratory common factor analysis are identified. Next, an illustrative example is used to describe a particular method of analysis that is suited to small sample applications. After the illustration the larger question of factor interpretation and inference is discussed. Then a small simulation study is reported to provide evidence on the broader applicability of such methods. Finally, this chapter contains a brief examination of certain extensions of this methodology as a means for elaborating and refining the basis for inferences about personal constructs.

BASIC ASSUMPTIONS

As a basis for rep grid analysis, common factor theory seems compelling for a variety of reasons. Most notably, this theory is founded on assumptions about data that are usually tenable for rep grids. The first assumption is that individual data records, or scores, are usually fallible. More precisely, scores are taken to be fallible in the context of what is termed an *additive model*. For most social or behavioral data this implies that, taken in isolation, one generally should not regard individual data points as either meaningful or interpretable. It follows that in the presence of fallible observations, *investigators should limit their aims to examinations of the general structural relations* among variables. For this purpose, both descriptive and inferential uses of common factor analysis are promising.

A second, related assumption underlying common factor models is that the common parts of manifest scores are a (linear) function of a *relatively small number* of underlying "common" factor variables; the common factors, and hence the common parts of variables, are necessarily unobservable. Such putative factors, it should be stressed, are *purely* theoretical — part of a formal analytical model. As such, even though typically modified with the adjective "common," one may quite reasonably assume that such factors are specific or unique to a single person's grid. Common factors may thus be construed as intervening variables, organizing principles, or perhaps personal (meta)constructs, when considered in the context of analyzing data from a particular respondent, one who has generated his or her grid on the basis of specific instructions. One need not assume that such underlying variables are common to any other grids, whether these are obtained from other persons or from the same respondent in a different context at a different time.

One can amplify the latter point with respect to prototypical rep grid analyses by noting that several aspects of the task of generating a grid entail considerable uncertainty about what a respondent has produced. Thus, an investigator will usually be wise to consider the mode of structural analysis as more or less exploratory. It follows that the more highly developed (confirmatory) structural analytic models, such as those frequently associated with the work of statisticians (Joreskog 1978), will usually be less well suited to analyses of individual rep grids than will exploratory common factor methods. However, the prospects for confirmatory analyses will be briefly assessed in the final section.

Reviews of research show that rep grid investigators generally grant the appropriateness of some form of multivariate "descriptive" method, especially those that produce row or column clusters (Shaw 1981). Although cluster analysis and interpretation usually entail the use of analytic processes that are analogous to those used in common factor analysis, the interpretation of cluster results depends on assumptions and techniques that by their nature are more restrictive than are their common factor analogues. Both principal component and cluster methods generally make no explicit allowances for data unreliability, and thus implicitly assume that data are wholly dependable. Multidimensional scaling methods also typically make no provisions for errors in the variables. Cluster methods in particular usually involve the assumption that structures are fully hierarchical. Common factor methods, and their superordinate structural analytic forms, make allowances for unreliability and do not require a structural hierarchy. It is also worth noting that the often-cited advantage of principal component analysis over common factor analysis — that components are wholly "determinant" but common factors are "indeterminant" — is illusory. McDonald (1979) discusses this point at length. (For elaboration of these points see Gorsuch 1974; Mardia, Kent, and Bibby 1979; or Seber 1984; for a comparison of cluster and principal component methods see Rump 1974 and Slater 1974.)

Of course, the above does not represent an argument in favor of the universal appropriateness of common factor theory or methods for rep grid analysis. Rather, the claim is that if a grid analyst finds purely *descriptive* (i.e., non-model-based) multivariate methods (including, especially, cluster and principal component methods) compelling or useful in a given context, he or she is likely to find some form of multivariate model-based method, especially its assumptions and mechanisms for inference, to be even more compelling or useful in the same context. Despite the general advocacy in this chapter of one class of analytic structural methods, it should be clear that in a given context of application, several different methods may serve complementary, not competitive, purposes. Justifications of methods based on abstract theoretical analyses alone are just as apt to be naive and misleading as the use of methods that have not been analyzed theoretically. The ultimate goal is to contribute to the understanding of substantive phenomena through the use of methods whose assumptions are appropriate in the context of their application.

In an attempt to avoid unnecessary abstractions and to direct the discussion toward rep grid applications, the next section will provide an illustrative analysis of a two-way array. Attention will be given to theoretical issues — in terms of both psychometric and statistical canons — as well as to issues of practicality — in terms of the efficiency and utility of computing algorithms. Considerations of accessibility of methods become especially important if they are to be applied interactively and conveniently on personal computers. In discussing theory, a major point will be made of the role of prior, or a priori, information in multivariate structural analyses.

AN ILLUSTRATIVE EXAMPLE

Suppose the 15 x 15 matrix of data in table 12.1 represents results of a rep grid elicitation in which, say, all bipolar scales were defined in terms of a five-point continuum. (In fact, these data were generated using a specific simulation model, a point that will be ignored for the moment.) One might conveniently view the columns as associated with constructs, the rows with elements.

Given the numbers in Table 12.1, our first objective is strictly numerical analysis; the aim is to learn whether some relatively simple — even simplistic — structure can be used to describe relations among columns of this array of fallible data. This aim closely parallels the goals

Table 12.1
Raw Data for Illustrative Example

Variable (Construct)														
1	2	3	4	5	6	7	8	9	10	11	12	13	14	15
3.	3.	1.	3.	3.	5.	4.	4.	3.	4.	4.	2.	3.	1.	4.
2.	5.	4.	2.	3.	2.	2.	2.	4.	3.	4.	3.	4.	3.	3.
2.	1.	2.	4.	3.	3.	2.	3.	4.	5.	2.	2.	3.	1.	4.
4.	1.	4.	3.	1.	1.	1.	1.	5.	3.	4.	2.	2.	3.	2.
1.	1.	1.	1.	3.	2.	3.	2.	3.	1.	2.	2.	3.	5.	3.
1.	3.	3.	1.	2.	1.	3.	2.	5.	5.	3.	3.	3.	1.	3.
1.	1.	3.	2.	1.	3.	2.	3.	2.	2.	4.	1.	4.	4.	4.
2.	1.	1.	1.	3.	1.	2.	1.	1.	1.	3.	2.	1.	1.	2.
1.	1.	1.	1.	4.	4.	2.	4.	2.	4.	4.	3.	5.	5.	5.
4.	3.	3.	3.	2.	4.	3.	2.	3.	1.	1.	3.	3.	3.	3.
2.	2.	2.	3.	2.	5.	2.	2.	2.	3.	2.	1.	5.	5.	3.
3.	3.	4.	3.	5.	5.	5.	5.	4.	4.	3.	4.	2.	2.	2.
5.	4.	3.	4.	5.	4.	4.	4.	3.	2.	2.	1.	2.	2.	3.
2.	1.	3.	2.	4.	1.	3.	1.	4.	1.	2.	3.	5.	3.	5.
2.	2.	2.	4.	5.	5.	4.	4.	5.	4.	5.	5.	1.	1.	1.

Source: Compiled by the author.

of conventional cluster and principal component analyses, which take into account nothing more than the numbers in such tables. Since content information will not be supplied in this example, all interpretations will be devoid of content references. In any event, subsequent discussion will note the principal limitations and caveats associated with method-based interpretations.

Starting from the 15 variables (columns) of Table 12.1, the matrix of Pearson product-moment correlations was computed. (The appendix at the end of this chapter contains a brief technical discussion of the relative merits and limitations of correlational methods for structural analysis of rep grids, compared with methods based on Euclidean distance measures that have become common in rep grid applications.) Table 12.2 displays the correlation matrix and its eigenvalues. The common factor model that was chosen for use in this context is based on the assumption that all population communalities (or uniqueness variances), for the different variables, are equal.[1] Communalities generally index the variances of the common parts of each of the variables, whereas uniqueness variances index the variances of the residual or "noncommon" parts. When an analysis commences from a matrix of correlations, each variable's total variance is unity of 1. By using a model that specifies only one communality or uniqueness parameter to estimate, the number of parameters is reduced by $p - 1$ (for p variables), in comparison to conventional common factor methods, for any value of m (the number of factors).

Whittle (1952) is responsible for the original common factor model used in this analysis. The algorithm is noniterative, and requires only the eigenvalues and corresponding eigenvectors of the matrix of correlations. Starting from the matrix of correlations, the algorithm was used to generate two matrices of factor coefficients. Columns (factors) of each of these were then transformed analytically using an orthogonal rotation algorithm based on a "simple structure" criterion to generate three and then four factor solutions. Table 12.3 presents only the four-factor solution, since this matrix suggested a somewhat simpler analysis and interpretation. Communality estimates (row sums of squares of the factor matrix) are given in the column labeled h^2. The average value of the communalities, taken across these 15 variables, equals 0.599; were these to be actual rep grid data, this result could be used to infer that the constructs had been rated or assessed with an average reliability *no less than* 0.60. Communality in the framework of classical test theory provides a lower bound to reliability; the bound may be regarded as a "close estimate" of reliability when the domain of variables (constructs) is sufficiently well sampled (McDonald 1979).

Table 12.2
Matrix of Intercorrelations for Columns of Table 12.1 and Corresponding Eigenvalues

Variable

	1	2	3	4	5	6	7	8	9	10	11	12	13	14	15
1	1.00														
2	.41	1.00													
3	.39	.44	1.00												
4	.65	.25	.27	1.00											
5	.16	.24	-.12	.26	1.00										
6	.24	.27	-.17	.57	.39	1.00									
7	.27	.43	.02	.32	.70	.54	1.00								
8	.12	.28	-.08	.41	.59	.79	.66	1.00							
9	.16	.24	.55	.34	.12	-.15	.21	.03	1.00						
10	-.17	.16	.04	.26	.12	.31	.12	.51	.46	1.00					
11	-.26	.00	.00	-.06	.05	.08	-.06	.29	.20	.43	1.00				
12	-.12	.15	.15	.04	.50	.14	.43	.26	.55	.30	.34	1.00			
13	-.40	-.09	-.02	-.31	-.24	.00	-.34	-.15	-.23	-.03	-.19	-.26	1.00		
14	-.27	-.26	-.07	-.36	-.27	.04	-.38	-.17	-.39	-.37	-.16	-.32	.67	1.00	
15	-.29	-.21	-.22	-.28	-.10	-.08	-.21	-.02	-.29	-.03	-.22	-.33	.80	.36	1.00

The Vector (D_2) of Eigenvalues of R

1	2	3	4	5	6	7	8	9	10	11	12	13	14	15
4.58	2.38	2.06	1.57	1.23	.88	.75	.48	.33	.27	.21	.19	.07	.00	.00

Source: Derived from data in Table 12.1.

Table 12.3
Rotated Factor Coefficients Matrix for Whittle CFA Solution

	Factor			
	1	2	3	h^2
1	.23	-.35	-.41	.70
2	.30	-.08	.05	.43
3	-.23	-.05	.11	.64
4	.45	-.24	-.07	.56
5	.66	-.25	.16	.53
6	.82	.08	.01	.69
7	.71	-.31	.10	.63
8	.83	.00	.28	.77
9	-.11	-.26	.54	.67
10	.26	.06	.68	.56
11	.02	-.12	.63	.44
12	.20	-.32	.61	.52
13	-.10	.87	-.04	.77
14	-.14	.63	-.26	.52
15	.00	.74	-.10	.58

Source: Compiled by the author.

For an orthogonal solution based on a matrix of correlation coefficients (as distinct from covariances), one can properly interpret factor coefficients as correlations between the original variables and the derived, but latent, factors. (Although superficially equivalent to their principal component analogues, such common factor coefficients tend not to reflect "self-correlations." Principal component counterparts of these coefficients are generally inflated to the extent that each composite/component is defined by variables with which it is correlated. Also, row sums of squares of coefficient matrices in PC analysis are not properly interpreted as reliabilities.) One can also interpret common factor coefficients like these as least-square regression weights for estimating the variables from the factors (not the reverse).

Given these facts, and the relatively small number of middle-sized coefficients, it should be clear that columns of the factor matrix in Table 12.3 admit to a fairly simple interpretation. The four column factors suggest four more or less independent variable clusters: the subsets correspond to variables 1–4, 5–8, 9–12, and 13–15. Only variables (rows of factor matrix, columns of original array) 1, 4, and 9 seem to have complexity greater than 1 (that is, to load highly on more than one factor).

Factor *score* estimates can serve as a further aid in the interpretation of factors or as device for "data reduction," especially when the factors are both orthogonal and more or less simple in form. Table 12.4 displays such score estimates for these four factors.[2] Rows of such a matrix — corresponding, say, to elements for a rep grid — provide a succinct expression of the similarities and differences among the "reliable parts" of the original observations. For factor interpretation using factor scores, the simplest procedure is to rank-order the rows (elements) based on the positive and negative scores for each factor, and to base one's interpretation on the relevant differences between the elements at the extremes of the ordering. When the factors are orthogonal, there should generally be no systematic association between different factor score variables; plots of such column coefficients can be used to help assess the viability of the linearity assumptions underlying the factor model.

Table 12.4
Factor Score Estimates for Rotated Whittle Factors

	Factor			
	1	2	3	4
1	1.29	.12	.12	-.28
2	-.78	.63	.82	1.22
3	.08	.25	.33	.20
4	-1.92	-.71	.11	1.20
5	-.32	-.12	-.64	-1.42
6	-1.11	-.07	1.53	.33
7	-.44	1.06	-.12	-.42
8	-.88	-2.02	-1.06	-2.04
9	.77	1.72	.89	-1.45
10	.04	-.16	-1.43	.91
11	.26	1.31	-.93	.07
12	1.41	-.55	.62	.74
13	1.31	-.53	-1.63	1.13
14	-.70	.76	-.16	.20
15	.98	-1.69	1.55	-.40

Source: Compiled by the author.

Numerous other graphical systems may also be effective in displaying row (element) features. It should be noted that in relation to standard hierarchical cluster methods, the points (in m-space) corresponding to elements' factor scores are not generally constrained to be hierarchically related to one another.

Factor score estimates (Table 12.4) together with factor coefficients (Table 12.3), provide a synthetic device for fitting the original observations (Table 12.1). (Actually, one fits the standardized score values that correspond to the array of raw scores [see Note 2].) When the data from this example were fitted, two of these rows (3 and 14) stood out as yielding residual values of relatively high magnitude. (If a multivariate normal sampling model is tenable, then the sums of squares of such row residual values can be assumed to follow the form of a chi-squared distribution with known degrees of freedom.) When this type of finding occurs, one should ask whether, for the model that has been used, the poorly fitted row(s) seem in retrospect to be fundamentally different, or to correspond to a different domain, compared to the other rows vis-à-vis content considerations. Given any such tentative common factor model to account for the original observations, an investigator should assess the model for its constructive value in describing and making inferences from the data, as well as for its inadequacies (in the framework of all its assumptions). Special attention should be given to judging the number of factors; for this purpose eigenvalue plots, or scree tests, are likely to be especially useful (Gorsuch 1974). But initial judgments are more likely to need revision when samples are small and when reanalyses are employed.

Reanalysis of the culled form of the original array (excluding the poorly fitting rows 3 and 14) yielded essentially the same pattern of factor coefficients, except that they tended to be larger, and the residual correlations (associated with lack of fit) were about 20 percent smaller. It seems reasonable to conclude that these four factor clusters would constitute a sound starting point for content interpretations, had these been actual rep grid data, conditional, of course, on the basic assumptions of the common factor model. Recall that communality estimates, when based on a "sound" estimate of the number of factors, provide quantitative evidence for deciding how reliably these constructs have been assessed. Comparisons of the (average) communalities across grids is likely to be of special assistance in some areas of grid research. To wit, one should be especially cautious about interpreting grid structures when average communalities are quite small (say, less than .5).

On the other hand, interpretations may be more confidently expressed when reliabilities are inferred to be relatively high (say, when the average communality exceeds 0.65). Again, communality estimates are always strongly conditional on the number of factors.

With samples as small as those in this illustration, one will often have to give up reliable information about the relative magnitudes, or even rank orders, of communalities within grids. Moreover, when *n* is small, single rows will generally have a relatively strong effect on the structural information about a set of columns; thus it may be useful routinely to see how communalities and structural results differ in a series of leave-out-one-row analyses. This implies the need for computer programs that facilitate convenient interactive reanalyses.

In choosing to perform a linear model analysis like this, one must be aware that any systematic nonlinear information among the columns will necessarily be ignored, or perhaps distorted. Although the Whittle method is the most parsimonious of all fully exploratory common factor methods, in terms of the number of parameters being estimated for a given number of factors, the procedure does not provide for variation among putative "population" communalities. However limiting such a procedure may be, it is a central principle that inferential forms of multivariate statistical analysis require that the number of parameters being estimated be kept to the barest minimum when samples are small.

SOME BROADER ISSUES OF STRUCTURAL INTERPRETATION

Perhaps the central question in rep grid contexts is whether clusters (or more generally, factors) such as those identified in the above example constitute a sound basis for structural interpretations. And under what conditions? The answers to such questions have been debated at length in the factor analytic literature, and space permits only a terse summary of that debate. The key point made by "rationalists" is summarized as follows: If one has a priori information — necessarily based on prior (psychological) theory, content considerations, or independently collected data — to provide a target pattern for the factor coefficients, and if one's data are found to conform strongly to this pattern, then the prior information demands due recognition in substantive theory construction (Rozeboom 1966: 291).

Although target patterns need not in principle be "simply structured," there are strong arguments growing out of the work of Jennrich (1973) for using relatively simple forms. In particular, Jennrich has shown that when population factor matrices are simply structured, sample factor coefficients will exhibit much less statistical variation when population values are estimated, than when population factor patterns are complex. This point is a corollary of the above-mentioned point concerning model parsimony: that is, when a population factor system can be simply portrayed — so that its idealized form has numerous zeros — then the number of parameters under estimation when sampling from this population will be reduced to the number of non-null factor coefficients. Of course, interpretations of either sample or population matrices will also tend to be simplified when construct–factor associations are portrayed by relatively simple structures.

For the most part (but of course, not always), if the basic methodological assumptions are not met, then the data will not conform to the preconceived pattern. In many such cases, including the above illustration as noted, there will be evidence that only some parts (here, rows) of the original array do not conform to a simple pattern. When this occurs, one may wish to eliminate, or at least "downweight" some observations to reduce their influence. Also, there may be advantages to weighting constructs differentially by performing analyses on rescaled correlation or covariance matrices (Pruzek and Rabinowitz 1981).

Further, one may reexamine the data after having applied say, nonlinear transformations to some variables (as when logarithms or square roots are used to reduce skewedness). Seen in the context of such possibilities, the restrictiveness of linear association measures (like product-moment correlations) — and indeed of linear models generally — can be seen as much less limiting than first appearances would suggest. When such operations are performed, the key point is to make explicit in reporting that the models were not fitted to the original, unmodified data. One of the major changes in data analytic practice in the last several years is the recognition that model-based analyses generally require interactive or iterative strategies (not just algorithms) to be broadly effective. (Alas, the same cannot be said of theoretical analysis of statistical inferential problems.)

In the present case of the data in Table 12.1, nothing has been said about an a priori pattern; and the method used a blind simple structure transformation procedure so that no a priori pattern was implied. But in fact the data in Table 12.1 were generated using a simulation factor model for which four disjoint, orthogonal clusters defined the population factor coefficients.[3] The simulation population factor matrix is given as that of

Population B in Table 12.6. In rep grid applications one would ordinarily construct a target pattern analogous to this, using prior theory. The magnitudes of the numbers in the target array are not crucial; it is rather their pattern that matters. Note that if one goes through such a process and determines that some variables (constructs) are essentially independent of all the rest — with respect to the elements under consideration — this would be evidence that one or more grid constructs should be added to the set to help ensure identification of extant structures. Alternatively, such constructs could be eliminated. The relevant finding from theoretical research on factor problems is that latent structures cannot even be uniquely defined, much less recovered, unless there are at least three (substantial sized) loadings on each factor *in the population*. Four or more such loadings are desirable. It follows that construct sets should be composed or assembled with special thought as to how they collectively sample the construct domain, as conceived using prior theory. (Some rep grid researchers have shown how prior data and theory can be used to generate specific structural hypotheses; for an example, see Rathod [1983: sections 3 and 4].) In some cases, of course, prior information will take the form of another person's, perhaps an expert's, grid. Or, the prior information could derive from a "modal" grid based on analyses of several other grids. Factor theory provides no guidance on issues of context.

A matrix of congruence coefficients, alternatively called *direction cosines*, was computed to quantify the association between columns of this population factor matrix (see Table 12.6) and columns of the sample factor matrix of Table 12.3. These congruence values are presented in Table 12.5; rows correspond to sample factors, whereas columns index population factors. Their pattern (see underlined values in Table 12.5), together with visual inspections of the correspondence between sample and population factors, seems to confirm strongly that, despite the small sample size (the number of rows of the array), sample factors 4, 1, 3, and 2 essentially reproduce the respective population factors from the original simulation model. It is important to recall that the cluster findings are based on a blind simple structure (i.e., nonprocrustean) transformation, so in some respects the correspondence is even more impressive than it would be had the prespecified pattern been used explicitly in the analysis.

Whereas the above example suggests that sample analyses can provide a means to recover "real" population structures when the number of grid rows (sample size) is as small as 15, it of course provides in itself

Table 12.5
Matrix of Congruence Coefficients

	Factor			
	1	2	3	4
1	.22	.89	.11	-.08
2	-.24	-.16	-.21	.86
3	-.12	.20	.89	-.17
4	.87	.10	.23	-.17

Note: Columns correspond to population factors, rows to columns of sample factor coefficient matrix in Table 12.3.
Source: Derived from Table 12.1 and information in text.

no more than a suggestion. What would be most useful at this point is a basis for describing the circumstances under which derived sample results such as this might be expected *routinely* to offer a reasonable chance of recovering population structures, when they exist. Equally important is to be able to recognize when a population structure is either weak or nonexistent. The theoretical statistical foundations of common factor analysis provide less assistance than one would like, because the theory is mostly asymptotic, justified only for large samples. Lacking a theoretical basis for demonstrating the inferential potential of small sample factor methods relevant to grid applications, a simulation study is used in the next section to begin to answer the question about factor recoverability. (The computer programs used in the illustration and in the simulation study below can be obtained from the author; these are being adapted for microcomputer applications as well.)

A SMALL SIMULATION EXPERIMENT

Four population structures were defined as a basis for simulating two-way arrays of the type often encountered in rep grid studies (see Note 2). Table 12.6 displays four related population factor coefficient matrices that were used for simulation. In rep grid applications, the pattern for any such population may be conceived as defining the essential structural correspondences for a single person's latent (i.e.,

Table 12.6
Population Factor Coefficient Matrices for Simulation Experiment

Factor 1	2	3	4
.94	.0	.0	.0
.94	.0	.0	.0
.94	.0	.0	.0
.94	.0	.0	.0
.0	.84	.0	.0
.0	.84	.0	.0
.0	.84	.0	.0
.0	.84	.0	.0
.0	.0	.78	.0
.0	.0	.78	.0
.0	.0	.78	.0
.0	.0	.78	.0
.0	.0	.0	.84
.0	.0	.0	.84
.0	.0	.0	.84

Population A

Factor 1	2	3	4
.88	.0	.0	.0
.88	.0	.0	.0
.88	.0	.0	.0
.88	.0	.0	.0
.0	.80	.0	.0
.0	.80	.0	.0
.0	.80	.0	.0
.0	.80	.0	.0
.0	.0	.71	.0
.0	.0	.71	.0
.0	.0	.71	.0
.0	.0	.71	.0
.0	.0	.0	.80
.0	.0	.0	.80
.0	.0	.0	.80

Population B

Factor 1	2	3	4
.83	.0	.0	.0
.83	.0	.0	.0
.83	.0	.0	.0
.83	.0	.0	.0
.0	.75	.0	.0
.0	.75	.0	.0
.0	.75	.0	.0
.0	.75	.0	.0
.0	.0	.71	.0
.0	.0	.71	.0
.0	.0	.71	.0
.0	.0	.71	.0
.0	.0	.0	.75
.0	.0	.0	.75
.0	.0	.0	.75

Population C

Factor 1	2	3	4
.50	.0	.0	.0
.50	.0	.0	.0
.50	.0	.0	.0
.50	.0	.0	.0
.0	.50	.0	.0
.0	.50	.0	.0
.0	.50	.0	.0
.0	.50	.0	.0
.0	.0	.50	.0
.0	.0	.50	.0
.0	.0	.50	.0
.0	.0	.50	.0
.0	.0	.0	.50
.0	.0	.0	.50
.0	.0	.0	.50

Population D

Source: Compiled by the author.

mental) constructs. In practice, of course, these would be unobservable and therefore unknown. The numerical values in such matrices may be viewed as indexing the correlations between manifest (i.e., observable) constructs and the underlying, unobservable (meta)constructs. For each population, ten independent random samples were simulated (see Note 3) to represent the types of rep grid arrays that one might obtain empirically. All samples were of size $n = 15$.

These population systems all use $m = 4$ common factors; all show independent, orthogonal clustering; and all have the same general appearance, except for the magnitudes of nonzero coefficient values. These magnitudes were selected to provide a realistic range of values with respect to the practical goal of recovering structures when intra-cluster correlations varied from a maximum of approximately .72 (the square of .85; cf. Population A, Table 12.6) to a minimum of .25 (.5 squared; cf. Population D). Such intra-cluster correlations are properly regarded as population reliability coefficients for individual variables — or as constructs in rep grid applications.

Table 12.7 summarizes the primary recovery statistics in the form of median and minimum congruence coefficients for each set of ten samples that were constructed using the simulation model. For each sample the strategy was to use the Whittle form of exploratory common factor analysis, including a blind, simple structure transformation algorithm (equamax), to generate a four-factor matrix of sample factor coefficients (Gorsuch 1974). Then congruence coefficients were computed between columns of the sample and population matrices. The largest values in the rows/columns of the 4 x 4 matrices of congruences (recall Table 12.5) were used for Table 12.7 computations. Rotations to maximum congruence were *not* employed, since these tend to lead to unrealistically large values and generally do not provide a sound basis for extrapolations in applied work.

For Population A, which depicts the highest measurement reliabilities, all but one of the median congruence values exceeded .90. Most samples for this population yielded congruence coefficients that ranged above .85; for the first factor only one value dropped below .90, and even for the third factor the median value was above .90. Factors 2 and 4 for Population A specified the same intra-cluster correlation (.71), and in all but one sample this led to congruence coefficients above .84. Inspections of the original, rotated sample factor coefficients suggest that when congruences are in the high .80's or above .90, then derived sample clusters essentially mirror the corresponding population clusters.

Table 12.7
Congruence Statistics for Simulation Study Comparing Four Population Structures

Population		Factor I	Factor II	Factor III	Factor IV
Population A	Mdn	.93	.91	.91	.88
		(.81)	(.30)	(.76)	(.62)
Population B	Mdn	.89	.89	.89	.82
		(.82)	(.18)	(.68)	(.54)
Population C	Mdn	.92	.84	.84	.83
		(.15)	(.66)	(.72)	(.26)
Population D	Mdn	.52	.48	.50	.52
		(b)	(b)	(b)	(b)

In each population, median values of matching sample/population convergence statistics are displayed for each factor; in each case, ten samples were simulated (see Note 3) using the population systems of Table 12.4. The values in parentheses are the lowest matching congruence coefficients across ten samples. $n = 15$ for each sample.

*In Population D the smallest congruence coefficients were all near zero or negative.

Source: Compiled by the author.

When congruence values drop into the low .80's or below, then population factor recovery could be said to be fair to poor.

For population systems B and C, congruence values suggest less adequate recovery of population structures, and in both these populations, factor 4 — the one with only three loadings — was essentially unrecoverable. Yet, based on median congruences, samples showed reasonable recovery of the first three factors for population B; except for the first factor in population C, samples yielded median congruence values in an unacceptable range with respect to population recovery. It should not be surprising that the third factor in population C was largely unrecoverable, since the constant population intra-cluster correlation was only .42 in this case. As might be expected based on the relatively low intra-cluster correlations, Population D results showed unsatisfactory recovery of all factors in terms of median congruence values, and in fact for *every one* of the ten simulation samples.

Four factors were specified for each population. Although all results are for uncorrelated factor systems, there is reason to believe that one could generalize from these results to situations where factors have low (say, .20 to .30) correlations with one another. Also, extrapolations to cases where a few of the population factors have more than one large loading for a few (say, up to 4 for $p = 15$) variables would not be unreasonable.

Some further simulation work was completed (no details are reported) using populations for which only a subset of the 15 variables loaded substantially on only two factors (ten variables, five on each factor), and the remaining five variables had zero communalities. Again, using samples of size 15, it was found that the "real" clusters for these subsets could routinely be recovered when the intra-cluster population correlations (read: grid construct reliabilities) exceeded .50. Variables having zero correlations with all others in the parent population structure tended to have complex loadings across factors, and relatively lower communalities.

Beyond the congruence values, inspections of individual sample factor coefficient matrices lent further support to the idea that without prior information, general interpretations of structure would ordinarily be highly problematical. Apparently one must have either at least four variables per cluster or unrealistically high intra-cluster population correlations to expect reasonable recovery of population structures with samples of this size. It is nevertheless constructive to find that, at least under some conditions, samples can often be expected to recover population structures when they exist, even for samples as small as these.

To amplify the point concerning the role of prior information, it is worth noting that several of the rotated sample factor coefficient matrices, especially for Populations D and C, yielded evidence of some structure, but it tended to be quite complex. In particular, numerous relatively large negative coefficients almost always occurred in those columns that may otherwise have suggested the known population clusters. If the analyst had good reason, based on a priori considerations, to know what structural information to ignore, or downweight, this could serve to facilitate sound interpretations in such cases. Specifically, if one had reason not to expect negative correlations among the pairs of columns of the original data matrix, then this information could provide a basis for focusing primary attention on the (positive) sample coefficients.

A converse point about the role of prior structural information is that if sample data deny one's prior structural views, especially by suggesting a substantially different alternative structure for interpretation, then the need for further evidence to support the alternative interpretation virtually always will require further (i.e., outside or external) information or data concerning the grid. Although it is possible to formalize the entire process under discussion, the central point is that, *especially for small samples, empirically derived structural interpretations cannot generally be trusted unless supported by independent (or prior) information, especially relevant theory.* Surely this idea is in the spirit of Kelly's original intentions of using rep grids to facilitate understanding of personal construct systems. It also has a bearing on prediction of future events, as will be noted in the following section.

SOME EXTENSIONS AND CONCLUSIONS

All of the preceding has been based on the concept of applying exploratory latent variable methods in situations where data from a single grid were concerned. The greater virtues and versatility of such methods lie in their extensions to situations where two or more grids are assessed and perhaps compared with one another. Suppose that at least a subset of the variables (say, constructs) for several different grids were to be compared across individually prescribed elements. Then one could advantageously "stack" the grids on one another to provide a larger number of rows across which to study column variables.

Standard latent variable methods exist either to examine column structures across the whole set of rows or to compare and contrast various structural interpretations for the different grids. For example, using methods described in Joreskog (1978), one could use derived cluster results from one grid to provide a structural hypothesis for the analysis of another, independent grid, if the rows and columns are mutually "compatible." This process could also be used in reverse, as in double cross-validation. (The number of rows, say for elements, must exceed at least the number of structural parameters under estimation, in order that the standard computational algorithms do not break down. Also with small *n*'s, statistical "power" can be expected to be relatively low, based on theoretical considerations. However, the importance of all such matters must inevitably be assessed contextually.)

Flexible models for testing specific structural hypotheses, or for exploring the data vis-à-vis more generalized structural hypotheses, are available (Joreskog 1978). This continues to be one of the most fertile areas for methodological research. Virtually every issue of *Psychometrika,* and several sociological periodicals, provides elaborations or extensions to the basic theory or algorithms for applications. Robustness studies have also been initiated to develop a better understanding of the circumstances in which structural analytic results may be invariant, even when there have been violations of their underlying assumptions (Boosma 1984).

A further virtue of these latent variable methods for structural analysis is that they provide a basis, through matrix inversion of covariance or correlation estimators, for unifying the concepts of structural estimation and regression estimation in the context of prediction. The methods of Pruzek and Frederick (1978) seem to be especially effective for improving predictions when samples are as small as those that arise in the single grids. (In fact, such methods were studied for the entire range of simulations described above and were almost always effective in generating reasonable regression equations, particularly when the derived sample structures turned out to be relatively simple.)

Formal Bayesian systems are also being developed to further enhance this prediction methodology (Chen 1979). Such new methods may be especially conducive to assisting an investigator who wishes to incorporate vague prior structural knowledge into analyses when the theory is in relatively early stages of development — which for a single rep grid elicitation could be said to be nearly always. Space limitations preclude elaborations, but the point is that several new methods of direct relevance to personal construct research are being developed within the disciplines of statistics and psychometrics.

Compared with component or cluster methods (as implemented with PRINGRID or FOCUS, say), the modern latent variable methods to which we allude seem to provide for more complete analyses in the sense that they are conducive to comprehensive description as well as to model testing, in a framework that may be tailored to the particular substantive theory considerations in each domain of grid research. In general, latent variable methods provide a basis not available with purely descriptive methods for quantifying the quality of inferences and for guiding both the design and collection of data to better support sound interpretations. It is hoped that this chapter will stimulate thoughtful applications of model-based methods in rep grid research.

APPENDIX

Given raw data in an $n \times p$ matrix x, for which n denotes individuals and p denotes variables, a conventional product moment analysis may be described as follows:

Compute raw cross-products among pairs of variables as

$$x'x, \tag{12.1}$$

from which the mean (outer products) can be subtracted to obtain deviation scores cross-products:

$$x_d'x_d = x'x - (1/n)x'\mathbf{1}\ \mathbf{1}'x \tag{12.2}$$

where **1** represents a vector of ones. Matrix 12.2 can be converted to a covariance matrix by dividing all entries by $(n - 1)$. Alternative covariance forms can be generated by rescaling; for example, the (dimensionless) covariances in Pearson product moment correlation matrix R can be obtained by diagonal normalization:

$$R = D_n\, x_d'x_d D_n, \tag{12.3}$$

where the diagonal matrix D_n contains reciprocal square roots of the diagonal elements in $x_d'x_d$. R can also be written as $Z'Z$, where Z is of the form X_dD_n, of order $n \times p$.

Theoretical analyses in mainstream multivariate analysis usually involve analytic factoring of R, or alternative covariance forms. However, typical rep grid analyses involve direct row/column permutations of x, based on Euclidean distances (cf. Chapter 7, this volume). Classical metric multidimensional scaling, as discussed in Seber (1984) or Mardia, Kent, and Bibby (1979), uses essentially the same information as do orthodox rep grid cluster methods.

There is a close algebraic (and geometric) correspondence between conventional methods for multivariate analysis and those used n multidimensional scaling or rep grid analyses. The key differences between the two forms of analysis have to do with the difference between analyzing distances between the endpoints of vectors in the raw data metric (cf. Chapter 5 in Seber 1984) and analyzing deviation score vectors in terms of certain linear combination vectors, as described in this chapter.

Numerous comparative analyses were used by this author to see whether standard rep grid *cluster* methods, based on row/column permutations, would yield clusters similar to those produced in a rotated factor solution (like Table 12.3, this chapter). Results were generally very similar, at least when variable metrics were comparable across column variables, as in our illustrative example. A major problem of the cluster methods, however, is that they often found clusters for the variables in a sample when, in the population, no such clusters existed (recall the simulation experiment). Moreover, for some relatively complex structures, the hierarchical form of the cluster results seriously distorted the known population structure.

By comparison, the chief virtue of the model-based methods is that they provide explicit quantifications of the degrees of uncertainty for interpretations and are thereby conducive to analytic testing of explicit structural hypotheses. Moreover, these methods do not presume a hierarchy and they provide direct, theoretically tractable (not ad hoc), linkages with more comprehensive analytical systems that may be of special benefit when comparisons across grids and related data are feasible.

NOTES

1. The $p \times m$ factor coefficients matrix can be written as $F_m = Q_m D_w T$, where $D_w^2 = D_\lambda^2 - \Theta I$ and T is the $m \times m$ (for m factors) orthogonal transformation matrix. D_λ^2 is the diagonal matrix composed of the m largest eigenvalues, and Q_m is the $p \times m$ matrix of corresponding column, unit-length eigenvectors of the correlation matrix R. The scalar Θ denotes the average of the $p - m$ smallest eigenvalues, chosen to minimize the off-diagonal fit statistic. Note that the presence of one or more zero eigenvalues has no effect on the viability of this algorithm; negative eigenvalues cannot occur as long as the original (grid) array is complete; that is, as long as no data are missing. This computing algorithm is closely related to ordinary principal component analysis, and is simple to program. See Pruzek and Rabinowitz (1981) for further details and discussion concerning Whittle's model for common factor analysis.

2. In the case of the Whittle model, the $n \times m$ matrix of factor score estimates is computed as $S = ZQ_m D_w^{-1} T$, where Z is the original $n \times p$ data matrix in standardized form ($R = Z'Z$); the remaining elements are defined in Note 1. The fitted data, say Y_m, can be computed as $Y_m = SF_m' = ZQ_m Q_m'$ for a given value of m, the number of common factors.

3. For the simulation study each p component data vector was constructed using the fundamental postulate of common factor analysis: $\boldsymbol{y} = F\boldsymbol{x}_c + U\boldsymbol{x}_u$. In this expression F is the input population factor coefficients matrix, of order $p \times m$; U^2 is the diagonal matrix of uniqueness variances, defined as $U^2 = I - \text{diag}\, FF'$ (so U is its square root); the elements of the common and uniqueness score vectors $\boldsymbol{x}_c$ and $\boldsymbol{x}_u$, of

order m and p, respectively, were constructed using a pseudo random number generator such that each element was drawn from a unit normal distribution independently of all others. Once each simulated data vector, y, had been constructed, it was converted to a five-point, discretized, variable by cutting the y values in such a way (i.e., with quantiles from a unit normal distribution table) that the probability of each of the scores 1 through 5 would be equal. Each simulated data matrix consisted of $n = 15$ rows of such discretized score vectors for each sample. Thus, for a sufficiently large sample, the y vectors so constructed should yield a correlation matrix that fits the simulation model precisely; the discretized vectors should be "minimally perturbed" with respect to this standard.

Bibliography

Abelson, R. P. 1981. Psychological status of the script concept. *American Psychologist* 7:715–29.
Acker, W. 1982. A computerized approach to psychological screening — the Bexley-Maudsley automated psychological screening and the Bexley-Maudsley category sorting text. *International Journal of Man–Machine Studies* 17:361–69.
Adams, J. 1979. Pet behaviour. *Practical Computing* 2:29.
Adams-Webber, J. 1970. An analysis of the discriminant validity of several repertory grid indices. *British Journal of Psychology* 61:83–90.
____. 1979. *Personal construct theory: Conceptions and applications.* New York: Wiley.
____. 1980. Differences between physical and psychological constructs in repertory grids. *British Journal of Medical Psychology* 53:319–22.
____. 1982. Assimilation and contrast in personal judgment: The dichotomy corollary. In *The construing person,* edited by J. C. Mancuso and J. Adams-Webber, pp. 96–112. New York: Praeger.
____. 1984a. Personal construct theory. In *Encyclopedia of psychology,* edited by R. Corsini. New York: Wiley Interscience.
____. 1984b. Cognitive complexity. In *Encyclopedia of psychology,* edited by R. Corsini. New York: Wiley Interscience.
____. 1985. Self–other contrast and the development of personal constructs. *Canadian Journal of Behavioural Science* 17:303–14.
Adams-Webber, J., and J. Benjafield. The relation between lexical marking and rating extremity in interpersonal judgment. *Canadian Journal of Behavioural Science* 5:234–41.

____. 1976. The relation between cognitive complexity and assimilative projection in terms of personal constructs. *Bulletin of the British Psychological Society* 29:219.

Adams-Webber, J., and D. L. Davidson. 1979. Maximum contrast between self and others in personal judgment: A repertory grid study. *British Journal of Psychology* 70:517–18.

Adams-Webber, J., and J. C. Mancuso, eds. 1983. *Applications of personal construct theory*. New York: Academic Press.

Adams-Webber, J., and E. Mirc. 1976. Assessing the development of student teachers' role conceptions. *British Journal of Educational Psychology* 46:338–40.

Adams-Webber, J., and Y. Rodney. 1983. Relational aspects of temporary changes in construing self and others. *Canadian Journal of Behavioural Science* 15:52–59.

Adams-Webber, J., B. Schwenker, and D. Barbeau. 1972. Personal constructs and the perception of individual differences. *Canadian Journal of Behavioural Science* 4:218–24.

Agnew, J., and D. Bannister. 1973. Psychiatric diagnosis as a pseudo-specialist language. *British Journal of Medical Psychology* 46:69–73.

Aldenderfer, M. S., and R. K. Blashfield. 1984. *Cluster analysis*. Beverly Hills, CA: Sage Publications.

Anazi, Y., and H. A. Simon. 1979. The theory of learning by doing. *Psychological Review* 86:124–40.

Anderson, J. R. 1983. *The architecture of cognition*. Cambridge, MA: Harvard University Press.

Anderson, J. R., and G. H. Bower. 1973. *Human associative memory*. Washington, D.C.: Winston.

Anderson, N. 1981. *Foundations of information integration theory*. New York: Academic Press.

____. 1982. *Methods of information integration theory*. New York: Academic Press.

Antonelli, D. 1983. The application of artificial intelligence to a maintenance and diagnostic information system (MDIS). In *The proceedings of the joint services workshop on artificial intelligence in maintenance*. Boulder, CO.

Ashbrook, R. M. 1982. Information search and cognition in psychopathy. Master's thesis, Ohio State University, Columbus, OH.

____. 1985. *Memory organization in attention deficit disorder children*. Ph.D. diss., Ohio State University, Columbus, OH.

Ashworth, C. M., I. M. Blackburn, and F. M. McPherson. 1982. The performance of depressed and manic patients on some repertory grid measures. *British Journal of Medical Psychology* 55:247–55.

Atkin, R. H. 1974. *Mathematical structure in human affairs*. London: Heinemann.

Atkinson, R. C., and R. M. Shiffrin. 1968. Human memory: A proposed system and its control processes. In *Advances in the psychology of learning and motivation research and theory*, vol. 2, edited by K. W. Spence and J. T. Spence. New York: Academic Press.

Attneave, F. 1959. *Application of information theory to psychology*. New York: Holt, Rinehart & Winston.

Averill, J. R. 1982. Anger and aggression: An essay on emotion. New York: Springer-Verlag.

Bainbridge, L. 1979. Verbal reports as evidence of the process operator's knowledge. *International Journal of Man–Machine Studies* 11:411–36.

Balogh, D., and R. Merritt. 1985. Susceptibility to type A backward masking among hypothetically psychosis-prone college students. *Journal of Abnormal Psychology* 94:377–83.

Bannister, D. 1962. The nature and measurement of schizophrenic thought disorder. *Journal of Mental Science* 108:825–42.

Bannister, D., and J. Agnew. 1977. The child's construing of self. In *Nebraska symposium on motivation 1976: Personal construct psychology*, edited by A. W. Landfield and J. K. Cole, pp. 94–125. Lincoln, NE: University of Nebraska Press.

Bannister, D. and F. Fransella. 1966. A grid test of schizophrenic thought disorder. *British Journal of Social and Clinical Psychology* 5:95–102.

Bannister, D. and F. Fransella. 1967. *Grid test of schizophrenic thought disorder: Manual*. Barstaple, Devon: Psychological Test Publications.

Bannister, D., and F. Fransella. 1980. *Inquiring man: The psychology of personal constructs*, 2d ed. Harmondsworth, England: Penguin.

Bannister, D., F. Fransella, and J. Agnew. 1971. Characteristics and validity of the grid test of thought disorder. *British Journal of Social and Clinical Psychology* 10:114–51.

Bannister, D., and J. M. M. Mair. 1968. *The evaluation of personal constructs*. London: Academic Press.

Barenboim, C. 1977. Developmental changes in the interpersonal cognitive system from middle childhood to adolescence. *Child Development* 48:1467–74.

____. 1981. The development of person perception in childhood and adolescence. *Child Development* 52:129–44.

Bargh, J. A. 1982. Attention and automaticity in the processing of self-relevant information. *Journal of Personality and Social Psychology* 43:425–36.

Barnett, G. 1985. A bibliography of Galileo material. Unpublished manuscript. SUNY at Buffalo.

Barrett, G. 1972. Reliability and metric multidimensional scaling. Unpublished manuscript. Michigan State University.

Bartlett, F. C. 1932. *Remembering*. London: Cambridge University Press.

Bavelas, J. B., A. S. Chan, and J. A. Guthrie. 1976. Reliability and validity measured by Kelly's repertory grid. *Canadian Journal of Behavior Science* 8:23–38.

Benesch, K. F. 1985. Processes affecting the congruency of personality descriptions: A personal construct approach. *Dissertation Abstracts International* 45:2355-B.

Benjafield, J., and J. Adams-Webber. 1975. Assimilative projection and construct balance. *British Journal of Psychology* 66:169–73.

____. 1976. The golden section hypothesis. *British Journal of Psychology* 67:11–15.

Berlyne, D. E. 1971. *Aesthetics and psychobiology*. New York: Appleton-Century-Crofts.

Bieri, J., A. L. Atkins, S. Briar, R. L. Leaman, H. Miller, and T. Tripodi. 1966. *Clinical and social judgement*. New York: Wiley.

Bieri, J., and E. Blacker. 1956. The generality of cognitive complexity in the perception of people and inkblots. *Journal of Abnormal and Social Psychology* 53:112–17.

Bonarius, J. C. J. 1970a. *Personal construct psychology and extreme response style: An integration of meaningfulness, maladjustment, and communication.* Netherlands: University of Gronigen.

____. 1970b. *Personal construct psychology and extreme response style: An interaction model of meaningfulness and communication.* Amsterdam: Swets & Zeitlinger.

____. 1977. The interaction model of communication: Through experimental research towards existential relevance. In *Nebraska symposium on motivation 1976: Personal construct psychology,* edited by A. W. Landfield and J. K. Cole, pp. 291–343. Lincoln, NE: University of Nebraska Press.

Boose, J. H. 1984. Personal construct theory and the transfer of human expertise. *Proceedings AAAI-84,* pp. 27–33. Austin, TX: American Association for Artificial Intelligence.

____. 1985a. A knowledge acquisition program for expert systems based on personal construct psychology. *International Journal of Man–Machine Studies* 23:495–525.

____. 1985b. Personal construct psychology and the transfer of human expertise. Boeing Technical Report BCS-G-2010-11, Seattle, WA: Boeing Computer Services.

____. 1986a. A grid tool for eliciting expert knowledge. In *Cognition and personal structure: Computer access and analysis,* edited by J. C. Mancuso and M. L. G. Shaw. New York: Praeger.

____. 1986b. Rapid acquisition and combination of knowledge from multiple experts in the same domain. *Future Computing Systems,* in press.

Boosma, A. 1985. Nonconvergence, improper solutions, and starting values in LISREL maximum likelihood estimation. *Psychometrika* 50:229–42.

Bousfield, A. K., and W. A. Bousfield. 1966. Measurement of clustering and sequential constancies in repeated free recall. *Psychological Reports* 19:935–42.

Bower, G. H., and S. G. Gilligan. 1979. Remembering information related to one's self. *Journal of Research in Personality* 13:420–61.

Boxer, P. J. 1981. Reflective analysis. In *Recent advances in personal construct technology,* edited by M. L. G. Shaw, pp. 95–104. London: Academic Press.

Brazleton, T. B. 1961. Psychophysiologic reaction in the neonate: I. The value of observation of the neonate. *Journal of Pediatrics* 58:508–12.

Brewer, W. F., and G. V. Nakamura. 1984. The nature and function of schemas. In *Handbook of social cognition,* edited by R. S. Wyer and T. K. Srull, pp. 119–60. Hillsdale, NJ: Erlbaum.

Broadbent, D. E. 1958. *Perception and communication.* London: Pergamon.

Brody, J. 1971. Information theory, motivation and personality. In *Personality theory and information processing,* edited by H. Schroder and P. Suedfeld. New York: Ronald.

Broughton, J. 1978. Development of concepts of self, mind, reality, and knowledge. *New Directions for Child Development* 1:75–100.

____. 1980. The divided self in adolescence. *Human Development* 24:13–32.

Bruner, J. S., J. J. Goodnow, and G. A. Austin. 1956. *A study of thinking.* New York: Wiley.

Buchanan, B. G., D. Barstow, R. Bechtel, J. Bennett, W. Clancey, C. Kulikowski, T. Mitchell, and D. Waterman. 1983. Constructing an expert system. In *Building expert systems*, edited by F. Hayes-Roth, D. A. Waterman, and D. B. Lenat, pp. 127–68. Reading, MA: Addison-Wesley.

Buchanan, B. G., and E. A. Feigenbaum. 1978. DENDRAL and META-DENDRAL: Their applications dimension. *Artificial Intelligence* 11:5–24.

Calvert, E. J., and R. C. Waterfall. 1982. A comparison of conventional and automated administration of Raven's standard progressive matrices. *International Journal of Man–Machine Studies* 17:305–10.

Cantor, N., and W. Mischel. 1979. Prototypes in person perception. In *Advances in experimental and social psychology*, vol. 12, edited by L. Berkowitz. New York: Academic Press, pp. 3–53.

Card, W. I., M. Nicholson, G. P. Crean, G. Watkinson, C. R. Evans, J. Wilson, and D. Russell. 1974. A comparison of doctor and computer interrogation of patients. *International Journal of Biomedical Computing* 5:175–87.

Carlson, W. M. 1979. The new horizon in business information analysis. *Data Base* 10:3–9.

Carroll, J., and J. Chang. 1970. Analysis of individual differences in multidimensional scaling via an N-way generalization of Eckhart-Young decomposition. *Psychometrika* 35:283–319.

Carver, C. S., and M. F. Scheier. 1981. *Attention and self-regulation: A control theory approach to human behavior*. New York: Springer-Verlag.

Cary, J. W. 1985. Information loss in grid analysis. *Sixth International Personal Construct Psychology Congress*. Cambridge, England.

Chamrad, D. 1982. *Letter detection of paranoid and nonparanoid schizophrenics*. Master's thesis, Ohio State University, Columbus, OH.

Chapman, L. J., and J. P. Chapman. 1973. Problems in the measurement of cognitive deficit. *Psychological Bulletin* 79:380–85.

____. 1978. The measurement of differential deficit. *Journal of Psychiatry Research* 14:303–11.

Chen, C. 1979. Baysian inference for a normal dispersion matrix and its application to stochastic multiple regression analysis. *Journal of the Royal Statistical Society, Series B* 41:235–48.

Chen, P. P., ed. 1980. *Entity-relationship approach to systems analysis and design*. New York: North Holland.

Chi, M. T. H., R. Glaser, and E. Rees. 1982. Expertise in problem solving. In *Advances in the psychology of human intelligence*, edited by R. J. Steinberg, pp. 7–75. Hillsdale, NJ: Erlbaum.

Clancey, W. J. 1984. Classification problem solving. *Proceedings AAAI-84* pp. 49–55. Austin, TX: American Association for Artificial Intelligence.

Cochran, L. 1976. Categorization and change in conceptual relatedness. *Canadian Journal of Behavioural Science* 8:275–86.

Cohen, B. H. 1963. Recall of categorized word lists. *Journal of Experimental Psychology* 71:858–66.

Cohen, B., and B. L. Murphy. 1984. Models of concepts. *Cognitive Science* 8:27–58.

Cohen, J. 1977. *Statistical power analysis*. New York: Academic Press.

Collins, A. M., and E. F. Loftus. 1975. A spreading activation theory of semantic processing. *Psychological Review* 82:407–28.

Cooley, C. H. [1902] 1964. *Human nature and the social order*. New York: Schocken Books.

Corter, J. 1982. ADDTREE/P: A PASCAL program for fitting additive trees based on Sattath and Tversky's ADDTREE program. *Behavior Research Methods and Instrumentation* 14:353–54.

Craik, F. I. M., and R. S. Lockhart. 1972. Levels of processing: A framework for memory research. *Journal of Verbal Learning and Verbal Behavior* 11:671–84.

Craik, F. I. M., and M. J. Watkins. 1973. The role of rehearsal in short-term memory. *Journal of Verbal Learning and Verbal Behavior* 12:599–607.

Cromwell, R. 1975. Assessment of schizophrenia. *Annual Review of Psychology* 26:593–619.

Cromwell, R., and W. Spaulding. 1979. A microprocessor-based psychopathology laboratory: I. Why bother? *Behavior Research Methods and Instrumentation* 11:241–42.

Cronbach, L., R. Gleser, T. Nanda, and V. Rajaratnam. 1974. *The dependability of measures*. New York: Academic Press.

Crowder, R. G. 1976. *Principles of learning and memory*. Hillsdale, NJ: Erlbaum.

Curtin, T. J. 1984. Coronary heart disease and Type A behavior: A personal construct approach. *First North American Personal Construct Network Conference*. Cincinnati, OH.

Damon, W., and D. Hart. 1982. The development of self-understanding from infancy to adolescence. *Child Development* 53:841–64.

Davis, R., and D. B. Lenat. 1982. *Knowledge-based systems in artificial intelligence*. New York: McGraw-Hill.

Dillon, W., N. Mulani, and D. Frederick. 1984. Removing perceptual distortions in product space analysis. *Journal of Marketing Research* 21:184–93.

Doster, J. A. 1985. Marital violence: A personal construct assessment. In *Anticipating personal construct psychology*, edited by F. Epting and A. W. Landfield, pp. 225–32. Lincoln, NE: University of Nebraska Press.

Eimer, B. N. 1981. *Children's conceptions of the purposes, outcomes, and styles of parental reprimand*. Ph.D. diss., State University of New York at Albany.

Elithorn, A., and A. Telford. 1969. Computer analysis of intellectual skills. *International Journal of Man–Machine Studies* 1:189–209.

Elwood, D. L. 1972a. Test-retest reliability and cost analyses of automated and face-to-face intelligence testing. *International Journal of Man–Machine Studies* 4:1–22.

____. 1972b. Automated WAIS testing correlated with face-to-face testing: A validity study. *International Journal of Man–Machine Studies* 4:129–37.

____. 1972c. Automated versus face-to-face intelligence testing: Comparison of test-retest reliabilities. *International Journal of Man–Machine Studies* 4:363–69.

Erlenmeyer-Kimling, L., and B. Cornblatt. 1978. Attentional measures in a study of children at high risk for schizophrenia. *Journal of Psychiatry Research* 14:93–98.

Eylon, B., and F. Reif. 1984. Effects of knowledge organization on task performance. *Cognition and Instruction* 1:5–44.

Feigenbaum, E. A. 1980. Knowledge engineering: The applied side of artificial intelligence. Report STAN-CS-80-812, Department of Computer Science, Stanford University.

Feldman, S. S., and S. C. Nash. 1978. Interest in babies during young adulthood. *Child Development* 49:617–22.

Fey, E. 1952. The performance of young schizophrenics on the Wisconsin Card Sorting Test. *Journal of Consulting and Clinical Psychology* 15:311–19.

Fiske, D. W. 1977. Personologies, abstractions, and interactions. In *Personality at the crossroads: Current issues in interactional psychology*, edited by D. Magnusson and N. S. Endler. New York: Wiley.

Flavell, J. F. 1963. *The developmental psychology of Jean Piaget*. (Forward by Jean Piaget). Princeton, NJ: D. Van Nostrand.

Forgy, C. L. 1981. *OPS5 user's manual*. Pittsburgh, PA: Department of Computer Science, Carnegie-Mellon University.

Francis, R. G. 1961. *The rhetoric of science: A methodological discussion of the two by two table*. Minneapolis, MN: University of Minnesota Press.

Frank, H. 1959. *Grundlagenprobleme der Informationästhetik und erste Anwendung auf die mime pure*. Quickborn: Schnelle.

Fransella, F. 1972. *Personal change and reconstruction: Research on a treatment of stuttering*. London: Academic Press.

____. 1982. Personal meanings and personal constructs. In *Personal meanings*, edited by E. Shepherd and J. P. Watson, pp. 47–58. London: John Wiley.

Fransella, F., and D. Bannister. 1977. *A manual for repertory grid technique*. London: Academic Press.

Fransella, F., and A. H. Crisp. 1970. Conceptual organization and weight change. *Psychotherapy and Psychosomatics* 18:176–85.

Frazer, H. 1980. *Agoraphobia: Parental influence and cognitive structures*. Ph.D. diss., University of Toronto.

Freeman, M. 1985. Paul Ricoeur on interpretation: The model of text and the idea of development. *Human Development* 28:295–312.

Freyd, J. L. 1983. Shareability: The social psychology of epistemology. *Cognitive Science* 7:191–210.

Gaines, B. R. 1984. Perspectives on fifth generation computing. *Oxford Surveys in Information Technology* 1:1–53.

Gaines, B. R., and M. L. G. Shaw. 1981. New directions in the analysis and interactive elicitation of personal construct systems. In *Recent advances in personal construct technology*, edited by M. L. G. Shaw, pp. 147–82. London: Academic Press.

____. 1985. Induction of inference rules for expert systems. *Fuzzy Sets and Systems* 18:315–28.

Gara, M. A., and S. Rosenberg. 1979. The identification of persons as supersets and subsets in free-response personality descriptions. *Journal of Personality and Social Psychology* 37:2161–70.

Gathercole, C. E., E. Bromley, and J. B. Ashcroft. 1970. The reliability of repertory grids. *Journal of Clinical Psychology* 26:513–16.

Gedye, J. L., and E. Miller. 1969. The automation of psychological assessment. *International Journal of Man–Machine Studies* 1:237–62.

Gentner, D. 1983. Structure-mapping: A theoretical framework for analogy. *Cognitive Science* 7:155–70.

Gentner, D., and A. L. Stevens. 1983. *Mental models.* New Jersey: Lawrence Erlbaum Associates.

Gergen, K. J. 1977. The social construction of self-knowledge. In *The self: Psychological and philosophical issues,* edited by T. Mischel, pp. 139–69. Totowa, NJ: Rowman & Littlefield.

____. 1985. The social constructionist movement in modern psychology. *American Psychologist* 40:266–75.

Gergan, K. J., and K. E. Davis. 1985. *The social construction of the person.* New York: Springer-Verlag.

Gevarter, W. B. 1983. Expert systems: Limited but powerful. *IEEE Spectrum* 18:39–45.

Gillham, J., and J. Woelfel. 1977. The Galileo system: Preliminary evidence for precision, stability and equivalence to traditional measures. *Human Communication Research* 3:222–34.

Glaser, R. 1984. Education and thinking: The role of knowledge. *American Psychologist* 39:93–104.

Goffman, E. 1959. *The presentation of self in everyday life.* New York: Doubleday.

Golden, C. J. 1978. *The Stroop color and word test: A manual for clinical and experimental uses.* Chicago, IL: Stoelting.

Goldfried, M., and C. Robins. 1983. Self-schema, cognitive bias, and the processing of therapeutic experiences. In *Advances in cognitive behavioral research and therapy,* vol. 2, edited by P. C. Kendall, pp. 33–80. New York: Academic Press.

Gorenstein, E. E. 1982. Frontal lobe functions in psychopaths. *Journal of Abnormal Psychology* 31:368–79.

Gorsuch, R. L. 1974. *Factor analysis.* Philadelphia, PA: W. B. Saunders.

Green, P. 1974. On design of choice experiments involving multi-factor alternatives. *Journal of Consumer Research* 1:61–68.

Green, P., D. Carroll, and F. Carmone. 1978. Some new types of fractional factorial designs for marketing experiments. In *Research in marketing,* vol. 1, edited by J. Seth. Greenwich, CT: JAI Press.

Green, P., D. Carroll, and S. Goldberg. 1981. A general approach to product design optimization via conjoint analysis. *Journal of Marketing* 45:17–37.

Green, P., V. Rao, and W. DeSarbo. 1978. Incorporating group-level similarity judgements in conjoint analysis. *Journal of Consumer Research* 5:187–93.

Green, P., and V. Srinivasa. 1978. Conjoint analysis in consumer research: Issues and outlook. *Journal of Consumer Research* 5:103–23.

Greenwald, A. G., and A. R. Pratkanis. 1984. The self. In *Handbook of social cognition,* edited by R. S. Wyer and T. K. Srull, pp. 129–78. Hillsdale, NJ: Erlbaum.

Grossberg, S. 1980. How does the brain build a cognitive code? *Psychological Review* 87:1–51.

Guidano, V. F., and G. Liotti. 1983. *Cognitive processes and emotional disorders.* New York: Guilford Press.

Harter, S. 1983. Developmental perspectives in the self-system. In *Handbook of child psychology,* vol. 4, edited by P. H. Mussen, pp. 275–83. New York: Wiley.

Hass, N., and G. Hendrix. 1983. Learning by being told: Acquiring knowledge for information management. In *Machine learning: An artificial intelligence approach,* edited by R. S. Michalski, J. Carbonell, and T. M. Mitchell, pp. 405–28. Palo Alto, CA: Tioga Press.

Hawkins, D. 1983. An analysis of expert thinking. *International Journal of Man–Machine Studies* 18:1–47.

Hayes-Roth, F., D. A. Waterman, and D. B. Lenat, eds. 1983. *Building expert systems.* Reading, MA: Addison-Wesley.

Head, H. 1920. *Studies in neurology.* London: Frowde, Hodder, & Stoughton.

Heerdt, W. A. 1982. The implicative structuring of self-role constructs and the formulation of reprimand that is relevant to the transgressor's construing of the transgressive event. Ph.D. diss., State University of New York at Albany.

Hinkle, D. N. 1965. *The change of personal constructs from the viewpoint of a theory of implications.* Ph.D. diss., Ohio State University, Columbus, OH.

Holbrook, M., and J. Huber. 1979. Separating perceptual dimensions from affective overtones: An application to consumer aesthetics. *Journal of Consumer Research* 15:272–83.

Honikman, B. 1976. Construct theory as an approach to architectural and environmental design. In *Explorations of intrapersonal space,* vol. 1, edited by P. Slater, pp. 167–82. London: John Wiley & Sons.

Horowitz, M. J. 1976. *Stress response syndromes.* New York: Jason Aronson.

Huber, J., and M. Holbrook. 1979. Using attribute ratings for product positioning: Some distinctions among compositional approaches. *Journal of Marketing Research* 16:507–16.

Hunt, D. 1951. *Studies in role construct repertory: Conceptual consistency.* Master's thesis, Ohio State University, Columbus, OH.

Huntzinger, R. S., and L. G. Space. 1979. A microprocessor-based psychopathology laboratory: IV. Software design. *Behavior Research Methods and Instrumentation* 11:253–56.

Isaacson, G. S. 1963. *A comparative study of the meaningfulness of personal and common constructs.* Ph.D. diss., University of Missouri.

Isaacson, G. S., and A. W. Landfield. 1965. Meaningfulness of personal versus common constructs. *Journal of Individual Psychology* 21:160–66.

Jaccard, J. 1981. Attitudes and behavior: Implications of attitudes towards behavioral alternatives. *Journal of Experimental Social Psychology* 25:41–78.

Jaccard, J., and M. Becker. 1986. Attitudes and behavior: An information integration perspective. *Journal of Experimental Social Psychology* 21:440–65.

Jaccard, J., M. A. Becker, and G. Wood. 1984. Pairwise multiple comparison procedures: A review. *Psychological Bulletin* 96:589–96.

Jaccard, J., and C. Wan. 1986. Cross-cultural analysis of behavioral decision making. *Journal of Cross-Cultural Psychology* 17:123–49.

Jaccard, J., and G. Wood. 1986. An idiothetic analysis of behavioral decision making. In *Perspectives on methodology in consumer behavior,* edited by D. Brinberg and R. Lutz, pp. 67–106. New York: Springer-Verlag.

James, W. 1890. *The principles of psychology.* New York: Holt.

Jennrich, R. I. 1973. On the stability of rotated loadings: The Wexler phenomenon. *British Journal of Mathematical and Statistical Psychology* 26:167–76.

Johnson, R. 1974. Trade-off analysis of consumer values. *Journal of Marketing Research* 11:121–27.

Johnson, S. C. 1967. Hierarchical clustering schemes. *Psychometrika* 32:241–54.

Joreskog, K. 1978. Structural analysis of covariance and correlation matrices. *Psychometrika* 43:443–77.

Kafrey, D., R. Jacobs, and S. Zedeck. 1979. Discriminability in multidimensional performance evaluations. *Applied Psychological Measurement* 3:187–92.

Kagan, J., S. Reznick, C. Clark, N. Snidman, and C. Garcia-Coll. 1984. Behavioral inhibition to the unfamiliar. *Child Development* 55: 2212–25.

Kahgee, S., E. Pomeroy, and H. R. Miller. 1982. Interpersonal judgments of schizophrenics. *British Journal of Medical Psychology* 55:319–25.

Kahneman, D. 1968. Method, findings, and theory in studies of visual masking. *Psychological Bulletin* 79:404–25.

Kanner, B. 1985. *Parent role repertories and reprimand constructions used by adolescents.* Master's thesis, State University of New York at Albany.

Kant, I. 1934. *Critique of pure reason.* London: Macmillan.

Kaplan, A. 1964. *The conduct of inquiry.* Scranton, PA: Chandler.

Keen, T. R., and R. C. Bell. 1981. One thing leads to another: A new approach to elicitation in repertory grid technique. In *Recent advances in personal construct technology,* vol. 81-94, edited by M. L. G. Shaw. London: Academic Press.

Kelly, G. A. 1955. *The psychology of personal constructs,* vols. 1 and 2. New York: Norton.

____. 1965. The role of classification in personality theory. In *Clinical psychology and personality,* edited by B. Maher, pp. 289–300. New York: Wiley.

____. 1969. Ontological acceleration. In *Clinical psychology and personality,* edited by B. Maher, pp. 7–45. New York: Wiley.

____. 1970. A brief introduction to personal construct theory. In *Perspectives in personal construct theory,* edited by D. Bannister, pp. 1–29. London: Academic Press.

____. 1973. Fixed role therapy. In *Direct psychotherapy,* edited by R. J. Jurjevich, pp. 394–421. Coral Gables, FL: University of Miami Press.

Kihlstrom, J. F., and N. Cantor. 1984. Mental representations of the self. In *Advances in experimental and social psychology,* vol. 17, edited by L. Berkowitz, pp. 2–47. New York: Academic Press.

Kintsch, W., and T. A. van Dijk. 1978. Toward a model of text comprehension and production. *Psychological Review* 85:363–94.

____. 1983. *Strategies of discourse comprehension.* New York: Academic Press.

Kirk, R. 1968. *Experimental design procedures for the behavioral sciences.* Belmont, CA: Wadsworth.

Klinge, V. and T. Rodziewicz. 1976. Automated and manual intelligence testing of the Peabody Picture Vocabulary Test on a psychiatric adolescent population. *International Journal of Man–Machine Studies* 8:243–46.

Knight, R. A. 1984. Converging models of cognitive deficit in schizophrenia. In *Theories of schizophrenia and psychosis,* edited by W. D. Spaulding and J. K. Cole, pp. 93–146. Lincoln, NE: University of Nebraska Press.

Kornetsky, C., and M. Orzack. 1978. Physiologic and behavioral correlates of attention dysfunction in schizophrenic patients. In *The nature of schizophrenia,* edited by L. Wynne, R. Cromwell, and S. Matthysse, pp. 196–204. New York: Wiley.

Lachman, R., J. Lachman, and E. C. Butterfield. 1979. *Cognitive psychology and information processing*. Hillsdale, NJ: Erlbaum.

Landfield, A. W., ed. 1971. *Personal construct systems in psychotherapy*. Chicago, IL: Rand McNally.

____. 1976. A personal construct approach to suicidal behavior. In *Explorations of intrapersonal space*, vol. 1, edited by P. Slater, pp. 93–107. London: Wiley.

____. 1977. Interpretive man: The enlarged self-image. In *Nebraska symposium on motivation 1976: Personal construct psychology*, edited by A. W. Landfield and J. K. Cole, pp. 127–78. Lincoln, NE: University of Nebraska Press.

Landfield, A. W., and L. M. Leitner, eds. 1980. *Personal construct psychology: Psychotherapy and personality*. New York: Wiley.

Landfield, A. W., and P. C. Rivers. 1975. An introduction to interpersonal transaction and rotating dyads. *Psychotherapy: Theory, Research and Practice* 12:365–73.

Landfield, A. W., and C. J. Schmittdiel. 1983. The interpersonal transaction group: Evolving measurements in the pursuit of theory. In *Applications of personal construct theory*, edited by J. Adams-Webber and J. C. Mancuso. Don Mills, Ontario: Academic Press.

Larkin, J., J. McDermott, D. Simon, and H. Simon. 1980. Expert and novice performance in solving physics problems. *Science* 208:499–512.

Leenaars, A. 1981. Drugs and people: Repertory grid structure and the construal of two different kinds of targets. *Journal of Clinical Psychology* 37:198–201.

Lefton, L. A. 1973. Metacontrast: A review. *Perception and Psychophysics* 13:161–71.

Lemon, N. 1975. Linguistic development and conceptualization. *Journal of Cross-Cultural Psychology* 6:173–88.

Lenat, D. B. 1982. The nature of heuristics. *Artificial Intelligence* 19:189–249.

Lerman, S., and J. Louviere. 1984. Using functional measurement to identify the form of utility functions in travel demand modes. *Transportation Research Record*, 78:673–76.

Lindsay, P. H., and D. A. Norman. 1977. *An introduction to psychology*. New York: Academic Press.

Livesley, W. J., and D. B. Bromley. 1973. *Person perception in childhood and adolescence*. New York: Wiley.

Louviere, J. 1983. Integrating conjoint and functional measurement with discrete choice theory: An experimental design approach. In *Advances in consumer research*, edited by R. Bagozzi and A. Tybout. Ann Arbor, MI: Association for Consumer Research.

Louviere, J., and G. Woodworth. 1983. Design and analysis of simulated consumer choice or allocation experiments: An approach based on aggregate data. *Journal of Marketing Research* 20:350–67.

Lucas, R. W. 1977. A study of patients' attitudes to computer interrogation. *International Journal of Man–Machine Studies* 9:69–86.

Lynch, J. 1984. *Adventures in paramorphic modeling: Models of consumer processing negative information*. Working Paper no. 39, University of Florida Center for Consumer Research.

____. 1985. Uniqueness issues in the decompositional modeling of multiattribute overall evaluations: An information integration perspective. *Journal of Marketing*

Research 22:1–19.
Maddi, S. R. 1984. Personology for the 1980s. In *Personality and the prediction of behavior,* edited by J. Aronoff and A. I. Rabin, pp. 1–41. Orlando, FL: Academic Press.
Magaro, P. A. 1980. *Cognition in schizophrenia and paranoia: The integration of cognitive processes.* Hillsdale, NJ: Erlbaum.
____. 1981. The paranoid and the schizophrenic: The case for distinct cognitive style. *Schizophrenia Bulletin* 7:632–61.
____. 1984. Psychosis and schizophrenia. In *Theories of schizophrenia and psychosis,* edited by W. D. Spaulding and J. K. Cole, pp. 157–230. Lincoln, NE: University of Nebraska Press.
Magaro, P. A., and R. M. Ashbrook. 1984. The application of an information processing model to the diagnosis and treatment of functional disorders. *Models and Techniques of Cognitive Rehabilitation IV: Fourth International Symposium,* Indianapolis, IN.
Magaro, P. A., and D. L. Chamrad. 1983. Information processing and lateralization in schizophrenia. *Biological Psychiatry* 18:29–44.
Magaro, P. A., P. Smith, and R. M. Ashbrook. 1983. Personality style differences in visual search performance. *Psychiatry Research* 10:131–38.
Maher, B. A. 1974. Editorial. *Journal of Consulting and Clinical Psychology* 42:1–3.
Mair, J. M. M. 1969. Some problems in repertory grid measurement 1: the use of bipolar constructs. *British Journal of Psychology* 58:261–70.
Mancuso, J. C. 1979. Reprimand: The construing of the rule violator's construct system. In *Constructs of sociality and individuality,* edited by P. Stringer and D. Bannister, pp. 43–97. New York: Academic Press.
____. 1986. The acquisition and use of narrative grammar structure. In *The storied nature of human conduct,* edited by T. R. Sarbin, pp. 91–110. New York: Praeger.
Mancuso, J. C., and J. R. Adams-Webber, eds. 1982a. *The construing person.* New York: Praeger.
____. 1982b. Anticipation as a constructive process: The fundamental postulate. In *The construing person,* edited by J. C. Mancuso and J. R. Adams-Webber, pp. 8–32. New York: Praeger.
Mancuso, J. C., and S. G. Ceeley. 1980. The self as memory processing. *Cognitive Therapy and Research* 4:1–25.
Mancuso, J. C., and B. N. Eimer. 1982. Fitting things into sorts: The range corollary. In *The construing person,* edited by J. C. Mancuso and J. R. Adams-Webber, pp. 130–51. New York: Praeger.
Mancuso, J. C., and K. H. Handin. 1980. Training parents to construe the child's construing. In *Personal construct psychology,* edited by A. W. Landfield and L. M. Leitner, pp. 271–88. New York: Wiley.
____. 1983. Prompting parents toward constructivist caregiving practices. In *Changing families,* edited by I. E. Sigel and L. M. Laosa, pp. 163–202. New York: Plenum.
Mancuso, J. C., and K. V. Hunter. 1983. Anticipation, motivation, or emotion: The Fundamental Postulate after twenty-five years. In *Applications of personal construct theory,* edited by J. Adams-Webber and J. C. Mancuso, pp. 73–92. New York: Academic Press.

____. 1985. Constructivist assumptions in the person theories of George A. Kelly and Jean Piaget. In *La psychlogia dei costrutti personali: Sggi sulla teoria di G. A. Kelly,* edited by F. Mancini and A. Semerari. Milan: Franco Angeli Libri.

Mancuso, J. C., and R. Lehrer. 1985. Cognitive processes in socializing reaction to rule violation. In *Thinking about parenting,* edited by R. D. Ashmore and D. M. Brodzinsky, pp. 67–93. Englewood Cliffs, NJ: Erlbaum.

Mancuso, J. C., and T. R. Sarbin. 1983. The self-narrative in the enactment of roles. In *Studies in social identity,* edited by T. R. Sarbin and K. Schcibe, pp. 233–53. New York: Praeger.

Mandler, G. 1984. *Mind and body: Psychology of emotion and stress.* New York: W. W. Norton.

Mardia, K. V., J. T. Kent, and J. M. Bibby. 1979. *Multivariate analysis.* London: Academic Press.

Markus, H. 1977. Self-schemata and processing information about the self. *Journal of Personality and Social Psychology* 35:63–78.

____. 1983. Self-knowledge: An expanded view. *Journal of Personality* 51:543–65.

Markus, H., and K. Sentis. 1982. The self in social information processing. In *Psychological perspectives on the self,* vol. 1, edited by J. Sols. Hillsdale, NJ: Erlbaum.

Marsh, H. W., J. Barnes, L. Cairns, and M. Tidman. 1984. Self-description questionnaire: Age and sex effects in the structure and level of self-concept for preadolescent children. *Journal of Educational Psychology* 76:940–56.

Mascolo, M. F., and J. C. Mancuso. 1985. The enactment of emotion as a self-defining role: A constructivist analysis. *Sixth International Personal Construct Psychology Congress,* Cambridge, England.

Massaro, D. W., and J. Schmuller. 1975. Visual features, perceptual storage, and processing time in reading. In *Understanding language,* edited by D. W. Massaro. New York: Academic Press.

McDermott, J. 1980a. R1: An expert in the computer systems domain. In *Proceedings of the First Annual Conference on Artificial Intelligence,* pp. 269–71. Palo Alto, CA.

____. 1980b. R1: An expert configurer. Report no. CMU-CS-80-119. Pittsburgh, PA: Computer Science Department, Carnegie-Mellon University.

____. 1982. R1: A rule-based configurer of computer systems. *Artificial Intelligence* 19(1):39–88.

____. 1984. R1 revisited: Four years in the trenches. *The A. I. Magazine* 5(3):21–32.

McDonald, R. P. 1979. The indeterminacy of components and the definition of common factors. *British Journal of Mathematical and Statistical Psychology* 30:165–76.

McGuire, W. 1976. Some internal psychological factors influencing consumer choice. *Journal of Consumer Research* 2:302–19.

Mead, G. H. 1932. *The philosophy of the present.* Chicago, IL: University of Chicago Press.

____. 1934. *Mind, self, and society.* Chicago, IL: University of Chicago Press.

____. 1938. *The philosophy of the act.* Chicago, IL: University of Chicago Press.

Michalski, R. S. 1980. Pattern recognition as rule-guided inductive inference. *IEEE Transactions of Pattern Analysis and Machine Intelligence* PAMI-2:349–61.

Michalski, R. S., J. Carbonell, and T. M. Mitchell, eds. 1983. *Machine learning: An artificial intelligence approach.* Palo Alto, CA: Tioga Press.

Michie, D., ed. 1979. *Expert systems in the micro-electronic age.* Edinburgh: Edinburgh University Press.

Mitsos, S. D. 1961. Personal constructs and the semantic differential. *Journal of Abnormal and Social Psychology* 62:433–34.

Morrison, D. 1976. *Multivariate statistics.* New York: McGraw-Hill.

Moto-oka, T., ed. 1982. *Fifth generation computer systems.* Amsterdam: North-Holland.

Murphy, G. L., and J. C. Wright. 1984. Changes in conceptual structure with expertise: Differences between real-world experts and novices. *Journal of Experimental Psychology* 10:144–55.

Neale, J. 1971. Perceptual span in schizophrenia. *Journal of Abnormal Psychology* 77:196–204.

Neimeyer, R. A. 1985. Personal constructs in clinical practice. In *Advances in cognitive behavioral research and therapy,* vol. 4, edited by P. C. Kendall, in press. New York: Academic Press.

Neimeyer, R. A., and G. J. Neimeyer. 1987. *Personal construct therapy case book.* New York: Springer Publishing Company.

Neisser, V. 1963. Decision time without reaction time: Experiments in visual scanning. *American Journal of Psychology* 76:376–85.

____. 1967. *Cognitive psychology.* New York: Appleton-Century-Crofts.

____. 1976. *Cognition and reality: Principles and implications of cognitive psychology.* San Francisco, CA: W. H. Freeman.

Nelson, K., and J. M. Gruendel. 1979. At morning it's lunchtime: A scriptal view of children's dialogues. *Discourse Processes* 2:73–94.

____. 1981. Generalized event representations: Basic building blocks of cognitive development. In *Advances in developmental psychology,* vol. 1, edited by M. E. Lamb and A. L. Brown, pp. 131–58. Hillsdale, NJ: Erlbaum.

Newell, A., and H. A. Simon. 1972. *Human problem solving.* Englewood Cliffs, NJ: Prentice-Hall.

Nisbett, R., and T. Wilson. 1977. Telling more than we can know: Verbal reports on mental processes. *Psychological Review* 84:231–59.

Norman, D. 1980. Twelve issues for cognitive science. *Cognitive Science* 4:1–32.

Nystedt, L., and D. Magnusson. 1982. Construction of experience: The construction corollary. In *The construing person,* edited by J. C. Mancuso and J. R. Adams-Webber, pp. 33–44. New York: Praeger.

Osgood, C. E., G. J. Suci, and P. H. Tannenbaum. 1957. *The measurement of meaning.* Urbana, IL: University of Illinois Press.

Painting, D. H. 1961. The performance of psychopathic individuals under conditions of positive and negative partial reinforcement. *Journal of Abnormal and Social Psychology* 62:352–55.

Palmer, S. E. 1978. Fundamental aspects of cognitive representation. In *Cognition and categorization,* edited by E. Rosch and B. Lloyd. Hillsdale, NJ: Erlbaum.

Pedersen, F. A. 1958. Consistency data on the role construct repertory test. Unpublished manuscript, Ohio State University.

Pekelman, D., and S. Sen. 1979. Measurement and estimation of conjoint utility functions. *Journal of Consumer Research* 5:263–71.

Phillips, E. 1981. Education for research: The changing constructs of the postgraduate. In *Recent advances in personal construct technology,* edited by M. L. G. Shaw, pp. 95–104. London: Academic Press.

Piaget, J. 1951. *Plays, dreams and imitation in childhood.* New York: Norton.

Pic'l, A., P. A. Magaro, and E. Wade. 1978. Hemisphere functioning in paranoid and nonparanoid schizophrenics. *Biological Psychiatry* 14:891–903.

Pope, M. L., and T. R. Keen. 1981. *Personal construct psychology and education.* London: Academic Press.

Pope, M. L., and M. L. G. Shaw. 1981. Personal construct psychology in education and learning. In *Recent advances in personal construct technology,* edited by M. L. G. Shaw, pp. 105–14. London: Academic Press.

Posner, M. I. 1978. *Chronometric explorations of mind.* Hillsdale, NJ: Erlbaum.

Powers, W. T. 1973. *Behavior: The control of perception.* Chicago, IL: Aldine.

Prechtl, H. F. R. 1963. The mother–child interaction in babies with minimal brain damage. In *Determinants of infant behavior,* vol. 2, edited by B. M. Foss, pp. 53–59. London: Methuen.

Pruzansky, S., A. Tversky, and J. D. Carroll. 1982. Spatial versus tree representations of proximity data. *Psychometrika* 47:3–19.

Pruzek, R. M., and B. F. Frederick. 1978. Weighting predictors in linear models: Alternatives to least squares and limitations of equal weights. *Psychological Bulletin* 85:254–66.

Pruzek, R. M., and S. Rabinowitz. 1981. A class of simple methods for exploratory structural analysis. *American Educational Research Journal* 18:173–89.

Pulleybank, J., T. Bisanz, C. Scott, and M. A Champion. 1985. Developmental invariance in the effects of functional self-knowledge on memory. *Child Development* 56:1447–54.

Rabinowitz, M., and M. T. H. Chi. 1987. An interactive model of strategic processing. In *Handbook of cognitive, social and neurological aspects of learning disabilities,* edited by S. J. Ceci, pp. 381–402. Hillsdale, NJ: Erlbaum.

Radley, A. R. 1974. Schizophrenic thought disorder and the nature of personal constructs. *British Journal of Social and Clinical Psychology* 13:315–27.

Rathod, P. 1981. Method for the analysis of rep grid data. In *Personal construct psychology: Recent advances in theory and practice,* edited by H. Bonarius, R. Holland, and S. Rosenberg, pp. 117–46. London: Macmillan.

____. 1983. Methods for the construction of interpersonal grids. In *Applications of personal construct theory,* edited by J. Adams-Webber and J. C. Mancuso. Toronto: Academic Press.

Reed, S. K. 1972. Pattern recognition and categorization. *Cognitive Psychology* 3:382–407.

Reid, F. 1975. A note on measures of similarity and scaling metrics for users of the repertory grid. Report no. 45, Oxbridge, England: Centre for the Study of Human Learning, Brunel University.

Reitman, W., ed. 1984. *Artificial intelligence applications for business.* Norwood, NJ: Ablex.

Rescher, N. 1969. *Many-valued logic.* New York: McGraw-Hill.

Ridgway, J., M. J. MacCulloch, and H. E. Mills. 1982. Some experiences in administering a psychometric test with a light pan and microcomputer. *International Journal of Man–Machine Studies* 17:265–78.

Rigdon, M. A., and F. R. Epting. 1982. A test of the golden section hypothesis with elicited constructs. *Journal of Personality and Social Psychology* 43:1080–87.

Riley, S., and J. Palmer. 1976. On attitudes and latitudes: A repertory grid study of perceptions of seaside resorts. In *Explorations of intrapersonal space,* vol. 1, edited by P. Slater, pp. 153–66. London: John Wiley & Sons.

Rodnick, E., and D. Shakow. 1940. Set in the schizophrenic as measured by a composite reaction time index. *American Journal of Psychiatry* 97:214–25.

Romany, S., and J. Adams-Webber. 1981. The golden section hypothesis from a developmental perspective. *Social Behavior and Personality* 9:89–92.

Rosch, E. 1975. Cognitive representations of semantic categories. *Journal of Experimental Psychology: General* 104:192–233.

____. 1978. Principles of categorization. In *Cognition and categorization,* edited by E. Rosch and B. B. Lloyd. Hillsdale, NJ: Erlbaum.

Rosch, E., and B. B. Lloyd, eds. 1978. *Cognition and categorization.* Hillsdale, NJ: Erlbaum.

Rosenberg, S. 1977. New approaches to analysis of personal constructs in person perception. In *Nebraska symposium on motivation 1976: Personal construct psychology,* edited by A. W. Landfield and J. K. Cole, pp. 179–242. Lincoln, NE: University of Nebraska Press.

Rosenberg, S., and R. Jones. 1972. A method for investigating and representing a person's implicit theory of personality. *Journal of Personality* 22:372–86.

Ross, B. H. 1984. Remindings and their effects in learning a cognitive skill. *Cognitive Psychology* 16:371–416.

Rozeboom, W. W. 1966. *Foundations of the theory of prediction.* Homewood, IL: Dorsey Press.

Ruble, D. N., A. K. Boggiano, N. S. Feldman, and J. H. Loebl. 1980. Developmental analysis of the role of social comparisons in self-evaluation. *Developmental Psychology* 16:105–15.

Rumelhart, D. E. 1975. Notes on a schema for stories. In *Representation and understanding: Studies in cognitive science,* edited by D. G. Bobrow and A. Collins, pp. 211–36. New York: Academic Press.

Rumelhart, D. E., and D. A. Norman. 1981. Analogical processes in learning. In *Cognition skills and their acquisition,* edited by J. R. Anderson, pp. 335–59. Hillsdale, NJ: Erlbaum.

Rump, E. E. 1974. Cluster analysis compared with principal component analysis. *British Journal of Social and Clinical Psychology* 13:283–92.

Saaty, T. L. 1980. *The analytic hierarchy process.* New York: McGraw-Hill.

Salmon, P. 1976. Grid measures with child subjects. In *Explorations of intrapersonal space,* vol. 1, edited by P. Slater, pp. 15–46. London: John Wiley.

Sameroff, A. J., and L. A. Feil. 1985. Parental concepts of development. In *Parental belief systems,* edited by I. E. Sigel, pp. 83–105. Hillsdale, NJ: Erlbaum.

Sattath, S., and A. Tversky. 1977. Additive similarity trees. *Psychometrika* 42:319–45.

Schaefer, E. S. 1971. Development of hierarchical configurational models for parent behavior and child behavior. In *Minnesota symposium on child psychology,* vol. 6, edited by J. P. Hill. Minneapolis, MN: University of Minnesota.

Schank, R. C. 1980. Language and memory. *Cognitive Science* 4:243–84.

Schank, R. C., and R. P. Abelson. 1977. *Scripts, plans, goals and understanding.* Hillsdale, NJ: Erlbaum.

Scheier, M. F., and C. S. Carver. 1983. Two sides of the self: One for you and one for me. In *Psychological perspectives on the self,* vol. 2, edited by J. Sols and C. S. Carver, pp. 123–57. Hillsdale, NJ: Erlbaum.

Schiffman, S. S., M. L. Reynolds, and F. W. Young. 1981. *Introduction to multidimensional scaling.* New York: Academic Press.

Schneider, W., and R. M. Schriffin. 1977. Controlled and automatic human information processing I: Detection, search, and attention. *Psychological Review* 84:1–66.

Seber, G. A. F. 1984. *Multivariate observations.* New York: Wiley.

Secord, P. F., and B. H. Peeves. 1974. The development and attribution of person concepts. In *Understanding other persons,* edited by T. Mischel, pp. 117–42. Oxford: Blackwell.

Selman, R. L. 1980. *The growth of interpersonal understanding.* New York: Academic Press.

Shapiro, D. 1965. *Neurotic styles.* New York: Farrar, Strauss & Giroux.

Shavelson, R. J., and R. Bolus. 1982. Self-concept: The interplay of theory and methods. *Journal of Educational Psychology* 74:3–17.

Shaw, M. L. G. 1980. *On becoming a personal scientist.* London: Academic Press.

____. 1981. *Recent advances in personal construct technology.* London: Academic Press.

____. 1982. PLANET: Some experience in creating an integrated system for repertory grid applications on a microcomputer. *International Journal of Man–Machine Studies* 17:345–60.

____. 1983. A computer aid to knowledge engineering. *Proceedings of British Computer Society Conference on Expert Systems,* pp. 263–71. London: British Computer Society.

Shaw, M. L. G., and B. R. Gaines. 1979. Externalizing the personal world: Computer aids to epistemology. In *Improving the human condition: Quality and stability in social systems,* edited by R. F. Ericson, pp. 136–45. Louisville: Society for General Systems Research.

____. 1980. Fuzzy semantics for personal construing. In *Systems science and science: Proceedings of the 24th annual meeting of SGSR,* edited by B. H. Banathy, pp. 146–54. Louisville: Society for General Systems Research.

____. 1981. Fuzzy entailment analysis. In *Applied systems and cybernetics,* vol. 6, edited by G. E. Lasker, pp. 3010–14. Oxford: Pergamon Press.

____. 1982. Eliciting entailment. In *Progress in cybernetics and systems research,* vol. 9, edited by R. Trappl, L. Ricciardi and G. Pask, pp. 425–35. Washington, D.C.: Hemisphere.

____. 1984. Application of personal construct theory to expert systems. *First North American Personal Construct Network Conference,* Cincinnati, OH.

Shaw, M. L. G., and C. McKnight. 1981. ARGUS: A program to explore intrapersonal personalities. In *Recent advances in personal construct technology*, edited by M. L. G. Shaw, pp. 125–34. London: Academic Press.

____. 1981b. *Think again*. New York: Prentice-Hall.

Shepard, R. N. 1980. Multidimensional scaling, tree-fitting, and clustering. *Science* 210:390–98.

____. 1984. Ecological constraints on internal representations: Resonant kinematics of perceiving, imagining, thinking, and dreaming. *Psychological Review* 91:417–47.

Shepherd, E., and J. P. Watson, eds. 1982. *Personal meanings*. London: John Wiley.

Shiffrin, R. M., and W. Schneider. 1977. Controlled and automatic human information processing: II. Perceptual learning, automatic attending, and a general theory. *Psychological Review* 84:1–66.

Showers, C., and N. Cantor. 1985. Social cognition: A look at motivated strategies. *Annual Review of Psychology* 36:275–305.

Sigel, I. E. 1970. The distancing hypothesis: A causal hypothesis for the acquisition of representational thought. In *Miami symposium on the prediction of behavior*, edited by M. R. Jones, pp. 99–118. Coral Gables, FL: University of Miami Press.

____. 1985a. A conceptual analysis of beliefs. In *Parental belief systems*, edited by I. E. Sigel, pp. 345–71. Hillsdale, NJ: Erlbaum.

____, ed. 1985b. *Parental belief systems: The psychological consequences for children*. Hillsdale, NJ: Erlbaum.

Signell, K. 1967. Cognitive complexity in person perception and nation perception. *Journal of Personality* 34:517–37.

Slater, P. 1964. *The principle components of a repertory grid*. London: Andrews & Co.

____. 1972. The measurement of consistency in repertory grids. *British Journal of Psychiatry* 45:45–51.

____. 1974. Cluster analysis vs. principal component analysis: A reply to E. E. Rump. *British Journal of Social and Clinical Psychology* 13:427–30.

____, ed. 1976. *Explorations of intrapersonal space*, vol. 1. London: John Wiley.

____, ed. 1977. *Dimensions of intrapersonal space*, vol. 2. London: John Wiley.

____. 1981. Construct systems in conflict. In *Recent advances in personal construct technology*, edited by M. L. G. Shaw, pp. 115–23. London: Academic Press.

Smith, E. E., and D. L. Medin. 1981. *Categories and concepts*. Cambridge, MA: Harvard University Press.

Smith, E. E., E. J. Shoben, and L. J. Rips, 1974. Structure and process in semantic memory: A featural model for semantic decision. *Psychological Review* 81:214–41.

Smith, S., and C. Leach. 1972. A hierarchical measure of cognitive complexity. *British Journal of Psychology* 63:561–68.

Sowa, J. F. 1984. *Conceptual structures: Information processing in mind and machine*. Reading, MA: Addison-Wesley.

Space, L. G. 1975. A console for on-line administration of psychological tests. *Behavior Research Methods and Instrumentation* 7:191–93.

Space, L. G., and R. L. Cromwell. 1978. Personal constructs among schizophrenic patients. In *Language and cognition in schizophrenia*, edited by S. Schwartz, pp.

147–92. Hillsdale, NJ: Erlbaum.

____. 1980. Personal constructs among depressed patients. *Journal of Nervous and Mental Diseases* 168:150–58.

Space, L. G., P. Dingemans, and R. L. Cromwell. 1983. Self-construing and alienation in depressives, schizophrenics, and normals. In *Applications of personal construct theory*, edited by J. Adams-Webber and J. C. Mancuso, pp. 365–78. New York: Academic Press.

Space, L. G., and R. S. Huntzinger. 1979. A microprocessor-based psychopathology laboratory: III. Hardware. *Behavior Research Methods and Instrumentation* 11:247–52.

Spaulding, W. 1986. Assessment of adult-onset pervasive behavior disorders. In *Handbook of behavioral assessment*, 2d ed., edited by A. Ciminero, K. Calhoun, and H. Adams, pp. 631–69. New York: Wiley.

Spaulding, W., W. Crinean, and T. Martin. 1983. Microcomputerized clinical and research laboratories in psychiatric inpatient settings. *Behavior Research Methods and Instrumentation* 15:171–76.

Spaulding, W., and D. Dras. 1958. Information processing in psychiatric patients, schizotypal college students, and normals. Unpublished paper, University of Nebraska.

Spaulding, W., D. S. Hargrove, W. J. Crinean, and T. Martin. 1981. A microcomputer-based laboratory for psychopathology research in rural settings. *Behavior Research Methods and Instrumentation* 13:616–23.

Spaulding, W., and L. G. Space. 1979. A microprocessor-based psychopathology laboratory: II. Research goals and design prerequisites. *Behavior Research Methods and Instrumentation* 11:243–46.

Spaulding, W., L. Storms, K. Goodrich, and M. Sullivan. 1986. Psychological principles and interventions in psychiatric rehabilitation. *Schizophrenia Bulletin* 12:560–77.

Sperling, D. 1960. The information available in brief visual presentations. *Psychological Monographs* 74, no. 11.

Sperlinger, D. 1976. Aspects of stability in the repertory grid. *British Journal of Medical Psychology* 40:341–47.

Sroufe, L. A. 1979. The coherence of individual development. *American Psychologist* 34:834–41.

Steffy, R., and K. Galbraith. 1974. A comparison of segmental set and inhibitory deficit explanations of the crossover pattern in process schizophrenic patients. *Journal of Abnormal Psychology* 83:227–33.

____. 1975. The time course of a disruptive signal in the reaction time performance of process schizophrenic patients. *Journal of Abnormal Psychology* 84:315–21.

____. 1980. Relationship between latency and redundancy-associated deficit in schizophrenic reaction time performance. *Journal of Abnormal Psychology* 89:419–27.

Sternberg, R. J. 1969. Memory scanning: Mental process revealed by reaction-time experiments. *American Scientist* 57:421–57.

Sternberg, R. J., and G. H. Bower. 1974. Transfer in part-whole and whole-part free recall: A comparative evaluation of theories. *Journal of Verbal Learning and Verbal Behavior* 13:1–26.

Stewart, B., and A. Stewart. 1981. *Business applications of repertory grids*. London: McGraw-Hill.

Stodolsky, D. 1970. The computer as a psychotherapist. *International Journal of Man–Machine Studies* 2:327–50.

Stringer, P., and D. Bannister, eds. 1979. *Constructs of sociality and individuality*. New York: Academic Press.

Stroop, J. R. 1935. Studies of interference in serial verbal reactions. *Journal of Experimental Psychology* 18:643–61.

Thomas, A., and S. Chess. 1977. *Temperament and development*. New York: Brunner/Mazel.

Thomas, A., S. Chess, and H. G. Birch. 1968. *Treatment and behavior disorders in children*. New York: New York University Press.

Thomas, L. F., and E. S. Harri-Augstein. 1985. *Self-organized learning: Foundations of a conversational science for psychology*. London: Routledge & Kegan Paul.

Thompson, J. A., and S. L. Wilson. 1982. Automated psychological testing. *International Journal of Man–Machine Studies* 17:279–89.

Thomson, D. M., and E. Tulving. 1970. Associative encoding and retrieval: Weak and strong cues. *Journal of Experimental Psychology* 86:255–62.

Thorndyke, P. W. 1977. Cognitive structures in comprehension and memory of narrative discourse. *Cognitive Psychology* 9:77–110.

Torgerson, W. 1958. *Theory and method of scaling*. New York: Wiley.

Tschudi, F., and R. Rommetveit. 1982. Sociality, intersubjectivity, and social processes: The sociality corollary. In *The construing person*, edited by J. C. Mancuso and J. R. Adams-Webber, pp. 235–61. New York: Praeger.

Tulving, E., and D. M. Thomson. 1973. Encoding specificity and retrieval processes in episodic memory. *Psychological Review* 80:352–73.

Tversky, A. 1977. Features of similarity. *Psychological Review* 84:327–52.

Tversky, A., and I. Gati. 1982. Similarity, separability, and the triangle inequality. *Psychological Review* 89:123–54.

Upshaw, H. 1962. Own attitude as an anchor in equal-appearing intervals. *Journal of Abnormal and Social Psychology* 64:85–96.

van den Broek, P. W., and T. Trabasso. 1986. Causal networks versus goal hierarchies in summarizing text. *Discourse Processing* 9:1–115.

Van Lehn, K., and J. S. Brown. 1980. Planning nets: A representation for formalizing analogies and semantic models of procedural skills. In *Aptitude, learning, and instruction. Vol. 2: Cognitive process analysis and problem solving*, edited by R. E. Snow, P. A. Frederico, and W. E. Montague, pp. 95–136. Hillsdale, NJ: Erlbaum.

Vernon, M. D. 1955. The function of schemata in perceiving. *Psychological Review* 62:180–92.

Volans, P. J., and R. Levy. 1982. A re-evaluation of an automated tailored test of concept learning with elderly psychiatric patients. *British Journal of Clinical Psychology* 21:39–47.

von Glasersfeld, E. 1984. An introduction to radical constructivism. In *The invented reality*, edited by P. Watlawick, pp. 17–40. New York: Norton.

Waterman, D. A., and F. Hayes-Roth. *An investigation of tools for building expert systems*. R2818-NSR. Santa Monica, CA: Rand Corporation.

Watts, K., A. Baddeley, and M. Williams. 1982. Automated tailored testing using Raven's matrices and the Mill Hill vocabulary test: A comparison with manual administration. *International Journal of Man–Machine Studies* 17:331–44.

Wegner, B. 1982. *Social attitudes and psychophysical measurement.* Hillsdale, NJ: Erlbaum.

Wertheimer, M. 1912. Experimentelle studien über das sehen von bewegung. *Zeitschrift für Psychologie* 61:161–265.

Wheeler, D. D. 1977. Locus of interference on the Stroop test. *Perceptual and Motor Skills* 45:263–66.

Whittle, P. 1952. A principal component and least squares method of factor analysis. *Skand. Aktuarietidskift* 35:223–39.

Wiggins, J. 1972. *Personality and prediction: Principles of personality assessment.* Reading, MA: Addison-Wesley.

Woelfel, J., and G. Barnett. 1982. Multidimensional scaling in Riemann space. *Quality and Quantity* 16:469–91.

Woelfel, J., and E. Fink. 1980. *The measurement of communication processes: Galileo theory and method.* New York: Academic Press.

Woelfel, J., and A. O. Haller. 1971. Significant others, the self reflexive act, and the attitude formation process. *American Sociological Review* 36:74–87.

Wolff, K. H. 1976. *Surrender and catch.* Dordrecht, Holland: D. Reidel.

Woods, W. A. 1975. What's in a link? Foundations for semantic artworks. In *Representation and understanding: Studies in cognitive science,* edited by D. G. Bobrow and A. Collins, pp. 35–82. New York: Academic Press.

Wyer, R. S., and T. S. Srull, eds. 1984. *Handbook of social cognition,* vol. 4. Hillsdale, NJ: Erlbaum.

Zadeh, L. A. 1965. Fuzzy sets. *Information and Control* 8:338–53.

____. 1977. Fuzzy sets. In *Encyclopedia of computer science and technology,* vol. 18, edited by J. Belzer, A. Holsman, and A. Kent, pp. 325–63. New York: Marcel Dekker.

Author Index

Subject Index

About the Contributors

JAMES C. MANCUSO is a professor of psychology at the State University of New York at Albany. He received his B.A. from Dickinson College and his Ph.D. from the University of Rochester. He has published *Schizophrenia: Medical Diagnosis or Moral Verdict* (Pergamon Press, 1980) in collaboration with Theodore R. Sarbin. His edited volumes, *The Construing Person* (Praeger, 1982) and *Applications of Personal Construct Theory* (Academic Press, 1983), with Jack Adams-Webber, are well known to students of personal construct psychology.

MILDRED L. G. SHAW is a professor of computer science at the University of Calgary. She received her B.Sc. and M.Sc. from the University of London, and her Ph.D. from Brunel University. She is a Fellow of the Institute of Mathematics and Its Applications and the British Computer Society and an Associate Fellow of the British Psychological Society. Dr. Shaw is a member of the editorial board of the *International Journal of Man–Machine Studies* and a managing editor of *Future Computing Systems*. She has authored over 70 papers and authored or edited five books on a wide variety of aspects of computer and human systems.

JACK ADAMS-WEBBER received his B.A. from Haverford College, his M.A. from Ohio State University, and his Ph.D. from Brandeis University. He is currently a professor of psychology at Brock University in Ontario. He is the author of *Personal Construct Theory: Concepts and Applications* (Wiley, 1979), and has co-edited *The Construing Person* (Praeger, 1982) and *Applications of Personal Construct Theory* (Academic Press, 1983).

RICHARD M. ASHBROOK is an assistant professor at Capital University (Columbus, Ohio). He received his B.S. from the University of Maryland, and his M.A. and his Ph.D. from Ohio State University. He completed a clinical internship at the University of Rochester School of Medicine and Dentistry. Following through on work that extends his doctoral dissertation, in which he examined attention and memory in subtypes of attention deficit disorder children, he continues to study cognition in childhood psychopathology and to investigate information-processing styles of personality types.

JOHN H. BOOSE is a Principal Scientist at the Boeing Artificial Intelligence Center in Seattle, Washington, where his major interest has been in developing knowledge acquisition techniques for knowledge-based systems.

JOHN E. CANNELL received his B.A. from the University of Denver and his M.A. and Ph.D. from the University of Nebraska. An Episcopal priest, he received his Masters of Divinity from Nashotah Theological Seminary in Wisconsin. Currently, he is with the Department of Psychiatry at the University of Texas Health Science Center at San Antonio. He has published in the areas of pastoral psychology and the relation of personal construct theory to psychoanalytic object relations theory.

RUE L. CROMWELL is the M. Erik Wright Distinguished Professor of Clinical Psychology at the University of Kansas. He took his Ph.D. at Ohio State University. After joining the faculty of Vanderbilt University School of Medicine, he studied nosological systems for emotionally disturbed children, and stress and outcome factors in myocardial infarction. His work on information processing, focusing on conceptual structure and personal construct factors, led to increased attention to the applications of computer technology. Besides having published numerous research articles, he has co-authored *Acute Myocardial Infarction: Reaction and Recovery* and *The Nature of Schizophrenia.*

BRIAN R. GAINES is Killam Memorial Research Professor at the University of Calgary. He received his B.A., M.A., and Ph.D. from Trinity College at Cambridge University. He is a Fellow of the Institution of Electrical Engineers, the British Computer Society and the British Psychological Society. He is editor of the *International Journal of Man–Machine Studies,* the *Computers and People* book series, and *Future Computing Systems.* He has authored over 150 papers and authored or edited five books on a wide variety of aspects of computer and human systems. His research interests include foundations of knowledge-based systems, knowledge transfer systems, and expert system applications in manufacturing, the sciences, and humanities.

JAMES JACCARD is a professor of psychology at the State University of New York at Albany. He has published numerous articles on the attitude–behavior relationship and decision making. His most recent research is on the development of idiographic approaches to the analysis of individual decision-making processes.

ALVIN W. LANDFIELD received his B.A. from the University of North Carolina and his M.A. and Ph.D. from Ohio State University, where he was a student of the late George Kelly, the originator of personal construct theory. Dr. Landfield is a professor of psychology at the University of Nebraska–Lincoln. His most recent books, *Personal Construct Psychology* (co-edited with L. Leitner) and *Personal Constructs in Use* (co-authored with F. Epting), carry forward his long identification with constructivist theory and method.

RICHARD LEHRER is an assistant professor of educational psychology at the University of Wisconsin–Madison. He received his B.S. in biology from Rensselaer Polytechnic Institute and a Ph.D. in educational psychology from the State University of New York at Albany. He presently investigates cognitive processes and systems of representation as these relate to classroom learning.

JOHN MITTERER received his B.A. from the University of Calgary and his Ph.D. from McMaster University. He is currently an associate professor of psychology at Brock University in Ontario. He is interested in the applications of computers in psychology and cognitive science.

ROBERT M. PRUZEK is an associate professor of educational psychology and statistics at the State University of New York at Albany. He received his M.S. and Ph.D. from the University of Wisconsin, Madison. His specialty is quantitative analysis, especially multivariate methods, and he carries his research over into applications in psychometrics and educational research. His current research deals with ways to improve conventional methods for structural analysis and regression in order to accommodate situations where there are many variables, relatively small samples, and semi-reliable measurements. His recent publications have appeared in the *American Educational Research Journal* and the *Psychological Bulletin.*

WILL SPAULDING is an associate professor at the University of Nebraska–Lincoln. He obtained his B.A. from Pomona College and completed his Ph.D. at the University of Arizona. He had an opportunity to extend his studies of the relationship of cognitive and developmental factors to patterns of severely disordered behavior when he worked with R. L. Cromwell as a postdoctoral fellow. His current research interests include the experimental and clinical psychopathology of schizophrenia and related disorders.

CHOI K. WAN, a native of Hong Kong, did his undergraduate studies in that city. He has a broad interest in the cross-cultural application of social and health psychology. He was awarded his Ph.D. at the State University of New York at Albany. Two of his main interests are the construct of social support and its relationship to well-being, and the ways in which people evaluate and compare their abilities relative to others.

GREGORY WOOD received his B.A. from Oakland University in Rochester, Michigan. He is currently a Ph.D. candidate at the State University of New York at Albany. His research interests focus on applications of decision theory to the analysis of consumer behavior.

JOSEPH WOELFEL completed his undergraduate studies at Canisius College, and his Ph.D. in sociology at the University of Wisconsin. He currently holds the position of professor of communication and public policy at the State University of New York at Albany. He is a Faculty Fellow at the Rockefeller Institute of Government at SUNY Albany. He has co-authored *The Measurement of Communication Processes* (with Edward L. Fink), and publishes regularly in the area of cognitive studies and information science.

www.ingramcontent.com/pod-product-compliance
Ingram Content Group UK Ltd.
Pitfield, Milton Keynes, MK11 3LW, UK
UKHW020236290926
15470UKWH00002B/578